PHILADELPHIA
FREEDOM

Also by David Kairys

The Politics of Law:
A Progressive Critique (editor and coauthor)

With Liberty and Justice for Some:
A Critique of the Conservative Supreme Court

Philadelphia Freedom

Memoir of a Civil Rights Lawyer

David Kairys

THE UNIVERSITY OF MICHIGAN PRESS

ANN ARBOR

2011   2010   2009   2008   4   3   2   1

A CIP catalog record for this book is available from the British Library.

Library of Congress Cataloging-in-Publication Data

Kairys, David.
    Philadelphia freedom : memoir of a civil rights lawyer / David
Kairys.
        p.   cm.
    Includes bibliographical references and index.
    ISBN-13: 978-0-472-11638-6 (cloth : alk. paper)
    ISBN-10: 0-472-11638-X (cloth : alk. paper)
    ISBN-13: 978-0-472-03310-2 (pbk. : alk. paper)
    ISBN-10: 0-472-03310-7 (pbk.)
    1. Kairys, David.   2. Lawyers—United States—Biography   3. Civil
rights—United States.   I. Title.
    KF373.K345A3   2008
    340.092—dc22
    [B]   2008015032

A Caravan book. For more information, visit www.caravanbooks.org.

To Antje Mattheus, my favorite person and the love and partner of my life, although her legal case didn't amount to much

CONTENTS

Photographs *following page 262*

INTRODUCTION

Under the Bridge

IT WAS AN OVERCAST EVENING in late February 1972, and mist rose above the Delaware River as I crossed the Ben Franklin Bridge, the ornate suspension bridge between downtown Philadelphia and Camden, New Jersey. As I slowed for the tollbooth on the Camden side, I could see the waterfront and the idle Campbell's Soup factories. I had driven around for an hour looking in the mirrors to see if the FBI was following me, but I mostly noticed I was not as nervous as I should be.

I went south on the New Jersey side about 10 miles until I came to the interstate that heads to Atlantic City if you go east or back over the Delaware River on the Walt Whitman Bridge to Philadelphia if you go west. I slowed down, looked around, and checked the mirrors again before taking the ramp onto the Walt Whitman Bridge. I got off at the first exit in Philadelphia and, as directed, made several turns that curled me around and onto a small, dimly lit street in a residential neighborhood under the Walt Whitman.

I was relieved to see I wasn't the first to get there. It was a few minutes before midnight, the meeting time we had set, and a car with windows up and engine running was parked at the designated corner. I recognized Toni Dewees behind the steering wheel. She had brown hair, big happy eyes, and the heavy lipstick and nail polish stylish in the predominantly Italian areas of South Philadelphia.

"Hi, Toni," I said as I got out of my van and she rolled down her window. "Thanks for doing this."

"No problem. It's all cloak and dagger, I guess." She smiled.

"Yeah, sorry I can't tell you more." Toni worked for the established law firm that rented a room in the back of their office to my partner and me for our fledgling law firm started a year earlier. She typed, did the books, basically ran their office, and she was a notary public, which meant she could witness the signing of documents and notarize them so they'd be recognized as sworn documents in legal proceedings. I had asked her to do me a favor—meet me at midnight at an out-of-the-way place to notarize a document, though I couldn't tell her what it was about. She suggested a corner in South Philadelphia under the Walt Whitman Bridge near her house.

At about midnight, two vehicles pulled up behind my van.

"What's a priest doin' here?" Toni said, as a small, thin man with reddish hair in informal priest garb emerged from the closest car.

"He's part of what I can't tell you."

I knew hardly any Catholics as a child, and I hadn't met many since, except in the civil rights and anti–Vietnam War movements, which always seemed heavily populated by Catholics and Jews. Father Michael Doyle was a local priest who fit my image of just what a priest should be. He was mild mannered yet incorruptible and unwavering in the things that matter most, with an understated spirituality and calm commitment grounded in the lives of common people, and a good sense of humor. He reminded me of Bing Crosby playing Father Chuck O'Malley in *The Bells of St. Mary* and *Going My Way,* movies from the 1940s that were already corny by the 1950s, although he didn't have the Crosby voice.

Bob Hardy, a tall, stocky man with thick reddish blond hair neatly combed over a wide, handsome face, came out of the driver's side of a beat-up van used for construction work that pulled up behind Father Doyle. He looked like a working-class Kennedy.

They approached Toni and me, and each shook my hand and nodded as I introduced Toni. Father Doyle was calm and quiet. Hardy looked nervous.

"This is it, Bob. You're making things right," I said.

"I know. Let's do it!" he replied, pursing his lips and looking away.

I felt relieved that he didn't raise any questions and seemed ready to go ahead. We stepped into the open side door of my van and took seats inside. I pulled a small box from under the rear seat.

A half year earlier, Father Doyle broke into the draft board office in downtown Camden in the middle of the night and tore up draft records. Bob Hardy was among the draft-board raiders, but he also worked undercover for the FBI. Hardy was in my van to sign an affidavit that would make the front page of the *New York Times* when I filed it two weeks later[1] because it explained how FBI director J. Edgar Hoover and Attorney General John Mitchell had set up the antiwar raid on the draft board in Camden.

The FBI orchestrated the crime, then ordered scores of FBI agents to hide while the draft records were destroyed before jumping in to make their arrests. The next day Hoover and Mitchell trumpeted their middle-of-the-night capture at an early morning news conference. The complex plan for the break-in, the unusual tools needed to pull it off, the walkie-talkies for communications, even groceries to sustain some of the plotters and the plot—all were provided by Hardy and authorized and paid for by the FBI. The FBI also paid Hardy an hourly wage for his considerable time, and Hoover personally sent him a bonus for a job well done.

Draft boards were where the Vietnam War touched the lives of Americans. The draft of young men to fight in the war became a focal point for antiwar activists, and its system of offices dedicated to the war effort in every community provided convenient targets for demonstrations and break-ins. The Camden draft-board raid needed FBI assistance because it was the only one that required a burglary of the top floor of a large, urban office building. Hoover and Mitchell made it happen to discredit the antiwar movement and to stem criticism of their earlier vague and not very believable conspiracy charges against antiwar activists.

The affidavit I had hidden in a box was the result of several secret meetings over a period of months with Hardy in which Father Doyle and I convinced Hardy to "flip"—testify against the government. If the FBI found out Hardy was meeting with a defense lawyer in the case, Hardy and his startling testimony, which might win the case for the defense, would be in jeopardy. The stakes were particularly high because Hoover and Mitchell had so publicly placed themselves at the center of this prosecution and because, as the affidavit said, Hardy was told by his FBI contacts that the Camden setup had been ordered by "someone at the little

White House in California," the retreat of President Richard Nixon in San Clemente.

It turned out well. The defendants, who quickly became known as the "Camden 28," were acquitted in what Supreme Court justice William Brennan later described as "one of the great trials of the twentieth century."[2]

But I had plenty of reason to worry as I looked around the unfamiliar area while Hardy initialed each page and signed at the end. I had been careful. I drove in circles prior to each meeting with Hardy to make sure I wasn't being followed, as I imagined James Bond would do in a dull scene, and I covered all discussions of the matter on the phone and in person with blaring rock music in case I was being bugged.

As Toni filled out the notary portion at the end of the affidavit and squeezed her plyers-like mechanism with a round seal on the end so it got engraved into the paper, I wondered how I had gotten to this moment in my life, puzzled by myself. I was only 29, just four years out of law school, and I was handling this historic challenge to abuse of power by the executive branch of the U.S. government, some of the leading civil rights cases of the time, and an odd assortment of other cases that regularly drew public attention. I had become a "movement lawyer"—a lawyer for a range of progressive civil rights and antiwar groups. Filing documents that upset powerful people was becoming a habit.

I was a middle-class kid from Baltimore who started college in 1960 studying mechanical engineering after a high school guidance counselor told me engineering majors didn't have to take any more languages. I envisioned a life immersed in engineering and business and, I hoped, making a lot of money.

I was at the 1963 March on Washington and heard Martin Luther King, Jr., deliver his inspirational "I Have a Dream" speech, volunteered to tutor poor black kids in East Baltimore, and marched against the Vietnam War. But civil rights and politics were among my many interests, "sidelights" in a life headed for personal wealth. Even as I entered law school in 1965, in part to avoid the draft, I never imagined that civil rights and political activism would become central to my work and life.

PART ONE

Beginnings in Crime

CHAPTER ONE

Georgia on My Mind

A SMALL ELEVATOR TOOK ME SLOWLY to the eighth floor of the old office building at Thirteenth and Market Streets in Philadelphia. Clients, almost all of them black, filled the seats and standing room in a cramped reception area just outside the elevator. Beyond them, a center area and a large hallway were filled with secretaries' desks, typewriters, and file cabinets. Lawyers' offices were in small, irregular-shaped rooms around the perimeter of the floor. Two or three old wood desks and an assortment of beat-up chairs and bookshelves were crammed into each office, leaving little room for people. The ceilings were very high, and the windows were large and surrounded by fancy wood moldings. It was all painted a drab off-white, but it had the feel of a once grand workplace. Now it was home to the Defender Association of Philadelphia, the local public defender office, where I reported for work the day after Labor Day in 1968.

I stopped for a moment and looked around, struck by how alien I felt among the clients and lawyers, all of whom seemed to know what to do. After a few brief introductions, a secretary led me to a desk and handed me a stack of the basic tools of the law trade, big yellow pads and pencils. As I sat down at my desk, I couldn't imagine anything I could write to fill a whole yellow page. I wondered if, as a lawyer, I would have enough to say.

But the metal desk chair and the banged-up old oak desk were sure signs that I had become a lawyer. I thought of my parents still in Baltimore, neither of whom had gone to college, who had made a sizable dent in the family finances to finance me and my career.

I soon found myself debating whether the pad should be lined up with the edges of the desk or at an informal angle. The lined up way looked orderly and symmetrical, but the angled pad made me look experienced and savvy, like a lawyer whose first day was some time ago. I felt embarrassed at my own thoughts.

Two other desks were in the room, covered with scattered papers and books. Whoever used those desks looked like they must be busy, which I felt I should be as soon as possible. I looked through the stack of forms left on my desk to greet me—forms for interviews, investigations, cases involving juveniles, and referrals to other departments. File folders for each case had blocks printed on the outside for detailed information about what happened at each stage of the process. Green files marked "Bail Case" were for clients out on bail; manila ones marked "Jail Case" were for clients imprisoned awaiting trial. I was eager to fill in some blocks.

I knew it would be some time before I got into a courtroom. I had taken the bar exam that July after graduation from Columbia Law School and wouldn't be admitted until late in December. Beginning that first September day and for the next few months, I spent my time interviewing clients, first those out on bail, the people waiting in the reception area, and later those held in prison. I learned a great deal, but it was mostly uneventful and frustrating because I took down the information and the defendants' stories but never found out how the cases turned out.

By the second or third week, I was getting bored when I happened to overhear an interview by one of the lawyers who shared the room with me. Stu had been a public defender for over a decade. He looked like so many white guys I had known in college and law school—medium height, brown hair in a crew cut, and always brown or black loafers. He was reserved, almost shy, but around the office he was known as one of the best in the courtroom. In court he became a different person, assertive, focused, often aggressive. Once I heard about his reputation, I began to observe how he worked.

That day, Stu was interviewing a large black woman whose voice caught my attention. It was gravelly and at the same time melodic and deeply resonant. She was sobbing, clutching a tissue in one hand and waving her arms as she talked to Stu. I picked up bits of their conversation. Her husband had just been arrested and was being held at the Detention Center for something that had happened in Georgia a long time ago. I started listening more intently.

"He accused of killing a man in 1944," she said, wiping tears from her face. "He escape from a chain gang." She explained that he had been arrested by Philadelphia police the day before when they had a loud argument and a neighbor called the police. When he was routinely fingerprinted, his prints matched those of an escaped fugitive.

"Was Mr. Jiles convicted for the Georgia murder?" Stu asked.

"They say he was."

"The police told you that?"

"Uh-huh."

Stu paused, looking down and away from her, then slowly back up to her face. "There's really nothing we can do, Mrs. Jiles," he said. "When someone is convicted and the state where it happened seeks extradition, that's the end of it. To extradite someone, all Georgia officials need to prove is that a crime was committed there and that the person held for it here is the same person they tried and convicted. That will be easy, since the fingerprints match."

"Lord help us," she gasped. She said she and her husband had four young children. "He was never in any trouble before. His work on construction support our family."

"I'm sorry, ma'am," Stu replied. "Our office advises clients to waive extradition. It can take months before the identification hearing, and your husband won't get any credit for the time he spends waiting here for extradition. If he waives and goes back to Georgia, at least he'll get credit for that time. I'll visit your husband in prison and explain it all."

She was sobbing and wheezing as if she had a bad cold. I stood up out of my chair, slowly, as I watched her leave. This murder her husband had been convicted of had happened almost 25 years ago, just about when I was born. Mary Jiles didn't know a thing about it until her husband was arrested. He had escaped, married, and made what sounded like a good life in Philadelphia for himself and his family. But now he would be sent back to a Georgia chain gang, probably for the rest of his life. She reminded me of someone I knew well, but I couldn't admit that yet, even to myself.

I had no reason to doubt Stu's assessment. He was experienced and one of the best. Yet I just couldn't accept it. There had to be something worth trying, though I had no idea what. I had a strong urge to intervene, although I was afraid it could anger him and I had no basis for thinking I could do anything that might help.

After a long silence, I casually asked, "Stu, would you mind if I look into it more?" I made the mistake of adding, "I've got nothing to do now but interview."

Stu bristled, looking more like I imagined he did in the courtroom. "Fine. You want a wild goose chase, go ahead," he said, as he held the file up in the air like something I would have to fetch. He added some good advice: "Don't let anyone hear you say you got nothing to do but interview. That's a vital function around here. We all do it, even the Ivy Leaguers."

The Ivy League comment reflected a tension in the office I would become familiar with. Until the 1960s, public defender work was usually not sought by graduates from the Ivy League. Most public defenders went to local schools, often, like Stu, at night so they could work and support themselves. Law practice is very hierarchical, and public defender work was near the bottom. This changed in the 1960s, however, as the nation turned its attention to civil rights, poverty, and the rights of people accused of crimes. Criminal defendants' rights are often discussed as if they were an innovation of the 1960s, but they were also the main subject of the Bill of Rights.

Just then, Mrs. Jiles came back into the room to get her purse, which she had left on a chair, making an awkward moment more awkward. "I will be visiting your husband in jail," I said, "to look into whether there is anything that can be done."

"Thank you, sir. May the Lord Jesus bless you," she said.

The word *Jesus* was startling. I never imagined that Jesus would care about me. It feels strange to be blessed so personally if you believe in a different religion or don't believe in any religion as much as the person blessing you. I felt her blessing deeply, although I had never been very religious. I was raised to be proud of my Jewish heritage and aware of the historic oppression of Jews, although my family seldom attended synagogue and I hadn't felt personally oppressed. Right then I thought I needed a good legal theory more than a prayer.

§§§

That night, I worked late at the law library in the office, but I was finding only what I had already been told: Georgia would have to prove just two things—that the crime occurred and that Jiles was the person convicted for it. He was, after all, a fugitive who had escaped from prison. That was the beginning and end of the analysis. It didn't matter that 25 years had passed, that James Jiles had led a good and productive life in Philadelphia, or that there might have been discrimination or unfairness in his trial. All of that was up to Georgia and could be presented in the Georgia courts and then the federal courts once Jiles was returned to the chain gang.

I started with *Corpus Juris,* a legal encyclopedia that covers just about everything, a good place to look when you don't know anything. It had a section on extradition and cites to many cases. I also found an article in *American Law Reports,* which summarizes the law on particular issues, on the requirements for proving the identity of a fugitive. Extradition was mainly a matter of state law. Pennsylvania had adopted the Uniform Extradition Act, standard in most states. From all these materials, I got references and citations to over 100 cases. I browsed the cases almost randomly, looking for some opening to challenge Jiles's extradition.

I found a 1963 New Hampshire case that refused to extradite a man to Massachusetts for failing to pay child support. This was because the guy had never been to Massachusetts, so that case didn't help. Recent cases in Wisconsin and Washington, D.C., mentioned the hardship an extradition could cause to family members but didn't refuse extradition on the basis of hardship. I was getting nowhere. I knew it didn't make much sense for the state where a prisoner fled after escaping to retry or pardon him, even if that's what he deserved. Maybe I was wasting time. That's always a hard call, particularly when you've got no experience.[1]

The list and definitions of crimes and available defenses are different in each state, and most law schools don't teach the laws of any particular state. Every state has crimes like murder, rape, burglary, and assault, but even those have differing definitions and defenses. I had no idea of particular crimes or defenses in Pennsylvania.

The library was only a little larger than my office, the walls lined with the numbered volumes of books I knew well from law school. There were hundreds of volumes of court decisions, statutes, general reference books, and practice guides. I liked the look of them. They held answers to puzzles I wanted to solve, but their sheer volume was daunting.

I settled on Title 18 of the Pennsylvania code, which covered the state's crimes. The list and definitions seemed pretty standard, but I noticed some strange ones. It was a misdemeanor in Pennsylvania to break the ice on a frozen pond or to tell fortunes.[2]

Anyone who "pretends for gain or lucre to tell fortunes or predict future events" commits a misdemeanor, said §4870, adopted in 1861. I liked the squiggly section marks—§—which reminded me of my earlier education in science. They look like a squashed integral sign in calculus.

I looked up the full opinions of a few cases. I was reading intensely when I had that feeling of being observed. I looked up, and there was Stu, peering in the doorway.

"Find anything helpful?" he asked, with a slight, knowing grin.

"No, but now I know all about the crime of fortune telling."

"Is that a crime?"

"Well," I said, happy that I knew at least one thing he didn't, "a faith healer, David Blair, was prosecuted in 1927 in Chester County for advising someone to avoid spells and restlessness by placing salt in his bed in the form of a cross. The court found the advice 'foolish' but let him off because he 'did not furnish the salt' and had 'assumed the usual attitude of prayer.' They exempted what looked like established spirituality."

"Are there more?"

"Yeah. One not-so-established fellow, Charles Dice, was convicted in 1924 for convincing someone that an invisible black dog was circling his house and casting a curse. The curse and the dog were removable for a fee of $36, of which $32 was for curse removal and $4 for the house call. Jeanne Viscount attempted to defeat a curse by burying animal hearts in a backyard and a cemetery. The court called this 'weird' and felt a duty to protect 'the ignorant, superstitious and credulous who, like the poor, are always among us.' It doesn't seem any weirder than a bed full of salt."

"I guess not. I'll stay away from black dogs and animal hearts," Stu said, "and maybe you should get some sleep and tomorrow get back to interviewing."

§§§

After an unproductive evening of law books and daydreams, I headed for the small second floor apartment I had rented on Spruce Street west of Rittenhouse Square. On the way, I stopped for dinner. I had a strong, almost urgent feeling that was familiar but no idea what to do about it. Whenever something seemed important, I couldn't wait. Any delay might change it, ruin it. My tendency was always to try to make things happen right away.

As I watched a black man mop the floor of the restaurant, something that had bothered me earlier came into focus. My thoughts centered on Mrs. Jiles. She was such an appealing person. She struck me as someone with real integrity, a religious woman deeply devoted to her family. But it was also clear that she was tough and had seen the harder side of life.

Now I understood why I had such a strong positive reaction to her. She reminded me of Queeny, my family's maid when I was a child growing up in Baltimore. The connection was embarrassing, though nobody knew it but me. Her nickname, Queeny, seemed a noble's title for a servant, as if mocking her place in life. After my father, who worked for a slipcover manufacturing company, was promoted to manager of the factory, Queeny had cooked and cleaned and taken care of me in my younger years, particularly when my mother was sick for a time.

I loved Queeny, who worked part- or full-time for my parents until I was seven or eight, though most of my concrete memories of her are gone except her face and her walk. I remember the time she let me watch her give herself insulin for diabetes. We were in the laundry room, down in the basement. The skin of her leg was so tough that she had to jab the needle in. Her fist wrapped around it, then her arm slammed it down. She had to do it every day. The shots I got for typhoid and tetanus seemed easy after that.

The civil rights and antiwar activists I had gotten close to in college and law school would find the relationship of this kind, hard-working woman to my family repugnant. So did I, although it provided the only real contact I had with black people until my high school was integrated in the late 1950s. Why is it some people have every opportunity, I wondered, while others have none? Here I was a lawyer, and before that I wanted to be an engineer. Maid or butler wasn't on my list, and engineer or lawyer wasn't on hers or her kids'. Knowing her was part of my bewilderment later in life that white people were so nasty to black people.

In the restaurant where I was eating, the black man continued to mop the floor so I and other patrons, almost all white, could dine in a clean place. Black people cleaned our homes and workplaces, cooked our food, parked our cars. I knew most whites didn't notice such things, and I often wondered why I did. Maybe it was all Queeny's doing, or maybe I was open to Queeny and saw the injustice of her plight because that's the way I am. Back then I thought I would probably never know, and perhaps I never will.

§§§

The day I planned to interview James Jiles, I pulled up in front of Holmsburg Prison. Three Philadelphia County prisons, the Detention Center, Holmsburg, and the House of Correction, held everyone imprisoned prior to trial and everyone convicted and sentenced to less than two years. Prisoners sentenced to two years or more served their time at one of several state prisons, most in remote rural locations. Most pretrial inmates were held at the Detention Center, the newest of the three. Holmsburg and the House of Correction held mostly sentenced prisoners, with one wing at the House of Correction for women and one wing, referred to as "Penny Pack House," for juveniles.

About 3,000 inmates were locked up at the three county prisons. Over half of them were being held prior to trial—which seemed like a lot of people to be imprisoned but not convicted of any crime.

Holmsburg was imposing. Its giant, old stone walls, maybe 20 feet high, had a medieval look. There was no moat, but it looked like there should be. Cars were parked all along the road in front of the gate on a neighborhood street, with row houses right across from it. Kids were playing jump rope and tag in the shadow of the prison, a strange place to grow up.

Inside, three large men, who looked like guards, worked behind a wooden counter in a narrow hallway. As I waited my turn, I noticed an architect's pen and ink drawing of the prison on the opposite wall, dated 1896. Holmsburg was laid out in the shape of a wheel, with a guard center in the hub and long corridors of cells like spokes. This seemed smart, since a small number of guards stationed at the hub could see down each of the cell corridors. I wondered if prisoners maneuvered to get out of sight of the hub.

I smelled a familiar locker room odor but also a pungent mildewy smell that made me feel like I might sneeze. Beyond the counter were what looked like interview rooms along a corridor that led to a door made of heavy metal bars. The door, with a solid metal panel about waist high that held a locking mechanism and a slot for a large key, led to an open or lighted area. Loud noise came from beyond the door, sounding somewhat like a high school corridor between classes. I wondered if the noise was constant throughout the day. Paint was peeling off the walls, and frayed electrical wiring was visible. The concrete floors had odd lines painted on them. Spending one's life in this place seemed inconceivable to me.

I introduced myself to a guard behind the desk, who led me to an interview room. "Mr. 'Carey,' you can set up in that last room on the left, right before the gate. Do you know how this works?"

"Actually, I don't. This is my first time up here," I said. I liked the sound of "mister" in front of my name, but its formality also made me uneasy.

He pointed toward the gate. I could see right away that it opened into the hub. In the center was a large structure, like a big counter. It was made of oak and stood about four feet high. Guards in gray uniforms stood inside the counter. About 15 feet outside the counter was a thick yellow line on the floor that encircled the counter. Several prisoners stood just outside the yellow line facing in, looking like they were waiting for permission to approach the counter. About 30 feet beyond the yellow line was a white line that extended almost to the outer stone wall that encircled the hub. Many prisoners were walking around the perimeter between the white line and the wall. Along the wall, large barred gates led to each of the cell-lined spokes and some smaller barred gates like the one I was peering through.

"I sent a pass down to the cell blocks," the guard said. "It'll take some time, but the prisoner you want will come to the gate on his block and be admitted to the guard station in the middle. They will send them to this gate, and you'll see them come in. If your inmate has a special assignment, it'll take longer to find him."

"You mean he might be working?"

"No, nobody works here. They just sit."

§§§

James Jiles walked into the tiny interview room slowly and sat across a small table from me. He was slender, medium height, much younger looking than his 43 years. He slumped over the table and had sad eyes and a blank look I later came to associate with longtime prisoners. He said little as I told him I had spoken to his wife, Mary. I knew I should not hold out much hope that anything could be done to stop his extradition. There were some uncomfortable silences as I tried to figure out how to say that while also saying that I would try everything I could think of to help him.

I read him the paperwork from Georgia, which said he was Louis Booker, who was convicted of murder in 1944 and escaped from his chain gang in 1945. I asked him if he was Louis Booker.

"I know Mary send you, sir, but I don't know if I should answer that," he said, bringing his right hand to his forehead, slowly moving his fingers in small circles as if he was massaging sore sinuses. His head sank down to where I couldn't see his face.

I didn't expect this, but it made sense. He had kept it all completely secret for almost 25 years. "I understand your hesitance," I said. "You know, as your lawyer, I'm not allowed to tell anyone what you say to me. The only way we're going to see if there's anything I can do for you is for you to tell me everything."

Jiles paused. "That be my given name, Booker," he said softly into the table, his head still down. I could barely hear him. "I guess I am the one they want, sir. No use hidin' it no more." He looked up, eyes squinting and brow furrowed, the muscles around his mouth and cheeks beginning to relax. "I wasn't in trouble except for that," he added, almost apologetically.

I told him, in the most official tone I could summon up, that it is very hard to beat an extradition, particularly for someone already convicted. I would do some legal research, but there might not be anything I could do about it.

He nodded, then said, "Well, sir, ya know, I was convicted, but it wasn't right." He looked me straight in the eyes for the first time.

"Why wasn't it right?"

He sunk down in the chair and paused for a moment. "Lemme see. I was 19 when we had the fight. Me and Perry work on a crew for the lumberyard. We was sent out, jus' the two of us, from Augusta to New Brunswick. In Georgia, you know. Perry was older, maybe 35, and everyone say he a bully. But they tell me to drive the truck. That make Perry my helper, you see. We was given a hut to sleep in, and we cook our food there every night. Perry got drunk that night. He kick the food I cook into the dirt. I was hungry, and we got to arguin'. He be carryin' on bad-mouthin' me, threatenin' you know. I get up and get my huntin' gun out the hut. He still talkin' that shit, and he come in at me, so I shot low to back him off. Some buckshot hit his leg, but it weren't bad. That be the beginnin' of the trouble.

"He got his leg fix up and come back to the hut the next day. He say he was goin' to kill me. I told him he better not try. Couple days later I'm with my girlfriend at her place on Boyd's Alley in Augusta. A woman up the street say Perry looking for me with a gun. I get my huntin' gun out and wait. Sure 'nuff he come down the street, holdin' his gun. I step out and he point the gun at me. I shot him dead where he stood."

I didn't expect anything like this story. Jiles was just a kid when it happened. He might even be innocent. "At your trial, did your lawyer argue that you acted only to defend yourself?"

"I don't get no lawyer, sir."

"You had no lawyer at your trial?"

"No, sir. No one but my kin saw me the whole time I was in jail waitin' for the trial. Somebody I never met sat at the table next to me during the trial, but he didn't do nothin'."

"Did you have a jury?"

"Yes, sir. They was all white men, like all the juries in Georgia. The whole trial didn't take but a couple hours. My family wasn't even there, 'cause they didn't tell 'em when the trial would be. They heard I was convicted after I was on the chain gang."

If this was true, the conviction should be reversed. But no judge was going to listen to any of it on an extradition. The story and my urge to immediately do something about it were nearly irresistible. I hoped that didn't show.

After a few months on the chain gang Jiles knew that couldn't spend the rest of his life there. "I knew I had to escape or die trying," he said. "I be dyin' there the rest of my life anyway." •

I asked him how he escaped. He said he was on a rural chain gang that bunked in a dilapidated former farmhouse. At night, there was an old guard who slept soundly and sometimes forgot to lock the front door. Escape was nearly impossible because the irons and chains on the prisoners' legs were not removed at night, the farmhouse was surrounded by a fence, and several bloodhounds roamed inside the fence at night. If a prisoner left the farmhouse at night, the dogs would attack and their barking would wake the guard. Even if he got out, an alarm set off by the guard would alert locals, who would shoot him on sight.

"I watch the dogs at night from the bunk window, tryin' to figure a way out. One night, I see the cows going out to pasture. They show me how to get out. The dogs don't even move when a cow walk by. They do everythin' by smell, and cows smell okay to them. A few nights after that, when the old guard didn't lock the front door, I rub cow dung all over me and walk right by them dogs, holdin' the chain 'tween my legs with one hand. I get over the fence and run to where I hear a train go by each night, hop it, and get to Philadelphia. It be awhile 'fore I smell right. That cow shit, you know."

"How did you get the chains off?" I asked.

"We find a bar in a rail yard. There be two of us, and we pry the chains off each other with the bar. One of the older men come with me, but he get so scared of bein' lynched, he turn himself in a few days later. I hear he still on the chain gang."

I asked him why he chose Philadelphia. "My people was from Carolina, Union, South Carolina," he said. "We was always told Philadelphia is the best place in the North. It ain't been bad to me, but I don't know why they said that. None of 'em ever been here."

For the first few years after his escape, he did farmwork in southern New Jersey. "I was pickin' tomatoes, cabbage, lettuce, all sorts of things. That's where I met Mary, waitin' for a train one day. The best day of my life." He smiled for the first time.

He got regular work with a construction crew. First he was digging ditches and breaking rock with a sledgehammer. "Weren't much different than the chain gang," he said. "I be workin' a jackhammer for 10 years by now, when they need me."

I paused, trying to figure out what to say next. "I'll look into this and come back to visit you soon," I said. My words felt insignificant after his story. I wished I had more to offer him and found myself trying to appear as if everything was routine.

"I be here, ya know," he said, smiling again as he got up and returned to his cell.

§§§

Jiles's story was part of the strange history of black migration to the North after the Civil War. Northern cities with growing industries were eager to recruit former slaves and unemployed young blacks for cheap manual labor. Many older blacks were hesitant to leave the South, but after cotton-picking machines were perfected, there wasn't much work for them there. Northern companies and cities sent recruiters to the South, offering blacks incentives to come up north, although often they didn't keep their promises. Cities competed; recruiters spun tall tales of plentiful jobs and housing almost free.[3]

Blacks from the Mississippi Delta migrated to form the large black communities in Chicago. Philadelphia recruiters focused on North and South Carolina, so for many blacks from those states, Philadelphia was the place to go. Jiles followed that trail, but for him the journey required an ingenious escape.

I was impressed with Jiles's resourcefulness and courage. What looked like waste or fertilizer to most people became a way out for him. As I drove back to the office, I decided to go through every case I could find to look for any decision that refused extradition based on the unfairness of a conviction; the passage of a long time in which a defendant led a productive, law-abiding life; or the hardship that extradition would cause a family.

I spent almost all that weekend in the law library at the University of Pennsylvania, so involved that the time passed quickly. Still, I caught myself daydreaming frequently, and I wasn't the only one there doing so. Experienced lawyers and well-published professors could be seen looking vacantly into the distance, with a finger gracefully inserted in an ear or a mouth hanging open. It was tempting to assume they were absorbed in creating some great theory or strategy. But I knew it was probably just that legal decisions are numbing, trance inducing.

Finally, I began to find some useful legal stuff. An article in the *Washington and Lee Law Review* published early in 1968 said "future irreparable harm" should be a ground for a court to refuse extradition. The article discussed hardships, rehabilitation of the person convicted, and invalid convictions. "Future irreparable harm" made it sound more official, I thought. I would use that phrase if this got anywhere. The article cited a case that was the best I had found yet. A recent federal court decision in Michigan focused on the difficulty and time required to challenge an invalid conviction. The case was helpful, even if it stood alone amid hundreds that went the other way, but the article itself didn't mean much. The article had been written by a student; even law review articles by professors are notorious for spinning theories that don't amount to anything. I had learned in law school that often you can't trust what books say.[4]

In several other cases I noticed references to the role of state governors in extradition cases. A Missouri Supreme Court decision in 1947 stated, "there might be a variety of circumstances which would justify a governor in refusing extradition." In 1943 the Illinois Supreme Court referred to the discretion of governors. My whole law school experience—which never included a mention of extradition—had focused on courts and judges, so I didn't understand why a governor would have anything to do with it. Law schools still generally operate as if the only significant legal event or action is the decisions of appellate courts, which does not prepare students very well to actually practice law. The role and discretion of governors seemed worth exploring.

§§§

I had done the basic research and had at least one interesting idea. It was time to talk to the person I knew could help me most with ideas and advice—Anthony G. Amsterdam, the law professor who had brought me to Philadelphia and the Defender office. Tony created an innovative program at Penn Law School that provided law students with some hands-on "clinical" experience with real cases, as medical schools routinely did for their students. Before Tony's program, law students got credit only for courses that focused on appellate court opinions. With funding by a four-year grant from the Ford Foundation, Tony hired three law school graduates a year who worked for the Defender office like other Defender lawyers but with the assistance of about 50 law students.

Though less than 10 years out of law school, Tony was already a legendary figure in the law. He had clerked for Supreme Court justice Felix Frankfurter, who referred to him as "one of the best brains to ever come down the tubes." His articles were already influential, and he was leading a nationwide challenge to the death penalty. He and others, mainly at the

NAACP Legal Defense Fund, had prepared a "Last-Aid Kit"—a set of legal documents for any person on death row, with full instructions and blanks to be filled in, that raised a range of constitutional challenges and included everything required to get a stay of execution at any stage of the process after a death penalty was imposed. The documents were so clearly drafted and at the same time so sophisticated and complete that probably anyone who could read and write could stop an execution. These efforts eventually stopped all executions in the country for about a decade and came close to invalidating the death penalty in Supreme Court cases often argued by Tony. I was honored to be chosen by Tony as one of the three graduates for 1968. I also couldn't tell why he picked me and worried that I might not live up to his expectations.

As I entered Tony's often open office at Penn, he was, as usual, deeply engrossed in a mass of documents. He looked up at me as I came in. He was thin and gaunt with a chiseled face, mustache, and deep-set eyes. Some used to call him "the hawk" because of the intensity of those eyes. He wasn't much into small talk, but he was always friendly and a focused listener to students as well as colleagues.

Desks and tables were arranged in an arc around Tony's swivel chair, and two big manual typewriters were on adjacent tabletops—one was for text, the other for footnotes. Tony would bounce back and forth between them, typing out the content of a legal scholar's typically long footnotes, usually with complete citations and page references, as he placed their numbers in the text. His typing was intense and fast—some described him as the fastest living typist—as words composed, edited, and retained in his olympian memory seemed to spill out.

I explained the problem and the results of the research I had done as Tony looked at me with his piercing gaze. He paused a moment, then said, "Dave, you've hit on the only possibility. A court challenge would be a waste of time. The governor route is possible but extremely unlikely. The governor of the state must sign what's called a 'governor's warrant' to validate an extradition. It's a technicality really, but a signed governor's warrant is a prerequisite to extradition. Governors sign them routinely. Once in a blue moon, a governor refuses."

"Are there reported cases where a governor has refused?" I asked.

"The instances where it's done are hard to find because they're not in any of the case reports. This body of law can't be found in appellate decisions. There was a law review article about it sometime in the mid-'50s.

Student law review editors wrote to the governors or attorneys general of every state and reported on the instances of governors' refusing to extradite." As he finished, Tony smiled and added, "Before you go much further, do you know who the governor is?"

"No." I was new to Pennsylvania, and it sounded like I wouldn't be happy with the answer.

"The new governor is a conservative Republican named Raymond Shafer. Governors in general and Republican conservative ones in particular don't like to appear to be helping convicted murderers. They also worry about retaliation by the other state because down the line they'll also be requesting extraditions."

This made sense. If Pennsylvania's governor refuses to send somebody back to Georgia, Axehandle Maddox might refuse to return some murderer to Pennsylvania. The Axehandle moniker for Georgia's governor, Lester Maddox, came from his standing in the doorway of his fried chicken restaurant with an ax handle in his hand, refusing to admit black people. This public act had launched him to the governorship.

"So you think it's not worth pursuing?"

"Your call. It's a worthwhile fight, but you should weigh the chances of success, which are minimal to nonexistent, and the other things you could accomplish in all the time it would take to do this."

"I'll think about it some more."

"Take care." He turned back to his mass of papers as I left.

I ran back to the law library. I couldn't wait to get at the *Index to Legal Periodicals*. The index contained long lists of law review articles, organized chronologically and alphabetically. I scanned the rows of thick red books and took down the volumes for the 1950s. There it was—an article entitled "Interstate Rendition: Executive Practices and the Effects of Discretion" in the 1956 *Yale Law Journal*.[5] It was over a decade old and written by a student. The handful of governor refusals to extradite had happened years earlier, some as far back as the 1930s. The most recent one cited was in 1952. Most disappointing, there was no instance of a Pennsylvania governor's refusing an extradition request. It had never been done in Pennsylvania.

But I had a theory. The article said the "foremost" bases for governors' refusing extradition was the rehabilitation of the fugitive and the "time lag," the time elapsed since the offense. Jiles's 25 years was as long as any of the successful cases. Other bases included hardship to the fugitive or his family and the unfairness of the trial. Trial issues were less favored, since they implied wrongdoing in the state where the crime was committed, which might upset relations between the states. In the rare cases in which extradition was refused on the basis of rehabilitation or hardship, the article said there were no hard feelings, bruised egos, or retaliations.

I felt the excitement in my stomach, where I often experience strong feelings. The article not only provided a catalog of unreported cases and successful theories. It also met the major argument against refusal. Refusals on grounds that don't imply wrongdoing have not caused a problem. And I thought I could frame the argument so the age of the favorable cases actually helped: Governors' refusing extradition was a traditional part of the established process, not some newfangled 1960s invention, and Pennsylvania's governors hadn't done it before because it wasn't something done lightly. An appropriate case simply hadn't come along, until this one.

§§§

I went to the office of the *Evening Bulletin,* Philadelphia's major daily newspaper at the time, to look at news clips and get some understanding of this Governor Shafer and maybe some idea of how to approach him.[6] Many microfilmed articles mentioned him, but they didn't say much about him. He had beaten the Democrat Milton Shapp.

Governor Shafer was born in 1917 in Meadeville, at the western end of Pennsylvania near the Ohio border. Before running for governor, he had been a prosecutor and state senator. His campaign literature described a Republican version of John Kennedy. He had even skippered a PT boat in the Pacific. I pictured the Pacific cluttered with PT boats, to accommodate the number of politicians who claimed to have skippered one. "Handsome in a rugged sort of way . . . never a loser . . . big in both body and mind," a campaign flyer said. A campaign ad in a newspaper described him as "big, tough, and likeable." Big and tough seemed important to the campaign strategy, perhaps because Shapp wasn't. Shafer went to college locally and then to law school at Yale. "Never a loser," he had, of course, been president of his college class.

There wasn't much about what he stood for—"development," "prosperity"—or any indication that he either opposed or favored the 1960s liberal reforms in criminal law. The only information on racial issues didn't sound promising, particularly since conservatism was more or less defined in those days by opposition to integration and to civil rights for blacks. Shafer condemned racism as a "brutal cancer" in a speech, which sounded like the moderate part of moderate-conservative, but the NAACP had boycotted a conference he sponsored on minority employment.

An interesting sidelight in the more recent articles was that Shafer had strongly backed the unsuccessful 1967 Republican candidate for mayor of Philadelphia, District Attorney Arlen Specter. Specter, most known as the leading proponent of the "single-bullet theory" of the John Kennedy assassination (and later as the U.S. senator who grilled Anita Hill at Justice Clarence Thomas's confirmation hearing), was the first Republican DA anyone could remember. This had possibilities. Any official in Philadelphia had to be concerned with black votes. Maybe the person to focus on first was Specter. He would be hard to convince, particularly as a prosecutor. But at least he would have to pay attention to issues important to blacks and liberal whites.

As I thought this through, it became clear that I would have to organize essentially a political campaign aimed at the governor. My argument to the governor and district attorney would be in terms of the traditional though seldom used discretion to refuse extradition and the factors for doing so identified in the law review article. The injustice of the conviction; the time lag; Jiles's productive, family-oriented life in Philadelphia—all were essential and doubtless appealing to most people. But they would not be enough to get this governor to refuse to extradite or this district attorney to urge him to do so. I had to make it politically appealing to refuse extradition or unappealing not to, or both.

It would take a lot of time and effort. Tony had said it was extremely unlikely to succeed, accompanied by a smile that I took to mean something like you may have to learn some things by making your own mistakes. Everyone I asked at the public defender office also thought it a waste of time that could be better spent on other cases, including the lawyer in Tony's program I was closest to and who would later be my law partner, David Rudovsky. Maybe I was too young, too stubborn, or too stupid (because, rationally, they were right) to listen.

§§§

I started formulating strategies and gathering evidence to reach and then convince the governor. I got a big break while talking to Mary Jiles on the phone. Sometimes luck or fate can seem to lend you a helping hand or to smack you in the head. It's tempting to see it as confirmation or repudiation of the rightness of one's cause or even of one's life. I haven't made up my mind whether it has spiritual origins, but it sure feels good when it goes my way.

I was explaining my strategy to Mary so she could help get evidence that James was a good person who was greatly needed by his family. I told her I wanted everyone in the black community to know about James, and I asked her to start with the churches, neighbors, and anyone else she could think of. I prepared a petition for her to distribute for signatures and asked her to get some people who knew James to tell me stories about good things he had done, what he meant to them, and the like, which I would write out in affidavit form.

"Okay," she said. "I be singin' and passin' petitions at every church in the city 'fore you know it."

"You sing in the choir?"

"Oh, yes, I do. You come to my church sometime and hear us."

"I would like that. Do you know anyone in the church who might know Arlen Specter, the district attorney?"

"No. James met Specter once though."

"He did?"

"Uh-huh. Specter spoke at the union hall, and James shake his hand. He told me 'bout it."

"He shook Specter's hand. That's good. Maybe I can use that as an opening with Specter, though he probably wouldn't remember James."

"He remember they for him."

"What do you mean 'they for him'?"

"For DA. They vote later that night in the meetin' to back him for DA. The TV say they the only union that back Specter."

"Mr. Jiles's union was the only union to back Specter when he ran for DA?"

"Uh-huh. Do that help?"

§§§

Local No. 57, Laborers' International Union of North America, AFL-CIO, had a reputation for tough work and tough workers and a renegade streak in politics that preceded its support of Arlen Specter in a town where labor was strongly Democratic. News clips at the *Bulletin* said Local 57 was already supporting Richard Nixon over labor-backed Hubert Humphrey in the upcoming presidential election. This wouldn't be easy. I needed a contact at the union who might support a resolution by the membership and provide an opening to Specter. People at the public defender office could arrange for me to have a conversation with Specter, but I was afraid that would make it, in his mind, a criminal, prosecution-versus-defense matter. I wanted him to see it as a union and black community issue.

Even if I got him to see it that way, he would be afraid of being labeled soft on crime or of being blamed if James were later charged with another crime. What I needed first was something to assure Specter and the governor that Jiles was not dangerous and to insulate them from blame in a worst-case scenario. The best way to do that was to get a report on Jiles by the court's Probation Department, which did such reports to aid judges in sentencing convicted defendants. One of the higher-ups at the Defender got me on the phone with one of the heads of the Probation Department. He seemed to want to do it after I told him the circumstances, but since there was no pending criminal case in the Philadelphia court, it was problematic. The Probation Department had authority and funding for cases in its own court, not extraditions to another state. Nevertheless, the Probation Department assigned an experienced, well-reputed probation officer, Earl Hall, who completed a report in two weeks.

The conclusion of Hall's report was clear and emphatic:

> It is respectfully recommended that the Subject's freedom be continued, as the Subject is completely rehabilitated and no useful purpose would be served by incarcerating him. He is an asset to his church and to his community, and the Subject's family would suffer severely if he is taken from the home.

This statement appeared on the last page. The first page discussed Jiles's arrest in Philadelphia and the argument between James and Mary that precipitated the arrest. This made sense, particularly given the doubts about whether the Probation Department could do a report at all. They started with the Philadelphia arrest, as a usual report would. But it bothered me. I thought the statements made in the report's conclusion should have been put at or near the very beginning and not be left to the end.

The argument against extradition should start there and be stressed throughout the rest of the report. Such details always bother me. I knew in this instance it was less important than it seemed, and I let go of it. Letting go of bothersome details has always been hard for me.

I was getting close to the most significant and challenging steps in this process: the calls to Specter and Shafer. I had the Hall report, and Mary was gathering petition signatures and stories about Jiles for affidavits. Tony Amsterdam gave me the name of a lawyer in Georgia who might help, John Ruffin, Jr. He agreed to get copies of the case file and trial transcript and to try to substantiate Jiles's memory of a lack of counsel and an all-white jury, which he said were common shortcomings of trials of blacks in Georgia in the 1940s. He also said the reason Jiles was not executed was probably the race of the man he killed. Georgia often didn't execute for killing a black man.

I was tempted to go to the media with the story, particularly the *Philadelphia Tribune,* a black community newspaper. A story there would get Mary more invitations to sing, and maybe they would run an editorial. I began to read the *Tribune* regularly and to keep track of reporters' names. I could also approach the big circulation, mainstream press. The *Philadelphia Inquirer* was very conservative in those days, but the *Bulletin* might do a good story. This was risky, though. An early negative story in the major press could kill it with the public and maybe with the DA and governor. I decided to go slowly and carefully with the media, starting with the *Tribune.*

I had one other idea that seemed strange but intriguing. There was no reason to leave Georgia officials out of this. Once I had the evidence of rehabilitation, I could ask Georgia to withdraw the extradition request. The chances of that happening were slight, but why not try? If Georgia said no, it could help in Pennsylvania because I could tell Shafer that Maddox got all the same evidence and refused to do the right thing. I decided that I would call Georgia when I had everything in hand, and I'd ask to speak to Maddox personally.

§§§

The union lawyer was cautious, but the leadership of Local 57 saw supporting Jiles as an opportunity for a union criticized for racial insensitivity to help a black member in a matter that would draw significant publicity. They arranged a meeting with Specter and told the union lawyer to accompany me.

Specter's office was upscale city hall, the woodwork in good shape and polished mahogany bookshelves lining one wall. Specter sat in front of a large semicircular window and greeted us cordially. His dark curly hair framed fine, almost delicate features. He was thinner and smaller than I expected.

Specter spoke as everyone sat down. "Nice to meet you, young man," he said to me. "I hear you're new over there at the PD. I want you to know that it's only through the graces of Local 57 that I've set aside this time for you. If something is important to them, it's important to me. But I must tell you that my people can't find any precedent for a governor refusing extradition, and I'm concerned this was a murder case." He sat back in his chair, looking squarely at me. He was smart and direct and gave a good politician's nod to the union.

I explained that at the time of the murder Jiles was 19, in a fight with a 35-year-old man, with both of them armed, when Specter interrupted.

"So why wasn't he acquitted?"

"You would be horrified by the record in the case," I said. "There was no defense lawyer, the trial took a few hours, and the jury was all white men."

"But if I accept all that, why not send him back to Georgia and let him raise these issues in appeals?"

I gave him the results of my research on the major errors in the trial, emphasizing that Georgia courts, including their appellate courts, were regularly affirming convictions even if the U.S. Supreme Court had reversed convictions based on the same error in other cases.[7]

Specter grinned. "Why doesn't that surprise me?" He leaned a little forward and relaxed, a good sign, I thought, feeling myself warming up. I decided to focus on the all-white jury.

"The Supreme Court recently reversed a Georgia case where a jury commissioner had noted an 'N' for Negro next to the names of blacks on the jury list," I said. "Yet a Georgia appellate decision refused to apply that precedent to a case where the commissioner had noted 'C' for colored. In both cases, the notations were used to exclude blacks from juries."

"Alright, but that's a problem for anybody convicted in Georgia," said Specter. "Why should I help this guy?"

"It would take Jiles several years and a topnotch appellate lawyer to get all the way through the Georgia courts to the Supreme Court," I said, "and, as you know, the odds against the Supreme Court even deciding to review any particular case are enormous. Meanwhile, his wife would lose her husband, and his four children would have no father. They'd probably end up on welfare—not in Georgia, but here. This trouble happened 25 years ago. He was a kid, and he's rehabilitated now."

"How do I know that?"

I handed him the Hall report, opened to the last page, and read him the conclusion. "James Jiles isn't perfect, but there's no question he's rehabilitated, if in fact he did the crime and needed rehabilitation."

Specter read the Hall conclusion. He looked up at me, slightly curling his lips on one side, his eyes squinting. "I'm going to be honest with you, Mr. 'Carey.' The guy doesn't sound dangerous, and I'd like to do you a favor. But it's risky."

"Why?" I said, looking at him eye to eye.

"Look, David," the union lawyer said, "maybe we should go."

I looked directly at him—I probably glared—took a deep breath, and turned back to Specter.

"Mr. Specter, I appreciate your honesty," I said. "You put it on the level of risk, so let me address it directly on that level. There is no risk to you and a lot of benefit. In the unlikely event he's freed and later does something bad, you can say you relied on the Probation Department report. Nobody's going to hold that against you. The report says he's no danger, and it's been 25 years since he was in trouble. On the other hand, you could be a hero on this, standing up for justice and civil rights. It'll help you win elections. I found out this morning that the *Tribune* is about to do an editorial asking the governor not to send Jiles back to Georgia. Blacks are over a third of the voters in this city, and they care about an innocent black man sent back to a chain gang, as do a lot of whites. You know, your role in this will be public, whatever you do and however it comes out."

"The *Tribune's* doing an editorial?" Specter said.

"Yeah. Look at the conclusion of this report again. You can't be faulted, and you'll get the credit for this as a leader who's willing to stand up. We'll all see to that."

Specter paused, thinking. "Well, you've made your best case. Now let me think it over, and we'll get back to you soon."

§§§

Almost a month had passed, and I hadn't yet heard from Specter. It was time to call Governor Shafer's office. If I let too much time go by, the governor's warrant might get signed routinely. I had to at least alert them that we were asking him not to sign it. I also wanted to request a hearing at which we could make our case to him face to face.

There was no procedure for this. I had trouble deciding whether I should get the name of some high-level adviser to the governor or attorney general or maybe call blind and not say much until I got to the higher-up. Either way, this strategy was aimed at getting to a higher-up quickly. An alternative was to purposely find somebody lower down. A high-level person would have power in the governor's operation. But I could imagine that someone lower in the operation and younger might be more likely to latch onto the case as a matter of principle and an important civil rights case and become an advocate to the governor and his advisers—someone who would take it on as a project of his own, would be more accessible to me, and might keep me posted on the goings-on in the governor's office.

A receptionist answered at the governor's office.

"Hello. I wonder if you could help me. I'm not sure who in the governor's office I should speak to." I had chosen the dedicated subordinate strategy and thought I'd enlist the help of whomever I got, including the receptionist.

"I'll try. What is it you want?"

"Thanks. I'm David Kairys, an attorney in Philadelphia. I have an unusual case involving an extradition."

"Extraditions go through the attorney general's office. Do you want that number?"

"I don't think so. This involves the governor directly, although it's a legal matter. Is there someone who advises the governor on legal matters?"

"Yeah, the attorney general . . . but, you know, one of the governor's new assistants is a lawyer. Hold on, I'll transfer you to—"

"What's his title? Hello, are you there?" I heard clicks and then the off and on ringing tone. She was gone.

"Hello, governor's office."

"Hello. This is David Kairys at the public defender office in Philadelphia. I have an unusual civil rights matter, and I'm not sure who I should be talking to." I worried that I should have said "whom" instead of "who."

"Well, shoot, and I'll tell you if it's me or someone else." He sounded direct, friendly, and young, and the mention of civil rights seemed to spur interest in his voice.

"I represent a black man who escaped from a chain gang in Georgia 25 years ago after being convicted without a lawyer by an all-white jury. He came to Philadelphia, married, and raised four kids. Georgia now wants him back—25 years later. At first, it looked hopeless, but I've come on one possible avenue of relief, and it involves the governor."

"How so?"

I explained that governors have a power they often are not aware of themselves since they must sign the warrants for an extradition to occur.

"I put a stack of them on his desk every so often. He signs 'em, though I doubt if he reads 'em. It's pro forma."

I asked if he knew that governors throughout the country have refused to sign on occasion, emphasizing that this is just the kind of case where it's been done. I asked for an evidentiary hearing before the governor, a chance to present evidence and argument before he routinely signs the warrant.

"I never heard of this. Lemme ask around here and get back to you."

Before he hung up, I found myself chatting with him. This sort of chat became familiar over the years, something I came to call lawyer banter. It can be about a case, a job, work in general, vacations, or the meaning of life. Sometimes it was strategic—to establish a relationship that could be used for particular purposes. I found it also humanized otherwise sterile and often hostile exchanges that consume most of a lawyer's day. Most often, it was both.

"I really appreciate your looking into this," I said. "It sounds like you're the right person for it. What are your usual duties?"

"I'm first assistant to the counsel to the governor, and I spend part of my time in the attorney general's office."

"Sounds like an interesting job. How long you been at it?"

"Oh, maybe 11 or 12 weeks. That's why I'm not sure. But it's a great job and an opportunity to see how government works."

"How long you been out of law school?"

"Three years. How about you?"

"I just graduated last June. I was doing interviews at the Defender, and this just fell in my lap."

"Sounds more like a novel than a legal case. Look, it's good talking to you. I'll get right on this and get back to you."

After years of law practice, I lost my taste for lawyer banter, at least when it goes beyond this kind of friendly chat, which it usually does if three or more lawyers gather together. I still have many friends who are lawyers, but I took to eating lunch with clients or friends or by myself rather than with other lawyers. I was aware that some lawyers saw it as an affront, not playing the game. For me lunch became a break from law practice, not an occasion for more lawyer talk.

§§§

I paused and then dialed again, trying to calm myself.

"Hello, governor's office."

"Hello. Could I speak to the counsel to the governor, please?"

"You mean special counsel, special counsel to the governor?"

"Yeah, that's it," I said. I thought I'd try the same title in Georgia. It was close, except in Georgia they're special, like FBI agents. All FBI agents are officially "special agents."

"Office of Special Counsel. Can I help you?"

"Yes," I said, "I'm calling from Pennsylvania. I need to speak to the special counsel for Governor Maddox as soon as possible about an interstate matter."

"Hold please."

I thought sounding like I expected it to be important to the special counsel and using an established-sounding category for it might get me put through. But I was on hold so long that I almost hung up. Then a man's voice came on.

"Hello, Frank Blankenship here."

"Mr. Blankenship, hello. I'm David Kairys, an attorney in Philadelphia, Pennsylvania, and I need to speak to the special counsel."

"That's me. Get to it."

"Well, I represent a man who did something awful in Georgia 25 years ago, then escaped from one of your prisons to Philadelphia, where he's led an exemplary life, working in construction, marrying, and raising four kids. He was just discovered as a fugitive, and I wanted to talk to you, and if possible to Governor Maddox, about the possibility that you might extend mercy in his case. I've heard the governor, though tough on crime, has an unusual record among governors for extending mercy when it's appropriate." One of the lawyers in the office told me he had read in a magazine story that Maddox pardoned a lot of mostly black prisoners each Christmas.

"Yes, that's right, and he's proud of that record. But I don't think we've ever granted clemency to a fugitive. He'd have to turn himself in down here, then ask for clemency."

"I understand that's the usual procedure. But that could take years, and it would destroy a family up here in Pennsylvania. They'd have to go on welfare without his income."

"Look, Mr. 'Carriage'—"

"Kairys."

"Give me his name and your phone number, and I'll look into it and get back to you."

"Thanks. He's Louis Booker, convicted of murder in a fight in 1944. I'd appreciate it if I could send you supporting materials, including a report of our Probation Department saying he's rehabilitated. What I'd really like is just a moment to talk to Governor Maddox personally on the phone."

"We'll see. Murder, huh. . . . What was that number?"

"LO-8–3190 in Philadelphia. Thank you."

Nobody gets my name right on the first try or often the second or third. My ancestors on both sides—the Lovetts and the Kairys—came from small Jewish enclaves in Eastern Europe, probably in what is now the Ukraine. Our original name was pronounced and may have been spelled "Kuris," meaning fisherman or something to do with fish. I'd prefer to think it didn't mean fishy, although at times I've wondered. Some immigration official probably thought it a garbled pronunciation of a not uncommon Lithuanian Catholic name pronounced "Care-reez." Kairys has been our name ever since.

I sent the materials to Blankenship—Hall's report, affidavits with the stories Mary had gathered, and the petitions. It didn't seem hopeful, until a couple weeks later when I got a call back.

"Mr. Kairys, Governor Maddox will talk to you, and he read some of the materials you sent. Hold on a minute. I'll get his secretary and see if he's still ready or got into something else."

More than a minute passed. I thought I might be dreaming.

"Is this Mr. 'Carey'?" a woman's voice said.

"Yes." I had given up on the pronunciation.

"Hold for the governor."

Another minute, maybe two. I felt myself sweating.

"This is Governor Lester Maddox calling from Atlanta." His southern drawl was extreme, his voice friendly.

"Hello, Governor Maddox. I really appreciate your taking the time to talk to me."

"Yes, young man, well I read what you sent, but I'm afraid I can't do anything for ya."

"Do you have any doubt that he's rehabilitated, governor?"

"Nah. I seen that probation report, and it's been a long time. I suppose he's as rehabilitated as the rest of us."

"Then why waste Georgia's money keeping him in jail?"

"I'm goin' to be honest with you, son. Every Christmas, I free some nigras from prison in the spirit of the holiday. My people collect the files of the best still in prison, and I pardon some of 'em, sometimes as many as a dozen. But this ain't Christmas and—"

"Governor, shouldn't we strive to keep that Christmas spirit alive the whole year through?"

"Well, that's creative young man, but I got a hell of a fight on my hands in the legislature. The assembly won't pass anything I send up. Those bastards would love to stick me with a soft-on-nigras story. Nobody can remember a governor down here pardoning somebody who's still a fugitive. Have him come back to Georgia, voluntarily. In a year or so, maybe I'll be able to do it."

"I appreciate that, governor. Can I tell the governor of Pennsylvania that you don't mind if he doesn't send the guy back?"

"Well, I don't know, you're playin' me every which way now. . . . Nah, it could get out down here. Now you come down here and visit us, son. You're doin' a fine job."

"Thanks, governor. Good luck with the assembly."

I hung up and sat back, not sure what had just happened. I liked his style and sense of humor. At the end I wished Maddox good luck with the legislature although I had no idea what the issues were between them. He might be pushing things I deeply opposed. And my Christmas-every-day-of-the-year argument was naive and felt embarrassing. I was trying to absorb what happened, but all I could think about was the absurdity of it all. He won't do it because it's not Christmas.

§§§

Several months went by, during which I was admitted to the bar and started arguing cases in court. I spoke to Mary a few times a week. On the morning of June 25, 1969, I left for the state capitol in Harrisburg with my car stuffed with stacks of legal papers. I wasn't worried about keeping my presentation to the governor short. I wanted the case for refusing extradition to be compelling, supported by mounds of evidence. However, I wasn't so sure about two things.

I still wore the beard I had let grow off and on since graduation. Beards were unusual among lawyers in those days, more associated with the hip or beat counterculture. There was a short article about mine in the *Evening Bulletin,* about a judge's telling me, during a legal argument, how his law clerk from Harvard was late because "his beard got stuck in an inkwell and he had to take time to clean it."[8] Inkwells were uncommon by that time, but I was apparently the only practicing lawyer in Philadelphia with a beard, although the walls of the courthouse were lined with pictures of bearded judges from the past. Some of my colleagues in the public defender office thought it unwise, even irresponsible, to retain my beard when I went to the hearing before the governor.

I wasn't trying to look hip or beat, but I was conscious that it looked and made me feel different than other lawyers and judges. The beard gave me some separation from them and confirmed my sense of integrity. It said, for me, something like, "I don't want to be a judge or care if I make a lot of money; I'm here because I believe in what I'm doing." There were also less noble and less self-conscious reasons—it saved a lot of time and money. I was liberated from the shaving industry, with its never-ending array of products for before, after, and during. I had made up my mind to keep it unless I got the sense that it hurt a client. So far, it had drawn comments and some jokes, but it didn't seem to have any significant effect on judges. Today, I still have a beard—I haven't shaved for 40 years.

My other worry that day as I drove to Harrisburg was coming in a separate car: James Jiles. I had used the rehabilitation evidence we gathered and a parade of community witnesses to convince a judge to release him on bail, although that was unusual for a fugitive who had been convicted of murder. Some in the office also thought bringing him was a mistake. There wasn't going to be a trial but rather an informal hearing or perhaps just a discussion with the governor. With no established procedure or precedent, I had no idea whether it would be held in a courtroom, conference room, or office. The governor might be offended by Jiles's being brought into an informal or attorneys-only setting. I took this seriously, and it worried me, because people who were more experienced and knew much more than me were deeply concerned. But their apprehensions also baffled me.

I wanted Jiles there because he was a soft-spoken, likeable guy who would seem nonthreatening, and he and Mary would make this case human and real. He said he would come if I thought it would help; he left it to me. I wanted to introduce Jiles to the governor and have them shake hands. I told him to try to make eye contact when he was introduced. I thought this would make it as hard as possible for the governor to send him back to a chain gang for the rest of his life.

The initial reception we got wasn't encouraging. The governor's staff told us the governor was too busy to preside at the hearing or to meet us. We would be heard by a deputy attorney general, Frank Lawley, Jr., who would come as soon as someone found a room. I told them we would need several chairs. After a while, we were led into a large ceremonial room to a very long table in one corner. I set up my notes and stacks of papers, and we waited.

Lawley walked in briskly and sat in the chair at the head of the table. The staff introduced me, and I immediately introduced James, Mary, and our witnesses. Lawley looked a bit surprised to see James standing in front of him, but he rather routinely shook James's hand and cordially but formally smiled at him. I thought it counted as contact.

Lawley asked if anyone was there to represent Georgia. His staff said no one came, although they were invited. He turned to me. "Proceed."

I handed Lawley my 16-page brief—on that silly-looking long paper, like the yellow pads but white—that presented five grounds for refusing to extradite James Jiles: rehabilitation, time lag and hardship, invalidity of the conviction, future harm because of the refusal of Georgia courts to abide by U.S. Supreme Court decisions, and timeliness (based on their missing some deadlines). I started with a short summary, emphasizing that extradition requests had been refused in other states without any resulting interstate problems. Then I called our witnesses and presented our documents.

Nolan Rochester was a neighbor and friend of James and Mary. He told Lawley that James saved him when he was attacked by two youths on the street. They beat him and crushed his eyeglasses into his eyes. James intervened, stopped the beating, and held one of the youths until the police came. Mr. Rochester said he realized only later how courageous this was, since any contact with police could result in James's return to the chain gang. He concluded, "If he is not a good friend and neighbor, then I don't know who is." Earl Hall summarized his report and strongly reaffirmed that James presented no danger and that Mary, who had asthma and had been ill in recent years, would probably have to go on welfare to support the children if James were sent back to Georgia. Lawley had no questions for them or for James.

I presented the petitions and letters or affidavits from four other neighbors, James's employer, the union president, and the pastor of his church. There was a unanimously passed resolution by the membership of Local 57 urging the governor to allow James to "remain among us as a free man." A lengthy editorial in the *Philadelphia Tribune* noted that James's conviction stemmed from a fight with the "town bully," that churchgoers contributed the money for his bail, that the conviction was unfair, and that he was rehabilitated. The editorial urged Governor Shafer to "refuse to sign the extradition papers which would send this man back to the slave labor Georgia chain gang."

The affidavit of John Ruffin and a letter from the clerk of the trial court in Georgia documented the deficiencies of the trial James told me about in our initial discussion. Two attorneys had been appointed to represent James just before trial, but neither of them had considered possible defenses, investigated, sought witnesses, or even interviewed James. One of them appeared at trial but asked few if any questions. The jury was all white. Ruffin had determined the race of all the jury members by comparing the jury list to the tax lists that identified the race of taxpayers. The clerk confirmed that there was not even a transcript of the trial.

I had one last piece of paper. I handed Lawley a copy of a letter sent a week before directly to Governor Shafer. Arlen Specter, resting heavily on Earl Hall's report, concluded that "the interests of justice would best be served if Mr. Jiles were not extradited back to Georgia."

Just as I was winding up, Lawley stopped me—probably fearful that more was to come, enough for several days. He said that the governor would make the final decision, but based on what he had seen, he would recommend that James not be extradited. James jumped up from his chair, as if thrown out by a big spring suddenly uncoiled. He stood speechless, looking at Lawley. Mary sobbed, "Praise the Lord."

§§§

A couple weeks later, the governor's office issued a press release announcing that he had refused to extradite James Jiles to Georgia, and I received a copy of a short statement by the governor and a formal opinion prepared by Lawley recommending that extradition be refused. Lawley emphasized rehabilitation, but he came down hard on Georgia—harder than I anticipated—for the trial and for flaunting Supreme Court decisions. It said he was "frankly impressed by the mass of evidence."

I liked that and enjoyed the subsequent celebration at the public defender office and the approval of the outcome expressed by stories and editorials in the media.[9] There's nothing like an early, startling victory to lift one's spirits and confidence. But it was also unsettling. I didn't have a method or approach to law practice; I didn't even know why I did what I did in Jiles's case. I had put to good use some lessons from my childhood—which was hardly in the distant past—my father Bernard's resourcefulness and sense that there is always a way, my mother Julia's strong but charming opinions and stubbornness, and my identification with outsiders and sensitivity to injustice from as far back as I could remember. But the public praise and pats on the back by colleagues were tempered by the sense that I didn't know what I was doing. I wondered if it was just a fluke.

I had to advise James not to leave Pennsylvania. If he were picked up in another state, Georgia could again request extradition, and Shafer's decision would not be binding. He never set foot outside of Pennsylvania, nor did he get in any trouble. I saw him a few more times, when he stopped in my office to say hello, before he died in 1991.

I saw Mary more often and remained close to her. We usually talked on the phone, or I visited her at home. Once I took her to one of the best restaurants in town, where she talked a lot about the difficulty of her early life and her sometimes rocky relationship with James, which had not come up earlier. Her health deteriorated, but she stayed active in her church and its choir as long as she could.

In 1994, a few years before her death, she invited me and my wife, Antje Mattheus, to the Sunday service at Oak Grove Baptist Church in North Philadelphia. We got there before the service began, as people entered the church and greeted each other with lots of big smiles and big hugs. The program on the seats contained prayers, events, and a list of the names and addresses of church members who were sick, with the heading "Please Remember Our Sick and Shut-in Members!" It was a community, with a mission, loyalty, and sacrifice at its heart, so different from the groups I was part of.

The church was now packed to the walls with members of the congregation. A door behind the altar opened, and nine women in long, pale-blue robes entered and stood on a stepped podium, three to a row. The last one out was Mary, who by then needed help walking. There was muted conversation and some milling around until piano music filled the room, at first softly and then with building depth and force. Several men in long black robes entered from the choir door and took seats on decorative wooden chairs on either side of the altar, facing the quiet but now packed congregation. No one spoke, but I could feel the shared anticipation in the room.

A large man rose from the chair nearest the altar and walked slowly to the pulpit. "Good morning, brothers and sisters," he said, smiling, his deep baritone voice carrying through the room. "Sister Charisse will offer today's morning prayer."

A slight woman rose from the congregation and read a short passage from the Bible. As she sat down, the blue-robed choir rose in unison. Their hymn started slowly, then built to a chorus:

Sing out, sing out, Oh Lord
Please do not pass me by.

They repeated the chorus, again and again, giving the "do nots" increasing emphasis with each repetition. I felt the music deep inside, so unlike anything I had heard in a synagogue. The harmony, the intensity, the unmistakable beat of every blues and rock 'n' roll song I'd ever heard moved me deeply.

The minister rose, announcing school and church events for the coming week in a low, almost whispered voice. Then he said, "You all know a lawyer came to the aid of Brother James and Sister Mary. Not a rich or famous lawyer, but a lawyer who cares about all God's souls. Welcome to you, David Kairys, and your wife beside you. Stand up, please stand up, and say something to us."

I didn't expect this. Loud applause surprised me more but gave me a moment to collect myself. "I'm deeply honored to be recognized by you and welcomed to your church this way," I said, feeling my voice crack and wondering if everybody could hear it. "I want you to know that we couldn't have won without Sister Mary, and many people in the community, several of whom I see here today, who helped. For me personally, knowing Sister Mary has enriched my life. She will always be an inspiration to me." My tearing eyes met Mary's, then I sat down quickly, very aware that I hadn't called her "sister" before.

"Thank you, brother," the minister said. "Now Sister Mary goin' to lead the choir in a hymn she's dedicatin' to Mr. Kairys." The piano played a soft rhythm as Mary stepped forward in front of the choir. Her heavy lidded eyes were barely open as she settled into position with some difficulty.

"Oh, Lord," her voice boomed deep and urgent,

Forgive us, forever. Forever.
For we shall obey Thy will.
Peace. Peace be still.

The choir joined behind her with thundering harmony, "Peace be still, peace be still." Several verses and choruses followed. By the time they were done, I was ready to be saved.

I don't believe I will ever receive a greater honor.

CHAPTER TWO

Bailed Out by the Great Writ

OR THE FIRST FEW MONTHS of my new job, my assignment was to interview a steady stream of clients, which is what I should have been doing when I overheard Stu interviewing Mary Jiles. The white interview form was as long as the yellow lawyer pads, with blanks for personal information and prior arrests and convictions on the front. Details about the crimes charged and possible defenses went on the back. The form made sense, but I didn't know anything about interviewing. Nothing in law school had prepared me for the most basic aspects of representing a client. When interviewing was discussed at all, the focus was what not to do, conduct that will get you disbarred. I worried that in the interviews I might miss some defense or a personal detail that might help on sentencing. I didn't realize until I got to do trials how right Stu was about the importance of the interviews. These interview forms were usually all the trial lawyer had to prepare for trial.

One of my first interviews was with a young man named Gerald Johnson, who was charged with burglarizing a house on his own block. He had just turned 18 and had dropped out of Germantown High School a year before. He was tall and thin with a big Afro hairdo. He wore a T-shirt with a faded picture of the face of Bob Marley, whose reggae music I loved. I got his name, address, and other personal information for the front side of the interview form.

Then I asked, "What happened when you got arrested?" I thought this was a good way to get started. Some clients took it as asking only about the arrest, while others started with what led up to the arrest.

"Don't I get no choice," he said, "'bout who's doin' my case? I don't want no PD. I want a real lawyer."

"PD" is what everyone called public defenders, often with a pejorative implication. I didn't expect that, and I had trouble understanding his English. "All the PDs are lawyers. We have to go to law school, take the bar exam, just like other lawyers."

"But PDs ain't the good lawyers, right? Ain't they part of the police or DA or somethin'?"

"No, we're completely independent, and I think we do as good a job or better as most the lawyers you pay. But if you want to hire a lawyer, that's up to you."

"Nah, nah, I ain't got no money for that. Go 'head."

"So what happened when you were arrested?"

"We was on our corner, and Train come by wit the stuff."

"The stolen stuff?"

"I guess. We don't know nothin' 'bout it."

"Who was on the corner with you?"

"Shawnee, that my brother, and Rico."

"Who's Rico?"

"Our corner boy."

"What did Train say?"

"He know Shawnee. He yell to him to hold the box for him. That was it. He go down the street."

"The box is the TV mentioned on the charge form?"

"Yeah, the TV. He got other stuff too. He just lay it all on us and run." Johnson shrugged his shoulders and looked at me like I should understand it by now.

"Okay," I said, "so what happened next?"

"The man come wit sirens. They jump out the red car and grab us. They say the box stolen from a house down the street and laugh when Shawnee tell them 'bout Train."

Johnson and Shawnee were charged with burglary, theft, and receiving stolen goods. I asked for details about Train.

"He a boy in the neighborhood, you know. He done some time at Graterford. He hang at the corner store a few blocks from our corner.

Train tell me 'bout the PDs. He say the guys wit big time at Graterford got PDs, the others go home."

"Do you know his real name and address?"

"Nah. He Train," Johnson said emphatically, with wide open eyes that met mine and another shrug. Then he looked away and added, quietly, "Shawnee maybe know more 'bout him."

I got all this down on the interview form and then filled out an investigation form. I was uncertain about the story, so I suggested that an investigator try to find Train by first speaking to Johnson's brother and then following up on leads. On my way to get lunch, I left the forms in the "Completed Interviews" and "Incoming Investigations" boxes near the elevator. I didn't want to part with them, though. I liked the look of the completed forms on my desk.

When I got back from lunch, there was a note on my desk: "See Vince right away." Vince was Vince Ziccardi, the deputy defender, who was rumored to be in line for the top job, defender. I was one of many assistant defenders. The defender titles seemed a bit overdone, but I got used to them.

Vince greeted me with a big handshake and a smile and repeated what he had said when I met him the first day. "It's great to have you here, and I'm sure you're going to be an asset to us."

Then his face tightened, and he looked at me under dark, bushy eyebrows with a slight frown. "But look, Dave, we have only a few real investigators and over 25,000 cases a year. The investigators are mostly retired cops, and some probably should retire again. We don't investigate stolen TV cases."

He paused, shaking his head as he leaned forward in his chair and got close to me, as if to tell me something confidentially. "You hear that bullshit about somebody leaving something just stolen and running off a few times a week around here. I called a DA I know, and he looked at the file for me. Johnson's brother already confessed. The three of them have been robbing houses in the neighborhood for a year or so. There ain't gonna be any investigation of this bullshit, and you clear any requests through me for a while. You alright with this, Dave?" He looked exasperated but tried to smile at me, maybe feeling he was angrier than he wanted to be.

"I guess so," I said, "but it would be nice to know these policies before I start. You may be right about this, but what about the poor guy who really is left with a TV by an acquaintance? It sounds like no one would investigate or believe him." I spoke with all the authority and certainty I could muster, but I wasn't sure if I was defending some hapless TV recipient or myself.

"Maybe you'll help us work up a manual or something, but meanwhile check with me on anything out of the ordinary."

"Okay," I said, wondering how I'd know what was out of the ordinary.

I hoped Vince wasn't serious about the manual. I didn't want to write manuals. I was there to try cases, and I was embarrassed. Being naive felt worse than being wrong. You're easily fooled, laughable, not good material for a Perry Mason audition.

§§§

Soon I graduated to the next stage: bail hearings, in which I would stand up in a court and represent clients. I found out that it wasn't much of a court, and it was hard to call it representation.

I was told to go to the bail court at Eighth and Race Streets. I walked from the Defender Association north and east toward the Delaware River, but I wandered too far north, fascinated by the dilapidated, mostly boarded up remnants of industrial Philadelphia. These factory and warehouse buildings had formed the backbone of the Industrial Revolution. Several blocks away in the small area next to the river that made up colonial Philadelphia were Independence Hall and Congress Hall, where the Liberty Bell was housed and the U.S. Constitution was written. A walk through these neighborhoods was a walk through American history.

At Eighth and Race I found the Police Administration Building, usually called the Roundhouse, because it looked like two five-story cylinders joined together and probably like a figure eight from above. A large parking lot was full of what everyone called "red cars," bright red police cars. They later phased out the red cars, because the color was seen as too provocative and they claimed that the color accounted for why so many feared the Philadelphia police.

Maybe a hundred officers stood near the red cars or walked in and out of the building. I had never seen so many police in one place. Some with "Highway Patrol" patches wore high jackboots and pants that widened at the upper leg, reminding me of storm troopers in old World War II movies. The whole assemblage looked like an army massed at its barracks. I felt out of place and a little scared.

I walked up to one of the officers who wasn't in jackboots. "Excuse me, officer, could you tell me where the bail court is?"

"You're right in front of it," he said, smiling as he pointed to the Roundhouse.

"But that's the Police Administration Building."

"Yeah, and the bail court is on the first floor. Just go in. You can't miss it."

The early stages of the criminal justice system up to the point of trial, Stu explained to me later, took place in police buildings and were intertwined with police operations. A person arrested was taken to a local police district and booked there, then taken to the basement of the Police Administration Building for fingerprinting and processing, and then brought up to the first-floor courtroom for a bail hearing. The highest ranking police officers and their centralized operations were at the Roundhouse. There were also police district headquarters and detective divisions in the various neighborhoods. Preliminary hearings were conducted by magistrates a week to 10 days later in courtrooms in police districts. Police milled about in the courtrooms as bail hearings and preliminary hearings were conducted.

I was nervous as I walked through the doors of the Roundhouse. I was a rookie public defender, and this was the domain of Frank Rizzo, the legendary police commissioner and later mayor. The walls inside were mainly cinder block with vertical strips of stained wood, probably put there to soften the stark stone surface and give the appearance of paneling, typical early 1960s construction. It felt stark and forbidding. A sign pointed to the courtroom on the first floor. It was a small room with the judge's bench elevated. A few floor-level desks were in front of the bench. Behind the desks was a small enclosed cell room with a Plexiglas front. To the judge's right, another enclosed area with a separate entrance from the first-floor lobby held about a dozen chairs for spectators.

When I entered, the judge's chair was empty and policemen stood around talking and exchanging papers. I walked up to one and asked if he knew where the judge was.

"Yeah, knock on the door behind the bench," the cop said. "He's in there smoking or playing with himself." The officers laughed.

I knocked, and the judge invited me in. "I'm David Kairys, a new public defender."

"Hi, I'm Judge Vito Spinelli." He was a short, stocky man with a friendly smile. "We'll start hearings in a few minutes. You'll get the hang of it. I really don't know why the PDs send anybody here, anyway. We just set bail. There's no right to a lawyer at the bail-setting stage and nothing for you to do here."

I knew the judge was right about the law. The Supreme Court had only five years earlier said, in *Gideon v. Wainwright,* that there was a right to a lawyer at criminal trials. Three years after that, the Court extended the right to counsel to certain interrogations in the *Miranda* case. But defendants had no right to an attorney at a bail hearing. The Defender Association sent lawyers only when we had sufficient resources to cover all the other stages of the process.[1]

I tried to explain to the judge why I thought the bail hearing was important. If someone doesn't make bail, they're imprisoned without being convicted of anything—often for a longer time than they would get if convicted and sentenced. You can lose your job in the time you're locked up awaiting trial or even lose your family. Besides, at trial it looks better for a defendant to walk in from the street rather than being escorted in from a cell.

"None of these criminals got a job to lose, son," Judge Spinelli said. "But you'll see. Here, lemme give you something that'll help you get into things." He handed me an index-sized card from a stack on his desk. It listed all the magistrates' names and phone numbers.

His casual labeling of all the accused as criminals and his assuming they were all unemployed annoyed me, and I wanted to question him about it. The Defender memos and reports said that most cases were dropped or dismissed before trial and that the Defender lawyers won most of the rest that went to trial.[2] But I thought I should learn more before doing any serious questioning.

"Thanks," I said. "How do I get to the cell room to interview my clients?"

"You don't need to do that. You just wait out there in the courtroom, and they'll bring up the prisoners."

§§§

The judge followed me out of the chambers. "Mr. Carey, is it?"

"Kairys, Judge."

"Okay, Kairys, you sit over there," he said, pointing to the desk at his far right.

I sat, feeling self-conscious. The courtroom was bustling with activity. Police led five handcuffed men into the enclosed cell. Four other people sat or stood behind the desks. A woman who appeared to be a clerk sat off to the judge's left and busily wrote on and arranged a stack of forms. A young man not much older than me who wore a fashionable suit stood by one of the desks, engaged in an intense conversation with a police officer. I guessed he was the prosecutor. Two other men looked like plain-clothes police or clerks. The desks were littered with multicolored papers. Everybody seemed to have a lot of forms and something to do but me. I wished I had brought a yellow pad or something in front of me on the desk so I would be an actor with at least one prop. I fiddled with the card the judge had given me. There was writing on the other side that said "Get out of Jail . . ." with a drawing and typeface that were familiar. It was a replica of the get-out-of-jail-free card in Monopoly, with the name, address, and phone number of a bail bondsman at the bottom. The judge was handing out ads for a bondsman.

The judge settled in behind stacks of forms. He looked from desk to desk, waiting until the DA sat down. "Alright, we're in session now," he said. "Bring up the first prisoner."

The prisoners were brought out to a bench in front of the Plexiglas cell. Their handcuffs had been removed. The uniformed officer yelled, "Richard Davis, step forward." A tall white man stood and walked slowly toward the desks.

There was a great deal of paper shuffling and muttering. The clerk handed a blue-green form to the prosecutor. Another man fumbled with the pasted together pairs of paper you got when copies were made by pre-Xerox "wet copy" photostat processes, separating some and handing them with other forms to the prosecutor and the clerk. The clerk passed several forms to the judge. Stuff was going every which way, some of it winding up in front of me. I had a carbon copy of the charge form and a still-wet copy of Davis's criminal record.

Davis, in his mid-30s, wearing a tie and wrinkled suit, was charged with drunk driving, and he had a prior arrest, also for drunk driving. The earlier charge was dismissed for reasons not explained on the criminal record form. He mostly looked down at the floor. When he looked up, his eyes didn't seem to focus on anything. There was a large stain on his jacket and pants, whitish with yellow streaks and specks of something. It looked like he had gotten drunk and puked on himself.

The judge looked up. "Alright, Mr. Davis, you understand you're charged with driving while under the influence of alcohol. This is not a trial. I'm merely going to set bail today. DA—" He looked to the DA.

"Yes, Your Honor, the defendant has a prior arrest for drunk driving. He lives in Cherry Hill, New Jersey. Mr. Davis, where are you employed?"

"I'm, uh, at a car place in Cherry Hill. I sell Nashes and Studebakers."

"Studebakers?" Spinelli said. "I didn't think they were around any- more."

"We sell a few leftovers, yeah, the last model was, uh, 1966. Nash is our main thing though." Tears were visible in his eyes; he seemed embar- rassed. He had the reddish complexion and swollen face I associated with alcoholism, and he was struggling to be coherent.

"Your Honor, we request bail be set at $300 and he be allowed to sign his own bond."

"Okay, that's right, $300 S-O-B. I'll accept that," the magistrate said.

Everybody started to write on their forms, recording the result. I thought I should too, but I hadn't been told what to record or bring back or what to say. I wrote "$300 SOB" on the charge form, which seemed to mean Davis would sign his own bail bond rather than having to post the amount himself or purchase a bail bond from a bondsman. The effect was to release him without any bail.

As they all wrote, the court officer announced, "Next, Terrence O'Neill—come on, move up there—burglary, robbery, theft, receiving stolen goods."

The judge turned to the DA again, as a young black man in jeans and a white T-shirt slowly stepped up. He had short, evenly cut hair, like most black men, and opaque plastic-rimmed glasses that looked worn past their time.

"Your Honor," the DA said, "this was a daytime burglary and robbery of a neighborhood hardware store in Roxborough. Defendant is almost 19. Two hammers, a box of screwdrivers, and an electric drill were taken, value over $100. That makes the theft a probable felony, Your Honor, along with the burglary and robbery. We recommend $2,500 bail."

"Okay, it'll be $2,500," Spinelli quickly responded.

I felt I should act, but I didn't know what to do. He had no prior record. That seemed a high bail for an 18-year-old to come up with, unless his family could help. He would probably sit in jail for months.

Nobody bothered to hear his side. I thought that was why I was there, so I might as well say just what I was thinking. But I was worried that my questions asked without having any idea how he would respond could hurt rather than help him. "Judge, could I quickly speak to him and see if there's something to be said that might lower that amount?"

"You don't need to speak to him, Mr. 'Carey.' We know everything we need to know. Besides, we're getting to the dinner hour. Just ask him what you want, right now. We're all friends here." They all grinned, except me and O'Neill.

I felt this was wrong. A lawyer should confer with his client in private and then figure out how to best present the client's case. The judge would only be aggravated by a direct challenge, though. I turned to O'Neill. "Mr. O'Neill, you live in this Roxborough area?"

"Counselor," the magistrate interrupted, smiling again, "his home address is in Germantown. The crime was in Roxborough."

O'Neill raised his hand, like a student in school. "Sir, Your Honor, can I explain somethin'?"

"Go ahead," Spinelli said, "explain, but make it quick." His expression, as he looked at O'Neill, was a mixture of skepticism and impatience. He didn't expect O'Neill could say anything worth listening to.

"I do live in Germantown, my whole life, and I go to Germantown High School. I was workin' at the hardware store after school in Roxborough 'til last week, when Mr. Matthews fire me. He say I too slow on my deliveries, and he won't pay me for my work all last week. I get upset and say I goin' to take some stuff from the store for what he owe me. Then they call the police. I sorry 'bout this, but I ain't no burglar or robber."

All noise and movement in the courtroom suddenly stopped. Not the best way for an employee to get paid, I thought, but it wasn't the burglary or robbery everyone pictured from the DA's summary of the charges.

Spinelli fiddled with his papers, avoiding eye contact with O'Neill or me.

I spoke, trying to sound conciliatory. "Judge, he has no prior record at all. He's a lifelong Philadelphia resident, and it sounds like he might have a good defense. I request that bail be set at $500 and he be allowed to sign his own bond." I thought it best to talk as if the bail hadn't already been set rather than ask him to change his earlier decision.

"Well," Spinelli responded, "I'll set the bail at $750. His people can find a bondsman."

"Judge, if I may," I said, "shouldn't we find out if he can afford that much?"

"No, Mr. 'Carey,' that doesn't matter. Now that's it; we're done with this case. We got a late start today. Send those three back down to the tank. We're breaking for dinner. Let's see, it's 6:15. We'll reconvene at 7:30."

The room was very quickly empty. I slowly gathered my few forms and went out the main entrance. The uniformed officer who called out the names was already standing beside the door, smoking a cigarette. "Counselor, don't take it too hard," he said. "You win some and you lose some in this game."

I realized I must look sad, which was how I felt, and the officer was trying to help me. Still, I wasn't ready for the casual lack of concern for people charged with crimes, the putdowns, or the humiliation of it all. Spinelli humiliated both O'Neill and me, with no apparent thought or understanding. I wanted to shout at him—to say something, but I wasn't sure what, and I suspected that this wasn't exactly the most opportune moment. It confused me, particularly since Spinelli seemed like a decent fellow. I didn't realize my feelings and confusion showed so openly.

"I'll try not to," I said to the officer, "but that kid shouldn't be in jail if what he said is true." I also didn't think it was just a game, but I didn't want to argue about that.

"Well, they all got something to say, but it don't turn out to be much."

"I guess I'll have to wait 'til I know more, to say whether I agree with that. Say, officer, where can I get something to eat?"

"Well, there's vending machines down the hall to the left. Just down the way there, though, that's Chinatown. Good food and pretty cheap." He pointed west, toward Race and Tenth Streets.

"Thanks. I'll see you in an hour."

§§§

Philadelphia's Chinatown looked a lot like New York's. You walk along a typical street, and then all of a sudden you're in another country. I picked the first place I saw with a bunch of ducks hanging in the window and quickly finished a large bowl of soup with noodles and wontons, topped with Peking duck. I sat there awhile with a pile of bones in front of me, greasy hands, and some spattered soup on my suit. I must have looked a bit like the drunk who puked on himself.

I thought about Terrence O'Neill, who was probably still in the Roundhouse tank or on his way to the Detention Center in Northeast Philadelphia. This part of my job was unexpectedly hard on me. When a trial or hearing is over, the defense lawyer—win, lose, or embarrassed—goes home or out to eat a good meal. The clients, when they lose, often go to jail. The disparity, the extreme difference of it, stunned and surprised me.

I was upset and realized it would be easy to feel guilty. But I had done my best based on what I knew to do. Maybe an experienced lawyer could have done more, but responsibility for what had happened was squarely on Judge Spinelli.

It didn't matter to Spinelli in the slightest whether O'Neill dined this night in prison or in Chinatown. He couldn't care less about O'Neill. To him, they are all, as he said, criminals, and so their feelings, their lives, were of no concern. I saw O'Neill as a kid who lost his after-school job, got angry, and chose a very foolish way to collect what he considered was due him—and then found himself treated like a murderer. O'Neill was a victim to me but a criminal to Spinelli. I wanted to yell about it—to Spinelli or whoever would listen—but I knew I had to control myself in the courtroom, understand the system in more depth, and think strategically about what to do.

I thought about justice, fairness, and "do unto others." Spinelli would be horrified if some judge treated his son that way or if the police arrested and charged his son for a botched attempt to get an earned week's pay. But O'Neill wasn't his son or a person he cared about.

I remembered one of my own brushes with teenage disaster. I was with a group of guys one night in the near suburbs of Baltimore when we came across a big housing development with maybe a dozen of the houses still under construction. It was the 1950s, and seeing so many houses that were just the same was new to us. As we joked about it and went inside some of the open, unfinished houses, I noticed that each house had a street address number on a piece of wood hanging in the front yard. Wouldn't it be funny, I thought, then said, if we took the numbers down, scrambled them, and put them back up? People might go to the wrong house.

The next day a construction crew came and started adding a room to the wrong house. I was in deep trouble. We committed some crimes—theft and trespass, maybe burglary that was, legally, not dissimilar to what O'Neill was charged with doing (burglary was usually defined as entering a building with intent to commit a felony). Someone recognized us. There were lots of phone calls, including some by a parent who was a lawyer; lots of upset parents; lots of apologies; and some scared teenagers. The people who got the unexpected new room liked it and were willing to pay for it, and the contractor therefore got to build two room additions rather than just one. The homeowners were angry, and we had violated the law, but explanations, excuses, and apologies got heard and understood. We were, like them, middle- or upper-middle-class whites and not threatening. There were no arrests, no bail.

§§§

The next morning, before my late shift at the Roundhouse started again, I called the Detention Center. O'Neill was there; he didn't make bail. I went to see Vince.

"I got this Judge Spinelli, and I could use your advice," I said. "He wouldn't let me interview the clients before the hearings. A kid got held on $750 who may only have taken some merchandise in full view of his employer as payment for his last week's work. I wasn't allowed to talk to him or figure out how to present his case. He handed me this card—"

"Hold on, Dave. I got it. That's par for the course. I never heard of any of us interviewing anybody down there. They don't want to hear us most of the time in any courtroom. They just hear the DA and pretty much do whatever the DA says. DAs kick ass; private lawyers at least get listened to; and us, we watch. That's the system. The most useful thing I can see we do at the Roundhouse is bring back copies of the criminal records."

"It's not just Spinelli?"

"Nah, no way. Spinelli's not so bad. They all got connections to politicians, and some are a little shady. Spinelli is a lawyer at least."

"Aren't they all?"

"No, the magistrates are political hacks who got their appointments for party work. They don't have to be lawyers, and many aren't."

"Would it be alright if I raise a few questions?"

"Do it nicely, Dave."

"I'm always nice, I think."

My priority as a lawyer wasn't to be nice. I hoped one could challenge injustice and still maintain respect for others and common decency, even toward one's adversaries. But the challenge was more important than being nice.

I called the Detention Center daily for over a week, and Terrence O'Neill was still there. I also called Germantown High School and spoke to a vice principal. O'Neill was in his last year there. A three-month stay in jail would cost him his senior year of school, in addition to his freedom and maybe his hopes for the future. He would be incarcerated in a facility in which he would be surrounded by older prisoners, some of whom were there for violent offenses, at a time that might determine the direction of his life. Who knew whether he would be able, or willing, to go back to school after that.

§§§

I was dumbfounded by the bail system. This kid had no prior record, he was working after school and about to graduate, and he would probably be acquitted once the trial came or at worst convicted on some very minor charge. The results of the bail hearing would likely be far more damaging to O'Neill than the results of the trial. Since bondsmen charged 10 percent of the bail amount, he was imprisoned because he didn't have someone to put up $75 for him. I wondered how many of the 1,500 or so prisoners held pretrial in Philadelphia were there for lack of such small sums of money.

I researched the bail system at the Penn Law library for several afternoons before going to the Roundhouse at 5:00 p.m. I found that the Supreme Court had only decided one case directly on the bail system, which was itself surprising. In 1951 the Court ruled that the only legitimate purpose for bail was to assure a defendant's appearance at trial. Likewise, the *Pennsylvania Rules of Criminal Procedure* stated, "The amount of bail shall be such as to ensure the presence of the defendant." Historical materials going all the way back to the time of the Constitution emphasized the posting of something of value to the defendant, such as a horse or a farm, which would be taken away if he didn't show up. They didn't ask for more than a person could post. That would defeat the purpose.[3]

I thought I should talk to Vince about it again. I stuck my head in his office doorway one day just before going to the Roundhouse for my 5:00 shift. He looked up from a pile of papers on his desk and in his lap and said to come in.

"I checked out the bail system, and all of the authorities say its only legitimate purpose is to assure that defendants show up at their trials," I said. "But we've got these magistrates setting bails too high for poor folks and not bothering to ask what a defendant could afford. Lots of our clients with minor charges sit at the Detention Center because they can't afford the low bail set."

"Yeah, I know, Dave," Vince said. "But you got to be practical. We all know some defendants are so dangerous they should just be held 'til trial. A mass murderer, like that guy who randomly shot people from that tower in Texas a few years ago. They've just broadened in recent years what and who is considered dangerous."

"But that doesn't explain the imprisonment before trial of these people," I argued. "These are people the magistrate thinks are a low risk of running or hurting anyone. If the prosecutor wants to hold someone prior to trial, we should define the grounds for a determination of danger, require proof of it from the prosecutor, and give the defendant the chance to disprove it." I sounded frustrated and angry.

"Alright, look, Dave, I'm with you. Maybe I'm too used to these things. Why don't you work something up, a memo on it?" He looked at me blankly with a slight smile, then looked again to his paperwork. Back to the "manual" again.

I headed for the elevator and my shift at the Roundhouse. What got me was the role of money in this process. O'Neill was still in jail even though Spinelli decided that he posed little risk because Spinelli expressed his decisions in terms of a bail amount, an amount of money, rather than just ruling that O'Neill posed little risk and should be allowed to go home. O'Neill was in jail although Spinelli really had not decided that he should be.

On one of my first nights at bail hearings, Spinelli had set bail in an attempted murder case at $10,000. That defendant stabbed his next-door neighbor because he cut down a tree between their houses. The defendant's wife paid a bondsman the usual 10 percent fee, $1,000 in cash, and her husband went home with her. He was free although the judge thought he posed a risk.

The translation of Spinelli's judgments into money amounts without considering ability to pay made the system completely arbitrary. High-risk defendants with financial resources were free, while low-risk defendants sat in jail because they lacked funds. Freedom and justice were for sale.

§§§

The next day I got to the Roundhouse at 5:00 p.m., but the courtroom was almost empty. I ate at the vending machines, peanut butter and cheese crackers, which I've always liked. I got a cup of coffee and sat on a bench, encircled by the machines. Even the vending area was round. I knew I couldn't just sit at the PD desk while poor people were paraded through the system and hauled off to jail without anyone hearing their side. There had to be something I could do.

The information needed to make a useful presentation at one of these bail hearings was minimal. I could quickly ask and write down each defendant's residence, length of time living there and in Philadelphia, and a few family details. Employment or school information would help. It wouldn't take a long interview to get enough to make some difference with the magistrates. Someone who has kids and lives with them would sound more likely to show up for trial and appear less threatening. Prior record was on the police form, but simply asking whether the defendant has a record would prevent a mistaken identity. This wasn't the time or place to find out the details of each defendant's story. But I could ask briefly if there was anything else I should know.

A lot of the information consisted of numbers or could be written down with a word or short phrase. I could jot it down quickly if I made a chart for it. That would also make it easy to present the information to the judge. I got out my yellow pad, now always with me, and started to draw columns. "Name, age, address," I wrote at the top of columns. Maybe I didn't need the complete address, just the neighborhood. "Time at that address" and "Time in the area" got two narrow columns, room for a two-digit number. I left a small column for "Family connections" and a digit column for "Number of kids." I created a small column for "Employment or school" next to a narrow column for "Number of years."

"Record" needed room for just yes or no. A small column at the end was enough for "Explanations."

I gazed at my long yellow chart, feeling very satisfied. It reminded me of my years studying engineering and science in college. I was once again recording the data, analyzing it, and presenting results. It could be a lab report or an experiment. Who knew those courses would help me practice law. I thought my bail chart, like a lab report, should be properly lettered and lined. I would get out my old drafting equipment that evening.

§§§

I went back to the courtroom. Spinelli showed up about 6:15 looking very full, probably of Chinese food. "Judge," I said, "can I see you in your chambers a moment?"

"Sure, Mr. Kairys, come on in." We walked into the little room behind the judge's bench. Spinelli took off his suit coat and sat down. "What is it?"

"Well, Judge, I've been thinking about how I could more effectively perform my duties down here. It's hard for me to get you the information you need if I haven't talked to the defendants. You remember the Germantown High School kid the first night I was here?"

"Yeah, I remember that kid." His voice dropped, like it wasn't a fond memory.

"If I'd known his explanation and background before you started, I could've given you the information right away. I really appreciated your rethinking that one, but you wouldn't have had to if I knew right off." I was trying to place the shortcomings of the process on myself, not the judge, and to stress that the judge could save time and do a better job with more information.

"Okay, so what's the point?" Spinelli said impatiently.

"Well, since we have these big delays between each group of prisoners brought up, I could interview them downstairs without any delay. Then I could present you all you need quickly at the hearing. I reduced it all to a chart—"

"A chart. Lemme see."

I put my yellow pad down on the desk in front of Spinelli. "I think I could fill them out in a few minutes for each defendant if you'd tell the police to let me in the tank."

"You do? Son, we got off to a bad start, but that don't mean nothin'. You're doin' a good job. But it's dangerous down there." He paused for a moment. "I'll tell you what. I'll order them to bring up the next group 15 minutes early. You sit with them in the fiberglass cell up here for 15 minutes, and let's see what you come up with."

"Thanks, Judge. I'm ready." I felt absurdly pleased.

Spinelli smiled. "Now, I gotta make a private call that's goin' to take just about 15 minutes."

"I'm on my way, Judge."

§§§

It was hot in the small Plexiglas cell, and I was crammed in beside three men and a woman. They looked at me like I shouldn't be there. I addressed them collectively. "I'm David Kairys from the public defender office, and I'll represent any of you who don't have private counsel at your bail hearing today. I need some information from each of you. We have to work quickly, so please try to answer as briefly as you can."

I turned to a young black man next to me, wearing a fashionable suit and tie. "Sir, what is your name?"

"Wayne. Look, I been through this, so don't bother. They're on their way to take care of me. I be right outta here, you understand."

"Okay, you sure about that?"

"Yeah, I'm sure."

I turned next to a middle-aged black man. I squatted uncomfortably in front of him, holding my pad on my knees. "What's your name, sir?"

"Alex Horne."

"Where do you live?"

"On Larchmont Street, near 49th."

"What neighborhood is that?"

"West Philadelphia. Don't you know that?"

"No, I'm new here. You live alone or with family or friends?"

"I live with my wife of 22 years and our three kids."

"How long you lived there?"

"Oh, 'bout 10 years in that house. My whole life in West Philadelphia."

"And how old are you?"

"Forty-eight, last I looked."

"Are you employed?"

"Sure am. I'm an insurance salesman with Prudential, for the last seven years."

"Now, what have they charged you with?"

"Drunk driving." I had noticed the smell of alcohol, but in the crowded cell room, I couldn't tell where it came from.

"You got any prior arrests?"

"Yeah, for drunk driving, about three years ago."

"Convicted?"

"Nah, it was just bullshit, like this one. They dropped it."

"Thank you. Now," I said as I shifted toward an older white man, "what's your name, sir?"

"Gus Stavros. 63. South Philly, near the Italian Market. Work at a newsstand for my cousin. Charge: numbers. Gus Stavros, this is your life." He looked at me, grinning. "Did I get it all for you, kid?"

I smiled back. "Yeah, Mr. Stavros, that was quick. Thanks. Record?"

"Sure. Numbers. Lots of numbers busts. I don't know, maybe 25 by now. Nothin' else."

"Okay, thanks." I figured numbers must be some kind of gambling.

"And your name, ma'am?" I turned to the last prisoner, a black woman.

"Lorette Jones."

"Address, Miss Jones?"

"It's Mrs. Jones, if you don't mind. We separated, but we still married."

"Sorry. Employment?"

"You kiddin' or you blind?"

I looked at her more carefully. She wore a short skirt, barely covering her panties, and a halter top that didn't cover much more. "Okay, I get it. What's the charge?"

"Prostitution, what else is new." She smiled.

"Prior arrests?"

"I do believe so, sometimes once a week, dependin' on what the cops up to. Usually, my man pay them, and there no trouble."

"Okay. Where do you live?"

"Venango Street, near Broad, wit some other girls."

"West Philly?"

"No, no way. North Philly."

"Okay, thank you all. I'm going to do my best to keep your bails down." I moved to the cell door, conscious that I could leave whenever I wanted.

§§§

"Call the first case," Spinelli said after everyone took their places.

"Gustave Stavros, Your Honor. Stavros, step forward."

The older man approached the desks. I stood up and moved next to him. I was his lawyer, so I should stand beside him.

"DA?" Spinelli said.

"Yeah, sure, Your Honor," a portly district attorney responded. "This is a numbers charge. The defendant had 47 three-digit numbers on a pad by the telephone at his newsstand. Anything over 10 numbers, we get the presumption he's a numbers writer, Your Honor."

"Yeah, I know all that. Mr. Stavros, you ever gonna quit this stuff?"

"Whadya mean, Your Honor? That was my shopping list. I don't know what the country's coming to. Ya can't even make a list of what to buy at the supermarket without getting busted. I didn't—"

"Alright, I know," Spinelli interrupted. "It's all a shopping problem, right." He looked around the desks at the court officers and DA, who all chuckled.

"You got it, Your Honor," Stavros replied.

"Alright. We need to move on. Nominal bail. You got a dollar?"

"Sure, Your Honor. I always keep one in my pocket, just in case."

"Well, just give it to the bail clerk and go home."

Stavros walked out the courtroom door, dollar bill in hand, happy to post bail at the bail clerk's booth in the hallway.

"Alright," Charley said, "Wayne Cross, step forward."

The first young man I had interviewed, or tried to, moved up to the desks. A middle-aged man in a suit who had been standing to one side of the desks walked over to stand next to him.

"Your Honor, I'm Thomas Miller, counsel for Mr. Cross. We ask that he be immediately released to—"

"Just a minute, counselor," Spinelli said. "Let's hear from the DA's office."

"Your Honor, defendant is charged with sale and possession of drugs, heroin. The detective's 49 Form says it's over 10 pounds, street value in excess of $50,000. Defendant has two other drug cases. He got probation in one, and the other is pending, also for sale and possession of heroin. We ask bail of $3,000."

"Your Honor," Miller said angrily, "that's ridiculous. This defendant was just riding in a car—a passenger, Your Honor, not the owner or driver—and he didn't know what was in the door panels. He's been in trouble before, but this is bogus, Your Honor. In the courtroom are his mother and aunt. Ladies, please stand up for the judge."

Two black women in the spectator section stood up. They wore worn, ragged clothes. I looked back at Wayne Cross, wondering if he cared about his mother. Spinelli nodded to the women. They sat down.

"Alright, bail is set at $2,000. Call the next one."

As Miller left, he pointed to a young man next to the two women, then moved his finger to point toward the door. The young man rose and walked into the hallway by the bail clerk's booth, where Miller met him. He peeled off 20 $100 bills from a large roll and handed them to the bail clerk. I assumed the young guy must be part of the same drug operation as Cross and that Miller was their lawyer. Cross knew what he was talking about. He would sleep at home tonight. Another miscarriage for the bail system, I thought.

"Okay, Alexander Horne, drunk driving charge," the officer said.

"Your Honor, we request $500 bail for this defendant. It's his second drunk driving charge."

"Judge," I said, rushing to Horne's side so I could talk before Spinelli ruled. "This man is a lifelong Philadelphia resident. He's 48, married to his wife for 22 years. They have three children. He's employed as an insurance salesman for Prudential. I request bail be $300 and Mr. Horne be allowed to sign his own bond."

"That was good, counselor. Quick and lots of info, like you said." Spinelli smiled at me. "The way you tell it, he sounds like a solid citizen. I'll set bail at $300."

"Thank you, Judge, but if I may, I don't know whether Mr. Horne has that much money with him, and the spectator section is empty. He may spend the night in jail although you set low bail."

"Well, Mr. Kairys, I can't do anything about that. They give 'em each one phone call. If he gets through, fine. Next case."

I remembered something from my first night at the Roundhouse that bothered me about Horne's bail. I knew Spinelli wanted to move on, so I decided to wait to raise it until after the last case in this batch was done.

"Your Honor, the last one here is Lorette Jones, prostitution." She walked up to the desks, and I stood next to her.

"Okay, you been here a lot lately, Lorette," Spinelli said. "Ain't found nothin' honest to do yet?"

"I guess not, Your Honor. I try, but nothin' work out."

"Alright, nominal bail. We're recessed until—"

"Judge, I'm sorry," I interrupted. "Can I see you a minute in chambers?"

"Mr. Kairys, you do a lot of chambers work. But alright, come up a moment." Everyone at the desks gathered their papers and left. I followed the judge into the room.

"Mr. Kairys, I like your interview thing, and I'm going to tell the president judge about it. If you get Herman, or is it Marty now, over in your shop to write to him, I wouldn't be surprised if we could make it a regular procedure." Herman was Herman I. Pollack, the longtime defender, and Marty was Martin Vinikoor, his successor.

"Gee, that's great, Judge," I said. I couldn't believe I had actually said "gee," like some corny sitcom character. I was going to have to watch the "gees." "Well, there's something else though, Judge, that I think you would want to know."

"Alright, what is it?"

"Well, Judge, back on my first night, there was another drunk driving charge. I believe it was a Mr. Davis. He was allowed to sign his own bond for $300. Maybe there's some difference I missed, but Mr. Horne—"

"You still on that Horne thing? That guy could be dangerous, driving drunk like that, and it wasn't his first time. There's one difference. I don't remember Davis."

"He was the Studebaker salesman from Cherry Hill."

"Oh, yeah, I remember, the guy out on the town who had a few too many. He wouldn't hurt anybody."

"It was also his second drunk driving charge, Judge. I think it might hurt just as bad to be run over by a drunk car salesman from Cherry Hill as a drunk insurance salesman from West Philadelphia."

"Yeah. Well, look, I don't remember the result in this Davis guy's case."

I thought I better tread lightly. "Judge, I just thought you'd want to be consistent, which isn't easy with all these cases."

"Okay, why don't we let Horne sign his own bond. I'm going to give you that one." Spinelli walked to the door and opened it. Though neither of us said it openly, I thought Spinelli had understood the racial inconsistency.

"Thanks, Judge," I said. "I'm really excited about this interview procedure we started."

"Well, don't get overexcited on me. Just go back and talk to Herman about it."

Spinelli and I liked each other in an odd sort of way. I was having an effect, and so far Spinelli didn't see me as a threat and wanted to accommodate me. That seemed effective as well as comfortable. I could have raised a ruckus about the race issue, but it wouldn't have done much good. I hoped there would be other opportunities to raise it in ways that might affect more people. I was just glad Horne could go home. But I was struck by Spinelli's perception of the two drunk driving defendants. Horne had lifelong ties to Philadelphia, which was supposed to translate into lower bail, while Davis was from New Jersey. Both men seemed like pleasant, decent guys, except when they drank and drove. The cases were basically the same, except Horne was black and Davis was white. Spinelli wasn't saying anything about race; he probably didn't take it into account in his own mind. He simply found the black man threatening, while he identified with the white man, whom he saw as a decent guy who'd had "a few too many." Spinelli didn't care if Horne spent the night in jail. He lacked empathy for the black man.

§§§

Another week went by, and Terrence O'Neill was still in jail. I combed the criminal procedure rules for some way to get a reconsideration of the bail set by Spinelli. The *Pennsylvania Rules of Criminal Procedure* weren't any help. I could file a habeas corpus petition, but that was a lot of paperwork and didn't yield a quick hearing. Sometimes local courts adopt their own rules, which they are allowed to do as long as local rules don't conflict with statewide rules. I thought I should check the Philadelphia local rules, kept in a loose-leaf binder in the office library. I found Rule *995, titled "Informal Applications for Bail."[4]

Local Rule *995 provided for an "informal oral" bail reduction hearing initiated by a written notice from the defense lawyer to the DA's office. The rule specified that the hearing would be in the Miscellaneous Court 24 hours after the notice is delivered. The defendant's presence at the hearing was not required, but the defense lawyer and the DA presented their arguments about the initial bail amount and a judge reconsidered it. All I had to do was deliver a formal written notice to the DA's office specifying the defendant's name, bail amount, and a time at least 24 hours thereafter I wanted the hearing before the judge sitting in Miscellaneous Court. The procedure was simple and sensible.

Miscellaneous Court, the usual place pretrial motions in criminal cases were heard, was in one of the large formal courtrooms at city hall. It was one of the first assignments for public defenders who graduate from bail hearings at the Roundhouse. The asterisk on the rule number, which meant the rule was only applicable in Philadelphia, was strange to me, particularly coming before the numbers. I showed the rule to Stu and others at the office, who were used to the asterisks in local rule numbers but not familiar with this rule.

I called the general number for the DA's office and got to an administrator who handled 24-hour bail hearing notices. Then I hand-delivered a notice for Terrence O'Neill specifying that the hearing would be the next afternoon. Later that day, the receptionist at our office gave me messages to call back Mary Jiles and "ADA Harvey Michael." ADA stood for "assistant district attorney," their counterpart to our assistant defender. I called Michael first, thinking it was about O'Neill, since no DA had any other reason to call me.

"Mr. Michael, this is David Kairys at the PD office."

"Oh, yeah, you sent that PD bail notice. Look, that procedure is just for private lawyers. It developed as a practice over many years. We would just tell the private lawyers to send us a letter, and then we arrange for the prisoner to appear in Miscellaneous Court a few days later. It got codified in the local rules later. But this is only a courtesy for private lawyers."

"Well," I said, stunned by his response, "it may have developed between your office and some private lawyers, but you can't have a procedure that's not available to poor people or their public defender lawyers."

"Why not? There's no constitutional right to a lawyer at a bail hearing and no constitutional right to another hearing in Miscellaneous Court. Anyway, that's our policy."

"Look, I understand what you're saying and the background of this. Maybe I should speak to someone in a policy-making position in your office."

"Be my guest."

"Who do you think I should call?"

"Probably Richard Sprague, first assistant district attorney, but you might wish you hadn't."

"Why?"

"You new around here?"

"Yeah."

"Well, Sprague is, shall we say, hard-nosed."

§§§

Stu came in and went to his desk as I hung up. "What're you up to today?" he said. I wasn't sure if I was proud or offended by his thinking I was always up to something.

"I have to call some higher-up in the DA's office named Sprague to talk about bail reduction hearings for our clients."

"Richard Sprague? Do you know who he is?"

"The DA I spoke to called him hard-nosed."

"That puts it mildly. He's a true believer and a dictator over there in the DA's office. He holds these legendary meetings of all the DAs on Fridays after court is over. If someone has lost an important case, he humiliates them."

"Sounds sweet. I might as well get it over with."

I dialed the number for Richard Sprague with Stu looking on with obvious anticipation. I didn't know what to expect. I was excited but thought I should be more scared than I was. I thought anybody that high in the DA's office would probably be hard-nosed but would realize that a procedure on the books had to be open to everyone. I would just tell Sprague why the procedure should be open to poor defendants as well as rich ones. If it got nasty, I would try to make sure that was Sprague's doing, not mine.

A secretary put me through to Sprague. Then a man got on and mumbled something I couldn't make out.

"Hello, is this Mr. Sprague?" I asked.

"Yeah."

"I'm David Kairys, at the PD office."

"Okay."

"Well, ADA Michael suggested I call you. I sent him a 24-hour notice under Rule *995 for a bail reduction hearing for one of our clients, and he said that procedure was only available to defendants with private lawyers."

"Yeah, that's right. So what's the problem?"

This guy doesn't use many words, I thought, and each one is a challenge. I was self-conscious about using too many words compared to him. There was something powerful about being in a position of needing only a few words to let others know what you want.

"The problem is, a procedure that could benefit defendants—get them out of jail—cannot be available only to ones who can afford private lawyers."

"Why not? We've got only so many resources for these hearings. It's a courtesy we extend to the bar."

"Well, I'm also in the bar, or I will be. Our lawyers are in the bar." I paused, realizing how silly that sounded. "I don't see how that's the point anyway. You can't have a procedure that's not available to some defendants just because they're poor."

"We can, and we do. Anything else?"

Sprague's viciousness, dressed in brevity and directness, was getting to me; I felt like saying "asshole" and hanging up, but I didn't. I collected myself as best I could.

"You don't see any problem with this, particularly when it relates to bail?" I said. "Poor defendants can't get out because they can't afford bail, and they can't get a bail reduction hearing because they can't afford a private lawyer. We might as well have them submit financial statements when they're arrested and send the ones below the poverty line directly to jail."

"If you don't like it, challenge it in court. I've got a lot to attend to. Good day." He hung up.

I still held the phone as I looked up at Stu, who was chuckling. I had struck out with Sprague, who treated me like a pesky gnat you swat away so you can do more important things.

Stu asked, smiling, "So what'd he say, Dave?"

"He said I should challenge it in court if I don't like it. It didn't bother him in the least."

"You bet it didn't." Stu wadded up a piece of yellow paper from his pad, squeezing it hard before tossing it, jump-shot style, into the wastebasket at the side of my desk. "The guy's not bothered by anything. As long as large numbers of bodies go to jail, he's happy. He's not interested in sorting out the innocent ones from the guilty ones."

"I guess you're right. I thought he might be a little embarrassed by it, at least. Maybe they're used to this procedure, but it's so obviously wrong."

"Ya going to file some challenge?"

"I don't know, but it isn't over."

I was mad and confused. I didn't expect the DA's office to roll over and give up, but the guy didn't take me seriously. I didn't admit it to Stu, but I felt personally insulted.

§§§

My first thoughts of what to do focused on a major challenge to the exclusion of poor defendants from a procedure specified in the local rules. I could file motions or maybe a civil lawsuit in state or federal court claiming a violation of the "due process" and "equal protection" clauses of the Fourteenth Amendment. The courts had not recognized a right to a lawyer at a bail hearing or to another hearing subsequent to the initial setting of bail. But some quick research in the office library confirmed that denying an important procedure to poor defendants because of their lack of ability to pay for it was probably unconstitutional. A filing fee for appeals had been struck down, and trial transcripts necessary for appeals had to be paid for by the government. There was no Supreme Court case right on point—invalidating the withholding of a court rule from defendants who are too poor to afford a private lawyer. But there was a good argument based on passages like this in an earlier Supreme Court decision: "In criminal trials a State can no more discriminate on account of poverty than on account of religion, race, or color."[5]

I thought I would eventually win, but it would take a long time. There would be appeals through the state and possibly federal courts before it was over, long before I could get a hearing for O'Neill. I wanted to challenge the exclusion of poor defendants from the Rule *995 procedure. But I didn't want to give up on O'Neill, and my usual impatience felt particularly intense because of the way Sprague had treated the issue and me.

Another approach came to mind. I could file habeas corpus petitions for O'Neill and others in the same boat, many others—flood the court with habeas corpus petitions. "Habeas," as we all called it, was a procedure guaranteed in the Constitution and recognized in the court rules. It went back at least to the Magna Carta. Now I understood why they called it the Great Writ and made such a big deal about it in law school. It provided a way to challenge the legality of any custody or confinement by requiring whoever "has the body"—habeas corpus—to justify it. I remembered that habeas corpus could be used even in family law, by a parent to challenge the custody of a child. The framers of the Constitution knew what they were doing when they forbade suspension of the writ of habeas corpus.

The downside of habeas was the paperwork required and the delay before the hearing. Some defendants would get to their trials before their habeas bail hearings. But no DA or judge would deny a habeas hearing to any defendant. The result would be habeas corpus hearings on low or moderate bail amounts that defendants were too poor to post, and each defendant would have to be brought to court for the hearings. The habeas hearings would be scheduled at least a week and sometimes a few weeks after the petitions were filed. But if I prepared a form habeas petition, with simple blanks to be filled in for each particular defendant, like Tony's "Last Aid Kit" papers, I could file lots of them.

This is where it got interesting, and I felt myself enjoying the idea. The habeas petitions could challenge both the bail amount set for each defendant, which, although low or moderate, was keeping him or her in jail, and the refusal to allow them to use Local Rule *995. But the force of the habeas petitions—and their potential to change things quickly—was not as a test case or prelude to an appellate decision on the matter.

The volume of habeas petitions, which could reach over 100 in a short time, would overwhelm the Miscellaneous Court. With the help of others at the PD office and the law students in Tony's program, I thought we could interview and prepare maybe 10 or 20 habeas petitions each day. If I filed as many as I could daily and sat back and waited, the judges who administer the courts, and perhaps the DA's office, might themselves

request an easier procedure, like Rule *995. It might also become important enough to command the attention of Richard Sprague.

§§§

The Detention Center, though only a few blocks away from Holmsburg,
was a different world. The painted cinder block so popular in the 1960s
could make almost any room look like a jail cell. At the Detention Center, seemingly endless corridors of cinder block cells were filled with
younger prisoners, almost all of them held pretrial. Though only five
years old, it was already overcrowded, and the youth and uncertainty
faced by the inmates were a volatile combination. Holmsburg felt old,
dank, and depressing; the Detention Center felt violent.

I was assigned to do full interviews of 10 prisoners, since I was going
up to the Detention Center anyway, and I added, with Vince's approval,
several who were held on low or moderate bail. Terrence O'Neill was first
on my list, but he came after several others.

O'Neill entered the interview room slowly and sat down, without
looking at me. His face was drooped down toward the floor, and he gazed
blankly, like he was about to go to sleep. The plastic frame of his glasses
had broken; the lens on one side was held in the frame by Scotch tape.

"Mr. O'Neill?" I asked.

"Yeah."

"I'm David Kairys. I was the PD when your bail was set."

He looked up. "Oh, yeah. What you doin' here?"

"I want to try to do something about your bail, so you might get out
of here. Have you made any calls to get someone to post the bail?"

"Yeah. They give me a phone call at the Roundhouse and up here, but
I didn't get nobody but my cousin stayin' at my house, and he don't have
no money."

"So I can tell a judge that you are not able to raise this bail?"

"Yeah."

"Look, I talked to the vice principal at Germantown High School, and
he said if you get out and go back right away, you could still graduate this
year."

"I don't know 'bout that. Can you get me out?"

"Give me some more details about you and what happened at the
hardware store, and I'll try."

§§§

"All rise. Oyeh, Oyeh, Oyeh." The words came from nowhere with great authority, ringing through the high ceiling of Courtroom 432 in city hall, the Miscellaneous Court. "This Honorable Court of Common Pleas for Philadelphia County is now in session, the Honorable Ethan Allen Meade, presiding. All who have cause, come forward, and you will be heard. Justice will be done. God save the Commonwealth and this Honorable Court."

I stood up out of respect and because everybody else did. The man whose voice rang out, called the "crier," was a heavyset, short fellow standing behind the bench, only the top of his bald head visible. He and the robed judge rose up behind the bench as they climbed the three stairs to the platform that held the bench and the large, wooden judge's chair.

The room was paneled with dark walnut. The platform was a few feet above the floor, with a short, stocky wood railing several feet in front. Two large oak desks were set against the railing. I felt like I was inside a hollowed out tree.

"Good morning, Your Honor," Stu said with a big, deferential smile as the judge took his seat. The two attorneys at the prosecutor's table immediately joined in, greeting the judge in unison. I stood next to Stu at the defense table.

"Your Honor," Stu said after everyone sat down, "let me introduce a new attorney in our office, Assistant Defender David Kairys."

"Mr. Kairys, welcome to my courtroom. I wish you well in your chosen career, which will bring you here often."

"Thank you, Judge. I appreciate that a lot."

I worried that my response wasn't formal enough and maybe too enthusiastic. I wanted to appear calm, interested, but unemotional, like I was taking it all in stride. I looked up at the judge for reaction to my comment. None was visible. I noticed the judge had clumps of dark black hair sticking out of his nose.

Stu turned to me and whispered, "Dave, stand up when he talks to you or when you say anything to him." I stood quickly, nodding to Judge Meade.

"Your Honor," Stu continued, "Mr. Kairys is just out of law school and hasn't gotten his bar exam results yet. I ask your permission for him to speak to some bail issues before you today, although he is not as yet a member of the bar. He did the research for our office on these petitions and knows them best."

"Well, I suppose, as long as it's about bail, nothing where a defendant has a right to a lawyer. Go ahead, Mr. Kairys. I guess I'll hear from you sooner rather than later."

"Well, thanks, Judge." I could hear my voice shaking. I took a deep breath and looked straight at the judge, trying to avoid the nose hair.

"There are really three things to address about bail, Judge. First is a series of habeas petitions we filed on behalf of defendants in jail pretrial on higher bail than they can afford. We tried to use Local Rule *995 to get 24-hour bail hearings, but the DA's office says the local rule just applies to rich defendants.

"Second, there's a petition for a young man named Terrence O'Neill, who's been in jail pretrial for a few weeks now. Maybe we should discuss Mr. O'Neill first and then—"

"Just a minute, Mr. Kairys. Slow down now," Judge Meade said. "I got these habeas petitions, maybe 40 or 50 of 'em by now. They're comin' in every day. You been layin' all this paper on the clerk's office and the court, young man?" He smiled slightly, along with a stern look that said I might be in trouble already.

"Well, yes, sir, I guess I have. Stu signed them, you know, 'cause I'm not in the bar yet."

"Now, we dealt with that a minute ago. I want to know why you keep filing the same petition for so many defendants, clogging up this court's docket?" He held up a stack of the petitions. The smile turned into a glare.

"Well, Judge, it's pretty straightforward, I think. I'm new around here, so I read through the local rules, and there was Rule *995, providing for a bail hearing in Miscellaneous Court 24 hours after a notice is served on the DA. I assumed—maybe rashly, Judge—that a procedure on the books is available to all defendants, not just the rich ones. So I—"

"Stop a second, Mr. Kairys. What does rich have to do with it?"

"It shouldn't have anything to do with it. But the DA's position, explained to me by ADA Michael, who's here today, and by First Deputy DA Sprague, is that this rule only applies to defendants with private lawyers—defendants rich enough not to have to rely on us public defenders. Now that—"

"Wait a minute, now. Mr. Michael," Judge Meade said, turning his attention away from me, to my relief, "is that right? You want me to apply that rule only to rich people?" He smiled at Michael, with a whimsical, knowing look.

Michael rose slowly. "Your Honor, 'rich' isn't the issue. That's Mr. Kairys's word and beside the point. This procedure arose because we wanted to accommodate the private bar by providing an expeditious procedure for their clients getting bail hearings. As you know, Your Honor, many private lawyers' clients don't deserve to be held in jail pretrial, and, anyway, they expect their lawyers to challenge their incarceration. So as a courtesy to private counsel, we started an informal practice that was later codified in Rule *995. This is a courtesy. We have no obligation to expedite, or even to agree to, a hearing for any defendant. There's no reason we should now be required to extend these hearings to the whole jail-house population. You'll be here hours extra every day if we do that, Your Honor."

The judge's smile turned to me. "What about that, Mr. Kairys? It may be so burdensome that, if you win, the DA's office will try to eliminate the procedure altogether."

"Judge," I said, "it won't be that burdensome if they're heard regularly, so they aren't bunched together like the pile before you today. I hope they won't try to eliminate the procedure, but if they did and were successful, private lawyers would probably do what I did, file habeas petitions. The overall burden on the court would be the same, just not as expeditious for the defendants.

"The problem before you," I continued slowly, looking directly at the judge and feeling that I had at least gotten him interested, "is that people with enough money to hire private lawyers have an expedited procedure for challenging unreasonably high bail; poor people don't. This is unacceptable, no matter how it came about. I attached a brief memorandum of law to the petitions, Judge. Would you like us to brief it further?"

"I don't think so, Mr. Kairys. Mr. Michael, you got anything more to say?"

"I agree, Your Honor. No briefing is necessary. As I said, this is just a courtesy. As long as there's no right to bail or a bail hearing, I don't see any reason for the court to change anything. Thank you, Your Honor."

The judge paused for a moment, looking away from all of us as if he was admiring the paneling. "Well, Mr. Michael, I'm afraid I have to agree with the new young man here. Mr. Kairys, submit to my chambers later today an order requiring the DA's office to comply with Rule *995 regardless of the financial status or representation of any defendant, and I'll sign it this afternoon. Meanwhile, use the rule for all these defendants, serve your 24-hour notices today.

"And Mr. Michael, meet with Mr. Kairys or whomever they designate to review the bail notices, 'cause some of the defendants described in the habeas petitions I went through look like they pose no threat to anyone. They're minor charges, and the bail is low. Let's not clog the jail or the court."

"Judge, are we done with that first issue then?" I asked. I wasn't sure about the judge's saying I had to submit something.

"I should say so, Mr. Kairys. You won, you know."

"I guess I did. Thanks, Judge."

"Don't thank me. I just call 'em how I see 'em. Now, didn't you say there's something else?"

§§§

When we got outside the courtroom, I had so much energy I found myself pacing in circles around Stu as we moved toward the elevator. "So was I okay, Stu?"

"You were good, 'cept you didn't seem to know when you won!" He grinned at me.

"You're right. I wasn't sure he was done. He kept skipping back and forth between me and Michael. It was chaotic, lots of places to talk or not talk. I didn't picture it like that in court, ordered and formal on the surface but so informal and chaotic at the same time. I liked it. I felt the momentum shift our way, we got an edge that I could almost taste, and Michael paused as if he felt it too."

"Yeah, well, you don't want to brief anything you don't have to, and judges don't want to read what they don't have to."

The elevator doors opened, and we exited city hall onto Market Street, heading east toward the Defender office.

"I'll remember that, about briefs," I said, as we passed Wanamakers, a huge department store started before the Civil War. "I can't believe it, though. What was he saying about me submitting an order?"

"They do that all the time. You won, so you draw up the order and the judge signs it. Saves the judge time."

Stu seemed to have more to say, but we walked silently. When we turned up Thirteenth Street to the entrance to our building, he spoke again. "By the way, you called him 'Judge,' not 'Your Honor.' Were you aware of that?"

"Yeah, I think so. I started doing that sometimes when I first spoke at the Roundhouse bail hearings. Is that a problem? 'Judge' feels kind of generic, like those new drugs you can get cheap without the fancy brand names."

"But what's the point? They expect 'Your Honor,' and might take offense."

"I guess that could happen." I paused, worried, but still uneasy about using "Your Honor." "I don't know, it's something about honor. . . . honor shouldn't be part of a job description; it's earned by what you do. Maybe honor is too important a word to be thrown around so much." My words sounded good, but I suspected it was the fawning to power that I resisted.

"Well, that's nice, but if you keep up the 'Judge' stuff, you may have to explain it one day."

"I'll think about it. Say, when will O'Neill get out?"

"The judge ruled O'Neill can sign his own bond. He'll be out tonight."

§§§

The DA's office decided to cooperate with our use of Local Rule *995, and I negotiated a workable procedure with them. They agreed to review the bail in all the cases we gave notice and to discuss them in regular meetings with us, so we could quickly gain release if there was no disagreement. We agreed to provide them three days' notice instead of only one day, since we presented them with an almost daily list and we wanted the opportunity to discuss each case with them. Interviewing clients at the Roundhouse before their bail hearings became a regular procedure, and we were able to use some of these interviews, and interviews at their preliminary hearings that come a week to 10 days after arrest, to prepare bail hearing notices for anyone who wasn't bailed out within a week of his or her arrest.

Initially, I did the additional interviewing, negotiating with the DAs, and representation at the hearings, with a lot of help from the law students in Tony's program. The law students eventually got to represent clients at the bail hearings, an exciting experience for them. They were effective, but their time and work was limited and erratic, not sufficient to sustain the effort. The numbers of prisoners, the meetings with the DAs, and the hearings were too much for a sporadic effort. Fortunately, a law student at Penn, and after him two law students at Villanova, took over and worked steadily.[6]

It evolved into a unique bail project. There were bail projects in several major cities that interviewed prisoners and developed criteria for determining the most "deserving."[7] We were providing all the prisoners counsel and getting them a chance to negotiate with the DAs and get a hearing before a judge. We made no judgments about who was deserving.

Over the course of a couple years, the bail project obtained the release of about 2,000 prisoners who were held on low or moderate bail. Later, it became institutionalized at the Defender office. While this was going on, I took test cases raising my approach to the constitutional issues through the Pennsylvania courts, and the media started covering and questioning the bail system.[8]

Initially, the Pennsylvania appellate courts refused to file my appeals without payment of the usual filing fees, which could not be afforded by defendants in jail for lack of funds to post low bail amounts. I challenged this in a federal lawsuit as a violation of due process and equal protection of the law. During the arguments in the federal case, the federal judge called a break and phoned the chief justice of the Pennsylvania Supreme Court. When the arguments resumed, the judge announced that the appeals would be accepted without filing fees. I assumed this phone-call justice was achieved by the federal judge telling the chief justice he was going to rule in our favor and offering him the opportunity to relent rather than be scolded by the federal court.

It was still procedurally difficult to get a ruling on the bail issues because trials would occur before I could get appellate decisions, making bail a moot issue. I used an unusual procedure in the Pennsylvania Supreme Court. Two of the seven judges agreed with me on the unusual procedure and the constitution. The majority opinion, with five justices on board, rejected the use of the unusual procedure without ruling on the constitutional issues and recommended that bail reform be taken up by a committee that would recommend rule changes to the courts.[9]

Terrence O'Neill got out the night Judge Meade allowed him to sign his own bond, and the charges against him were dropped after the owner of the hardware store failed to appear for the trial. Maybe the owner regretted getting O'Neill arrested and charged with a crime, or maybe he just had better things to do. I don't know whether O'Neill got paid for his last week of work at the hardware store or whether he was able to put his life back together.

CHAPTER THREE

Sexual History, Going Out for Ribs, and Juries without Peers

T HROUGH THE WINTER OF 1969 I was assigned to preliminary hearings in courtrooms in the police districts and to pretrial motions in the Miscellaneous Court at city hall. By spring, I was actually trying cases. These stages of the process focus on witnesses and evidence, and the lawyer's main functions were to present and cross-examine witnesses and to make short, convincing arguments on legal issues. Law school didn't pay much attention to any of this vital lawyer stuff. My image of cross-examination was formed by television, and the standards were high. Perry Mason regularly—every week as I remember—got his clients acquitted by grilling a witness for the prosecution until the witness admitted to lying and then confessed to committing the crime himself. I never did get to do that, and I don't believe I ever saw it in a courtroom. The reality was usually, or at least very often, more complicated and less clear. The most basic lines were often hard to draw—truth or lie, guilt or innocence, justice or injustice.

I walked into the police district building at Fifty-fifth and Pine in West Philadelphia ready for my first preliminary hearings. Instead of the courtroom I expected, there was a large room that looked and sounded more like a high school gym. At one end, a desk for the judge and small tables for the prosecutor and defense were roped off from an open area with fold-up chairs and standing room. Police were everywhere, going in and out of the "courtroom," having often loud discussions as they went to and from assignments.

In one of my early preliminary hearings, I represented Wayne Smith, who was charged with the rape of a 19-year-old neighbor, Delores Cross. He had not been interviewed, and I had only a few moments to talk to him in a cell in the police district building. We sat next to each other on a grimy bench. I was holding his file, which had been handed to me at 5:00 p.m. the day before. It only contained his criminal record and the DA's form setting out the formal charges.

Smith was a short, light-skinned black man in his mid-30s, with a record of theft and minor property convictions. He hadn't previously been accused of any violent or sexual crime. He told me he was a friend of the accuser's family and was there that night.

"Man," he said, "I go over there most nights. This is ridiculous. I didn't rape that girl or have sex with her that night."

"Then what's going on here, why did she tell the cops you did it?"

"Look, man, I gotta tell you, she retarded. She don't go to school or nothin', she a mess."

"You mean retarded literally?"

"I don't know what you mean 'bout literally. She slow, you know, she don't think right."

"Okay, what happened?"

"Alright, look, I had sex with her before, but not that night. We do it every week or so, and she love it. That night her mother found out she was havin' sex with boys in the neighborhood. Look here, I got somethin' you can use." He handed me a handwritten list with several names. "Delores have sex with all these guys."

I looked away from Smith at the dingy, dirty cell and took in a big breath of stale, moldy air. The surroundings fit the story. I was repulsed by what Smith told me and admitted to, whether or not he also raped the young woman.

Smith wanted me to question his accuser about each of the men on the list. He and I both knew that was an allowable avenue of defense— the argument was she's doing it with others, so she would do it with any man and must have consented. I had seen a rape trial where the famous Philadelphia defense lawyer Cecil B. Moore cross-examined a woman who testified that Moore's client raped her. He demanded the details of sexual encounters with four other men she "admitted" she had sex with. These sexual relationships sounded like they were with men she was dating, but Moore made each one seem lurid and sinful. At the end of the cross-examination, as he returned to his seat, he mumbled softly but so all could hear, "Rape, shit!" The jury acquitted his client.

At preliminary hearings, held a week to 10 days after arrest, the prosecutor had to present enough evidence to justify going ahead with the case to a trial. The magistrates almost always ruled for the prosecutor, but it was still useful for the defense. It provided the opportunity to find out what evidence the prosecutor had, to cross-examine witnesses, and to commit witnesses to a specific version of the events that could be mined for inconsistencies later.

"Miss Cross," the DA asked the young black woman standing by the rope in front of the judge's desk, "tell the judge what happened between you and Wayne Smith a few evenings ago."

"We always at the house, every evening," she said slowly. She appeared to be younger than 19 and looked down at the floor.

"What do you do in the evenings?"

"My mom read to me, we watch television. I'm not sure what evening." She turned around and looked at an older black woman standing behind her. "That right, Mama?"

The woman behind her held her index finger up and put it to her lips. "Shhhh," she said in a whisper.

"Miss Cross," the prosecutor said, "please talk to the judge. You have to say what happened, without your mother helping."

"Well, you know, he stuck his thing in me."

"His penis?"

"Judge," I said, "I object. He's leading the witness."

The judge glared at me. "I'll allow it," he said emphatically.

"Was it his penis?" the DA asked.

"Uh-huh."

"Where did he stick it?"

"In my pussy."

"Who did that?"

"Wayne. We thought he a friend, but he rape me."

"Did you want Wayne to do that?"

"No." She shook her head emphatically back and forth several times as she answered.

"Did you consent?"

"What you mean?"

"Did you tell Wayne he could do that?"

"No. He fuck me."

"Your witness."

"Mr. Kairys," the judge said, "cross-examine."

The prosecutor had enough of a case. The young woman testified there was penetration and it wasn't consensual. There was something likable about Smith, but he struck me as a hustler. I didn't take anything he said as true, and I didn't want to ask this young woman about the details of her sex life. But my instinct was that there was not a rape that night.

"Miss Cross, did you have an argument with your mother that night?"

She looked back at her mother briefly, with tears in her eyes. "Uh-huh."

"What did you argue about?"

"Your Honor," the DA said, "what does an argument between mother and daughter have to do with these charges?"

The judge looked at me again. "Mr. Kairys, this is just a preliminary hearing, and they've got enough evidence. Let's not waste time."

"It is a preliminary hearing, and that means we get to cross-examine the prosecutor's witnesses. If you hear only the witnesses' responses to the prosecutor's questions, we might as well go by the witnesses' written statements to the police and not have hearings at all."

"Alright, but this better connect to these charges pretty soon."

"Miss Cross, what did you and your mother argue about?"

"She hear bad things 'bout me from the woman next door."

"What bad things?"

She started to sob and looked back again at her mother. I waited until she gained some composure. "Miss Cross, there was a big argument between you and your mother, right?"

"Yeah."

"And in that argument, who used the word *rape* first, you or your mother?"

"I don't know. I guess she did."

"What did she say?"

"She say Wayne rape me."

"And then you said Wayne raped you?"

"Uh-huh."

"And that ended the argument. You didn't have to hear your mother yell at you anymore once you said Wayne raped you?"

"Uh-huh."

"You agreed with your mother about the rape so she would stop yelling at you?"

"Yeah, I guess I did."

"But Wayne didn't really rape you, did he? You don't want him to go to jail for something he didn't do?"

"No, I don't want him to go to jail."

"Because he didn't rape you, did he?"

"No, I guess he didn't." She stood there sobbing.

The judge looked at her a moment, then said, "Okay, the defendant is discharged. Mr. Smith, you stay away from her and her house, you understand?"

"I do, Your Honor. You won't hear from me again."

The judge didn't hear from him, but I did. He wanted me to represent him when he got in trouble again, which he did a few times. I couldn't do that, even if I wanted to. I was assigned to particular courtrooms and handled whatever cases were there. Based on the subsequent charges, he seemed to move from stealing to drugs, and I heard later that he was shot and died during a drug deal that went bad.

The Friday after Wayne Smith's hearing, I went to Vince's office and caught him still there at 5:30.

"Vince," I said, with a tone that probably sounded a bit ominous, "I need to talk to you about rape cases."

"Come in, Dave. What's up?"

"Well, I had a rape defendant this week who gave me a list of all the guys he knew who had sex with his accuser."

"Yeah, an actual list is unusual, but that's fair game."

"That's what I want to talk about. I don't think it's fair."

"You gonna go feminist on me?" He smiled.

"Well, maybe that's a good description, but I'm also worried about our clients. I don't think I can cross-examine a woman about her sex experiences."

"Why not?"

"I don't think it's relevant or should be allowed as a legitimate line of defense, and it's demeaning. It's like victimizing her again. She's raped, and then you expose her as also sinful and immoral. It's like sex is sinful, for women anyway. You know, the double standard."

"But an active sex life makes it more likely she consented?"

"I don't know why that would be so. Do the women you know who have had sex consent with anybody they meet? That makes women who have sex fair game for rapists. It should be about what happened—either the defendant raped her or he didn't."

"Look, I might agree with you if we were in the legislature setting policy, but we've got defendants to represent, and this provides them with a defense."

"That's the problem, Vince. Since I don't want to do this—I wouldn't, or I'd do it half-assed—the defendants I represent on rape charges wouldn't get the full defense they're entitled to."

"So, what are you saying? You don't want to do rape cases?"

"Yeah."

He paused and looked straight at me. I thought we were going to have a big problem. "Dave," he said, "you're in Tony's program, and Penn is paying your salary. Why don't we say that because of that I'm agreeing that you won't do rape cases. If someone on our regular staff asked, I don't know what I'd do."

"Fair enough, Vince."

"Now, we don't need to broadcast this, right?"

"Right."

Smith's was the first and last rape case I handled. Several years later, the Pennsylvania legislature passed a "rape shield" law, which prohibited proof of prior sexual activity by rape accusers in most cases.[1]

§§§

"Alright," Judge Meade said, "we'll start with search and confession motions in one of your cases, Mr. Kairys." Pretrial motions were heard in the Miscellaneous Court, where I was often in front of Judge Meade. The motions covered a range of issues, but most challenged the constitutionality of a search or a confession. Just several years before, in 1961, the Supreme Court adopted the controversial "exclusionary rule" in *Mapp v. Ohio*, which excluded from trials evidence that was obtained unconstitutionally.[2] At the motion hearings, a judge heard witnesses testify to how evidence was obtained and decided whether the evidence should be excluded or "suppressed."

"It looks like we'll hear them together," Meade continued. "Is that right, Ed?"

"Yes, it is, Your Honor," the ADA said. The ADA that week was a rookie like me. He was a friendly guy who spent a lot of time talking to everyone in the courtroom. In the mornings, I'd be reviewing files and thinking about how I'd approach cases, while he'd be shaking hands and chatting up the clerks, stenographers, police, and sometimes even defendants and their families gathered in the public seating. He reminded me of the class president of my high school.

"Call your officer."

"Thank you, Your Honor. The Commonwealth calls Officer Brian Kelly."

A medium height, seriously overweight uniformed officer walked up to the witness box and stood with his hand on the Bible on the ledge in front of him. "Officer," the clerk said, "do you swear to tell the truth and nothing but the truth so help you God?"

"I do, Your Honor," said Kelly, already starting to sit down.

"Officer Kelly, were you on duty near Twentieth and South on August 25 last year?"

"Yes, sir, I was."

"Tell us what happened with respect to this case."

"Your Honor, I was on patrol alone in my red car about 7:30 at night, going east on South Street, when I saw a group of young black males on the southeast corner of Twentieth and South. I decided to question them, since this is a high-crime area. As I drove on South by these males and was about to pull over, one of the males looked right at me. It was this defendant, named . . . I don't remember, Your Honor, but it's this case. He looked at me, and then right away I saw him turn toward me and throw something small. I don't know where he was trying to throw it, but it came toward me and landed on the edge of the sidewalk, in plain view. I continued by these males and then pulled over. As I started toward them, one yelled, 'The pig comin',' and they all ran in different directions. I could only go after one, so I took off after the one closest to me, this defendant. I caught him in the next block. Then . . . do you want me to do the confession now or later?"

"Continue, officer," ADA Rendell said.

"I handcuffed the defendant and took him back to my red car. Once he was secured in the locked backseat of the car, I walked over to where I first saw him and saw what he had thrown in plain view. It was a small glycine packet with two hand-rolled joints. I came back to the car and read the defendant questions on the *Miranda* card.[3] He answered 'yes' to one, 'yes' to two, 'no' to three, 'yes' to four, 'yes' to five, 'no' to six, and 'yes' to seven. He then confessed they were marijuana. When I asked him if he had anything to do with a string of robberies in the neighborhood, he confessed to one the week before. I arrested him for burglary, theft, receiving stolen goods, and possession of marijuana."

"No further questions, Your Honor."

"Mr. Kairys," Meade said.

"Officer Kelly, so you saw the young men on the corner and you decided to question them?

"Yes, that's right."

"And then as you went by them, you saw Mr. Jenkins throw something to the sidewalk?"

"Yeah."

"And you could see this as you drove?"

"Yes."

"Including where it landed?"

"Yes. It fell on the sidewalk where I found it."

"How far from Mr. Jenkins were you in the moving red car?"

"Maybe 15, 20 feet. It was just across the street."

"How do you know the packet wasn't there already?"

"It looked the same; it glistened."

"You could see it in his hand glistening from your moving car?"

"Yes."

"When you just described it, it was just 'something small' you picked up because it was in the place he had thrown it. If you saw more detail and recognized it, why testify it was small and you got to it by its location?"

"I didn't say that. I recognized it as what I had seen thrown by the defendant."

"Would the stenographer please read back the officer's testimony on direct examination about the packet."

The stenographer grabbed a pile of the slim, folded white paper in the tray at the back of his steno machine, leafing through until he found the testimony.

"Question by Mr. Rendell," the stenographer said. "'Tell us what happened with respect to this case.'"

"Answer by Officer Kelly, skipping down: 'I saw him turn to the side and throw something small. I don't know where he was trying to throw it, but it came toward me and landed on the edge of the sidewalk, in plain view.' Then continuing later: 'I walked over to where I first saw him and saw what he had thrown in plain view. It was a small glycine packet with two hand-rolled joints.'"

"So you did say that?" I asked.

"Well, I wasn't saying all I did. I saw it and recognized it when I got back to it."

"Okay, that's your testimony," I said. "Officer, you also testified that you decided to pull over and question these young men before anyone threw anything, isn't that correct?"

"Well, maybe it was before or maybe after."

"Officer, shall we have the stenographer read that part back too?"

"No, alright, it was probably before."

"So all you knew about these young men at the time you decided to question them was they were standing on a corner and black?"

"I guess so."

I was tempted to push him further on the lack of any cause and the racial assumption, but I had found it was better not to push further when you get an admission like that. I could argue later that it was an admission. "Okay, officer. Is South a small residential street or a main street?"

"There are some houses, but it's got lots of stores. It's one of the main streets in that part of town."

"So there's a lot of traffic?"

"Yeah."

"And police cars would come by fairly frequently?"

"Sure, we patrol it regularly."

"So this young man would see many red cars go by if he stayed on the corner for a while?"

"Yeah."

"And if he were going to throw his marijuana as soon as he saw a red car, he wouldn't be likely to stand on a corner on South Street, would he?"

"Objection," Rendell said.

"It's okay, continue," Judge Meade responded.

"If that's what he was going to do," I continued, "he might as well throw the marijuana away before he sees a red car, so he wouldn't get arrested, right?"

"I don't know."

"How long have you been on the force?"

"I been on the force a decade come next January."

"In that period, have you noticed a change in the behavior of criminal defendants? Have they starting throwing dope at officers, since maybe about 1961?"

"I don't know what you mean—"

"Alright, Mr. Kairys, I get it," Judge Meade said, smiling at me. "Move on."

"When you read Mr. Jenkins his *Miranda* rights from the card, what exactly did he say?"

"Like I said, 'yes' to one—"

"Stop there, please. I want to know what he actually said. In response to question one, was it 'yes' or 'yeah' or 'okay' or maybe 'I'm not sure what you mean'?"

"I don't know what he said that way. I don't keep track of it."

"So you can't tell us what he said?"

"Not like that, no. I never been asked before."

"So you always just write the seven yes-no answers?"

"Yeah."

"Where did you write it? Can I see it, please?"

"I didn't really write it. I mean, I just know that's what he answered."

"You just know?"

"Yeah."

"Is your testimony the same as to the confession? You didn't write it down or have it signed, and you don't know the words Mr. Jenkins uttered?"

"That's right. Well, he said, 'I done that burglary,' and pointed to the house."

"Your testimony is you asked if he burglarized a house on the block and he just said right away, 'I done that burglary,' and pointed to the house that was broken into?"

"Yeah."

"He used the word *burglary*? That's not your word?"

"Yeah, burglary, that's what he said."

"And he kind of volunteered it as soon as you asked?"

"That's right."

"Did you ask him about other crimes in the area, since he was so co-operative?"

"No."

"Okay. Did you have any discussion with these young men about their radio and their food?"

"They was eating, and some bones were in the gutter next to them. What kind of discussion?"

"About the bumper sticker on their car?"

"Yeah, I seen that Black Power sticker, and I know the face on it is one of those Black Panther guys."

"Isn't that what happened first? You pulled over because you saw a group of young black men eating and listening to the radio blaring from a car with a Black Power bumper sticker?"

"I saw that and heard the radio, but I came over to just ask them what was going on. One called me a 'pig,' then they all ran."

"You left out something, didn't you? You didn't include in that sequence of the events Mr. Jenkins's throwing anything at the sidewalk."

"Yeah. That too."

"And you just testified that you heard the radio as you drove by?"

"Yeah."

"You didn't tell us that earlier, did you?"

"I didn't say everything at once."

"No further questions, Your Honor." I was focused on Officer Kelly but noticed I said "Your Honor" without realizing it. It was contagious.

"Alright, you done, Mr. Rendell?"

"Yes, Your Honor."

"Mr. Kairys."

"Judge, I call the defendant, Mr. Jenkins."

Jenkins, a thin young man dressed in a formal suit and tie it looked like he borrowed, was sworn in and sat in the witness chair nervously looking at me. "Mr. Jenkins," I said, "were you at Twentieth and South on the evening of August 25?"

"Yeah."

"What were you doing there?"

"We go to BeBe's, ya know, on South down the way from there. We hungry and got some slabs."

"Slabs of ribs?"

"Yeah, that all BeBe got, and they good. We drive up from Tasker to get ribs."

"Tasker housing project, south of Twentieth and South Streets?"

"Yeah."

"You live in the Tasker project?"

"Yeah."

"Have you ever been in any trouble with the law before?"

"No, sir."

"Alright. Tell the judge what happened that evening."

"We got our slabs and fries and bread and rode a little way to Twentieth and South. We get out the car and ate on the corner, with the car doors open so we hear the radio."

"Who was there?"

"Four of us. We hang at Tasker. Hank, he got the wheels."

"Okay, then what happened?"

"The red car come. He goin' pretty fast, 'til he see us. He pull over just past us, get out the red car, and cross the street walkin' to us. We stood there, not eatin' no more, scared. He say, 'Whose car is that with that Black Power stuff on there?' and he point at the bumper sticker."

"What was on the bumper sticker?"

"It say 'Black Power' and got a picture of Huey P. Newton."

"Who is Huey P. Newton?"

"I don't know much 'bout it. He a Black Panther and that picture all over. I seen a big fancy one of him in our library at school."

"What happened next?"

"Hank, he say the car his. Then the cop move right to Hank and try to grab him. Hank pull away, and everybody run. He got me 'cause I was sittin' on the hood of the car next to him. He grab me as I got down."

"Then what?"

"He say, 'Up against the wall and spread 'em.' I lean on the wall next to the car with my hands high up on the wall and spread my legs. He pat me down and stick his hands in my pockets. He say he find the joints in my back pocket."

I didn't want to touch the last comment about the marijuana. For this motion and hearing, it didn't matter whether Jenkins actually had the marijuana. "Okay, did you confess to anything?"

"No, no way. He talkin' when we in the red car 'bout robberies and break-ins. I didn't say nothin'."

"Did he say anything about your rights not to speak or to a lawyer?"

"Nah, he don't be talkin' 'bout my rights. He just tell me what to do."

"Your witness."

Rendell paused and looked down at his paperwork, then back up. "No questions, Your Honor."

"Alright," Judge Meade said, "let's hear argument. Mr. Kairys, it's your motion to suppress."

I stood and moved to the podium between the DA and defense tables built into the small wood wall that separated the tables from the bench. The stenographer and several clerks, positioned in front of the bench, were right in my face, and I hadn't yet gotten used to ignoring them. I tried to focus on the judge.

"We have several questions for you to resolve, Judge. But credibility—who's telling the truth and who's not—is at the heart of the matter, because the law on these issues is pretty clear. If Mr. Jenkins threw the marijuana to the sidewalk in plain view of Officer Kelly, I have to concede that the courts have ruled, over and over, that there wasn't even a search, so you don't have to decide whether it was a constitutional search. The law is, unfortunately in my view, that by throwing the packet away Mr. Jenkins abandoned it, so it's no longer his property. Officer Kelly can pick it up without conducting any search and use it as evidence. And if Mr. Jenkins waived his *Miranda* rights and confessed the way Officer Kelly testified, his confession is admissible.

"However, those are big ifs, Judge, and for you to rule that way, you have to be willing to accept these pat stories from the police we hear a dozen times or more each day in this motions court. Apparently, if the police are to be believed, there was some momentous shift in people's behavior, in Philadelphia and I hear around the country, sometime around 1961. All of a sudden, people started throwing dope at police as soon as they saw them. They didn't do it before 1961. Maybe it's a fad or it's connected to rock 'n' roll. Some sociologist or anthropologist might be able to figure it out, Judge, whoever studies—"

"Alright," Judge Meade said, "I get that. It's pretty funny, I have to admit, but let's move on."

"The point, Judge, is that, once the Supreme Court excluded evidence obtained by a bad search in *Mapp v. Ohio* in 1961, police have regularly used a legal loophole to negate the Court's mandate. Property thrown away can for some purposes be considered abandoned, and if it is in plain view rather than, say, in someone's pocket, it can be picked up by the police. Either the police are regularly lying to establish facts that allow them to use this loophole, or you have to believe that people just started throwing dope at officers in 1961. I'm sorry to bring up the sociologists, Judge, but it's a new social phenomenon or a pattern and practice of police lying, one or the other. It seems quite clear at this point that the police are using this narrow, technical interpretation of abandonment and the law of property—along with a willingness to present false testimony—as a way to circumvent and negate the Supreme Court's clear mandate.

"Similarly, the *Miranda* warnings don't mean anything if their effect can be negated by police reciting yes and no answers to seven questions, which is the testimony we hear in this court day after day. The Supreme Court said in *Miranda* that the rights they were establishing could be waived, without saying how. Courts should require at least a written waiver signed by the defendant rather than repeatedly accept police testimony that negates what the Supreme Court has mandated."

Judge Meade looked down at me, and he wasn't smiling. He was used to defense lawyers questioning the credibility of police testimony, but I knew my saying there was a pattern or policy of police lying was on a different level. He turned to Rendell. "DA's response?"

"It is absurd and insulting to suggest that there is a pattern of police lying," Rendell said. "Officer Kelly was a credible witness, and that's all you have to decide, Your Honor."

"Judge," I said, "I don't see how you could decide that without considering whether, as the judge who hears these motions day in and day out, you've repeatedly heard pat testimony that doesn't seem believable and appears to be police policy or an informal practice passed on among officers."

"Okay, I think I've heard enough on this. I can't say it hasn't occurred to me that I hear the same testimony an awful lot, particularly the abandonment testimony that makes *Mapp* and the exclusionary rule irrelevant. But I don't know enough to say it's a policy or pattern, and Officer Kelly seemed credible. Of course, you can raise doubts about the confession at trial, but it's admissible. Motions to suppress denied."

I left the courtroom feeling good about setting this out to the judge, but I don't know whether it did any good. It was sometimes hard to tell when I was just taking a satisfying moral stance—challenging something because I believed it was wrong and should be confronted—and when I also had a decent strategy that might result in real change. It was obvious early on that I would lose effectiveness if I challenged everything I thought should be challenged, particularly since I represented so many defendants before the same judge all day, all week, sometimes all month. I had to weigh each challenge, like I had become accustomed to weighing when and how often I asserted a defendant's innocence. It was hard to say more than once or twice a day that a defendant was innocent and conviction would be an outrage.

I didn't repeat this argument for each search and confession motion in front of Judge Meade. But I did sometimes refer to it indirectly—by throwing into my arguments "it's another dope throwing case." Or, "that's our dozen dope throwing cases for today." Meade would smile, and it might have had some effect. I did notice that he would more often grant motions to suppress, but only when an officer gave some basis for granting them in his testimony. I never saw him or any other judge grant a motion to suppress because he just didn't believe police testimony like this, no matter how many times they heard the same post-1961 story.

Jenkins probably also lied about the pot in his pocket. I didn't think he was guilty of the burglary, particularly since the only evidence the DA had was the confession. The emphasis on confessions was a very American phenomenon. In many other Western democracies, whose legal systems are most like ours, confessions in police custody are not allowed at all or are viewed as presumptively coercive and of doubtful value. The Philadelphia police seldom used the usual investigative tools—like finding witnesses not at the scene when they arrive or using fingerprints or other scientific evidence. They honed in on the person they thought did it and then pushed to get a confession from that person.[4]

The motions court brought out a reality that was more evident there than at any other stage of the process—there is a lot of lying in court, on all sides.

§§§

I took a break from the motions court one day to watch a more experienced lawyer in Tony's program try a case before a jury. Lou Natali, whom I would join many years later on the Temple Law School faculty, was trying a robbery case. The jury was picked and seated in the jury box as the ADA began his case by leading the complaining witness, the owner of a convenience store in Northeast Philadelphia, through his story. He said the defendant, a black man in his 20s, came in with a gun in his hand around closing time, demanding the money in the cash register. He complied, and the defendant left. The defendant was picked up a few days later with a small amount of drugs and taken to the store in a police van for the owner to identify.

Lou believed they had the wrong guy, so he was questioning the witness's ability to see the defendant's face well or for long. After a few questions and answers, the witness stopped talking in midsentence and slowly stood up, with a blank stare on his face. He got almost erect, his face tensed and looked pained, and his hands tightly gripped the front rail of the jury box. He leaned slightly forward and then fell over the front of the jury box onto the floor below, knocking over the stenographer's machine and then the stenographer. He lay there motionless for what seemed like a long time. Lou jumped up and ran to him, turned him on his back, and started doing mouth-to-mouth resuscitation. The judge set off an alarm, but it was over 15 minutes before help came. Lou continued giving CPR that whole time, but the man was dead, killed, as the rumors in the PD office later had it, by Lou's tough cross-examination.

After medics came and took the body on a stretcher, the judge sent the jury out for an early lunch and told the lawyers that the case would resume in an hour and a half. Lou, obviously shaken, had to resume the defense lawyer's role. He demanded that the judge declare a mistrial and retry the case before another jury, since he hadn't completed his cross-examination and the jury just saw the complaining witness die right in front of them. The judge said a new trial might not be possible without the complaining witness. Lou argued forcefully that there may not be a second trial but that the alternative of proceeding with this jury was unacceptable and would be reversed on appeal.

The judge relented, but only after the ADA seemed to agree with Lou. We left the courtroom not in the mood for lunch, and Lou said he wanted to go immediately to Wanamakers. I thought it an odd time to shop. He bought a toothbrush and toothpaste and brushed his teeth and washed his face in the men's room at Wanamakers for a half hour, while neither of us said much. I never heard Lou discuss the case with anything other than a deep sadness.

As Lou did CPR in the courtroom, I found myself glued to the jury. They were horrified, of course, but looking at juror to juror brought home how white, male, and old they were. This wasn't the time for thinking up challenges to the judicial system, but I couldn't help but notice that there were only a few women and only one black person. Some of the men looked like retirees; maybe a few were in their 30s or 40s. The rest were 55-year-old white men. They were supposed to be representative of the community, but this defendant, whether innocent or guilty, had no peers on the jury.

The faces—and the unrepresentativeness—of the jurors stuck with me. Each time I saw another jury, it was the same—too many 55-year-old white men, too few women and minorities. It started to feel like an exam question in one of my engineering courses. I had read in the newspapers that Philadelphia was about a third black and thought it was, presumably, about half women. How far off cross-sectionality was the jury system and why?

§§§

In late 1970, I got some answers. The jury system was administered by the Jury Selection Board, headed by its clerk, Paul Tranchitella. I dropped in his office one day and told him I was interested in how the jury system worked. He was more than cooperative and seemed honored that some-one connected to Penn Law School was paying attention to his work. But the system was surprising, to say the least.

Tranchitella told me they started with the list of about a million reg-istered Philadelphia voters divided into voting wards. Each ward was as-signed to a specific trial judge and sheriff and allotted a specific number of persons to be selected. No method or standards for picking from the ward lists were required or suggested. That was up to each of the judges and sheriffs or to their clerks and secretaries, who sometimes were as-signed the task. Four masters of the Jury Selection Board sent question-naires to every person selected from the ward lists. After eliminating a substantial number based on answers on the questionnaires, each was called in for an interview with the master. After the interviews, there were usually about 16,000 names placed in the jury wheel, which was about the number of jurors needed for a year.

The judge and sheriff selection stage looked something like the "key man" systems mainly in the South, which I knew about from a paper I wrote in law school. Key men in the community—officials, ministers, politicians, leaders of organizations—were asked to suggest names of up-standing people for jury service. They and the people they suggested were usually all white men. The Supreme Court had not invalidated the key-man system, but it was discussed as suspect in recent decisions. I had never heard of interviewing jurors, and it wasn't at all clear what the interviews were supposed to accomplish. This seemed to collide with the whole purpose of representativeness—the jury system is supposed to reflect all the people, not anybody's version of the most suited or best.

In October 1970 I filed a motion challenging the juror selection system as unconstitutional. To prevent the challenge from being mooted out by trials, I filed the motion in several cases that had proceeded through preliminary hearings but not indictment by a grand jury and sought a stay of grand jury proceedings pending the outcome of the motion. Grand jurors and trial jurors were chosen by the same process and picked from the same pool of people, and so the same issues were raised by a challenge to either the grand or trial jury. I realized how charged the issue was when just the filing of the motion got prominent news coverage.[5]

As a pretrial motion, it came before Judge Meade, who granted the stay and ordered the Jury Selection Board to provide me with the information about the system needed for the challenge. He set a hearing date and asked the president judge to specially assign a judge to hear the motion. This was a good development—it meant a judge's calendar would be cleared sufficiently to allow a full hearing on the motion. But the judge assigned was James T. McDermott.

McDermott was proud of his nickname, "No Streets," meaning defendants he tried never saw the streets again. His regular assumption was that any defendant convicted would get the maximum sentence, and he sometimes referred to his sentencings as "doomsdays" when he imposed sentences like 130 to 260 years. In political circles, he was known for doing the Republican Party a favor by running in a hopeless campaign for mayor against an unbeatable Democrat in the early 1960s. This engendered gratitude and helped elevate him to the Pennsylvania Supreme Court in the 1980s.[6]

I had no illusions about winning the challenge before McDermott, but he made it clear from the beginning that he would give me a full hearing without limiting my evidence. We also hit it off in an odd sort of way. He took frequent, long breaks during the hearing and increasingly invited me back into his chambers, where we would chide each other's politics in a friendly way. He called me radical and I called him reactionary, both said with smiles.

One morning the newspapers were full of headlines about the state attorney general, Fred Speaker, dismantling the electric chair, which had not been used in some time, as a symbolic rejection of capital punishment.[7] McDermott was angry but in his articulate, sometimes eloquent manner.

"I guess you're happy this morning," he said after he had me called into chambers.

"You mean about the electric chair?"

"Yes. Now the freakiest of our citizens are free to pillage and rape without facing the wrath of that chair."

"They'll still sit in jail, and we'll all be spared the government's killing folks and the penchant for picking the blacks and poorest among them for execution."

"I knew you'd like it. I'm in mourning after what that liberal did."

He seemed genuinely sad. "I have an idea, Judge," I said. "I could contact Speaker, you know, liberal to liberal, and ask him if he would ship the electric chair to your chambers for reassembly right here."

"That's excellent."

"You could look at it anytime you want with the hope that someday you'll be able to use it. You could sentence them to death and then take them back here and execute them right away. You could pull the switch yourself."

"I'd like that." He was smiling, and we were kidding, but I got the distinct impression that he would like pulling the switch.

§§§

After gathering all the information and data about the jury system I could get my hands on, I was mostly frustrated by what I didn't know. I got the proportion of the 21-and-over population that was black—34 percent—from census data. But race wasn't shown on the juror questionnaires, so I didn't have the black percentage of the jurors to compare it to. I proposed, and the ADA on the case agreed, that I use student volunteers, mostly from Tony's program, to conduct a telephone poll of randomly selected jurors. This established that the jurors were 23 percent black while the population was 34 percent black.

The other major hurdle was how to argue that 23 percent was unconstitutionally low when the population was 34 percent black. This was a familiar mathematical problem from my engineering studies. But the

Supreme Court cases on the issue didn't help much. They were adamant that a cross-section of the community was required and that a "substantial" underrepresentation established a case for unconstitutionality, but they didn't provide any specific method or criteria for distinguishing minor underrepresentation from unconstitutional ones. I decided to argue that the court use the "statistical significance test," though it was difficult for non-scientists to understand. A statistician at Penn volunteered to do the analysis and to present the data and explain the statistical test at the hearing.[8]

The statistician testified that jurors chosen randomly from the population would be expected to be 34 percent black but that, in any particular selection of thousands of names, some variance from the exact percentage would also be expected. If you flip a coin 10 times, he said, you expect 5 heads, but 6 or more or 4 or less would occur fairly often. If you flip a coin 1,000 times, there will also be variation, but it should be closer to 50 percent because of the large number of flips. Statisticians can calculate the probability of getting 6 heads in 10 flips or any number of heads in any number of flips. If that probability is very small (the usual cutoff is 5 percent), statisticians conclude that it isn't an expected statistical variation—something is amiss with the coin or the flipping process.

The statistician calculated the probability that a random drawing of 16,000 names from the 34 percent black population of Philadelphia would yield a pool that is 23 percent black. He testified that the probability was "less than 1 out of 10,000," so he concluded that the juror selection system was skewed and seriously unrepresentative.

I noticed that the wealthier and whiter areas of the city were seriously overrepresented, while the poorer and minority areas were seriously underrepresented. To get beyond the numbers, which were hard for anyone but a statistician to comprehend, I got out my old drafting equipment. On a map of the city, I colored in the significantly over- and underrepresented areas; the impact was clear for anyone who knew the city's neighborhoods. A graph demonstrated that the jurors' median income (obtained in the phone survey) was about 50 percent higher than the population's median income and that the income distribution of the population had two peaks, roughly representing the middle class and the working class and poor, while the jurors had only one peak—at the same income as the population's middle class. The statistician testified that the difference between the juror and population income distributions was also statistically significant.

The masters of the Jury Selection Board testified that they had discretion in the interview stage and were looking for "good character," which got a range of definitions: "works or has a job," "moral or ethical values," "belief in an almighty," "physical appearance," "his mannerisms, the way he speaks." Tranchitella testified to a more elaborate standard for elimination of jurors: "doesn't believe in the jury system, law and order, judges, or anything else."

The evidence and legal arguments were set out in a 57-page brief, on the long legal paper, accompanied by another 50 or so pages of appendices with charts, maps, equations, and graphs. The brief had 45 often-long footnotes, which were difficult to place at the bottom of the pages before computers and word processors. A top typist in the Defender office who also became interested in the case, Geri Melvin, was able to eyeball when to stop typing text and start typing footnotes on each page so it came out looking near perfect.

McDermott was not moved. But a strange thing happened. The loss and the publicity generated by the challenge and the hearing resulted in the same reform of the system as a win would have. They dropped the judge/sheriff selections and the interviews in favor of a random selection from the voter lists. Juries were soon significantly more representative.[9]

§§§

My first taste of an actual trial came in the Municipal Court, which was created in 1968 to hear cases with a maximum sentence of less than five years. These were minor charges—gambling, minor property crimes, scuffles, and assaults not involving a weapon or any serious injury. The magistrates got a new title—they became judges of the Municipal Court—and many more were added.[10]

There was no preliminary hearing or jury trial, but a defendant unsatisfied with the result could request a new trial before a jury. This made the Municipal Court ideal for a novice lawyer like me. If I really messed up, the defendant could start over and get a jury trial. But it seemed a waste of time to go through a trial before a judge and then do it again later before a jury—until I was there awhile and saw that convicted defendants were rarely sent to jail. They would get probation, a fine, or a warning. So jury trials, which any defendant charged with a crime that had a maximum sentence of six months or more had a right to, were seldom worth the time or aggravation.

The Municipal Court was created to deal with the huge number of criminal cases and the resources and time required to put each through the full criminal law process. That process, evolved from the common law in Britain, included a preliminary hearing, an indictment, and a jury trial. If every defendant demanded his or her full rights to the whole process, the court system would have quickly ground to a halt. As the number of cases swelled, courts created new processes that required fewer resources and less time. Criminal defendants were offered incentives for voluntarily using them and disincentives for not doing so.

My first months of Municipal Court cases were uneventful. I was handed a pile of 20 or 30 case files for each day at the end of the day before. I got a quick dinner after work and then read the interviews and other paperwork and made notes about how I would approach each case. Many looked like a guilty plea deal made sense, many others presented good defenses, and some made me wonder why the charges were brought. I separated them into three categories: explore guilty plea, probably not guilty or at least worth contesting, and not enough information to make an evaluation.

First thing in the morning, I huddled with the ADA for the usual discussion of the day's cases. I asked what the ADA was looking for in each case, focusing first on cases I thought they might agree to drop. I didn't offer any guilty pleas, particularly since I hadn't talked to any of the defendants yet, but the ADA regularly encouraged them with offers of agreement to light sentences. Then I'd find the defendants in the busy courtroom and talk to them before the trials started or in breaks as we went along. It was chaotic, but after awhile I felt I had the hang of it.

That changed toward the end of the first week I was before Municipal Court judge Robert Latrone, a stocky man with dark shiny hair that looked like he used Brylcreem, a men's hair preparation popular in the 1950s. The first few days, as I looked up at him in the morning, I could not get out of my mind the jingle on the radio from my high school days, "Brylcreem, a little dab'll do ya." Latrone had a tough reputation, including his widely known practice of carrying a handgun in a shoulder strap under his judicial robe. He was unusually friendly and courteous to the lawyers and defendants, however. I never saw him send anyone to jail, but he found a much higher proportion guilty than did the other Municipal Court judges.[11]

The morning started out normally. Latrone took his seat on the bench as we all stood and heard the usual "Oyehs" intoned by the clerk. Municipal Court courtrooms had just been constructed in city hall. The judge's bench was recessed into a stained, paneled wall, with a built-in look that reminded me of the built-in desk in my bedroom when I grew up. The judge entered through a doorway outside of the courtroom, so he would appear behind the bench rather than have to walk up, as in the older courtrooms.

"Okay," Latrone said, "let's hear any applications from private counsel." The private lawyers always went first in the courtrooms. Judges considered our PD cases only after all the private lawyers were done. A couple private lawyers stood and asked that their cases be "continued." Latrone, like most of the judges, granted one postponement in a case, but he bristled at attempts to get a second one. There were no private counsel trials that day, and so Latrone turned to the PD, me.

"Mr. Kairys, let's start with any continuances and then go to guilty pleas."

The ADA and I had both been before Latrone that whole week, and so we knew the drill how he liked it. We presented the continuances and guilty pleas and completed a few trials before lunch. Trials were quick in Municipal Court. Usually, the ADA called one or two witnesses; I cross-examined; then I presented a couple witnesses, whom the ADA cross-examined; and Latrone told us his decision—which was almost always guilty.

In the afternoon, we completed the rest of the cases I had prepared and were left with defendants who had not been interviewed. About 50 cases were listed in each Municipal Court courtroom each day, about 10 of which were handled by private attorneys. For the rest, which were assumed to be assigned to the PD office, the defendants often hadn't been interviewed as yet. Usually, this was not a problem. I'd interview them during breaks, or the judge would give me time to do so at the end of the other cases. This day we got through trials or continuances for all of the rest of the cases, except one.

Glenda Charles, a middle-aged black woman wearing a green dress with a formal shawl, had been charged with assaulting her daughter's sixth grade teacher. We talked in the back of the courtroom during a break.

"Ms. Charles, what happened between you and the teacher?"

"It's Mrs. Charles. Miss Morse was giving my daughter Charlene a hard time. She say Charlene a discipline problem, and she keep her after school lots of times. I went in to talk to her 'bout it, to get her to lay off Charlene."

"So what happened?"

"She telling me 'bout things she say Charlene done. I didn't think Charlene done all that, but there weren't any trouble 'til she say, 'Your daughter a lying thief, and she been cheating.'"

"Cheating on a test or something?"

"Yeah. She say Charlene copy answers from the girl who sit next to her while Miss Morse go to the bathroom. Then she look in Charlene's desk and find a bracelet she say not Charlene's, but I gave Charlene that bracelet. We was standing by her desk. I was upset. I step closer to her, and I say, 'Don't you call my Charlene a cheater or a thief.'"

"She say, 'Don't you shake your finger at me.'"

"Were you shaking your finger?"

"Yeah."

"Were you touching her?"

"No."

"How close?"

"My finger, maybe a foot or two. Then she yell, 'Get away from me,' and she push me with both hands on my stomach. I push her back. Then other teachers come and pull us apart."

"She pushed you first?"

"She did."

"Were there witnesses?"

"Yeah. Lots of the kids there, they back me. Some teachers I guess hear us, 'cause we got loud. Teachers over there with Miss Morse." She pointed to a group of five or six well-dressed white people standing and talking at the other end of the courtroom. "One of the teachers say he see her push me first, but he not here."

"Are any of the kids who saw it here?"

"No."

"Would the kids and the teacher come to testify for you?"

"Yeah. I believe so."

"Okay. You said you work sometimes at a bank?"

"Yeah, Provident National Bank, downtown."

"What do you do there?"

"I'm a teller, but I'm laid off now. They probably call me back soon."

"Now look, Mrs. Charles, this is a judge who wouldn't send you to jail, but he finds almost everyone guilty, and I imagine that might hurt you at the bank. I want to ask for a postponement so you can come back with your witnesses and probably get a different judge. Is that what you'd like me to do?"

"Yeah. They may not call me back to the bank if I found guilty."

I looked up at Judge Latrone and nodded that we were ready. He called the court to order.

"Judge," I said, "I request a continuance in the case of *Commonwealth v. Charles*. Mrs. Charles is accused of assaulting the sixth grade teacher of her daughter. We had no interview, so I talked to her in the courtroom just now. She has witnesses that are not here because she wasn't interviewed prior to today. The witnesses for the prosecution are here."

"Mr. Kairys, so they got witnesses. Let the accuser testify and maybe a witness or two briefly. Then your client will tell her side, and we'll be done with it. If the testimony conflicts, I'm going to decide based on who I believe, the teacher or the defendant."

"Judge Latrone, I know you would decide like you decide any other case, but she can't present her side fairly in this situation. I don't know why a criminal charge was brought in the first place. It seems the teacher and the parent got upset and there was some pushing. But it has been brought as a criminal charge, and more is at stake than whether anyone goes to jail. A conviction might hurt her in her profession."

"What profession?"

"She's a bank teller, currently on a layoff."

"Well, I'll take that and everything else into account. Let's get started." He turned to the DA. "Call your first witness."

"Judge," I said, before the DA could begin, "I ask, once again, that you continue the case so that the defendant can get a fair trial and I or another PD can function effectively as her counsel. We've already continued several cases today, some requested by lawyers who had interviewed their clients. This is the first listing of this case."

"Continuance denied. DA, call your witness."

"Judge Latrone," I interrupted again. "With all due respect, I cannot participate in this trial as counsel for Mrs. Charles because you have made it impossible for me to defend her. I've not signed the appearance form, and I refuse to do so." The appearance form, a small piece of paper sitting on the clerk's desk, was the formal way an attorney officially acknowledged he was representing a client.

"Mr. Kairys, you are an officer of the court, and you appear here on behalf of a publicly funded agency. I order you to sign the appearance form and conduct yourself as defense counsel for this defendant, as you have done quite effectively this whole week."

"Judge, I appreciate the compliment, but no attorney could be effective in these circumstances. *Gideon v. Wainright* first established a right to counsel for criminal defendants only six years ago. I'm not going to participate in depriving that monumental development in the law of real meaning."[12]

"Mr. Kairys, I've ordered you to proceed with this case. If you continue to refuse, I'm going to hold you in contempt of court."

"You have that power, Judge, and I may spend the night in jail, but I think an appellate court will think differently about it." He was glaring at me at this point, his face a dark shade of pink. I didn't want to directly challenge him this way, but I was determined not to proceed with the case.

He shook his head back and forth, still glaring at me. "Mr. Kairys, I'm going to take a recess for 10 minutes. I expect you to get on the phone with the defender, Vince Ziccardi, and come back with a little more sense in your head and proceed with this trial. Otherwise, I will direct the court officers to escort you to the tank upstairs. Do you understand me?"

"I understand, and I will call Vince."

"Court's adjourned for 10 minutes." He pounded his gavel on the bench louder than usual.

I left the courtroom calmer than I thought I should be, mostly worried about Vince's reaction. Vince had just been elevated to the top job, defender, at the request of Mayor James Tate. The Defender Association started in 1934 as a private group organized by the Pennsylvania Prison Society that recruited volunteer lawyers to provide "politically independent representation to impoverished clients." Funding for the Defender Association, which came mostly from the community chest, something like today's United Way, was erratic and inadequate for the large, full-time staff needed to satisfy the new right to counsel in criminal cases. Earlier in 1969, Tate agreed to provide substantial city funding if there was a restructuring that included the exit of Marty Vinikoor and the installation of Vince. Vince was a longtime Defender lawyer, but I wasn't sure where his loyalties would lie in my conflict with Latrone.[13]

By the time I got to the pay phone in the hallway outside, found 10 cents, and got through to Vince, Latrone had already called him. "What's going on over there, Dave?" Vince said as soon as I got connected to him.

"He's threatening to hold me in contempt and send me to the tank, Vince. What happened is, I refused to enter an appearance or go along with a trial after he refused a continuance. The defendant is a woman who works as a bank teller, and she's accused of assaulting her daughter's teacher. There was some pushing between them in the midst of a heated argument. Our client says she was pushed first and has witnesses, but she wasn't interviewed and no witnesses are here for her. The teacher came in with several witnesses. You know what Latrone will do. Guilty with probation. She may never work again as a teller."

"Alright, Dave, I get it. He will send you to jail, you know. He's done it for less. He can't handle being challenged. You ready for that?"

"Not eager, but if he does it, I'll be alright, Vince. My question is will you back me? Will you call him back and tell him you support my position?"

"I will call him back and tell him I won't order you to proceed, that it's up to you. Good enough?"

"Yeah, I guess."

"I'll also send someone over right away to represent you should he hold you in contempt. We'll appeal right away. I'll see if any of your comrades in Tony's program are around. You know, Dave, I like what you're doing, but you're a lot of work."

"Sorry about that. Thanks."

I stayed in the hallway more than the 10 minutes. I wanted to talk to Mrs. Charles and to wait until I had a lawyer. Mrs. Charles, leaning on a wall in the hallway, was upset and dabbing tears from her eyes.

"I'm sorry about this," I told her. "Whatever happens to me, he won't send you to jail, and you can request a jury trial later. So hang in there as best you can."

"I will," she said, wiping away more tears. "I appreciate what you did for me. Are you goin' to be in trouble?"

"I'll be fine. It might help me understand this lawyer work better if I spend a little time in the tank."

She smiled slightly as we headed back into the courtroom. Dave Rudovsky arrived to represent me. I told him quickly what was going on and gave him my wallet and watch.

"Alright," Latrone said, "we're back in session and on the record. Mr. Kairys, are you ready to represent this defendant?"

"I'm very ready to represent her, but I can't if you force us to trial now. I request a continuance."

He looked at me. I saw less pink or red, but I didn't know how to read him. I was ready to go to jail.

"Mr. Kairys, you will leave my court immediately, and I don't want to see you in any case before me in the future. You understand?"

"Yes, I understand," I said. I started walking toward the door, glad I wasn't heading for the tank. I felt relieved, almost giddy, as I realized that this was also a great benefit to all my future clients. They would never have to endure or be found guilty by Judge Latrone. But I was worried about Mrs. Charles.

Latrone immediately appointed one of the private lawyers in the courtroom to represent Mrs. Charles. Judges have the power to appoint an attorney for a person who can't afford one, and the court pays an hourly fee to the attorney. There was no shortage of lawyers in the courtroom; word had spread around city hall about the fireworks in Latrone's room. The lawyer entered his appearance and tried the case on the spot. Latrone found Mrs. Charles not guilty. It wouldn't have looked good to convict her after all that had happened, and I suppose he thought acquittal would demonstrate how wrong I was. Anyway, Mrs. Charles probably did better than she would have with or without a postponement. My future clients also fared well. I had a few cases listed before Latrone, and each time they were continued or sent to another judge.

The middle-class white folks I grew up with would never stand for the kind of representation Mrs. Charles got, and Latrone and the other judges would only impose it on people they viewed as below them. The basic public defender structure would be unacceptable to middle-class whites or anyone with money. Our office played what looked like a zone defense in basketball. Lawyers were assigned to places, particular courtrooms, spread out to cover the various stages in the process. We represented every poor client that came through the courtroom we were assigned rather than representing particular clients throughout their entire cases. Clients got a different lawyer at each stage of the process. It was efficient and handy for training new lawyers, since we could be assigned to each successive stage and gain knowledge and experience.

Our lawyers were as good as, often better than, the private lawyers I saw each day, and we managed to provide good representation despite the zone defense. But it was a system dictated by insufficient funding, efficiency, and only minimal concern for poor defendants. We PDs were there to provide needed representation, but we were also, as Latrone viewed us, cogs in a large machine. Sometimes sorting out the two roles wasn't easy.

CHAPTER FOUR

Civility, Stop Smiling, and a Surprise Jury Trial

I WAS LIVING IN A SECOND-FLOOR WALK-UP apartment in a small stone building on Twenty-third Street near Spruce in Center City. The 20-minute walk to and from the Defender office took me through Rittenhouse Square, two square blocks of greenery and fountains surrounded by fashionable stores and apartment buildings that in the 1960s became a hangout of choice for artists, musicians, and hippies. There was usually good music, sometimes the faint smell of marijuana, and always a lot of hair—sure signs of the lifestyle and politics of the time usually called the "counterculture." I fit in with the hippies when I wasn't in one of my lawyer suits, though I saw it more as a symbolic rejection of mainstream culture than an alternative way of living.

One day in early 1969, I got to my apartment after the usual stroll through the counterculture and found the door half-open. I was sure I had left the door locked. I stuck my head in, not knowing what to expect.

"Hello, hello," I half-yelled, half-mumbled into the doorway, wondering if there was anybody there to hear me.

"What the hell is it now? I'm working down here," came back at me in a deep, resounding voice rising from somewhere inside and under the floorboards.

"Sorry, I just live here. Who are you?"

"Okay, kid, hold on a second. I'm coming up."

I moved toward the voice, which seemed to come from the bathroom. A huge man was vaguely visible in the near darkness next to the bathtub.

Only his head and bare chest, covered with grime and a lot of blondish curly hair, rose above the floor. He was climbing out of some kind of hole down into the first-floor apartment. A portable radio in the sink, with caked-on plaster and a bent antenna held up with electrical tape, softly played classical music.

He emerged from the hole slowly, an immense, sandy-haired man with a surprisingly childish grin. In his cupped hands he cradled a large ball of dripping black gooey stuff.

"I found the problem," he said with an even wider grin, "down in the main drainpipe. It looks like one of those new tampon things some jerk flushed down the toilet. Backed up the whole system. I'm Phil, the plumber for the guy that owns the building. They didn't tell you there was a problem and I was coming?"

I thought the guy talked a lot for someone I just met in a hole in my bathroom. "No," I said.

"Well, you'll have to work it out with them, because this ain't going to be done for a while."

"I go to work early in the morning, so why don't you finish then?"

"What kind of job you got, kid?"

"I'm a public defender," I replied, a little tentative for no reason I was aware of.

"What you want to do that for?" Phil asked. "Anyone the cops got, might as well keep 'em for good, as far as I'm concerned."

"Well, maybe we'll talk about it sometime." I could see some of the toilet goo stuck to his face. "Can't you get sick from that drain goo all over you?"

"Nah, plumbers become immune to it all. You get sick a lot the first few years, but then there's no germ you haven't confronted and beaten." He started back down the ladder that was coming up from the first floor but stopped and rested his butt on the floor and looked up at me. "Ya know, you should forget these criminals and do some lawyering on construction. I have a doozy of a story."

He disappeared into the hole, and I thought I was done with him.

§§§

I asked Tony if we could work on civil as well as criminal cases. I wasn't interested in construction law but rather in the Philadelphia legal services office, Community Legal Services. CLS, as everyone called it, provided attorneys for a range of poor people's legal problems—evictions, utility shutoffs, debts, job terminations, bankruptcies, and welfare benefits. It was another controversial innovation of the 1960s (and still is). Before that, landlords, utilities, creditors, employers—anyone with resources who dealt with poor or low-income people—could send their lawyers to courts and get just about anything they wanted from unrepresented poor people. I thought I would learn a lot, and I could use a break from crime.

Tony liked the idea, but there was a practical problem. He had gotten a special rule of the Pennsylvania Supreme Court that allowed us to practice as part of the program if we were in the bar of any state, so we could come to Philadelphia from all over the country without having to take the Pennsylvania bar exam. However, the special rule referred only to criminal cases through the public defender office. Tony said he'd think about it. Two weeks later, the Pennsylvania Supreme Court handed down an amendment to the special rule that included civil cases through a legal services office. Tony had called one of the justices, who spoke to the rest, and they adopted the amendment.[1]

West Philadelphia CLS and its head lawyer, Larry Lavin, welcomed me as a volunteer lawyer, and I was soon interviewing a stream of clients at their office on the first floor of an old storefront near Fortieth and Market Streets. The entrance and waiting area were renovated to look roughly like a law office, but the back had a couple small rooms and a large open area that wasn't very useful. Larry had been pushing administrators to finish renovations, but with the limited resources available, he didn't think it would happen anytime soon. After a few weeks interviewing with two other lawyers at desks in the noisy open area, we exaggerated our experience with building wallboard walls and suggested to Larry that we build the offices ourselves. The administrators came up with funds for the materials, and we had fun doing it together. The gaps between wallboards, which demanded some skill with tape and joint compound, were a little lumpy, but it looked okay, and each room was quiet and private.

Tackling the civil legal problems of poor people didn't come as easily. CLS had created some teams of lawyers in the main office that specialized in particular issues. But in the branch offices, lawyers had to know it all. One client would come in with a mortgage foreclosure, the next with an eviction, or the one after that fired. Often they came in to the office for some immediate problem that turned out to be several problems.

One client, Teresa Ramos, came in and sat in the chair beside my desk without saying anything. She was young with long, dark hair. Two girls about four or five clung to her, and an energetic little boy looked like he was enjoying his newfound ability to walk.

"Jorge, come stand here next to me," she said to the boy, who kept going like he didn't hear. She looked up at me. "I'm sorry," she said, as she handed me our paralegal's intake interview form that said she got a gas cutoff notice, which was stapled to the form.

"Don't worry, Ms. Ramos," I said, quickly reading the notice. "The kids won't bother me." She nodded in response, seeming too nervous or shy to say anything. "These papers say that you haven't paid the gas company, PGW, for three months."

"I haven't, I know. Julio, the father of my kids, left four, five months ago now. I go to the welfare office to get help, but they say he around and should pay support."

"Do you have gas heat?"

"Yeah. The stove is gas, too, and the hot water, I think."

Once she got going, she was talkative. She had a distinct Hispanic accent but spoke as if she had gone to high school in English. "Do you know where Julio is?"

"No."

"Could he pay some support?"

"Yeah, he do alright cleaning offices downtown 'til he got fired."

"So he doesn't have income now?"

"I don't know. He don't want to be with us, if it make us poorer anyway, so I stay in the apartment with our kids. I filed for support 'cause welfare tell me to."

"You did? Did it go to some court or hearing?"

"Yeah," she said, "you all did it for me. Here, you know."

"Oh, I'll look for that file. You've managed to pay your rent, though?"

"No, but he won't evict me for a while."

"How do you know?"

"He send me an eviction, but I don't think he'll do it. My cousin know his family."

"You got an eviction notice?"

"Yeah."

"Let me look into this and make some calls. I'll call you later today. The form has your neighbor's phone, is that right?"

"Yes. Thanks." She gathered the kids and left.

I cut the interview short because I realized I didn't know much about the law on any of her problems. There might have been limits on the gas company's right to shut off the gas, and she might have been entitled to welfare.

It sounded like she and Julio could get by as long as he had his job, but once that was gone, their finances, and their relationship, were in trouble. It was easier to get welfare as a single mother with children if Julio wasn't around, particularly since he was the father of the children. This gave poor women an incentive to break off relationships and made it hard to establish new ones.

I had encountered a harsher version of this, called the "man in the house" rule, the summer of 1966, after my first year of law school. I was working for CORE, a civil rights group often at the forefront, in East Baltimore. I was the closest thing to a lawyer at the CORE office in the city's poorest neighborhood, performing much the same intake and screening role as the paralegals at the CLS office. I interviewed people and, if I thought we could help, referred them to volunteer lawyers. Some women with children complained of being dropped from welfare because a "midnight raid" had discovered they were sleeping with a man. Welfare caseworkers, often accompanied by police, would visit the homes of women on welfare in the middle of the night. One would go to the front door while others waited at other doorways. They knocked and announced who they were, which was often quickly followed by a man hardly dressed running out of the house or apartment.

If there was a man in the house, the children were dropped from welfare—whether or not he was the father, was actually providing financially for the children, or could or would do so. State statutes and regulations that established these rules were often explicitly morally based—aid could not go to mothers having sexual relations because they were "unworthy," "immoral," or not providing a "suitable home." Congress, according to Senate and House reports on the act first establishing welfare in 1935, had authorized each state to "impose such other eligibility requirements—as to means, moral character, etc.—as it sees fit." Malcolm X called it genocide. The Supreme Court invalidated the man in the house rule in 1968 but let stand the searches of homes of welfare mothers without probable cause or a search warrant. Welfare officials could enter a welfare recipient's home looking for violations of welfare regulations and for evidence of any crime, without any cause or basis.[2]

The more Teresa Ramos spoke, the more urgent legal problems emerged. I didn't know where to begin. Should I start with support, welfare, or the gas company? And should I rely on her sense that the landlord wouldn't evict her? She wouldn't go to jail, but an awful lot in her life, and the lives of the three children, depended on effective legal help. I asked the CLS lawyers for some direction. I got an extension from the gas company, and a long talk with her welfare caseworker seemed to put her back on track for the next month's check. I told her to talk to her landlord and assure him she would pay all her rent rather than hope he wouldn't throw her out.

After a few weeks, I realized that I was asking the CLS lawyers what to do, whom to call, or what the law was on almost every case. I wasn't contributing much, and it would take a long time before I knew enough to be useful. I suggested, and Larry agreed, that I dig into some particular issue rather than try to represent incoming CLS clients. Something unexpected soon came along.

§§§

A lawyer in the CLS office, Janet Stotland, worked mostly on housing issues. Among her clients were several community groups opposing expansion of Penn and the Drexel Institute of Technology into residential communities in West Philadelphia. Similar disputes led to protests at Columbia in 1968 while I was in my last year of law school. In November 1969, Janet asked me to accompany her to an evening meeting of those groups in Powelton Village.

Powelton was a small area north of Drexel and Penn known for racial integration that preceded the civil rights movement and as the home of choice for many antiwar and civil rights activists. When Janet described the neighborhood, I immediately wanted to live there (and did a couple years later). The meeting was at the home of Ernie and Edith Parent on Race Street between Thirty-third and Thirty-fourth Streets. The house was a typical "Philadelphia twin," two large stone houses, usually three or four stories, joined at a common wall with a substantial yard in the front and back of both.

About 20 people were gathered in the living room, surrounded by beautiful stained Victorian woodwork. Edith was a nurse; Ernie, a handsome French Canadian, was between jobs; Gerry Goldin taught physics at Penn. Two elderly black women lived on Summer and Winter Streets, in a small, predominantly black community. Several young white men and women lived in "communes," group houses of usually five to eight people that formed around political issues or lifestyles. There was a bus driver, an architect, a veterinarian, and a dental student. CLS could represent the groups and any of the individuals who met the low-income standards for legal services offices.

"For those of you who are new to this, it goes back a decade," Gerry said, starting the meeting. "There were hearings before city council and negotiations with the city's Redevelopment Authority aimed at placing limits on Drexel's expansion."

"Why negotiate with the city?" someone asked.

"The city had a crucial role because only the city can condemn the land and throw out the owners and residents of the houses, which include some of the best Victorian houses in Philadelphia. In 1964 we reached an agreement with the Redevelopment Authority on a policy of selective clearance. The community would welcome Drexel as an integral neighbor, and most of the houses would be preserved. But Drexel would not go along with it, and the city—whose obligation should be to the public—caved. Then the community went to court. Janet, our CLS lawyer, is here. Do you want to explain that?"

"Sure. A federal judge placed a temporary freeze on the federal funding of this 'redevelopment' project because agencies adopted plans without consulting the community, which is required under federal law. By claiming that the area was 'blighted,' they could get federal funds to tear down buildings and relocate residents. While the freeze was in effect, Drexel continued to buy and neglect properties, to support its position that the area is a slum and should be torn down."[3]

"They've done their best to make it a 'slum,'" Gerry said. "Some homeowners have given in and sold to them, and then they let those properties deteriorate. After a decade of this, east Powelton is pocketed with abandoned buildings and vacant lots. But the community is still here—over a hundred attend general meetings, and we can put up a sizable picket line when we need to. Al, you've got the latest Drexel plan, don't you?"

"Yeah, we finally got a copy of Drexel's long-secret new plan," Alan Johnson said as he unrolled and laid on the floor a large drawing showing Drexel's plan and the existing housing. He was an architect with shoulder-length dark hair wearing jeans and a white T-shirt. "At this point, they plan to take out at least 25 twins, including Edith and Ernie's, and all of Summer and Winter Streets." The two elderly women from that area gasped. "The houses that will go are shown with dashed lines."

"What do the new Drexel buildings look like?" Ernie asked.

"It's the same thing they've been pushing from the beginning. They haven't listened to a word we've said. All the buildings are single purpose—there's a math building, a chemistry building, you know—and every building except the dorms is only two or three stories. Here's the alternative plan I've drawn up."

He unrolled another large drawing and placed it next to Drexel's plan on the floor. "Here I've met all the needs Drexel claims—the square footage of space for offices, classrooms, the whole gamut is the same as in their own plan. I've used three- or four-storied, multipurpose buildings, so physics and chemistry might be in the same building, and maintained all of the existing residential housing. It's a campus somewhat integrated into the community, with a lot of open spaces."

"That's the basic problem," a small woman from a commune said. "They've designed a campus one might see in a rural or suburban area. Low, single-purpose buildings and big open spaces between them. The problem is we're in the city; people live here. We've got to make it a public issue and demonstrate!"

"You got it, Melissa," Al said. Most everyone nodded or voiced their agreement.

She had summed it up well, and I found myself looking at her intensely for a moment. She was pretty, with long brown hair and no makeup, wearing a peasant blouse and jeans skirt. I wouldn't have expected such an emphatic, edgy analysis from her. Her look was very hippie and counterculture. Many of the women I grew up with in suburban Baltimore were as smart and articulate, but you'd never know it. They wouldn't speak up like that or take a leading role in a meeting like this. I was glad I had left suburban Baltimore and the mainstream, middle-class life I would have lived there.

"So what are we going to do?" Ernie asked. "They've already torn down what they need to build the dorm across the street. Construction is expected to start soon. That's their game—get buildings down as fast as possible."

"We have to do our best to nonviolently stop the construction of the dorm, because that's what's happening now," Melissa said. "Maybe we can gather enough support to stop it or negotiate the rest of this stupid plan."

They talked out plans for demonstrations and nonviolent civil disobedience to start once Drexel began the dorm construction. Volunteers took on various tasks—setting times for meetings, activating a phone chain to inform all their supporters, making picket signs. I liked the energy and informality of the group and their commitment to their community.

§§§

I didn't hear anymore about it for a couple weeks, when Janet told me a judge had issued injunctions against them. "They were demonstrating at the dorm site and asking Drexel's president or some other high official to meet with them to negotiate. Drexel refused, so they walked from the dorm site down to the Drexel campus and gathered at the student activities building. From there, they moved toward the main administration building to see the president of Drexel. When they were kept from entering the administration building, they went back to the student activities center and sat down. For 10 hours."

It became a sit-in, a tactic used successfully by the civil rights and antiwar movements. As a college student, I had sat in at a segregated restaurant and a segregated amusement park in Baltimore. It scared me—I was vulnerable to whatever the authorities had in mind for me. At the amusement park, we sat huddled together on the ground surrounded by police with billy clubs, guns, and dogs. But there was strength, unity, and a deep sense of making a difference that came from the same source as the fear—putting our bodies on the line. That's why it can work. Everyone knows you are risking your body and your freedom while not endangering anyone else's, because you deeply believe there is an injustice that should be addressed.

Two temporary injunctions had been gotten by Drexel and its dorm contractor, Cubic Construction Corp. of New Jersey. The Powelton groups and several of the individual residents were prohibited from entering or blocking access to the construction site. These parts of the injunctions were legal. The Powelton neighbors had a right to demonstrate on the sidewalks around the site, but there has never been any right, based on First Amendment free speech or anything else, to go on someone else's land or to block access to it. Such forms of civil disobedience can be quite effective, but trespassing or blocking a doorway for the purpose of drawing attention to a problem did not make it protected free speech or legal.

But I thought the content of the injunctions and the process by which they were obtained violated free speech rights. The injunctions also forbade the Powelton neighbors from "directly or indirectly," "in any manner," or "otherwise" interfering with the construction and from "insulting" or "annoying" Drexel. Also, Drexel and Cubic had gone to a judge in city hall to get the injunctions without any notice to the neighbors or their lawyers, although they knew where to find them.

A hearing was set for December 9 on whether the injunctions should continue. Such a hearing was required soon after a temporary injunction was issued. The CLS lawyers, Janet and Larry, asked me to take the lead at this hearing, since free speech and civil rights were more my areas. I hadn't yet litigated any civil rights issues except in the criminal law context. I was hesitant, but I thought this was just what I wanted to do, so I might as well do it.

When Janet and I came into the courtroom, the judge, Leo Weinrott, was on the bench sitting quietly as we took out our papers and settled in our seats at our counsel table. He had white hair and wore horn-rimmed glasses that looked big on his small head. He didn't look up to his fierce reputation. He was most known for and proud of swearing in Frank Rizzo as mayor and imposing injunctions and large fines on unions.[4]

Nine or ten lawyers for Drexel and Cubic were already settled in seats at the other counsel table, extending back from the table in rows of three or four. I noticed the number of them and their fine tailored suits. I was self-conscious but also proud of my nice but inexpensive suit from Joseph Banks Clothier in Baltimore, a warehouse-like place that claimed to sell the top-labeled suits without the labels. They never looked the same, at least not on me. My father had taken me there before I moved to Philadelphia so I would look like a real lawyer. I didn't think it worked, particularly with my beard and long hair.

Drexel and Cubic, the plaintiffs in this civil lawsuit, sought what was called "equitable relief"—an injunction prohibiting the Powelton neighbors, the defendants, from interfering with what were claimed as Drexel's and Cubic's rights. In the heyday of English common law, going back some centuries, there were separate civil courts and judges for "law" and "equity" cases (and sometimes for religious cases). They were merged in the course of U.S. history, so there were no longer separate courts or judges in most states, but the distinction survived.

In "law" cases, the plaintiff claimed the defendant violated his or her rights and usually sought compensation in the form of damages—money. A negligence claim based on a traffic accident is an example. In "equity" cases, the plaintiff usually sought to make the defendant do or stop doing something. They also involved rights and claims, but equitable relief involved a more serious incursion on the rights of a defendant than paying money.

So in an equity case like this one, the plaintiff had additional burdens, and the judge was supposed to balance the "equities"—the various interests and consequences. Among the common requirements for an injunction were "irreparable injury," an injury that cannot be adequately compensated by money, and "clean hands," dealing with the defendant forthrightly and in good faith.

Weinrott started the hearing with a lecture about how important institutions of higher education were and how we attorneys for the neighbors should be concerned about Drexel since we went to college and law school. He seemed to think that all attorneys, since they are educated, should side with Drexel and that none should represent the Powelton neighbors. I didn't respond.

But he went on. "We have to stop this sort of thing from happening in Philadelphia," Weinrott said. "When bad things happen, I'm available at any time of day or night to enjoin them." He paused and then asked me, "Did you think about these things when you decided to represent these people?"

I felt angry and wanted to scream the most one-upping, cutting responses I could think of—starting with, "How could you call yourself a judge?" But I was discovering that wanting to yell at judges was going to be a fact of law practice for me. I restrained myself and tried to channel the anger into a creative, principled response. I was determined not to avoid or ignore this level of judicial indecency but also to be effective.

"With all due respect, Judge Weinrott," I said, "I am honored to represent these residents of a fine Philadelphia neighborhood who are willing to speak out to preserve their community."

Weinrott's face and shoulders tightened as he leaned down toward me and pointed his finger straight at me. "You're part and parcel of the whole thing. You were there—you also violated the injunction."

"I was there as counsel for the neighbors, like some of the lawyers on the other side, who were also there as counsel for their clients."

"Well, I have a matter to settle with you later. I'm not sure you're even a member of the bar."

That sounded like he planned to hold me in contempt of court. "I don't know what you're talking about, Judge, but for no good reason you have been intimidating counsel and urging us to abandon our clients. I assure you that I won't do that. I move that you disqualify yourself as biased against the Powelton neighbors and their counsel."

"I will not. That's ridiculous and insulting." His face was getting that pink-reddish hue I was becoming accustomed to. I wanted to name it, maybe "judicial red."

"Well, why were you talking about stopping bad things from happening in Philadelphia when you haven't heard proof of anything illegal and before you even hear our side?"

"You'll get your chance to present your side, and my mind is open. Present your case and your argument."

He quickly collected himself. He must have realized it was looking like he was biased. I was conscious of how the transcript of the hearing would read, and he seemed conscious also but tended to lose his cool. We would lose in front of Weinrott, and the transcript would affect how we did in any appeal and how I would do if I were held in contempt. I noticed the stenographer stopped transcribing sometimes when Weinrott went off on his weirdest tangents. Many stenographers were regularly with the same judge and sometimes viewed themselves as serving the judge rather than the court or the public. Some protected their judge. Fortunately, the fireworks between me and Weinrott drew the press, and newspaper articles covered much of it.[5]

Later, one of Weinrott's clerks came in the courtroom holding a small file, and Weinrott stopped the proceedings. "You got it?" he said to the clerk.

"Yes, Your Honor." The clerk handed a file to Weinrott.

"You're not on the alphabetical list of admitted lawyers, Mr. Kairys. Do you have anything to say before I have the sheriff take you into custody?"

"Judge, I don't know what would lead you to even look into my bar membership. Do you think no bar member would represent these defendants? But if you thought I'm not a member of the bar, why raise it in the middle of this hearing?"

"I just wanted to check, a hunch you could say."

"Well, again with all due respect, I believe we're here for a hearing about two injunctions you issued, not bar membership hunches. But to move us along, if you have your clerk check bar admission Rule 12½ of the Rules of the Pennsylvania Supreme Court and ask the prothonotary of that court whether I am admitted under that rule, he will tell you I am. I would like to proceed, Judge, with the hearing, if we could. But first, I again move that you disqualify yourself."

"Young man, I'm going to look into this, and if I find any problem, you're going to be out of here. I will never disqualify myself."

And so it went. I was sometimes confused about what Weinrott was getting at or unsure of how to respond, but less so than I would have thought. It felt like being bullied as a kid, which I resisted and had learned to talk my way out of. I found myself enjoying the back and forth and felt basically in control of the situation. I was making my principled points directly without being disrespectful. I worried that I was too confrontational and wanted to make sharp, edgy responses only when he went too far.

Weinrott's one-sidedness and explosive diatribes were interspersed with testimony by witnesses and the trappings and language of judicial formality. Drexel and Cubic presented testimony by Cubic personnel; a police official; Drexel security personnel; and William Hagerty, president of Drexel. Hagerty testified that Drexel rightfully owned and was developing the land according to a plan approved by the city and federal governments. The Cubic witnesses testified that on December 6 about 75 people demonstrated at the dorm site. Most all were on the sidewalk or street, but some went on the edge of the site property. A part of the fence around the site was down at another place, but they didn't know how that happened or whether it was connected to the demonstrators.

Lt. George Fencl, head of the Philadelphia police's Civil Disobedience Unit—civil disobedience was so common in those days that they had a separate police unit assigned to it since 1964—testified that there was no violence or harm to property. Demonstrators shouted out his attempt to read the injunctions, but when the injunctions were read, the demonstrators left, as they did later in the day at the Drexel student activities building. Drexel security witnesses testified that the neighbors were orderly, that there was no damage or disruption at the student activities center, and that the center is open to the public.

None of the Drexel or Cubic witnesses specifically connected any of the neighbors or groups to any illegal act. They admitted that they knew where the defendants and their lawyers could be found and that the individual defendants named in their complaint were picked because they were quoted in the newspapers as critics of Drexel's expansion. This established that Drexel and Cubic could have given notice before they got the injunctions from Weinrott and that they were seeking to enjoin the protected speech of their critics.

I thought we were doing quite well, and I was happy with my cross-examinations of the witnesses. I emphasized the peaceful nature of the Powelton demonstrators, their acting within their free speech rights, the lack of connection of any of them to anything illegal, and Drexel's refusal to negotiate or even inform or listen to its neighbors about plans that would destroy their homes and community—the "unclean hands" that could defeat a request for an injunction.

But Weinrott had one more surprise. Instead of ruling from the bench that the temporary injunctions were to continue in force as long-term injunctions—as everyone expected—he said he needed to consider his ruling and asked both sides to file briefs in a week. He left the injunctions "temporarily" in force—in the period the Powelton neighbors most needed their free speech rights—while making appeal procedurally difficult by not giving us a decision to appeal.

A litigant in a trial court could not appeal from a ruling or order simply because it went against them or violated their rights. In general, appeals were limited to the end of cases. This made sense; it avoided the time and resources required for many appeals before a case was over, and it avoided any appeal before the lower court decided who won. There were exceptions, and it was sometimes difficult to decide what was the "end," but it looked like we couldn't appeal from the temporary injunctions while Weinrott's decision on extending them was still pending.[6]

And we'd have to appeal first to the Superior Court of Pennsylvania, an intermediate appellate court known for approving almost anything the trial court judges did. Then we could go to the Supreme Court of Pennsylvania. I read all the recent Pennsylvania Supreme Court decisions on free speech, and they seemed pretty good. I counted at least four of the seven judges who could potentially decide our way. But the dorm might be built by the time we had a shot at a favorable decision by an appellate court, and we might go that route and not find out for months whether an appeal was allowable at this stage.

Federal court was another possibility. Federal courts had jurisdiction over federal civil rights claims based on the First Amendment. But the federal judges weren't as good on free speech as the Pennsylvania Supreme Court judges were, and the federal court would likely also require us to wait until Weinrott decided.

§§§

I combed the rules and decisions on the jurisdiction of the Pennsylvania Supreme Court and noticed that, going back to common law brought here from Britain, there was "original" jurisdiction to hear writs of "mandamus" and "prohibition." This was familiar from law school, since the first case we read in constitutional law, *Marbury v. Madison* (which established judicial review), focused on similar jurisdictional provisions. I knew original jurisdiction meant the rarely used jurisdiction appellate courts have to hear some cases filed originally with the appellate court rather than appealed from a lower court. Mandamus was a writ used to force a government official to perform certain acts that were routine for their office. I had never heard of a writ of prohibition, so I looked into it.[7]

Prohibition was a common law action filed in an appellate court to challenge a lower court's acting beyond its jurisdiction or abusing its jurisdiction. It developed as a procedure by which a trial court that was hearing a case that it did not have jurisdiction to hear could be immediately stopped. It made sense that there be a way to stop a trial court in some cases without a drawn-out appeal. The action was filed against the judge whose jurisdiction was challenged, which had an added appeal—it would be a lawsuit against Weinrott personally. But over the years the Pennsylvania Supreme Court had rarely heard prohibition cases.

I had three ways to connect the Powelton neighbors' case to jurisdiction. First, the failure of Drexel and Cubic to give notice to the neighbors that they had filed lawsuits and were seeking the temporary injunctions from Weinrott raised a jurisdictional issue. Notice to the defendant was often a prerequisite to valid jurisdiction.

Second, according to decisions in some states, the bias of a judge was considered an "abuse" of jurisdiction that could be heard by a prohibition action. The Pennsylvania appellate courts had not ruled on the use of prohibition to challenge a biased judge. Since this was a common law writ that was part of the law in every state, I could use the cases from other states, but they weren't as good as a Pennsylvania decision would have been.

Finally, improper assignment of judges was recognized as a jurisdictional issue that could be challenged in a prohibition action. The procedure for obtaining a temporary injunction was to go before the civil motions judge, who was not Weinrott. Lawsuits aimed at stopping various activists or protests were regularly heard by one of three or four Philadelphia judges, including Weinrott, who had said at the hearing he was "always available." Either the motions court judge was always assigning these cases to a small number of judges or, more likely, Drexel's and Cubic's lawyers waited till after 5:00 p.m., when civil motions court was closed, and called Weinrott.

Even if one or all of these worked, the basic free speech issue—the injunctions prohibiting protected speech—wasn't jurisdictional. I could argue that, as the cases sometimes said, on occasion prohibition could be used to remedy a grave injustice unrelated to jurisdiction. Or I could emphasize the jurisdiction-related issues when I discussed prohibition and assume that the court would decide the free speech issues if it heard the case.

I worked around the clock for a few days, which resulted in a 36-page brief on the long lawyer paper that cited over 70 cases.[8] Recent decisions by the U.S. Supreme Court adamantly protected peaceful picketing and gathering for purposes of communicating ideas on public streets, sidewalks, and parks. An injunction prohibiting these protected activities was particularly disfavored because it constituted a "prior restraint"—it barred speech before it occurred. Overly broad or vague prohibitions of speech deterred open dialogue and ran afoul of the First Amendment. A very recent case also decided that lack of notice to defendants who were subjected to an ex parte (from one side) injunction involving their free speech rights itself raised a free speech issue. Such notice should be provided unless it is "impossible" to do so.

Since the injunctions did not explicitly ban picketing or demonstrations, I emphasized the broadness and vagueness of their provisions. A peaceful demonstration could "interfere" by swaying public opinion, but that is the essence of free speech. This language was also vague, which had a "chilling effect"—speech was deterred because speakers could not know whether their protected speech is prohibited.[9]

These arguments can be difficult to make convincingly in the abstract, but we also had a concrete example. The demonstration at the dorm site was peaceful and did not block access to the site or obstruct construction. Yet, Drexel, Cubic, and the Philadelphia police viewed the Powelton neighbors' protected speech that day as prohibited by the injunctions.

The brief focused on these free speech issues, after tracing the history of the Drexel-Powelton dispute, the current crisis at the dorm site, and the history and basics of the law on writs of prohibition. I emphasized that Weinrott's maintaining the temporary injunctions while not ruling on the whether they should be continued indefinitely left us without the ordinary avenue of appeal. The only other option would be for the neighbors to engage in peaceful demonstrations and raise the First Amendment as a defense if they were charged with contempt of court for violating the injunctions. But this was foreclosed by a recent U.S. Supreme Court decision. Although you could "test" the constitutionality of a statute or executive branch action by violating it and raising the Constitution as a defense, the Court decided that no constitutional defense was allowable for violating a court order.[10] This decision made no sense to me; if a government action is unconstitutional, it's supposed to be void and of no effect.

My "Petition for Writ of Prohibition" and the brief and other paperwork supporting it were strong, and I was ready to file, but there was one more strategy decision. I had prepared a motion asking the court to expedite the case and to grant us immediate, temporary relief. Expediting would make the case move faster than usual, and the temporary relief would restore the free speech rights of the Powelton neighbors until the court considered the case fully and ruled. We could file the papers and wait and see what response the Pennsylvania Supreme Court had. Since it was an extraordinary writ with a request to expedite, it would come to the attention of the justices quicker than regular appeal papers. But it could also sit there for some time. Alternatively, once the papers were filed, we could contact a justice and request an immediate ruling on the motion to expedite and to grant immediate, temporary relief.

Any justice had the authority to entertain such a request, but there was nothing in the rules about which justice you should call. An experienced appellate lawyer told me the practice was to call the chief justice first and then go in order of seniority until one of them agreed to hear me. The one who agreed to hear me would be the only one I could ask. He (they were all men) might contact some or all of the rest before deciding, particularly if he was tending to grant temporary relief, but they didn't have to. Which justice you spoke to was obviously very important, and I knew I had a problem.

The chief justice, whom I would call first, was John C. Bell, Jr.[11] He was an arch-conservative, a term applied to ideological conservatives in that time, who came to prominence in the Republican Party because of his staunch opposition to the New Deal—opposition to Social Security, unemployment benefits, benefits for disabled people, that sort of thing, which didn't exist before the 1930s. He was also what was widely termed a WASP, a white Anglo-Saxon Protestant, whose ancestors probably sailed on the *Mayflower*, which entitled him to his membership in the Sons of the Revolution. I might have qualified for membership in something like the Sons of the Bearded Guys Fleeing from Eastern Europe. I had heard of his brother, Bert Bell, the commissioner of the National Football League in the 1950s, but that didn't help. A call to Bell wouldn't go well for our side.

There were other justices who would likely be receptive. Conservative and liberal labels might not mean so much on an issue like free speech, but Bell's brand of conservatism seemed deadly with a university pitted against demonstrators over land owned by the university.

§§§

"Chief Justice Bell's chambers," a cheery woman's voice said.

"Yes. I'd like to speak to Chief Justice Bell to make an oral application on a pending case filed today. May I speak to his law clerk or whoever is appropriate?"

"I'll put you through to the law clerk in chambers now." It was a few minutes after 5:00 p.m.

"Hello, who am I speaking to?" The voice was a young man's about my age.

"Hello, this is David Kairys. I'm a lawyer with CLS in Philadelphia, but mostly with the public defender office, and working through a new kind of clinical legal, law school program. I'm admitted under a special rule—"

"Okay, let's get to it. I'm on my way out the door."

"Well, we have a situation here in Philadelphia. A lawsuit was filed against some residents of the Powelton neighborhood. Do you know the Philadelphia neighborhoods?"

"Not really."

"Well, we filed a petition for writ of prohibition today, and I have to speak to Chief Justice Bell immediately about temporarily suspending temporary injunctions issued—"

"Look, the chief justice is gone for the day, and I know he's hearing arguments tomorrow morning, maybe all day. Why don't you call back tomorrow?"

"I could, but you're saying it won't be possible to talk to the chief justice today or tomorrow morning?"

"No. Look, I don't know if he'll talk to you at all. But I have to go, alright?"

"Sure, thanks. Good-bye."

Bell was not available, a result I tried to make as likely as possible by calling after 5:00 and babbling a bit. I went down the list, and a couple justices later I had Justice Herbert B. Cohen on the phone.

"Justice Cohen, thank you for taking my call. I tried Chief Justice Bell and went down the list in order of seniority, and you're the first who could hear me."

"Go on."

"We have an urgent and potentially explosive free speech problem in Philadelphia. A judge has issued ex parte temporary injunctions that prohibit residents of a fine community being partially demolished from peaceful demonstrations to voice their opposition. The judge won't rule on extending the injunctions, so we can't appeal. We filed a petition for writ of prohibition today, because the lack of notice to the residents, the bias of the judge—he said in open court that he's available to issue injunctions day or night—and the same judge's repeatedly issuing such injunctions, rather than have the civil motions judge hear them, all raise substantial jurisdictional issues."

"Still," he said, "writs of prohibition are rarely allowed. Who issued these injunctions?"

"Judge Leo Weinrott, who was just reversed by the Third Circuit for another injunction limiting free speech."

"What case is that?"

"It's the Grove Press case, involving a movie. We attached a copy of the opinion to our petition. I don't believe that case went through your court."

"What do the injunctions say?"

"They prohibit the residents in very expansive language from 'insulting' or 'annoying' Drexel, it involves Drexel's expansion into the Powelton Village community, and from interfering with Drexel's plans 'in any manner,' 'directly or indirectly,' or 'otherwise.' It's been interpreted by the police and Judge Weinrott to bar a wholly peaceful, nonviolent gathering on the sidewalk with picket signs. They've effectively muzzled the Powelton neighbors, who are trying to gather support from the public and—"

"All of this is set out in your petition and motions?"

"Yes, there is a motion for expedited consideration and for temporary restoration of the neighbors' free speech rights while the court decides."

"I'll look at it, and you'll hear from the prothonotary."

There was a click on the line, and he was gone. I couldn't tell how I had done. His reactions were dry, all business, but he gave me some time and asked the right questions. There was nothing else to do but wait, which I didn't like at all.

It didn't take long. Several days later—and just a total of nine days after the hearing before Weinrott—I got a call from the prothonotary's office. "Mr. Kairys, Justice Cohen has entered an order today granting your motion for expedited consideration. Judge Leo Weinrott has been ordered to file a response in three days. Further, Justice Cohen handwrote the following on the expedition order: 'All proceedings, orders and decrees restraining the First Amendment rights of the defendants are stayed pending action on the within petition.'"

"Thank you. Is that all?"

"No. Justice Cohen set a date for consideration of your petition, a few weeks from now."

After Justice Cohen's order, the demonstrations resumed, the media covered the neighbors' plight favorably, and a city councilman joined the fray on the side of the neighbors. New negotiations with Drexel resulted in a "moratorium" on destruction of houses and compromises and a Drexel "restudy" of the plan. I was surprised how much the free speech issue, the successful legal challenge to Weinrott's injunctions, and the fireworks between him and me drew media attention and aided the neighbors in their efforts to preserve the community, far beyond simply restoring their free speech rights.

About six weeks later, I got another call from the prothonotary of the Pennsylvania Supreme Court. The court completely invalidated Weinrott's two injunctions, in a decision written and signed by John C. Bell, Jr., chief justice.[12]

§§§

The negotiations between Drexel and the community broke down periodically. The Powelton neighbors would take to the streets, and Drexel would head for Judge Weinrott. Once the Supreme Court had reversed him and thrown out the initial injunctions, he had to start over. But there was no change in his rulings or attitude toward the Powelton neighbors or me.

The controversy reached its height in early February 1970. Drexel ended a moratorium, and construction crews arrived at the dorm site. The neighbors entered the site by climbing over the fence around it and stood or sat in front of cranes and bulldozers, conduct that was not included in any of their First Amendment rights. At one point, four elderly women, including Emma Hammond from the Summer and Winter Streets area, sat in the scoop of a bulldozer. Work was stopped for a few days.

Weinrott issued new injunctions, with notice to the neighbors and us lawyers and without the prohibitions of protected free speech. Lt. Fencl and his Civil Disobedience squad arrested the neighbors on the site, sometimes over 20 at a time. They were taken to the lockup at city hall and brought before Judge Weinrott.

When it was her turn, Mrs. Hammond took the stand, turned to face Weinrott, and said, without any questions being asked, "I'm 90 years old. I was never in a courtroom in my life. Drexel is coming in and kicking us out of our homes and giving us nothing. I thought it was my time to protest. That's why I'm here."

Weinrott looked straight back at her, saying nothing with his mouth open, seemingly stymied. "How'd you get over the fence and into the scoop of the bulldozer?" he asked.

"They put up a ladder for me on the fence. I climbed up the ladder and went over. They were helping me, but then I fell flat." She smiled and looked out at the people in the crowded courtroom, who mostly smiled back. "It didn't hurt much."

That was the only sign of hesitation I saw from Weinrott, and it didn't last long. At the beginning of one of the sessions, he angrily condemned the demonstrators and declared, "This is an American courtroom, and sit-ins are un-American." A front-page story in the *Philadelphia Inquirer* the next morning had the headline "Sit-Ins Un-American, Weinrott Rules."

Then he turned to me. "Mr. Kairys, will you join me in maintaining law and order." He had a slight, satisfied smile.

"Law and order are important," I replied, "but sometimes justice is more important, and sometimes good, decent people like Mrs. Hammond have no option but to nonviolently violate a law to seek justice because all the cards are stacked against them."

He stared at me, with a little of the judicial red hue in his cheeks. Then he continued with the testimony, until he suddenly stopped a witness in midsentence.

"Just a moment," he said to the witness and then turned to me. "Mr. Kairys, what are you smiling about?"

"I'm talking, in a whisper, to my cocounsel, Judge."

"But what were you saying that was so funny?"

"With all due respect, Judge, a conversation between cocounsel about a case is privileged and, frankly, not your business." I was aware that I was preceding the biggest challenges to him the same way—"with all due respect"—when I didn't respect him or believe any respect was due him. It felt like a cushion and like what I was saying was principled, not personal. The transcript might read better with it. Anyway, it somehow made the challenges more comfortable.

"Don't smile in my courtroom, Mr. Kairys. It irritates me."

"Judge Weinrott, you are the judge here, and you make the rulings, set the schedule, even call the bathroom breaks. But I am not aware of any power you have—or any reason for you to be concerned—over smiling."

"We'll see what power I have. Go ahead, resume the testimony."

The witness continued testifying, but after a few moments I interrupted. "Excuse me, Judge Weinrott, but the middle lawyer in the second row for Drexel just smiled, and I thought you'd want to know."

As soon as I said it, I knew this time I had gone too far, but I had difficulty resisting the comment when it popped into my head. Maybe it was my youth, a rush of testosterone, or just inexperience. In hindsight, I wouldn't do it again, but I'm glad I did. It felt good.

His response wasn't as bad as I expected or as it could have been. "We're going to discuss some things after the hearing is over, Mr. Kairys. I don't want to hear anymore about smiling, you understand?"

"Sure, I do."

He never did discuss anything with me at the end. He didn't even treat the Powelton neighbors who sat in harshly. They were let out with a lecture from him after spending usually most of a day in the can. Gerry Goldin got the biggest lecture, because, as a teacher, he should support Drexel. Mrs. Hammond was allowed to go right home, and if I'd have requested a police escort for her, he'd probably have granted it. He probably thought it wouldn't look good to go after the neighbors or me in the wake of being reversed by the Pennsylvania Supreme Court.

The dispute between Drexel and the neighbors had its ebbs and flows, although there were only occasional, small sit-ins after that. In December 1970, Janet and I got another judge, Fred DiBona, who issued more injunctions against sit-ins, to also prohibit Drexel from making "any building" in the area "less habitable by any means whatsoever," which slowed Drexel down for some time. The Drexel plan was changed, and quite a few of the houses were saved, but Drexel got just about what it wanted. And it's still not over—as I write this, the current neighbors are fighting Drexel's plan to build student apartments on a plot previously designated for recreational use.[13]

§§§

Early one Saturday morning in late 1970, I was awakened by pounding on my apartment door. I moaned and glanced at my bedside clock, which read 7:00 a.m. "Just a minute," I yelled. I got up and unlocked the door. It was Phil, the classical music, Jewish plumber I met months earlier in a hole in my bathroom.

"Good morning," Phil said. "Come on, let's get up and get going."

"Okay, Phil. Come in. I wanted to sleep late, but I might as well get dressed now."

"Don't go formal on my account. I'm used to underwear."

I put on some jeans and went into the small kitchen. "Want some orange juice, Phil?"

"Sure, don't mind if I do." He plunked down into a kitchen chair.

"So, Phil, you do floors too. I thought you were strictly a plumbing guy and some carpenter would come for the hole."

"Oh, I do it all. You kidding? A few years back, I was buildin' whole homes in a development in Montgomery County, just outside the city. I thought I was out of plumbing for good."

"What happened?"

"Well, that's what I come about. I'm in trouble. You know anything about construction financing and what happens when the market slides?"

"No."

"Well, I was partners with this guy who had a lot of money. He put up the money, and I built the houses. See, on construction loans, they only give you the money in stages. When you get so much done, you get some money. Get to the next stage, you get some more of the money. The problem is, you got to pay the contractors and workers to get things done, and you got to get things done to get the money to pay them. Get it?"

"Yeah, I think. Sounds like risky business."

"I'll say. Well, my douche bag partner started getting cold feet. The market was down in the mid-'60s, so houses weren't selling. When the finished ones sit, there's no money to work on the ones still being built, so you can go on to the next stage and get the loan money. All we needed was him to put up a little more money, but he wouldn't. The whole thing went down."

"What do you mean *down*?"

"That was it, kaput, bankrupt."

"You, personally?"

"You bet, me personally. Those sleazeballs came and took every goddam thing we had 'cept my house and my car. My wife had a nervous breakdown. She still ain't right. And I'm back pushin' shit around. But, hey, what can you do? We had a shot at real money."

"That's too bad, Phil." I didn't know quite what to say. I regretted my comment about doing floors. "What's this trouble you're in now?"

"I got charges on me."

"Criminal charges?"

"Yeah. The douche bag went to the cops, sayin' I took money that should have gone into the houses we was buildin'."

He handed me a charge form. He was charged with four counts of embezzlement and fraudulent conversion. "Phil, the trial date is next week."

"I know. I've been a mess about it. I thought I was going to hire this big shot lawyer, but I can't get the money." He paused and dropped his head into his hands, sobbing.

I wanted to tell him it would be alright, but I didn't know that. "Phil, what happened to the money they say you stole?"

"Every damn cent of it went into the houses. I was tryin' to get the houses to the next bank payment stage."

"Why didn't the douche bag like that?"

"He told me to stop the building. I thought he was wrong and I could make it go if we could just get some more done."

"Did you wind up with any of that money?"

"No, no way. It went down the construction drain, like everything else. I paid it out for work and materials. I didn't steal it."

"So how can I help?"

"Try my case. I know you're young, but you're smart and you care about things. I saw your name in the paper around that Drexel stuff you did, you know."

"Well, we'd have to run you through the public defender operation. With the bankruptcy, you won't have too much money. Are you sure you want me to do it, Phil? I've done some trials, but I am new."

"You're all I got."

§§§

I wondered if I was going too fast with this one and was maybe in over my head. "All I got" was not inspiring. But when I started to look into the case, I got interested—and angry. Douche bag was very rich. He lost some significant money but nothing like the hit Phil took. And there were documents supporting Phil that showed that he didn't put anything in his own pocket. The problem was they had a written agreement that money couldn't be spent unless they both agreed, and Phil acknowledged that douche bag specifically told him not to spend any more. Phil did it anyway, thinking he could salvage the project.

When we walked into the courtroom of Judge Harry Rosenberg, I felt ready. It was a trial "list" room—cases more serious than Municipal Court but heard by a judge in a similar fashion. I got myself assigned everything in the room that day, a total of about a dozen cases. Most were continuances. After those, the judge called a sentencing, a case in which there was an earlier conviction and the matter was listed again just for sentencing.

I read the file the night before. Kenny Smith was a 19-year-old unemployed black man who took a license plate off of an abandoned car that had sat in his neighborhood for months. There was a question about whether it was theft, since the car and tag were abandoned. Judge Rosenberg had found him guilty after a short trial a few weeks earlier.

"Alright," Rosenberg said, "we're in session and on the record. This is the sentencing in *Commonwealth v. Kenny Smith*. Mr. Smith, do you have anything to say?"

"No, Your Honor. I'm jus' sorry I did this. I wasn't gonna do nothin' wit' it but put it in my room, on the wall."

"But, Mr. Smith, it belonged to someone else. We have to have respect for private property."

"Judge," I said, "his mother, who is here today, told me he has several old tags on his wall in his room. It looks like he was collecting them."

"Well, okay. But I think there is a lesson that has to be learned here. Mr. Smith, your sentence is 11½ to 23 months at Holmesburg."

Smith, standing next to me and staring at the judge, started swaying in small circles. Then he dropped to the floor, like a piece of rope that was held up and then let go. His mother screamed and came forward as he fell.

"Alright, stand back now," Judge Rosenberg said. "Give him some room."

The court officers helped Smith back to his feet, but he still looked dazed.

"Judge, if I may," I said, "that was an unexpectedly long sentence. This is his first conviction of any crime, it involved no violence, and the property was of little value and abandoned for a long time. I ask that you reconsider and place him on probation."

"Reconsideration is denied. Sheriff, take Mr. Smith into custody. We're in recess." He left the bench quickly as two sheriffs led Smith out the side door to the lockup.

I talked to Phil, who was waiting for his case in the courtroom. "Dave," he said, "that does it for me. Can I still get a jury? That's what I want anyway."

He had preferred a jury, but I convinced him to waive it because of the risk of a tough sentence if the jury convicted. That rang hollow after he saw what happened to Smith. I also talked to the other clients I had that day.

"Alright, we're back on the record," Rosenberg said. "*Commonwealth v. Phillip Miller.*"

Phil walked forward and stood beside me in front of Rosenberg. "Judge," I said, "Mr. Miller has decided not to waive a jury trial. He requests a jury."

"Okay, we'll send this case up to Room 625, the calendar room. Next, *Commonwealth v. Juan Alvarez.*"

Phil moved back, and Juan Alvarez came forward. "Judge, I've spoken to Mr. Alvarez, and he also wishes to have a jury trial."

"Mr. Kairys, if I call the rest of the public defender cases, am I going to get the same response?"

"I believe so, Judge."

"Counsel will see me in chambers." He headed out the side door to the chambers, which was a small room with a desk and a few chairs, with the ADA and me behind. It had a strong odor of cigarette smoke.

"What's going on here, Mr. Kairys?"

"Well, Judge, they were all in the courtroom during the sentencing, and after they saw what you did to that young man, they wanted jury trials."

"They decided this on their own, without encouragement from you?"

"I agreed with and supported their decisions. I suspect the calendar judge will be surprised to get this stream of cases for jury trials from your room."

Rosenberg was eliminating the incentive to waive a jury trial—light sentences, particularly in minor cases not involving violence. The calendar judge would notice the stream of cases, and Rosenberg and I knew it would reflect badly on him. I felt like I was on strike, using the pressure I could muster to get Rosenberg to change the "working conditions" in his courtroom.

"Well, maybe I've made my point with Mr. Smith and he's gotten the message," Rosenberg said. "He fainted, didn't he?" The judge was smiling, like he was proud he'd had such an effect.

"Yes, he did."

"I'll reconsider if you will or if your clients will, of course."

"I believe they will, Judge, except Mr. Miller."

"I'll change the sentence for Mr. Smith to three years' probation."

The rest of the defendants decided to go to trial in front of Rosenberg. Another public defender came over to the room to handle their cases. I went with Phil to Room 625.

§§§

In the calendar room, a long list of major cases were taken up each day to determine which courtroom they would be assigned to for trial. The seating area was filled with lawyers and defendants out on bail. Defendants held on bail they couldn't make were brought in as their cases were called. When the first case was called, a well-dressed lawyer approached the podium between the defense table on the left and the DA's table on the right.

"Your Honor, Kenneth Lipscomb for the defendant. The defendant is out on bail and in the courtroom. Mr. Smythe, stand up." A middle-aged white man in a suit stood up in the back of the room.

"Your Honor, I request a continuance. It's Rule 1, Your Honor."

"Okay, Mr. Lipscomb," the judge said. "Mr. Smythe, come up here." Smythe walked up to the podium next to his lawyer and looked up at the judge. "Mr. Smythe, this is the second listing. I'm going to give you another continuance, but next time this case is going to trial, no matter what."

I whispered to the PD sitting next to me, "What's Rule 1?"

"It means the defendant hasn't paid the lawyer yet. Defense lawyers insist on payment before trial. Rule 1 is the way they tell the judge that they haven't been paid, and the judge usually encourages the defendant to pay up."

"Next available date, Your Honor," a large clerk bellowed out from his seat at a desk below the judge's bench, "is six weeks away, February 22, Your Honor."

"Okay. Next case."

"*Commonwealth v. Darrell Jones,* Your Honor, burglary, robbery, and receiving stolen goods. PD is on the case." The young PD next to me stood, and a young black man came up and stood beside him.

"Your Honor, I'm Mitch Corson, assistant defender. The DA claims the homeowner was at home during the burglary, so they've added the robbery charge, which raises some issues. The defendant is undecided about a jury, but I see there aren't many cases before Judge Harris this morning. Perhaps you could send it there, and I'll talk to the defendant."

All the lawyers came to know the reputations of the various judges. Court administrators regularly assigned the toughest, hardest sentencing judges to jury trials, which meant that a defendant took a gamble if he demanded a jury trial. The jury might be more likely than a judge to acquit, but if convicted, the sentence would be long. Corson was signaling the calendar judge that his case involved unusual legal issues and if it was sent to Judge Harris, known to have more of an intellectual bent than most and to believe in reasonable doubt, the defendant would waive a jury.

"Alright," the judge said, "we'll send this case to Judge Harris's courtroom."

The calendar room seemed something like the floor of the New York Stock Exchange, chaotic but folks in the know could deal to their benefit. Phil's case was called just before lunch. I said it would be a jury trial, and we were sent to Judge Sloane, who Corson told me was one of the toughest.

§§§

Sloane got to our case by mid-afternoon. Jury selection went quickly, an hour at most. I had no idea whom I was selecting or challenging among the cast of white men in their 50s. The trial was also fast and mostly a blur.

My cross-examination of Phil's partner went well. I managed to avoid calling him "douche bag," which I was afraid I would do since Phil and I regularly called him that.

"Mr. Dubois, did Mr. Miller take any of the project's money and keep it for himself?" I asked him.

"He took several thousand dollars as things were going badly, and I told him not to."

"Did the several thousand dollars wind up in his pocket?"

"No, I guess not."

"You don't have to guess, Mr. Dubois. You know that he used that money to try to complete more of the project, didn't he?"

"Yeah, he did. But I told him we were done, not to spend more."

"So there was a disagreement about whether to quit and take a big loss or to try to do more of the work, which meant spending more of the partnership money, with the goal of getting the next stage of the bank construction loan?"

"Yeah, but we had a contract. No money was supposed to be spent unless we both agreed."

"I understand that, Mr. Dubois, and you probably have a contract claim against Mr. Miller for damages. But he didn't steal from you or the partnership, and he's not a criminal."

"Objection," the ADA said. "That calls for a legal conclusion by the witness."

"Sustained," Sloane ruled.

"Did any of the partnership money go to Mr. Miller or to anyone or anything other than legitimate construction costs?"

"No."

Phil's testimony wouldn't add much, and on cross-examination he could easily be made to look bad—he was directly told not to spend the money. So he didn't testify.

My closing argument to the jury stressed the where's-the-crime theme; the fact that the money belonged to the partnership, which was half Phil's; and its use for partnership purposes, not for Phil personally. The ADA repeatedly used "thief" and "stolen" in his closing.

The jury came back with a decision after a couple hours, just before 5:00 p.m. on the second day of the trial. Phil and I stood side by side as the judge asked the jury for its verdict.

"Mr. Foreman," Judge Sloane said, "what say you on count one, embezzlement by officers of corporations or associations?"

"We find the defendant not guilty."

"What say you on count two, embezzlement by officers and agents of banks, corporations, or associations?"

"We find the defendant not guilty."

"What say you on count three, fraudulent conversion of partnership, etc., property?"

"We find the defendant not guilty."

"What say you on count four, fraudulent conversion of property?"

"We find the defendant guilty, Your Honor."

I was shocked by the last verdict. Phil and I looked at the jurors, who avoided eye contact with us, and then we turned toward each other. He was pale, and his face seemed drawn and frozen.

"This is it. I'm done." His eyes looked down at his feet, and he slowly shook his head side to side.

"Hold on, Phil. Like we talked about, he will probably grant you bail pending our motion to set aside the verdict and our appeal, particularly since you were convicted on just one count. Sit down while I check something."

"I ain't goin' anywhere," Phil said, as he slumped back into his chair.

While the jury was led out, I went over to the clerk who had the form the jury foreman wrote the verdicts on and asked to see it. The only conviction was for fraudulent conversion, like I thought I heard it.

I went back to the defense table and fumbled through my large catalog case, looking for the folder with my legal research on the case. Once the jury was out, I looked up at the judge, while still half bent over and looking for the research folder.

"Judge, I move for arrest of judgment on the ground that there was not evidence to sustain the charge of fraudulent conversion. I have here, if I might have a moment, a case that is right on point, *Commonwealth v. Moyer.* I can't seem to put my hands on it, Judge, but the court ruled—"

"Mr. Kairys, file your motion, we'll get a response from the DA, and I'll list it for argument."

"I request that Mr. Miller's bail be continued, Judge. It is a minor charge, Mr. Miller's first offense; he's always lived here and is not going to flee; and if I could find the *Moyer* case, it establishes a solid ground for the motion."

"Bail is continued. We're adjourned."

None of the judges wanted to overturn the result once a jury had spoken, particularly not a proprosecution judge like Sloane. It was only done rarely, since you had to convince the judge essentially that there was no evidence at all to prove a necessary element of the crime or that no reasonable jury could have convicted.

I found the case and reread it in the hallway outside the courtroom. Moyer was also convicted of fraudulent conversion of property for use of partnership money. The conviction was thrown out because, like in Phil's case, partnership money was not, as fraudulent conversion requires, property "belonging to any other person," since it was jointly owned by the defendant himself as one of the partners. And Moyer, like Phil, didn't "convert [it] for his own use" but put it to partnership uses. Fraudulent conversion of partnership property may have fit the facts, but the jury acquitted Phil on that charge.[14]

Judge Sloane granted my motion. Phil was free and grateful, and I was relieved.

§§§

Phil and I kept in touch, and things got better for him, although he never did make the fortune he dreamed about. Over a decade later, the heating system in my house in West Philadelphia stopped working in the middle of winter. Phil was there an hour after I called him. After he put in a new boiler, we sat in the kitchen in the back of the house. He was grimy, and we drank orange juice, like the first time around.

After a long silence, Phil said, "Dave, you know, you saved my ass."

"Thanks, Phil. We got a little lucky, you know, both of us. The jury seemed to reach some kind of compromise, but if the one count they got you on was any one of the other three rather than fraudulent conversion, you'd probably have a conviction."

"Yeah, I remember all too well. You knew they fucked up, though, right after the verdict."

"Yeah, I had no idea they'd do that, but I had read all the cases in the area. After all, I was nervous. It was my first jury trial."

"Whadya mean? I knew you were young and inexperienced, but you never been before a jury before that?"

"No."

He smiled, and his voice got louder. "That should be fuckin' malpractice."

"Somebody's got to be the first, Phil."

"But not me. I'm gettin' nervous again just thinkin' about it. I'm glad I thought you knew what you were doing."

PART TWO

A Small Civil Rights Law Firm and a Big War

CHAPTER FIVE

Rizzo's Police

I HAD NOT COME TO PHILADELPHIA thinking I would stay, but as my three years in Tony Amsterdam's program drew to a close, I felt connected to the civil rights and antiwar communities, activists of many stripes who sat in on bulldozers as well as at lunch counters. The "movement" groups, as we called them, felt different in Philadelphia. Perhaps it was the influence of the fervently antiwar and pro–civil rights Quakers, whose national service organization as well as many members were centered in Philadelphia. Whatever it was, I easily found comrades and friends in Philadelphia—in various Quaker-based organizations like the American Friends Service Committee and the Pennsylvania Prison Society, the unusually active and effective Philadelphia branch of the ACLU led by Spencer Coxe, local civil rights and black and Hispanic activist groups like the Black Panthers (who mostly ran school breakfast and education programs for kids), antiwar groups like Philadelphia Resistance, and the Powelton housing groups. They all needed legal representation, and there would be no shortage of important work and challenges in Philadelphia because of one man—Police Commissioner and later Mayor Frank Rizzo.

Philadelphia had also grown on me as a city. I liked the big-city but manageable downtown where, unlike New York, you could still see the sky; the ethnic neighborhoods; the often raucous city politics; and the inexpensive old stone houses in friendly, integrated neighborhoods like Powelton and Mt. Airy.

I left Tony's program with the deepest respect for public defenders and legal services lawyers but ready to move in a new direction: police abuse; free speech; protection of antiwar and civil rights activists and communities like Powelton; and whatever problems and conflicts quirky Philadelphia would yield. It seemed an ideal place to base a civil rights law practice. I didn't know I would stay the rest of my life (or at least until I wrote my memoir), but it doesn't surprise me that I'm still here.

§§§

Frank Rizzo was a tough street cop who became the first police commissioner of Italian ancestry in a department previously dominated by Irish and German Americans. Rizzo's father joined the police force to avoid being drafted to fight in World War I. Frank, a high school dropout, got an appointment to the force in 1943, the year I was born, through what we now might call Mob-related connections. He patrolled tough neighborhoods on foot, earning a reputation as a cop who was dangerous to cross and the nickname "Cisco Kid," which was said to reflect his quick draw.[1]

For the Rizzo family, and other white ethnic immigrants, the police department and other city jobs provided an opportunity to overcome prejudice and to step into the middle class. Once they got a foothold in the department, Italians hired more Italians, like the Irish and Germans had done before them. Although there were surely ethnic rivalries, these practices functioned as an informal affirmative action plan that didn't seem to bother anyone until it was African Americans' turn to benefit. Within the police department, Rizzo's rise to commissioner was controversial not because of his tough reputation but because he was of Italian ancestry. Some in the department didn't think an Italian could handle the top job.

Rizzo was a down-to-earth, straightforward "guy from the neighborhoods," as he was widely referred to in those days. Everyone knew which neighborhoods: the white, Italian areas of South Philadelphia, in which Italian was still often spoken in the 1960s, and the white working-class areas like Northeast Philadelphia. He was very popular among working- and middle-class whites and seriously disliked and feared among African Americans, other minorities, and liberals and most moderates.

Rizzo rose through the ranks with widely publicized, usually violent arrests and wordy, polarized conflicts. In the 1960s, he clashed with beatniks reading poetry and snapping their fingers at coffeehouses around Rittenhouse Square, gays in Center City, media critics, and pretty much anybody who criticized the status quo or whose politics or lifestyle he didn't like. These clashes were often violent and often led to arrests, though no crime had been committed—more as media stunts than law enforcement.

Rizzo was appointed police commissioner in 1966 after the previous holder of that office balked at Mayor James Tate's insistence that the police force be politically mobilized for Tate against his rivals. Rizzo's police harassed reporters who criticized Tate or Rizzo and state police who investigated corruption in the police force. Corruption was rampant during Frank Rizzo's time as commissioner, although he was never proved to have personally received illicit money. The Pennsylvania Crime Commission concluded that in this period police corruption was "ongoing, widespread, systemic, and occurring at all levels" and "in every police district." Rizzo had "an understanding" with Mob boss Angelo Bruno; illegal gambling would be ignored as long as there weren't drugs or violence.

Rizzo was known for a bluntness that tickled his ardent supporters. The night he was elected mayor, he famously told reporters, "I'll make Attila the Hun look like a faggot." It was never clear to me whether such moments of verbal clarity were strategic or showed lack of minimal self-control. One of his most notorious confrontations was a police raid on three headquarters of the Black Panthers, who in Philadelphia were mostly known for a before-school breakfast program for poor kids and for, like most Americans, possessing guns. The police forced 14 Panthers to strip completely naked on the street outside their office, in front of waiting media cameras. Rizzo was roundly criticized, but he said the media and politicians who were his critics had it all wrong. "The Black Panthers were the ones who dropped their drawers, and they all exposed their rumps to the photographers," Rizzo said. "The police didn't do that."

His most defining moment came in 1967 at a peaceful demonstration of a few thousand black high school students in front of the Philadelphia Board of Education. This nonviolent action sought more diversity in the high school curriculum and inclusion of the role of blacks in American history classes. There wasn't any trouble, but the unexpectedly large number of students led Lt. George Fencl, in charge at the scene, to call for more police. Rizzo came with buses and vans full of police and lined them up in the street like an army. Everything had been calm, but, by most accounts, when a student broke the antenna on a police car, Rizzo yelled to his police, "Get their black asses!" Hundreds of armored, almost all white policemen rushed the unarmed, peacefully gathered black students and clubbed and beat them with nightsticks, breaking open heads and leaving much blood in the street. Dozens of students were injured. The next day Rizzo denied he had said "get their black asses," but a local TV station had him on film saying just that.

During Rizzo's time as police commissioner and mayor, police use of force was controversial in many cities, but Philadelphia became known nationally as much for police brutality as for cheesesteaks. Eventually, community groups that had long spoken out began to be heard, various law enforcement agencies began investigations, and politicians and the local media began to criticize Rizzo. A 1977 Pulitzer Prize–winning series in the *Philadelphia Inquirer* called "The Homicide Files," by William Marimow and Jonathan Neumann, found routine beatings and coerced confessions from defendants and witnesses in homicide cases, routine cover-ups of police crimes, and routine lying by police in court testimony. I helped expose and successfully challenged the brutality and corruption while consuming at least my share of cheesesteaks.

§§§

In 1971 I started a small civil rights law firm with my colleague and friend in Tony's program, David Rudovsky. A firm offered the opportunity to do the civil rights cases and represent the progressive groups I believed in and the freedom to pursue the odd and seemingly unwinnable cases I was sometimes drawn to. It was ideal for channeling out-of-the-box thinking into a law practice. I could have gotten more money and more security at an existing law firm or at one of the established civil rights legal organizations. But I felt surprising clarity about the importance of not working for others and of taking on issues, clients, and cases I would chose. It didn't matter that no one gives you a salary or benefits when you start your own firm—we would earn only what we made from our work, which was likely to be minimal for some time. I had no fear or doubt that I could make enough money to live decently no matter what I did, and money wasn't a particularly important goal.

This was surely a sign of the times. The 1960s so reviled by conservatives past and present was very much about a youthful quest for meaning in one's work and life that might transcend the materialism and regimentation of the 1950s, as well as a youthful revulsion at our racially segregated and warlike elders. But for me it was also a lesson learned from an elder, my father. Unlike most of my cohorts in the 1960s, my rebellion was never against my parents. They supported my civil rights and anti-war activism, although they worried about my safety and my "career." My father, Bernard Kairys, worked hard for a company owned by others and succeeded, making enough money so we lived the middle-class dream— nice house, fancy cars, expensive colleges, and a lush country club for Russian Jews (separate from another lush one for German Jews). But as time went on he dreaded the work and wished he had struck out on his own. I liked the middle-class dream he provided, except Woodholme country club, where I never felt comfortable, but his experience and his feelings about it deeply affected me.

While money wasn't the goal, it was important if the firm was to succeed. I took on, and enjoyed, the job of managing the finances and controlling the costs, perhaps satisfying an entrepreneurial side I could also trace to my father. I was surprised, and a little embarassed, to find that I liked keeping the books and writing the checks to pay the bills.

Succeeding financially didn't look easy. Since few of our clients would have the resources to pay us a fee, we would have to rely on winning a lot. We would get contingent fees—a proportion of what the client won in a case, usually one-third. In some cases, counsel fees could be recovered from the other side, but only if a statute provided for them. Either way, if we lost a case, we got nothing, and we would have to absorb the sometimes huge expenses. There was a popular perception then (even more so now) that plaintiff's lawyers had it easy and made fortunes based on little work. Very few did. Defense lawyers in civil cases, who often represented insurance companies or wealthy institutions or individuals, were paid good hourly fees, win or lose, but plaintiff's lawyers generally took significant risks, and there were no parachutes.

Fortunately, our lifestyles didn't demand much. The same year we started our firm, I moved into a "collective" house with five other people on Hamilton Street near Thirty-fourth in Powelton, a three-story stone Victorian twin. Each of us had a room and cooked, ate, and hung out on the common first floor. I had bought the house since I was the only one with a good enough credit rating and job (although partner in a law firm sounded better on a mortgage application than the financial reality of the fledgling operation). We split living expenses and the costs of the house, which amounted to only $30 per month total for each of us, including utilities, a small sum even in those days.

When Kairys & Rudovsky opened, we had one source of funding. I had volunteered and worked one of the summers during law school with the well-known New York firm Rabinowitz & Boudin. Victor Rabinowitz and Leonard Boudin had litigated some of the most significant civil rights and international law cases going back to the 1940s. Leonard called me after he saw a December 1965 open letter to President Lyndon Johnson in the *New York Times* that challenged the Vietnam War. The letter, at an early stage of opposition to the war, was signed by almost 100 Columbia law students, who were mostly known for getting good jobs with Wall Street law firms. Leonard asked a friend of his on the Columbia faculty who was responsible for the letter and invited a few of us who had organized it to lunch. He asked us to help him with some research—on the widely publicized exclusion of civil rights activist Julian Bond from the Georgia legislature, whose case, like so many others, they would win in the Supreme Court. Later, Leonard and Victor asked me to work there for a summer. It seemed almost a dream to work with them on major civil rights cases and on some odd ones like the labor negotiations for the musicians in the New York Philharmonic Orchestra.[2]

I got particularly close to Victor, although I could never convince him that the best way for him and me to quickly get to appointments in New York City was on my motorcycle. He was a short, stocky man with a neatly trimmed beard, whose sharp legal mind and get-down-to-business attitude were accompanied by a friendly smile and manner. Victor got start-up funding for a new student law journal I founded and led as editor in chief, the *Columbia Human Rights Law Review*. When Kairys & Rudovsky started, Victor and Leonard arranged for the National Emergency Civil Liberties Committee (NECLC) to make us its Philadelphia counsel, for which it paid us a small monthly retainer.[3]

NECLC had split from the ACLU in the 1950s, with Leonard and Victor as its primary lawyers, to take on a series of cases refused by the ACLU—people accused of being communists or socialists who were fired from jobs, dragged before legislative committees (the most famous of which was run by Senator Joseph McCarthy), or jailed. Many of these people had done no more than attend meetings about unemployment, poverty, or racism during the Depression years or join groups whose agendas were enactment of the safety net achieved not long after with President Franklin Roosevelt's New Deal. Most doubted the virtues of un-fettered capitalism after living through the extreme poverty accompanied by extreme wealth, and booms and busts, it produced. Some favored some form of socialism or communism, and some subscribed to the teachings of Marx, Lenin, or Trotsky. They mainly worked for New Deal–type programs while they talked and debated various alternatives to unrestrained capitalism. They didn't attempt or train for overthrow of the government. There were no guns, no military training, not even aerobics-for-commies classes.

These people had done no more than several folks in my family, and I remembered the silly sting of anticommunism in the 1950s when my parents told me not to play with my friend Gilbert, whose father had been named by one of the anticommunist legislative committees. I liked being on the NECLC side of this and being their Philadelphia counsel. The ACLU, which before and after this period so effectively championed the rights of everyone, later officially repudiated their temporarily succumb-ing to the rabid anticommunism of the 1950s, so the rift healed.[4]

Rudovsky, or Rudy, as many called him, was a terrific lawyer whose political leanings, lifestyle, ambitions, and Russian Jewish ancestors were similar to my own. He was tall, thin, and athletic, with brown hair that had a reddish tint. We originally met before Tony's program, as law students at a civil rights conference where he represented NYU students and I represented Columbia students. We had a very easy personal relation-ship, enjoyed talking out legal and political issues and hanging out to-gether, and had deep confidence in each other's work.[5]

There were differences, however, mainly of personality and style. I tended to be direct and open (sometimes more direct and open than oth-ers appreciated), enthusiastic, friendly but often reserved, and not gener-ally enthralled with lawyers. Rudy was less direct or open, kept his thoughts more to himself, and tended to avoid conflict except in the courtroom. He was unusually friendly and attentive to almost everyone he encountered, particularly lawyers. People often thought he was a good friend of theirs when he didn't even know their names. It was a trait I as-sociated with politicians, but he seemed to do it with more integrity than politicians usually do.

Kairys & Rudovsky opened its doors, or door, really, in May 1971. We rented a small room in the back of a criminal law firm, Segal, Appel & Natali (Lou Natali from Tony's program), in a second-floor walk-up above stores along Walnut Street near Broad, very close to city hall; hired a secretary/typist to whom we committed a salary and benefits; and got stationery—I didn't feel it was a law firm until we had paper and envelopes with our letterhead. We shared the criminal law firm's interview and conference rooms, copy machine, and law library.[6]

This arrangement allowed us to get a start without any clients. We also had a little help from our friends. Civil rights and antiwar activists, led by Joe Miller, a successful businessman in finance and real estate, donated desks and chairs and most of our other equipment. The desks came from storage in the attic of Joe's office building, where Rudy and I pulled them out of a dusty pile and rolled them early one morning on flat wood wheelies down a few blocks of Walnut Street to our office. An IBM typewriter was a gift from my parents. It was a carbon-ribbon model that produced clear, vivid type, something like that achievable now with a laser printer, by using a shiny carbon-copy type ribbon that was usable only once rather than the more common fabric ribbons that could be used many times. We bought a stack of long lined pads and lots of pencils, the yellow lawyer stuff, from a stationery store.

We were in cramped quarters but had the essential lawyer equipment. Our desks were on opposite walls, so close that if we both leaned back in our swivel chairs, our heads would hit, as they did several times. It didn't help that Rudy was six feet tall and I was six foot three. Aside from more space, all we needed were some clients and some cases. I remember sometimes in the early weeks sitting there in our small room, all geared up to litigate, with nothing to do. I wondered if the phone would ring.

§§§

The phone did ring. At first it was mostly our movement friends, who needed us to negotiate and attend their almost weekly demonstrations against the Vietnam War. But then, within a few months, something big came in the door with a man named John Hilfirty. He was a young, tall, muscular, mustached, Hollywood-handsome white guy. He had called before he came in to say he was having a problem with the police.

We shook hands, and as he sat down he said, "Look, call me Jack. I seen your name in an article in the papers a while back and wrote it down. Maybe I knew something was about to go down. Now the Rizzos are after me—and after I worked hard to get Frank elected mayor. I'm losing my job and Vince, another fireman, is recovering from a beating that put him in a coma." He looked me straight in the eyes, his lips pursed, like he was under a lot of stress and a bit confused. "I'm not sure where to start."

"Try the beginning, when you think it started," I said, with what I hoped was a casual smile.

He smiled back and slowly nodded a few times. "Okay. It sounds stupid, but it started over a parking problem. This past New Year's Day, January 1, 1972, we was called to a false alarm. I'm the lieutenant at Engine 47, Grays Ferry Avenue near Thirtieth, you know. I'm in charge of the firehouse. They say I'm the youngest fireman ever to make lieutenant." He settled in and was talking easily, with almost a swagger about him.

"So we checked the firebox that was pulled and the area around it, but there wasn't any fire. As we was leaving, I saw a car parked in front of a fire hydrant, so I waved to the uniformed cop called to the scene—every time a box is pulled, an engine and a police car are sent. So I told him to ticket the car. That was it. I don't think I said anything else, and he didn't say anything.

"About 20 minutes later, we're getting comfortable back at the firehouse, and the same cop knocks on the front door. He told the guy who answered the door that two cars, which it turned out were mine and fireman Vincent Marvasi's, were parked illegally in front of the fire station. He said we had to move them. They called me, as the commanding officer, to the door. I introduced myself to the officer, whose name is Earl Shorty. He's a big, black fellow who looked angry. I explained that we had fire department permission to park there."

"Who gave you that permission?" I interrupted.

"The chief's office, downtown," he said. "There wasn't enough spaces for us near the firehouse otherwise."

"So what happened next?"

"Okay, so he got all riled up, telling me to move the cars 'or else.' I told one of the guys to call the 17th Police District and get a sergeant or somebody with authority to deal with this guy. That's the district that covers our firehouse; we know them well. Then Shorty threatened to 'get anybody' who got him in any trouble and left. But he returned soon, with another cop who was out of uniform and drunk. They was both yelling at us, and before long Shorty came at me with a blackjack in his hand. He pushed me against a wall. It took four or five of my guys to grab the arm with the blackjack and pull him off me. I had a shoulder injury and was out for two weeks."

Hilfirty looked and sounded like a guy who doesn't take that kind of challenge easily, particularly as a young, new lieutenant in front of his men. "In all the yelling, did you say anything?"

"I got in a few words. I was mainly tryin' to calm him down, but then I got pissed."

"No one would blame you if you spoke back in that situation. It's important that I get a good idea of what happened."

"Yeah, I said somethin' like, 'Don't you come in our house talkin' like that,' and maybe, 'What the 'f' you think you're doing comin' in here shoutin' like that?" He smiled.

"Okay, but that was after he was already yelling at you."

"Yeah. He was insulted because I told him to ticket the parked car. At one point in all the shouting, he said, 'No one tells me how to do my job.' I gave a statement with more details 'cause the police looked into it and brought formal disciplinary charges against Shorty. For my safety, at my request, I was transferred. A few of us from Engine 47, including me and Marvasi, testified in March against Shorty at a Police Board of Inquiry. They found him guilty and suspended him for five days without pay. But after his suspension, they put him back on duty in the 17th, back where Engine 47 is."

I paused a moment. I knew the Philadelphia police seldom if ever brought disciplinary charges against a cop based on a citizen complaint. The charge and result were probably because this victim was a fireman. "He wasn't transferred?"

"No. He was back where a lot of the guys who testified against him were. But it gets much worse. In late June, Vince went out to get sandwiches for all the guys, in his same car that was parked in front of the firehouse. We all do that, take turns, you know, gettin' food. On the way back, a police wagon with its siren and lights going pulled Vince over just a hundred feet from the firehouse. There was two cops in the wagon. The cop drivin' the wagon was Shorty, but he acted like he didn't recognize Vince. He said Vince was speeding and went through red lights, but he didn't issue any tickets. He asked Vince for his license and owner's card.

Vince had left them in his civilian pants at the firehouse, which was so close they could see it."

Hilfirty tensed up as he spoke, clenching one hand into a fist while he poked air with the other. Some veins bulged out in his neck. "Shorty wouldn't let Vince get the cards," he continued, shaking his head slowly. "He handcuffed Vince and threw him in the back of the wagon. Then he got Vince alone in an interview room at the 17th and beat him bad with the blackjack. Vince lay unconscious for some time in the hospital."

Hilfirty stopped, as if he were absorbing it, like me, for the first time. He looked like he would cry if he ever allowed himself to cry. "Did they discipline Shorty again?"

"You bet. He got a 30-day suspension, and the DA has brought criminal charges."

"Assault?"

"Yeah, something like that. Vince is off duty, they say recovering, but I don't think he can be a fireman anymore."

Criminal charges against a cop were unusual, if not unprecedented, again, I thought, because this cop beat a fireman. "And how about you?"

"They're in the process of firin' me. They said it was insubordination or somethin' like that. We all know what it was. When the police put Shorty back to work after his 30-day suspension, I and some of the other guys complained to the commissioner, you know, Joe Rizzo."

"Frank Rizzo's brother, right?"

"Yeah. Frank promised the fire department before the election that he wouldn't make Joe commissioner, but he did it. Joe flunked an examination for promotion some time ago. Anyway, instead of backin' us and gettin' the police to put Shorty off duty or off the street, he backed the police. We was told it was a police matter and we should let them handle it. They weren't handlin' it. We thought we'd get beat like Vince or killed."

"So what did you do?"

"When the big shots in the fire department wouldn't help, I went to the *Daily News,* the state police, and the state attorney general's office, 'cause I had heard good things about them on the news."

I had seen some of the *Daily News* articles and other publicity on it. "Did you know that the attorney general has been critical of the Rizzo administration and that Rizzo viewed him as a political rival?" I asked.

"I don't know. I knew somethin' about that, but the guys and Vince's wife was all over me about doin' something. I was looking for anybody who could help us."

"Understandably. What's the 'insubordination' about?"

"I'm off duty temporarily now, by Joe Rizzo's order. They at first suggested and now ordered me to see the fire department psychiatrist, and they're sayin' I don't dress right. I don't need no psychiatrist. They just want to discredit me and build a case that I'm unfit for duty, which is bullshit."

"It sounds like that's what they're up to. Postpone the psych visit as long as you can. Maybe the first thing we should do is get you evaluated by a well-reputed and unbiased psychiatrist. We can submit his report to the department."

"You got a shrink in mind?"

"I do, but let me think about it and make some calls." I was thinking about Richard Lonsdorf, a professor of psychiatry and law at Penn, but I didn't want to mention anybody until I knew they were willing to do it. "Who's been giving you these orders?"

"Usually a deputy commissioner or someone high in the bureaucracy, sometimes Joe Rizzo himself."

"Tell me what Joe Rizzo has said."

"Well, let's see. I was ordered to see him in July, about two weeks after the *Daily News* articles and other press. He said he was goin' to 'squash' me. That's one of his favorites, I guess, squashing, 'cause I heard that a lot. Then in August, I was at headquarters and was told to go back to work. But just after I walked out the door, Joe rushed out behind me. I guess he heard I was there. He was cursin' at me right there on the sidewalk, something about his brother, Frank, and he told me he'd 'squash' me again. He ordered me to get a haircut and come back in an hour. When I got back, they put me off duty for another 30 days, and they gave me the order to see a shrink."

"Did you get a haircut?" His hair wasn't long for young men in those days.

"No."

§§§

I returned to our little room after the interview. "Dave," I said, "we're in. The fireman wants me to bring his lawsuit, and it's unbelievable. It's that case in the news where another fireman was badly beaten in the 17th District. We may get that fireman, too."

"Alright," he said, holding up the palm of one hand waist high for me to slap as I sat down. This particular sports gesture preceded the high five and chest-to-chest collision. "What happened to the cop?" he continued, "Nothing, right?"

"That's what I thought, but he was disciplined, suspended, and there's even a criminal assault charge pending."

"No kidding. I guess we can't say they never discipline."

"It's probably because the victims were firemen. Also, the cop is black. The usual racial context is flipped."

"That's unusual, but this is just what we want. Firemen plaintiffs make the best test we could imagine."

From the beginning, police misconduct was one of our major concerns. Rudy was referring to the doubt we had heard expressed by civil rights lawyers and activists that a Philadelphia jury would ever come down against the police in a police brutality case. We had also heard that black cops can be particularly tough and controlling on the streets, to prove to white cops that they are cops first and black second. But race might figure in our favor in a perverse sort of way, if a jury was more likely to believe a black cop would use force without good cause or to identify with the assaulted white firemen.

I checked out psychiatrists and researched the law on the order to see a psychiatrist and on federal civil rights claims Hilfirty could make. His case was strong, but it depended on the facts. If his version of events was believed, he would win. The Rizzo brothers and the city would have a different version. I knew it would be hard to prove that the order to see the psychiatrist was a setup and that they were after Hilfirty because he went public, made Frank Rizzo look bad, and helped a Rizzo rival. The case was stronger, and the damages bigger, if Marvasi was also a plaintiff. His beating by the police was the basis for a claim that didn't depend on any wrongdoing, or guessing about motives, in the fire department. Hilfirty thought Marvasi was hesitant to sue but might do it if he saw no alternative. He said he would talk to Marvasi about it.

§§§

Meanwhile, we worked mostly on demonstrations and cases started earlier. Rudy's ongoing and so far successful challenge to the awful conditions in the Philadelphia prisons kept him busy and went on for decades. The major cases I had were civil rights suits against the Philadelphia police—one for harassing the *Philadelphia Free Press,* a small local weekly that opposed the Vietnam War, favored civil and labor rights, and couldn't stand Frank Rizzo; and another for the brutal police beating of a black man named Arthur Davis that later settled for a considerable sum.[7]

Small movement newspapers like the *Free Press* thrived for a time in the 1960s and early 1970s, with usually unpaid reporters and editors and strong political positions. They had a consuming fervor for political theories about social change and revolution that envisioned an overthrow of the capitalist system. But they were not armed or organized to do more than talk or write about such things and to act on more local, concrete issues, like police brutality.

The *Free Press* couldn't have had a circulation of more than a few hundred, who mostly already agreed with (and weren't put off by) its often doctrinaire perspectives and heated rhetoric. It's hard to understand why Rizzo paid any attention to it—the paper and its staff hadn't done anything except express their views. But Frank Rizzo had a surprisingly thin skin. He couldn't stand criticism, particularly harsh, personal criticism like that dished out by the *Free Press,* no matter how few people read it or cared.[8]

Rizzo's police, and the Rizzo media machine, went into action against the *Free Press.* Police followed the paper's leader, Bill Biggin, and other *Free Press* folks almost everywhere they went. Plainclothes and uniformed police openly staked out and searched the apartments of Biggin and another leader, Roger Tauss, and then rented apartments across the street from their apartments to watch them around the clock. At many public events, *Free Press* reporters were surrounded by police and not allowed to cover the events or move around; sometimes they were taken into custody and released several hours later with no charges. Officers openly brandished their guns on several occasions and threatened Biggin with violence if he didn't leave Philadelphia.

Al Gaudiosi, a police reporter who would become Rizzo's campaign manager when he ran for mayor a year later, wrote a three-part series for the *Evening Bulletin,* called "The New Revolutionaries," that focused on the *Free Press* and Biggin. It's amazing that a major newspaper published these articles. Gaudiosi quoted only "police sources" and unnamed informers and vaguely described police documents saying how dangerous Biggin and the *Free Press* were.

Gaudiosi unveiled his most frightening and concrete claim in the final article of the series: a bomb plot tied to the *Free Press* and to the other great threat to Philadelphians, those Powelton residents upset with Drexel's expansion into their neighborhood. Two months earlier, the article said, Terry Caldwell, "a shaggy-haired, blond, ex-mine worker," stopped in Philadelphia with his pregnant wife and two daughters on their way to California. "Sources within the revolutionary movement" said that while the family stayed a few nights in Powelton, Caldwell, who had some knowledge of bombs since he worked in mines, drew bombs and discussed bombing some particular targets with young men associated with the *Free Press* and the Powelton housing dispute. Apparently based on this informant's information, the FBI raided the building where Caldwell stayed, with a warrant that accused Caldwell of a bomb plot that included his teaching bomb making and marking targets on a map of Philadelphia. The article said the FBI also found marijuana seeds and a revolver. Caldwell signed a statement, quoted at length in the article, that admitted to the bomb plot and the gun (he denied having marijuana).

Gaudiosi reported that "police told Caldwell to get out of town as quickly as possible." There were no charges against Caldwell or the other bomb plotters specifically identified in the article. The inflammatory headlines and rhetoric of the series were not backed up by any concrete wrongdoing. But the message was clear: Only Frank Rizzo stood between these violent revolutionaries and the fine folks of Philadelphia.[9]

This is how Rizzo and his minions in the media operated. If a man, shaggy-haired and headed for California, or not, actually had been caught by the police and FBI with marijuana and a gun, and he admitted in a signed statement to participation in a bomb plot, they would charge him and the others with several crimes. And why whisk him out of town, except to make him unavailable when the story would be used for a media smear? The *Bulletin* editors didn't ask these, or any other, questions.

When Caldwell was released after police questioned him, a few weeks before the *Bulletin* series, he went into hiding in the Philadelphia area before heading for California, and he told the *Free Press* about the raid and the police and FBI interrogation. Biggin ran an article in the *Free Press* about the raid and Caldwell that described Philadelphia as "the city of police-fabricated brotherly bomb plots." He and the Powelton groups quickly contacted me and asked me for legal help.

I knew some big coverage of left movements was coming soon in the *Bulletin* because they had interviewed many activists about it. I didn't know when or whether the phoney bomb plot would be part of it. I considered possible lawsuits. A civil rights lawsuit was plausible but difficult because the police would say that Caldwell told them about the plot and signed a statement and the *Bulletin* reporters would say that the police told them. There can be a defamation claim if one is called a revolutionary, but government officials were immune from defamation suits, and any issue of the *Free Press* would prove the label accurate.

I thought the best focus of my efforts was on the forthcoming *Bulletin* articles and on Terry Caldwell. Caldwell wouldn't come to my office, but he agreed to talk to me on the phone before leaving for California. He completely repudiated the police statement as false and coerced. I would have liked to get his repudiation in another, signed statement, but that wasn't possible, so I asked him to send me a signed letter. We talked on the phone for an hour about the content of his letter. I got Caldwell's letter in the mail, and I called the *Bulletin* and demanded, with the threat of a lawsuit, that the letter and the responses of the supposed plotters identified in Caldwell's police statement be covered prominently if there was any coverage of the raid or the statement.

I was directed to Gaudiosi, who talked about the objectivity and balance of *Bulletin* coverage of all topics, and to an editor, who listened without much reaction. I didn't think I got anywhere with either of them, but somebody at the *Bulletin,* perhaps an attorney, since I threatened a lawsuit, thought this shouldn't be ignored.

The final bomb plot article in the series was accompanied by a long article that started: "There is a second version of the recent visit here by Terry Caldwell." That article said Caldwell was in the Philadelphia area to visit his family and stayed a few nights with his wife and children in Powelton. He got drunk one night and talked about drugs and his mining experience with explosives. There were no bomb classes, no targets marked on a map, and no bomb plot.

In a letter to "David Kairys, 27, a lawyer," the article continued, Caldwell said the statement was written by the police and he was coerced. He signed it only because they threatened to charge him with drug and gun crimes and to keep him from leaving Philadelphia with his family if he didn't. The *Bulletin* reassured its readers that it had unnamed "independent sources" that supported the police version. Frank Rizzo was quoted—"Mr. Caldwell was not a police plant"—but there was no sign that the reporters or editors asked him any questions. No charges were ever pressed against anyone.[10]

Later, Rizzo decided to settle the *Free Press* lawsuit, although settlement was embarrassing to him, by agreeing to an injunction against the police. This made further harassment of the *Free Press* punishable quickly in federal court by a contempt of court proceeding, and their complaints of harassment stopped. My civil rights practice got off to a good start, and our firm had its first major victory against police misconduct and violation of freedom of speech and the press.[11]

§§§

"Ex-Fireman Prayed When Beaten by Cop," the banner first-page headline read in the *Daily News* after the first day of the trial. Vince Marvasi had testified, his head bent down and his eyes barely open, "I prayed to God and asked for my kids as I was punched and dropped to the floor. The next thing I remember was the blackjack coming down on my head." His thin, short frame looked even smaller slouched into the big wood witness chair.[12]

Hilfirty was also a good witness, though less dramatic. The fourth day of trial was about to commence with my calling Joe Rizzo to the stand. I had some promising material to go through with him.

Our psychiatrists, including Penn professor Lonsdorf, concluded that the vicious beating and the failure of the fire department to back or support Vince had left him unable to function as a fireman. They described his condition as "post-concussion syndrome"—what we would now call posttraumatic stress disorder. The city psychiatrist who evaluated and treated Vince, Richard Fitzgibbons, agreed. But the city initiated proceedings that would terminate Vince's health and disability benefits— Vince would have to go back to work as a fireman or walk away with nothing.

The city was claiming in the lawsuit that, although Vince's injury happened while on duty and was work related, he hadn't returned afterward because he was a "malingerer" wanting to cash in on his civil suit. The problem for the city was Joe Rizzo's statements at an informal fire department hearing on termination of Vince's benefits that I had recorded, with their consent. Since there was no medical or psychiatric basis for denying Vince's condition, I had prodded Joe, who reacted angrily that Vince shouldn't have filed a lawsuit and that they terminated his benefits because he did. This established a major civil rights retaliation claim. They also had to deal with Dr. Fitzgibbons's courageous testimony at a deposition that city officials had told him to "reevaluate" Vince and had pressured him to agree with the malingerer conclusion but that he had refused to change his diagnosis.

The only support the city had for its malingerer defense was a psychiatrist, Dr. Lord Lee-Benner, hired as a consultant after Vince's benefits were terminated and we brought the lawsuit. He concluded that Vince was "lying" and "manufacturing a series of complaints in order to obtain financial gain." His expert report, which didn't mention the contrary conclusion of all of the other doctors, including the city's own treating psychiatrist, was based on Vince's conduct revealed in nurses' notes. Vince tried to stand in the hospital a while after the beating, and later when asked to undergo a hospital stay of several days for evaluation, he said he wanted to speak to his lawyer, me, before complying, which Dr. Lee-Benner found "inappropriate" and "demanding" behavior.

Dr. Lee-Benner sealed his conclusions with an emphasis on what he called Vince's "family predilection for poor career patterns." This was based entirely on the fact that Vince's father was a medical doctor in Italy but did other work in the United States and eventually went back to Italy to practice medicine. From this, Dr. Lee-Benner concluded that Vince's father did not practice medicine in the United States because he was lazy or a "malingerer" (without considering obvious licensing and job availability problems), that Vince's whole family had this problem, and that it left Vince lazy and a malingerer. I looked forward to going through this with Joe Rizzo, including what looked to me like Lee-Benner's baseless negative stereotypes of Italians.

And there was some strange behavior by Joe Rizzo not publicly known. When Joe became fire commissioner, he ordered all firemen to wear white underwear at all times. No pale blues, stripes, or plaids. It reminded me of my mother telling me not to wear underwear that had even the smallest hole to school because I might get called in to see the nurse. He had also adopted regulations requiring that sideburns not be longer than a specifically set-out relationship to the ear and had hired a sculptor to remove the sideburns from a statue of a 19th-century fireman outside of fire headquarters. I hadn't yet figured out how I would work these matters into my examination of Joe, but I thought it would come to me.

§§§

I had gotten used to keeping my outer demeanor cool even when I was jumping inside. I couldn't wait for the examination of Joe Rizzo that I thought would win the case. As we sat in the courtroom waiting for the judge to emerge and resume the testimony, I looked back at the packed spectator seats the publicity from the first few days had produced. I noticed a new face at the city's counsel table. It was Sheldon Albert, Frank Rizzo's city solicitor, who was to law roughly what Rizzo was to law enforcement. A short fellow with a frequent smirk, he was regularly polarizing and full of bombast in situations that called for calm and communication. He frequently stumbled for the words he wanted to say, which were often unnecessarily belligerent. I couldn't figure out if he just wasn't very bright or used that as a persona he somehow saw to his benefit.

The judge entered, all rose, and we were about to get going. Albert stayed standing as everyone else sat down. "Your Honor," he said, "could counsel see you in chambers before we start this morning's session?"

"Certainly," federal judge Raymond Broderick said, then turned to his clerks seated below his bench. "Tell the jury there will be a short delay this morning."

Albert, the assistant city solicitor trying the case, and I settled in comfortable chairs in front of the judge's desk. Broderick greeted each of us warmly and informally, as judges regularly did in chambers. When he got to me, he said, "Didn't you handle that Georgia extradition case a few years back?"

"Yes, I did, Judge. James Jiles was his name."

"You know, I was lieutenant governor then."

"I didn't know that. Were you involved in that case?"

"Not really, but I'm proud of what we did." He paused, then turned to Albert. "So what is it we owe your presence to this morning?"

"Your Honor, the mayor and I have followed this case, and we think the extensive counsel time and court time to finish it to a verdict could be avoided since it ought to be possible to settle it. Would you allow me to take Mr. Kairys to breakfast, if he hasn't already had his, anyway, to talk, you know, for maybe an hour before the trial resumes?"

"I believe the case should be settled, but I believe that about every case," Broderick said, looking back and forth at Albert and me with a slight grin. "Do you agree, Mr. Kairys?"

"It's certainly worth a try, Judge. They wouldn't talk settlement at all before the trial started, but let's see what develops. I'd like a moment to talk to my clients before we go." I thought the best response was to be open but dubious.

"Why don't we say trial will resume at 10:30, giving you an hour and a half."

"Thank you, Your Honor," Albert said.

There wasn't much in the way of eateries in those days near the federal courthouse at Ninth and Chestnut, even though it was close to Independence Hall. Albert suggested a coffeehouse in a nearby hotel. I had had my usual cup of coffee and Danish, but I was ready for a real breakfast.

We sat at a corner table uncomfortably saying little while we read menus and ordered. I decided I wouldn't do much talking and certainly not start things off. So I was waiting for my western omelette and for Albert to get to the settlement discussion.

Eventually, he did, after considerable chat about where we each grew up and how we got into law. "Look, Dave, can I call you that?"

"Sure."

"Dave, we've followed this case, and the mayor sent me down here to try to settle it. I discussed it with our assistant who's trying the case, and I don't know why we didn't make any offer earlier. But look, I'm ready now. I heard you asked for $50,000 as your demand for your clients prior to trial. I talked to the mayor, and if they will leave the fire department, which makes sense for everybody, we're willing to give you that, although it's an awful lot of money."

I had mentioned $50,000 as a demand to open settlement discussions, but they showed no interest and made no counteroffer. "Sheldon," I said, "did your assistant tell you several jurors were crying when Fireman Marvasi testified? I'm new at this civil jury stuff, but crying jurors should be worth something."

"I heard that, and reading the *Daily News* accounts, I can see why. We're sorry this happened. You know, $50,000 is more than four years' salary, so that's more than two years for each of the firemen. That gives them a good start on some new job, and we'll write them glowing recommendations. So let's go back and tell the judge we've settled it."

I pictured a letter of recommendation for Vince that said he was the most competent malingerer in the fire department. "I don't think so. Vince and Jack are ready to move on; they're not eager to return to the Philadelphia Fire Department, but that means they have to start over, as you said. They'll need a lot more than that. We'll take $200,000, for all the claims and counsel fees."

"You're kidding, aren't you? Don't read too much into my coming down here. How about if I ask the mayor if he'd go to $75,000?"

"Ask him if he'd go to $200,000." I thought my best strategy was to pick a number and stick to it. Before we went to breakfast, I told Vince and Jack I'd ask for $200,000 for starters, and I suggested we divide whatever we won if we settled into half for Vince, a quarter for Jack, and a quarter for my little law firm. I knew Vince and Jack would settle for far less than $200,000, and I thought we'd have to. But I didn't want to discuss that with Albert, and I wanted to be able to say truthfully that was the lowest amount they authorized.

"That's as low as we're going to go," I continued. "Look, if that's something you have to talk over on your end in more detail, let's resume the trial, and you and I can talk tonight or tomorrow morning." I wanted to appear unconcerned about the outcome and to see how much they wanted to avoid Joe Rizzo's testimony. I thought that might be driving their change of tune as much as the crying jurors. We both knew Joe was likely to embarrass the administration, and it would be widely covered in the press.

"You know, you're throwing away an opportunity that won't be there if we have to go through the trial. I'll make the call and see if I can get $100,000."

"If you're making a call, ask for $200,000, 'cause that's what it's going to take." I was a little worried that we might regret refusing $100,000. Juries were always unpredictable. Many of the jurors were from the white working-class areas of the city that loved Rizzo. Even if they were convinced that Vince and Jack were seriously wronged, they might be hesitant to go back to their neighborhoods after a widely publicized verdict against the police and the Rizzos. And the amount they'd award, if we won, was tricky. I'd seen interviews of jurors who thought they'd awarded a large sum since it was two or three times their personal annual salary, while the litigants viewed it as small. But the offer was likely to be repeated after the first day of Joe's testimony—I planned to have him on the stand for at least two days. I thought I'd play this out at least right up to beginning Joe's testimony and then maybe ask for more time for Vince, Jack, and I to discuss things.

We went back to the judge's chambers and told him we were unable to agree to a settlement. I continued to act eager to get on with the trial—which wasn't hard to do—and confident of a big win. We went back to our seats in the courtroom, and I chatted casually with Jack and Vince. Joe Rizzo was there, seated just behind Albert. Albert was fidgeting in his seat and not smirking. We all rose again, the judge emerged, and he asked that the jury be brought in as we sat.

"Your Honor," Albert said as he bounced back up, "I'm sorry, but let me make one more call before we resume."

"Sure, Mr. Albert. I'll return to chambers, and you send in word that either the case is over or we resume right away."

"I will do that, Your Honor."

We all rose again as the judge left, and Albert headed for a phone. I thought he might come back with $125,000. After a few minutes, he came back in and asked me to talk to him outside in the hallway for a moment. His face was tensed, and as this process developed, he increasingly swayed in jerky little motions and looked at me intensely. He seemed frustrated, angry, like a kid in a schoolyard face-off who wanted to take a swing.

"Look, Dave," he said, "I want us to be clear about this. Marvasi and Hilfirty are willing to leave the fire department for good if we agree to an amount of money?"

"Yeah."

"Alright, I got $200,000."

I was surprised, happy, and disappointed. I'd have to forego the Joe Rizzo show. The jurors I was able to talk to were sure we would have won, but they had no idea how much. Vince and Jack were elated, although the reality of moving on and starting over hit them later. It seemed easier for Jack, who used some of the money to buy some land with a nice house in a rural area of Pennsylvania, which he had wanted to do for some time. I heard from him once in a while. Vince was a bank teller for some time. Eventually, I lost touch with both of them, but they still mean a lot to me.

The settlement cost the city over half of what it paid out in civil cases for the entire year, drew a lot of attention to police brutality, and made it easier to settle other lawsuits against the police. The brutality and law-lessness of the Philadelphia police became a staple of our law practice, which at one point included three different cases in which young black men had been shot in the back by police. Rizzo's police regularly shot and killed civilians at about twice the rate as New York police (per officer or per population), who were not known for being particularly soft.

CHAPTER SIX

War without End, or a Declaration by Congress

NOT LONG AFTER WE STARTED Kairys & Rudovsky, I got a call from Edith Tiger, the executive director of NECLC.

"Hello, Philadelphia counsel, how's it going down there?"

"Fine, Edith, how are you?"

"We got something. We want you to file a case in Philadelphia. Challenge the war."

Edith, a middle-aged woman with a heavy New York accent who often spoke in short phrases, was seldom interested in chitchat or personal matters. She talked about civil rights and politics and getting things done.

"The declaration issue?" I asked.

"Yeah. We want to file it in several places, get the media and the country talking about it."

The Vietnam War focused attention on something about the Constitution I learned in grade school—the power to decide whether we go to war was with Congress. The issue had broad appeal beyond war opponents. A massive war without a declaration by Congress seemed an affront to the Constitution and the rule of law.

"Victor and his shop are working on a complaint and brief. We'll get it to you in time."

"In time for what?"

"Bastille Day. The filing date."

"Are you serious?"

"Yeah. It's the people rising up. With the Constitution, you know."

Bastille Day is the French celebration every July 14 of the storming of the Bastille prison in 1789. I appreciated the connection and liked the political impact the suit might have, win or lose, but the Bastille connection might be unnecessarily off-putting to judges.

When a case came to both Rudy and me, usually one of us handled it, and if we both wanted to do it, we flipped a coin. This happened mostly in the early years. As time went on, cases came to one or the other, and we did few cases together, although we talked about all of them a lot. I won this flip.

§§§

The NECLC draft complaint and brief were well researched, argued, and written, mostly by Michael Krinsky, a lawyer about my age at Rabinowitz & Boudin. I had researched the issue off and on for years. I made some changes and shortened it, though it still came to 49 long legal pages that had to be typed out on our IBM.

The argument seemed straightforward since it dealt with one of the most specific and clearest clauses of the Constitution. The Constitution is a short document with mostly broad-brush, generally phrased provisions. The generality and vagueness of the provisions open them to a great array of possible interpretations and applications to particular situations.

Lawyers argue that "the law" favors one side or the other of a dispute by articulating interpretations and meanings of some language. In constitutional law, it's the language of the Constitution. In other areas, it's the language of a statute, a contract, a prior judicial opinion—language from some source of law. It basically comes down to each side offering interpretations, meanings, and applications to the particular case. Then judges decide.

The array of interpretations and meanings is usually reduced if the language is specific and clear, but it doesn't go away. The question of which branch of the federal government has the authority to take us to war is about as specific as the Constitution gets. In the list of the powers of Congress, the Constitution includes the power "To declare War." I always liked the overboard capitalizations, but meanings of words, like styles of capitalization, change over time. This phrase, however, meant to its writers what it meant in 20th-century America.

The framers were unusually clear about the meaning and purpose of this clause. The initial draft used the word *make* instead of *declare*. James Madison thought *make* blurred the distinction between the power to "repel" attacks, which should be up to the executive, and the power to "commence" war, which they wished to assign only to Congress.[1]

The clarity of the language and intent are particularly striking because of the difficulty and time required in those days to gather Congress for a decision. Communications were much slower, and the president would have access to the best information; was commander of the military; and could make a quicker, informed decision. So what did the framers have in mind?

Presidents deciding when and against whom to go to war was precisely what the framers didn't want. They had seen leaders go to war for little or the wrong reasons—a border dispute, a marriage dispute among royalties, an insult, internal politics, pride. They knew the usual consequences—young men would die or return scarred in large numbers, the treasury would be depleted, trade and the economy would be disrupted, and often the world would become a more dangerous place.

The framers wanted to make it cumbersome, difficult, and time-consuming for presidents to go to war, and they wanted a national debate on the necessity and wisdom of doing so before it happened. Some said it emphatically: George Mason favored "clogging rather than facilitating war"; Oliver Ellsworth thought it "should be more easy to get out of war, than into it." Later, Abraham Lincoln put it this way: "Kings had always been involving and impoverishing their people in wars, pretending generally, if not always, that the good of the people was the object. This our Convention understood to be the most oppressive of all kingly oppressions . . . [and] frame[d] the Constitution that no one man should hold the power of bringing this oppression upon us."

The interpretation, meaning, and application of this provision seemed obvious and easy, but the stakes—a pending war—were obviously daunting. Challenges to the lack of a declaration of the Vietnam War had been raised for many years and in many cases, but none had succeeded. Courts either upheld the war or refused to rule on the issue. The Supreme Court had not ruled at all, although this was the leading constitutional crisis of the time.

§§§

Using NECLC's and our contacts, we got together some impressive activists to be the plaintiffs. Joe Miller was one, and another, David Gracie, was an Episcopal priest who became a friend and not infrequent client. Gracie was a solidly built, handsome man about a decade older than me with dark, thick hair. His presence and speaking skill communicated extraordinary integrity and vision and made him a natural leader. For somebody who didn't care much about religion, I was strangely drawn to civil rights and antiwar activists who blended their activism with a deep (but nonproselytizing) faith. I could have listed activist clergy as one of my specialties, but I never thought of it.

We didn't file until September 1971, so it wasn't a Bastille Day lawsuit. Federal court cases were assigned to judges by the old drawing-from-a-hat method. It wasn't a hat anymore, but the clerk stuck his hand into a box that had a token for each sitting judge, and the judge's name was stamped on the filed complaint. We drew Joseph Lord, III, chief judge (by seniority, so he'd been around awhile) of the U.S. District Court for the Eastern District of Pennsylvania, which covers Philadelphia. He was a liberal on most issues, although I wasn't optimistic that any judge would stick his head out on this one.

His initial ruling wasn't encouraging. The government, represented by the attorney general's office, moved to dismiss the case as to President Nixon on the ground that he was immune from suit, a position repeated not long after in response to the Watergate scandal. Judge Lord rejected that argument, but he dismissed Nixon anyway since any remedy we might get could be enforced through Melvin Laird, the secretary of defense. The case became *Atlee v. Laird*.[2]

§§§

The next decision was procedural, but it opened us to a number of grounds for dismissing the whole case. Much often happened under the procedural label that involved and resolved underlying issues. I requested that the district judge to whom the case was assigned convene a "three-judge court" to hear the case. A federal statute and many decisions provided that a three-judge court was appropriate if a case credibly raised the unconstitutionality of a federal statute. The idea behind it was that invalidation of a statute as unconstitutional shouldn't be left to a single district judge. The three judges usually consisted of the district court judge to whom the case was assigned; another district court judge; and a judge from the Circuit Court of Appeals, the appellate court between Judge Lord and the Supreme Court.

"I've read the briefs from both sides," Lord said, letting Gilbert Unger, the Department of Justice (DOJ) lawyer, and me know what was obvious in the circumstances: that he expected our arguments to be brief. He had squeezed us in during a break in the trial he was hearing, and the papers of the lawyers on that case were spread over the counsel tables. We stood on either side of the lectern in front of the judge. "Mr. Unger, do you agree that if I don't dismiss the case, I should convene a three-judge court?"

"I don't concede that, Your Honor. But I believe you should dismiss this case." Judges often used oral arguments to seek concessions from the attorneys and narrow the issues in a case.

"Tell me why, in a nutshell."

"We have four grounds, Your Honor. First, the identical suit has been filed in several district courts around the country. Counsel are clogging the courts, and their multiple suits should be dismissed or be resolved in one case, and some were filed earlier than this one. Second—"

"Just a moment. Mr. Kairys, some of these complaints look identical, as the DOJ brief says, and your brief is very similar to some others."

It was the Bastille Day problem, but no one had noticed the filing date of some of the other suits. I decided to make light of it. "Lawyers have specialties and tend to work with other lawyers in the same field. Many suits raising the same issue are not uncommon, and you know how we lawyers use a good brief when we find one. The plaintiffs are different in each case. In any event, Judge, my understanding of the law in this area is that you should consider only jurisdictional grounds for dismissal at this stage."

"Mr. Unger, my reading of the cases is that I am limited to jurisdictional grounds. Do you disagree?"

"I read the cases more broadly, Your Honor, as our brief explains. Anyway, the second ground goes to jurisdiction. That's the 'political question' issue. The Supreme Court has held that some issues—like foreign policy and the conduct of a war—are beyond second-guessing or resolution by courts, beyond their jurisdiction."

This was the basis for dismissal of most of the earlier challenges to the war based on the lack of a declaration by Congress. I knew we'd have to confront this, but I didn't want to at this stage.

"Judge Lord," I said, "you have jurisdiction over this case unless the constitutional challenge is weak—courts have framed it in terms of 'insubstantial,' 'frivolous,' or 'sham' constitutional challenges. This challenge is none of those. There's a clear constitutional provision, and the language and intent of the framers are also clear. The question of whether this is about foreign affairs or how to conduct a war is separate; that's the political question issue. But we don't challenge a foreign affairs decision, the decision to go to war, or how the war is conducted. The sole focus of the case is whether the executive branch can, under the Constitution, initiate a full-fledged war without a declaration by Congress. In any event, that question is not jurisdictional."

Lord turned back to Unger. "Your Honor, I don't think there could be a more appropriate case to dismiss under the political question doctrine," Unger said. "We can't have judges deciding foreign policy or interfering with the president's duties and responsibilities in wartime."

"I think I understand both of your positions on that. What are your remaining points, Mr. Unger?"

"Sovereign immunity, Your Honor. This is really a suit against the government, which is barred unless there is a statute passed by Congress waiving sovereign immunity. And, finally, standing. A person cannot bring a lawsuit just because they don't like something the government is doing. They must have a personal stake in the action, event, or controversy. Otherwise, our courts would be flooded with suits."

Lord turned back to me. I looked down at my notes for a moment and took a deep breath, thinking how I might respond with a strong moral edge and without many words or a hint of doubt that he should rule our way. Of these last two issues, standing was more a problem for our side, and its focus on war and the rights of the people presented an opening.

"There is a recognized exception to sovereign immunity, Judge, if the government is acting in violation of the Constitution, and that's exactly what this case is about. On standing, we've claimed standing as taxpayers, citizens, and voters. There are, of course, limits on suits that a plaintiff may bring, but Mr. Unger overstates them. Courts have struck a balance between too many lawsuits, which would clog the courts, and too few, which would allow the government to continue operating in ways that violate the Constitution or other law.

"The plaintiff's interest does not have to be unique to him or her, and courts consider injuries that are noneconomic as well as economic, including aesthetic and environmental harm. Economic injury doesn't have to be large—in one case it was a poll tax of $1.50. This war is devastating the treasury, causing or increasing inflation, and displacing other needs for governmental funding. It has caused widespread death and injury to the people—over 45,000 dead so far, Judge—depleting the country's human resources. And the country and the world are less safe. There is an increased possibility of personal harm—here in the United States, traveling abroad, and perhaps everywhere since the superpowers with their nuclear arsenals have locked horns."

I stopped there and looked straight at Lord. I couldn't read him one way or the other. "Alright," he said, "I understand your positions. I'm not going to rule now but will issue an opinion."

I felt satisfied that I had placed it all on a moral playing field, which was our best chance and where it should be placed. But I worried that I might have gone too far. I wanted to motivate him as much as possible without making him uneasy about whether the law, as well as morality and the needs of the country, supported our side. It was a touchy balance. The complex mixture of rules and considerations mandated by many prior cases could be lined up to adequately support a decision either way on each of the four issues. I thought my task started with pointing out how best to line them up our way and convincing him that our interpretations and applications of the rules are supported by prior cases and yield a better way for courts to operate. But I also thought it vital to give him a good reason to do so.

I could feel the same push and pull and vying for the "edge" that was apparent the first time I argued in criminal cases in front of Judge Meade, but it was different. My focus was the lack of a declaration of war and the Constitution. But the government wanted to talk about complicated procedural issues and to dispense with the case without reaching the major issue. The struggle took a form I would see regularly in my civil rights lawsuits. The government's mission, though its lawyers might not see it this way, was to move the focus away from the basic issues, while mine was continually to draw the focus back to those issues.

§§§

At about the same time, Candace Falk, a young sociology professor at Stockton State College in southern New Jersey, sat at her desk hurriedly writing a letter. "To The Army Reserve Unit," she typed out quickly on her Stockton stationery. "Stockton students release you from your 'duty' to recruit. We are against the Vietnam War and Army's role in it." She signed her name and wrote "Instructor" under her signature. Falk, a thin, medium-height white woman with brown hair, ran downstairs and passed the letter around to about a dozen students waiting in the first-floor commons. They all signed below Falk's signature, then she handed it to Sergeant Steven Smoger, a large, fit man in full army uniform who stood with his army recruiting team in front of the students.

Smoger read the letter, then looked up at Falk, shaking his head back and forth slowly. "I'm just doin' my job here, ma'am, and we got a war to fight, whether it's popular on campus or not. But if that's what you want." He paused and then quickly added, "Have a good day, ma'am." They turned, walked out of the building, got into their car, and drove away.

About two weeks later, I got a call from Professor Falk. "Some friends in California, where I'm from, told me I should call you. I'm in trouble."

She told me about the letter and the recruiters who went away. "It's amazing that they left," I said.

"Yeah, I didn't expect it, though I'm not sorry. I felt I should say what I believe, but I thought they'd go on in and recruit."

"So," I said, "what's the problem?"

"They're firing me, the college. They say I misrepresented who I was and threw the sergeant off campus without authority."

"You got a notice of your termination?"

"No, they are trying to discipline me for violating the college code of conduct. I have a hearing set for about a month from now. If I lose, I'll be fired. I moved all the way from California for this job. I'm a wreck. Can you help?"

I said I would represent her. The sergeant may have read the letter as a college decision to exclude him, but the letter didn't say that. I researched cases on faculty discipline and termination. There was helpful law, mostly on state colleges, which Stockton was. Most Americans think our constitutional rights are general and enforceable against anyone or anything that would limit them, but the First Amendment limits only government actions that infringe on speech.

Cases from the 1960s offered some protection of free speech rights of teachers at public schools and universities. Falk was simply speaking her mind, but the charge against her would be that she spoke for her university without authority and misstated the university's position. They would put it in terms of an employee who has exceeded her authority and misrepresented a policy of her employer. It also didn't help that the successful cases were almost all procedural—courts reversing colleges' disciplining faculty because there wasn't a fair hearing. I would look carefully at the procedures at Stockton, but a procedural win didn't win much. Usually, the court only required the college to start over with a fair hearing, which didn't change the outcome. Few cases overturned college discipline based on the grounds for disciplining, leaving colleges broad discretion in faculty matters generally and faculty discipline specifically.[3]

She could be fired for speaking privately and peacefully to the sergeant and presenting herself as just what she was, a professor of sociology, because he misunderstood what she said and by what authority she said it. The whole thing seemed out of proportion. But that wasn't unusual for the times. The war polarized most everything, at universities, corporations, and institutions pretty much across the board. Dissent against the war was usually considered threatening and, for many, unpatriotic.

§§§

Lord issued his opinion on March 28, 1972. He rejected all of the DOJ's procedural arguments and concluded that the constitutional challenge was substantial and merited a three-judge court. The plaintiffs had standing, the other similar cases did not bar this one, and the government was not immune to this suit. He left final resolution of the "political question" issue to the three-judge court but emphasized that the case did not involve courts or judges in foreign affairs or in war and peace decision making. It dealt with only the "textually demonstrable commitment" of the decision to commence a war to Congress. "[T]his assignment of power to

Congress was not a mere happenstance without purpose," Lord wrote. "It was the intention of the framers of the Constitution to make it more difficult for the nation to engage itself in war with all the suffering this entails for its citizens."

No other case got this far during the Vietnam War era or since. It also raised a difficult question: What could judges do about an unconstitutional undeclared war? If they issued orders the president refused to follow, the resulting constitutional crisis could undermine the courts. This came into focus when a law clerk for one of the judges asked casually in the midst of some chitchat during a break at one of the proceedings, "So what would you ask the court to do if you won?" It could have been an innocent, curious question. But I thought I should treat talking to the law clerk as if I were talking to the judge. I started with some humor but worried later that might not have been the best tactic.

"What I'd suggest is that the judges pick the most unpopular guy in the marshal's office, hand him an order to stop the war, and put him on a train down to the Pentagon with instructions to knock on the door and serve the order like they generally do. He might say, 'You are running a war here and you're going to have to stop it. I have an order from a judge in Philadelphia that says it's illegal.' He might never be heard from again."

The law clerk smiled, a little nervously. "What else, say, if the judges wouldn't do that?"

"I would recommend that the court start with as unintrusive a measure as possible. Maybe set a specific time in which Congress could declare war or not, enough time to make it realistic. If they declare war, the case is moot. If not, the court could extend the time and suggest, again, deliberations by Congress. Ultimately, it could come to an ordered end to the war with stages of withdrawal to be determined by the military and with all due precautions for the safety of the troops."

"Interesting."

§§§

"Good morning, ladies and gentlemen. This is the case of *John S. Atlee v. Melvin Laird*," said Arlin Adams, from the Third Circuit Court of Appeals, seated next to Lord and Daniel Huyett, another district court judge. I was in front of the three-judge court.

Adams and Huyett were moderate to conservative, not extreme conservatives. But they were generally cautious, which might be worse in this case. The Vietnam War was polarized in liberal versus conservative terms, but the declaration of war clause could reach across that divide, if conservatives so inclined didn't place more importance on the war than the Constitution and liberals stood by the democratic principles in the Constitution.

The courtroom was packed. I was more nervous than usual, not because of the large number of people or the media but because of the presence of so many antiwar activists. They were there to see me carry the torch for our side, and I didn't want to let them down. It helped that I would split the argument for our side with a veteran seated next to me, Victor Rabinowitz, my one-time employer and now NECLC colleague and friend.[4]

The side making a motion—here the government's motion to dismiss the whole case—would argue first and then the other side would respond. Gene Fenner, from the Civil Division of the DOJ in Washington, made the same four points Lord had heard. He spent a lot of his time, a total of an hour for each side, on all four, although the judges made it clear that they were most interested in the political question issue. Usually it's advisable to follow a judge's interest and answer questions when they are asked. Instead, he emphasized that the current cases challenging the lack of a declaration of war, like the many that preceded them, "have been decided favorably to the United States for some or all of the reasons which defendant is advancing here today." He had to rub it in. Bastille Day wasn't changing anything.

"You concede our jurisdiction," Adams interrupted, when Fenner got to the political question issue and seemed to combine it with jurisdiction. In appellate arguments, judges interrupted constantly and you had to be ready to immediately answer questions away from your train of thought.

"No," Fenner said.

"You are suggesting to us: Even though we have jurisdiction, we ought not to exercise it?"

"Yes, sir, Your Honor." Adams got one, a concession that would narrow the issues. There now was little doubt that this would boil down to the political question issue.

"The foreign affairs and war-making power generally is constitutionally committed to the executive and Congress," Fenner said, "and the kind and degree of participation in this shared power by each branch is at their discretion. The courts really have no role in the resolution of this question."

"Suppose," Lord asked, "Congress should enact a law that would say, 'For this session of Congress, the president shall have the power to declare war'?"

"It would be a nonjusticiable political question."

"Are you suggesting," Adams asked, "that no court in the United States can ever adjudicate whether the executive has exceeded war-making powers set forth in the Constitution?"

"No, I am not saying that."

"You don't go that far."

"I would submit that view should be adopted—it's totally outside the power of the judiciary—and has been adopted by most courts. But there is another view that allows the court to determine whether there has been a sharing of this power, to see that one is not simply acting totally on his own."

"I am suggesting courts can examine that. You are saying that if there is some action by both Congress and executive, courts may look no further."

"That is correct."

"I have a little difficulty drawing these lines as black and white. One of the cases you cited said a court could examine whether there has been an escalation of the war that might violate the declaration of war clause. Suppose we began using nuclear weapons in Southeast Asia?"

"I would reach the same result."

Lord leaned toward Fenner. "I am concerned that we are overlooking the very genesis of the war-making power. The clause and thinking of the framers are clear. The executive has the power to repel a sudden invasion. But when it comes to a declaration of war, the Constitution is explicit."

"'Make war' was changed to 'declare war.' Congress only has the power to declare war. The president has the power to make war, to wage a war," Fenner said, reversing the meaning of this language change. "Congress has the power over the purse, to grant or withdraw finances."

"In your brief," Adams said, "you suggest that Congress has declared war by its defense appropriations for the war and the Draft Act, that taken together various legislation amounts to a declaration of war."

"No. A declaration of war brings about treaty obligations and other consequences, and that has not been done. I am saying that Congress has collaborated with the executive in bringing about the activities that are currently going on in Southeast Asia. They have done all they need to do, and that makes it a political question."

"Doesn't your argument," Huyett said, "that the war is authorized short of a formal declaration lead you into the merits of the matter and so take it out of the political question area?"

"I don't think the court should go that far, but if it does it is a small point."

"Does the government contend that war declaration by Congress is now an obsolete concept, given modern-day facts of life?"

"It is foreseeable that there may never be another declaration of war, but there may be a different situation that requires one."

Fenner returned to his seat and sat down.

§§§

Victor stood up and walked to the lectern. "May it please the court," he began in the traditional way, which always sounded like a form of fawning that came out of some book on manners. "Mr. Kairys and I are dividing the argument this morning. I propose to cover three of the issues, standing, sovereign immunity, and the similar lawsuits filed elsewhere. Mr. Kairys will discuss the political question doctrine issues."

Victor looked shorter than usual standing in a big expanse of rug in front of the lectern that came almost up to his chest, and his New York accent was more apparent in this Philadelphia courtroom than I remembered it in New York. But he got right to it.

"This war is probably the most important issue that has confronted the American people certainly since the days of Reconstruction. It is the longest war in our history, probably the most expensive, and may very well be the most destructive. Except for the Civil War, it has had the most devastating effect on national morale and unity. For the first time in our history, or at least since the War of 1812, we find the country sharply divided on a question of support of its own government in a foreign war."

He went through the three issues smoothly and effectively, but the judges weren't very interested. At one point, Adams said, "We would rather hear argument on the so-called political question."

"Your Honors are almost asking me to sit down, and I like it here," Victor said to general laughter in the courtroom.

Before he sat, he responded to a question about the "constitutional crisis" that a judicial decision could create. "I suppose it's conceivable that that could happen," Victor said, "but I don't believe it would be any greater than the constitutional crisis that confronts us at this very moment. We heard the suggestion from Your Honor that maybe the declaration of war provision is obsolete—"

"I certainly didn't suggest that," Huyett said. "I just wanted to see the government's position on that."

"Yes, sir. I must say I found the government's response disturbing. The government suggested here today that the president has the right to conduct this action in Vietnam, not call it a war, without a declaration."

Victor headed back to our table as I rose and slowly walked to the lectern. The judges seemed moved by Victor, although I didn't like his little confrontation with Huyett. But confrontation, pushing them, seemed right and necessary. They seemed, except for Lord, headed for the safest ground they could find. The only chance we had was to move them with the sense that our way of reading the Constitution was historically sound and best for the country and to motivate them to take what was an awfully big step. Victor's comment about Huyett's question pushed them with moral force, and it went to an important issue that was mostly under the radar—the sense that the declaration of war clause may be outmoded. But Huyett was right that all he did was ask a question about an issue in the DOJ brief and in the case, so it came off as an unfair criticism of the judge. I thought I'd start off light and remind them that they liked Victor and that he said some important things.

"That's a hard introduction to follow," I said, to smiles from the judges, including Huyett, and laughter from the audience.

"I was going to say you've got a tough assignment," Adams responded. He also thought it time to lighten things up.

I paused and gathered myself. "I know. I would like to start, Your Honors, our discussion of the political question doctrine with what it has meant historically, as compared to what the government now urges as its meaning before the court." I decided to skip the *may it please the court,* but as soon as I said it I knew it was going to be hard to avoid the *Your Honors* in this formal setting.

"The political question doctrine," I continued, "historically and up to very recently was never regarded as a doctrine of nondecision or a discretionary device for courts to avoid difficult questions. It has been a substantive rule of decision used by courts to decide what branch of government has authority to do what, exactly what we ask the court to do here.[5]

"Going back to 1890, the Supreme Court had before it two parties who each claimed some hides Pancho Villa brought into the United States from Mexico. Which one owned them boiled down to a question of which of two rival regimes in Mexico was recognized by the United States. The Court decided that recognition of foreign governments was within the powers of the executive branch—a political question for resolution by the president, not any court. The hides went to the party who claimed them through the Mexican regime recognized as its government by our president. The Court *decided* which branch had the power to recognize governments and examined whether that power had been exceeded, while it refused to second-guess the president as to whether he might have made the best decision in recognizing one regime's legitimacy over the other's, which was a political question.

"During the Korean War, President Truman took control of the steel mills as a matter of national security to prevent labor and other disputes from interrupting the flow of steel. Nothing at the time was more politically charged. Yet, the Supreme Court *decided* whether the president had that power and concluded that he didn't.

"In 1967, when Adam Clayton Powell was excluded from his seat in the House of Representatives, the government argued to the Supreme Court that it would be unthinkable for a court to look into the authority of the House to disqualify one of its members. Yet, the Court did *decide* whether there was a "textually demonstrable commitment" of authority to a branch of government and the scope of that authority. Powell won his seat back.

"In the civil rights cases in the last decade, the Supreme Court *decided* that Tennessee's apportionment scheme, though formulated by a legislative, political process, had to comport with the Fourteenth Amendment requirement of equal protection of the law.

"I've read all the cases on this issue, more cases than I wished. The political question doctrine does not stem from language in the Constitution; it is a judicial creation, so the early cases should be particularly important. Prior to the recent, Vietnam War–era cases, there isn't one single case in which the Supreme Court used the political question doctrine to *refuse to decide* a question of constitutional power between Congress and the executive. What these cases mean and reaffirm is that, at least since *Marbury v. Madison* established judicial review, the power to make the ultimate decisions about what is or is not constitutional is firmly lodged with the courts. With that power comes a duty and responsibility of the courts to decide questions of interpretation of the Constitution, particularly basic ones like which branch has which powers."

"Mr. Kairys," Huyett interjected, "I understand your view on the political question doctrine, but this war has gone on for seven years, and you have appropriation bill after appropriation bill, the Draft Act, the Gulf of Tonkin resolution, and so on. Why do you believe Congress hasn't done enough to satisfy the declaration of war clause?"

"Judge Huyett, I thought that was one of the government's main arguments until I heard them repudiate it this morning. Anyway, these actions by Congress are not sufficient. First, the Supreme Court has generally held that appropriations, even with knowledge of what the executive branch intends to do with the money, are not considered congressional ratifications. This application of the principle seems among the clearest. Failing to appropriate money to feed, house, and arm the troops is not an alternative Congress would or should entertain. This argument reverses the roles of Congress and the president set out in the Constitution. The president could initiate wars, and Congress would have to repudiate them explicitly or by refusing funds to protect the troops, which is hard to imagine Congress ever doing. Congress could phrase a declaration in many ways, but the Constitution requires that it be explicit and intentional and that Congress be aware when they vote that they are discharging their duty under the declaration of war clause, Article I, Section 8."

"Suppose," Adams asked, "a president is elected and he inherits from his predecessor hundreds of thousands of troops abroad in a skirmish that he doesn't particularly like. He wants to get those troops home as quickly as he can. But his attorney general says he should get Congress to declare war. The president thinks that's the last thing he wants, since he'd like to get out of it. What then?"

"Well, why doesn't he just withdraw them?"

"He wants to do it over several months."

"If he wants to leave them there for a long time and if it's a war under the Constitution, I agree with the attorney general—he needs a declaration."

"Is that a political question?"

"What he decides to do—continue the war, withdraw slowly, end it quickly—is a political question, but the Constitution requires a congressional declaration of war. A court should grant the president some time and protect the troops, but I don't see that as a political question."

"What if, as the government says," Huyett asked, "the war is limited and winding down and casualties are declining?"

"We've been told it's limited and winding down for almost a decade. We are still bombing highly populated areas, defoliating farmland, dropping napalm. We just blockaded a neighboring country's harbors. Casualties are declining only if you don't count Asian people. According to the *Philadelphia Bulletin,* last week 3,278 people died, one of the highest weekly totals for the war."

"I think," Lord said, "the government means it's winding down as far as we are concerned. The *Bulletin* didn't say who they were, did it?"

I knew mentioning the deaths of non-Americans wouldn't help with the judges, but government and media reports regularly only included American losses, and I had made up my mind not to let it pass if it came up. "That was a total of everyone who died in that week, and if one is to assess the casualties of a war, we should include more than just Americans."

The judges asked more questions, and I gave the best responses I could muster. Then I paused a moment, thinking it was time to finish. "This is an appropriate place for me to conclude my argument," I said, looking directly at them as intensely as I could. "I believe it is the highest duty of this court at this time to reach the merits of this issue. The American people have waited long enough for this to be decided."

§§§

We requested that Candace Falk's disciplinary hearing be public. The Stockton College administration first opposed it but then relented. The crowd of students gathered to view the hearing was larger than could fit in any of their rooms, so it was held in an open area of the same commons in which Sergeant Smoger had been greeted by Falk and a dozen students.

The formal charge against Falk, set out in a letter to her from the Campus Hearing Board, was that she "acted without authorization as a college spokesman and representative to 'Evict' from the campus Army Reserve Recruiters, contrary to the Campus Conduct Code in the College

Handbook." The letter quoted the code provision: "Each member of the campus community has the right to identify himself as a member of the campus community and a concurrent obligation not to speak or act on behalf of the college without authorization." I read the handbook carefully, and the provision was quoted accurately, but it was under the heading "Statement of Rights and Responsibilities," an introductory section that preceded the sections entitled "Violations" and "Campus Code," which spelled out specific offenses.

I planned to emphasize Falk's right to express her views and her presentation of herself as just who she was, a faculty member speaking for herself rather than as an official authorized to kick anyone off the campus. But I had some additional defenses to work with from the charge and code provisions. There was long-standing authority, which I also had used in the Powelton-Drexel dispute, that offenses generally, particularly those that limit free speech, must be specific, narrow, and spelled out clearly as offenses. I found some cases applying these principles to school disciplinary codes. Also, the handbook said that anyone violating the code "shall receive warning that his conduct violates or threatens to violate the Code." Falk had gotten no warning.

The sound of so many students standing around in the commons and talking among themselves was deafening. It reminded me of recess in elementary school. The chair of the Campus Hearing Board of two faculty, two students, and an administrator, Professor William Lubenow, had trouble quieting the crowd. He summarized the charges and the provisions of the code as the students settled down.

"Before we begin," I said, "I have some preliminary issues to raise that in a full criminal proceeding might be called pretrial motions."

"What is it, Mr. Kairys?" Lubenow asked.

"I don't believe the panel was legally or fairly constituted. As I understand it, the administration handpicked all of you members. I understand further that some of you have expressed derogatory views about Professor Falk's conduct. Whether or not that's true, and despite the lack of bias you may accurately believe you have, this is not a properly constituted panel."

Lubenow and the others quickly conferred. The crowd resumed its loud discussions, and someone yelled, "You're like Julius Hoffman," referring to the judge in the notoriously repressive Chicago 7 trial. I thought a large number of students would help our side, but I didn't expect this. Some pressure on the panel and the realization that disciplining Falk would create a serious problem with students were to the good. One of the reasons I pushed the prehearing issues was to pressure them and put them on the defensive. But I worried that the students and their comments might feel too threatening.

"We've conferred, Mr. Kairys," Lubenow said, "and we're satisfied that this is an appropriate panel."

The crowd booed loudly. I interrupted them. "Secondly," I said, "in your summary of the proceedings you referred only to the code. Doesn't the Constitution also apply to these proceedings, so Professor Falk has, for example, First Amendment rights?"

Lubenow made no response. "Do you have any response?" I asked.

"No," he said. "Our responsibilities are in the handbook, and we'll abide by that."

"Finally, I received a copy of the 1971–1972 handbook, and it seems to apply only to men. The provision Professor Falk is charged with violating refers to 'identify himself.' I'd like to know, is there another handbook for women?"

The student audience burst into laughter, even louder this time. Lubenow half grimaced and half smiled at me. He held his hands up, asking for quiet. "This is the college handbook."

The administration relied on the testimony of James Williams, the head of security, and Richard Chait, an administrator, who jointly had brought the charges against Professor Falk. Williams, a black man in his 30s with a flattop haircut and long sideburns, said a group of about 15 students and faculty had greeted the recruiters.

"The group stated they didn't want the recruiters on campus," Williams said. "Sergeant Smoger replied, 'Well, we don't want to be here, either. This is our duty.' Miss Falk asked, 'What would it take to have you leave?' 'Something in writing,' he said, 'to signify that we're not wanted.' Some of the protestors went off and came back with a typed note on Stockton stationery, signed by a dozen or so, and they gave it to the recruiting team. The recruiters read the note and left. There was no contact or any loud talking or hostility."

"Did you have any prior experience with Professor Falk in this type of situation?" I asked.

"Yes, she assisted us in an uncomfortable situation at a demonstration some time ago."

"Didn't Professor Falk advise the recruiters that they—the group of students and faculty—intended to protest and that they—the group again—did not want the recruiters on campus?"

"That's correct."

"Did she at any time say anything to suggest she was an administrator or spoke for the college?"

"No."

"Did she identify herself as an instructor?"

"Yes, she did."

"Did you decide to make the complaint yourself about obstructing or misrepresenting in this proceeding?"

"It is a joint complaint."

"Did you at the conclusion of these events believe there was any violation or believe a proceeding should be brought against Professor Falk?"

"No."

"You saw no need for disciplinary proceedings against Candace Falk?"

"At that time, yeah."

"What changed your mind?"

"I didn't say I changed my mind."

The students roared. Lubenow waited for them to settle down and then said to me, "More questions?"

"What else can I ask?"

Chait was next. He was a young white man with longish dark hair and big bushy sideburns. I asked him, "To your knowledge, was Miss Falk warned that what she was doing violated the code?"

"Not to my knowledge."

"There is a code provision on warnings," I said, "in the men's code." I couldn't resist. "Did you believe Mr. Williams just now—is he an honest man?"

"I have no comment."

"Ohhhhh," the students roared.

"Why are we here, Mr. Chait? Why did you bring these charges?"

"I perceive violations."

"You mean the letter. She signed it and wrote 'Instructor' under her name."

"That's correct."

"Is she authorized to use the stationery?"

"Yes."

"Do you expect her to write 'This is not the administration speaking' at the bottom?"

"No."

"You have the letter in front of you. 'Instructor' is under her name, 12 students also signed, and someone wrote at the bottom, 'and several others.' Does that sound like it's the way an administrative determination would be expressed?"

"No."

The hearing went on like this for a full day. Sergeant Smoger didn't appear, but he earlier sent a letter saying he was "surrounded by hostile students" and didn't want to "risk injury or possible civil unrest."

A couple days later Candace Falk got a letter from Lubenow announcing that the board unanimously decided that there was "insufficient evidence" of a violation for three reasons. The letter didn't establish a misrepresentation, the handbook provision was not in the violations section of the code, and there was no warning. Candace, who became a close friend, now heads a research institute, the Emma Goldman Papers, at the University of California at Berkeley.

§§§

On August 7, 1972, I got a call from the clerk of the district court in Philadelphia. "Mr. Kairys, the court has reached a decision in *Atlee v. Laird,* and the opinions will be mailed to you today."

He said "opinions," plural, which meant there was a dissent.

I ran from my office several blocks to the district court. There was one opinion, not two, typed on long, white, legal paper. I saw on the first page that Adams wrote it. Opinions often went on for some time before they said which side won, so I was used to looking at the last page first to find out what happened. The last page said a dissent by Lord would be filed shortly.

Adams, with Huyett in agreement, had dismissed the case based on the political question doctrine. The opinion was long, covering the history of the political question doctrine, which he described as "born of pragmatic considerations." Adams detailed several criteria for determining when it should be applied that he drew from recent cases and then applied them as if our suit requested review of the decisions to go to and

maintain the war rather than the power to do so in the absence of a declaration of war. For example, the first was "information in a foreign policy case comes from multiple sources and might be, by sheer bulk alone,
unmanageable for a court." We challenged no foreign policy decision. He
would have to decide only a question of constitutional interpretation,
which belonged in the judiciary. He also said it would be hard to determine whether there was a war in Southeast Asia, although everyone knew
there was. Courts commonly decide many thorny issues, like whether
there is an "impasse" in labor negotiations. This one seemed easy by
comparison. I was, and still am, disappointed, particularly at the weak-
ness of his reasoning.

Two weeks later, Lord issued his dissent. "The effect of the majority
decision is to remove an entire provision of the Constitution from judicial scrutiny," Judge Lord wrote. "The duty of a court to judge whether
acts of the other branches conform to the requirements of the Constitution has been established since *Marbury v. Madison.*" The political question doctrine was being misused as a "device for judicial avoidance."
Courts should decide "whether there has been a textual commitment" of
a power to a particular branch, which is not the same as "second guessing the wisdom" of another branch's political or policy determinations.
"It is rather a constitutional question concerning the division of power
within our system."

Lord's dissent had an impact as the strongest statement of the time on
the necessity of a declaration of war by Congress, which he, like the
framers of the Constitution, saw as vital to protect the people. He also
pressed the somehow controversial principle that courts should do their
duty even when it's difficult.

The Supreme Court never ruled on the issue. Judge Lord's initial
opinion and later dissent drew national attention. *Atlee v. Laird* got the
best result and most emphatic statement of the declaration of war principle during, before, or after the Vietnam War.[6]

CHAPTER SEVEN

"One of the Great Trials of the Twentieth Century"

I WAS EXHAUSTED THE NIGHT in late August 1971 I returned to my apartment on Spruce Street after five weeks in the wilderness with two close friends. They had quit their jobs and were touring North America in a van, playing out a common dream in those days. They called in July from a campground in Montana and asked me to meet them a few days later in another campground next to the Missouri River. I had to make a quick decision. Four airplanes later, I landed at the Missoula airport. We began a trek that took us north through British Columbia and out to Vancouver Island.

I was on the road for a month or more most every summer camping, hiking, and backpacking in wilderness areas. I felt the most relaxed and present I can remember on those trips. That night, I was ready to get back but sensitive to the sights, sounds, and smells of the city, particularly from the oil refineries as I drove from the Philadelphia airport to the city. I turned on the TV to catch the news while unpacking. The bantering and flirting of perfectly dressed local newscasters and the imposing light of the TV were startling. I turned the volume down and mostly paid attention to my dirty laundry.

But one of the lead stories drew me to the TV. There were riots in Camden, New Jersey, across the Delaware River east of Philadelphia. Riots weren't all that unusual then, particularly in areas like Camden, where minorities lived in extreme poverty. The event precipitating this one was not uncommon—police had shot and killed a Hispanic man pulled over for a traffic stop. But in the middle of the night, the FBI arrested antiwar activists who had broken into the draft board office in the federal courthouse building in Camden. They had destroyed the records of the Camden-area draft board. Video clips showed the handcuffed activists being led away, the fire escape they used to climb up to the draft board on the fifth floor, and the ransacked draft board office. In the early morning hours right after the arrests, FBI director J. Edgar Hoover and Attorney General John Mitchell held a news conference in Washington. I wondered if they ever slept.

I remembered Hoover as an icon of my youth. I believed the TV show *The FBI*, starring Efrem Zimbalist, Jr., as the clean, courageous, humorless FBI man who, though his hair never moved, always got the bad guys.

I didn't know then that Hoover's career had largely been built on exaggerated crime fighting and repression of dissenters and immigrants. In the 1960s, I heard him actively oppose and undercut the civil rights movement. As part of the effort, the FBI wiretapped and harassed Martin Luther King, Jr., whom Hoover regarded as a communist. They sent phony letters to King's wife in an attempt to divide them, and they tried to provoke King to suicide with threats of a scandal about his personal life. This didn't seem like law enforcement.

The *New York Times* reported on its front page the day after the Camden raid that the "[g]overnment obviously set great store by the Camden arrests," emphasizing that they had caught "adherents of the Catholic Left" in the act, "dressed in dark, . . . their faces and arms blackened with charcoal, carr[ying] burglar's tools." They boasted that an FBI informer had been working with the defendants for over two months. The story quoted federal magistrate Charles Rudd, who when he set high bail said, "I don't want to see my country destroyed. God bless the FBI; they've done a wonderful job."

In all, 28 defendants, who quickly became known as the Camden 28, were arrested and charged with several crimes carrying a maximum sentence of 47 years—8 who entered the draft board, several at the scene, and others who the government claimed assisted or conspired in various ways.

Hoover and Mitchell used the occasion, as the Nixon administration used all antiwar activities, to condemn the broader antiwar movement.

But I knew they had an additional reason and agenda for gloating. In early 1971, Hoover and Mitchell were widely criticized for attempting to suppress war opponents with vague, baseless conspiracy charges.

Hoover had gone public with what he called a Catholic Left criminal conspiracy to kidnap Secretary of State Henry Kissinger and to blow up utility tunnels under Washington. Hoover had been advised by the Justice Department (DOJ) that they had insufficient proof of this for criminal charges—only the testimony of a questionable informant, without any substantial corroboration. But once Hoover went public, the DOJ and the Nixon administration backed him with an indictment. The eight antiwar activists charged, including well-known priest Phillip Berrigan, preached and practiced nonviolence. The charges were preposterous, and in 1972 even a jury from conservative Harrisburg, Pennsylvania, the location for the trial chosen by the DOJ—hence the moniker Harrisburg 8—was hung with 10 of 12 jurors favoring acquittal. The DOJ declined to retry the case.

Then in March 1971, someone broke into the FBI field office in Media, Pennsylvania, took a lot of FBI files, and sent copies to journalists and academic researchers. The Media Papers, as they were called, were revealing and devastating for the FBI. They exposed FBI actions and programs explicitly aimed at undermining progressive activists and organizations rather than at enforcing the law, including the FBI's Counterintelligence Program (COINTELPRO). One document stated that the FBI sought to "enhance the paranoia of the new left" and "convince them that there is an FBI agent behind every mailbox."

The FBI's furious investigation of the Media raid focused on Philadelphia antiwar groups and the Powelton neighborhood. We filed a suit challenging their harassment of both, *Resistance v. Mitchell,* in mid-July, just before I left for Montana.

At the August 22 news conference, Hoover and Mitchell sought vindication. The Camden draft board raid was no vague conspiracy—the defendants were caught in the act after destroying draft board files. The FBI considered the Harrisburg case, the Media raid, and the Camden draft board raid one big conspiracy, combining them in one file named "MED-BURG-CAMDEN." The immediate arrests of the culprits were also trumpeted as showing how effective the FBI was. However, there was at least one early sign that Camden might not serve to restore the FBI's reputation: though they had advance notice and at least 40 FBI agents lay in wait in the building to make the arrests, they hadn't brought enough handcuffs. Father Michael Doyle, the local Camden priest arrested inside the draft board who later met me under the Walt Whitman Bridge, had to be cuffed with his belt.[1]

§§§

A few days later, Bernie Segal, the criminal lawyer in whose office we rented a room, asked for help representing so many draft board raid defendants at their bail reduction hearings. A few local lawyers, including Rudy and me, volunteered. I did not know any of the defendants, few of whom were from the Philadelphia area. Bernie gave me a list of several to interview in jail and to represent at their bail hearings, including a local defendant from the Italian working-class area of South Philadelphia, Kathleen Ridolfi. Some of the FBI documents added after her name "aka Cookie," which was their usual way of making nicknames seem like sinister aliases.

The bail hearing was uneventful, except there were a lot of priests in the audience and the walls were lined with federal marshals. It looked like a Vatican gathering under military occupation. At one point, after a priest from New York testified that the defendants were honorable, reliable people who would show up for their trial, the prosecutor, assistant U.S. attorney Joseph Audino, asked him, "You know several of the defendants very well?"

"Yes, I'm proud to say I do," the priest answered.

"When did you last see any of them before the raid?"

"I don't recall."

"Where were you on the night of the draft board raid?"

"I was—"

"Judge Cohen," I said, "I object."

"On what ground?" Judge Mitchell Cohen said, looking at me like he didn't think there was a good answer.

He was probably right, but I thought 28 defendants was quite enough. "I don't know what his answer would be, but it might make him the 29th defendant."

"Your Honor," Audino chimed in, "Mr. Kairys does not represent this witness and has no standing to object on his behalf."

"You don't represent him, do you Mr. Kairys?" Cohen asked.

"I don't, but I am a member of the bar and an officer of the court. I'm simply informing you, Judge, that this man might incriminate himself in response to the line of questions being pursued by the prosecutor. He is unrepresented by counsel and may not know that he has a right to refuse to testify on the grounds that it may incriminate him. Perhaps you should inform him."

"Alright," Cohen said. "I'm not going to get into your standing to object. Mr. Audino, continue the cross-examination but proceed on another line of questioning."

"Very well, Your Honor."

Cohen lowered the bail amounts, but they were still far too high for these defendants or their supporters to post, and he denied our request that they be allowed to post 10 percent, which was a common practice in the federal court. We appealed to the Third Circuit Court of Appeals, which lowered the amounts again and allowed posting of 10 percent. All of the defendants were released by two weeks after the raid, and I thought that would be the extent of my involvement.

§§§

Several weeks later, Cookie Ridolfi invited me to dinner at her mother's house in South Philadelphia to discuss the case. On the way to the house, we walked along a narrow street lined by parked cars in front of row houses that went on as far as I could see. I noticed three men in suits coming the other way on the other side of the street. As they approached, one of them, a trim man with dark, slicked-back hair and a silk suit, silk shirt, and silk tie of varying shades of white, stepped over the curb and moved toward us. He looked like he came from a casting call for a Mob movie.

"Cookie," he yelled, "what the hell you doin' breakin' in a fed building wit' those antiwar weirdos? I seen it in the *Daily News*. You crazy?"

"No," she said, smiling, "it's what I believe. I'm just putting myself on the line, sayin' I won't accept it."

"Well, shit," he said, coming closer. "Guys in the neighborhood are dyin' over there, so you can go fuck wit' a draft board?"

"I want to stop the dyin'," she said, as he got close and I got a little nervous.

When he was right in front of her, he put his hand around the back of her neck and pulled her head down close to him. He was shorter up close than he looked from across the street, much shorter than Cookie, but he had hold of her neck.

"I don't want to hear all that protest shit," he said, "but you let me know if those feds mess with you, okay?"

"Thanks, Joey. I will." They both smiled, and he walked away with his companions as we continued toward Cookie's house.

"Who's that?" I asked.

"A family friend from the neighborhood."

"Did he mean it?"

"He might get into it if someone was hurting me. But mostly it's his way of saying he's with me no matter what I do. Even if I'm stupid enough to raid a draft board."

Cookie's mother, tall and attractive like her daughter, was mostly interested in how long I thought Cookie would be in jail, as well as how much I liked her ravioli, which I loved. I told her there was no way to know. Cookie seemed less concerned about the details and resigned, almost calm, about going to jail. She said little about the case or the trial.

A few days later, Cookie called. "David," she said, "John Grady is in town, and he wants to talk to you and would like you to come to a meeting of the defendants in Camden."

Grady was the undisputed leader of the Camden 28 and much of the Catholic Left. I had met him at the bail hearings. He was thoroughly Irish or what I knew as Irish. A stocky man of medium height with curly hair, he had a hardy handshake; a ready smile; a loud, cheerful voice; and a strong Irish brogue. He had a book distribution business and had once run for Congress from New York, but it wasn't clear what he was currently doing except raiding draft boards. Over 350 draft boards were raided during the Vietnam War, and I had the impression he had a hand in many.

§§§

Almost all of the 28, as well as some supporters, sat or stood roughly in a circle against the walls and windows of a large, open room somewhere in rural South Jersey. Several were dressed in priest's garb, but otherwise it looked pretty much like any gathering in that time of about 50 people mostly in their 20s.

As I came into the room, I was greeted warmly by Terry Buckalew, a big bear of a defendant who came from Philadelphia. We discovered we knew a lot of people in common. While we talked, someone I recognized from the bail hearing as a defendant came up to us. "You're Terry Buckalew, right?" she said.

"Yeah, in the flesh." They talked briefly, and then she moved on to talk to others.

"You didn't know her, Terry?" I asked.

"Nah. A lot of us have never met. It's not the well-oiled machine Hoover makes us out to be. Some came a few days or weeks before the raid. Some are not from the Catholic Left or Catholic."

"So how was it organized?"

"Word spread through an informal network that help was needed for a draft board raid in Camden, and folks came from Massachusetts, New York, Washington, Philadelphia. That's how it works. A core organizes it, spreads the word, and others come in to help."

"How did you get in it?"

"Bob Williamson called me, said they need help. I came over to meet folks in Camden with Bob and Keith Forsyth a couple weeks before the raid. I met Bob Hardy—you know, the FBI guy—then but only talked to him a few times. Right away I got his macho, ex-marine routine. He talked like I was in his gang or something. What an ass."

Hardy had set them up for serious jail time. He had fooled them into thinking he was one of them. They were all angry about it in the conversations before and after the meeting. But they didn't talk about him much once the meeting started, and they seemed resigned to lengthy jail terms.

The meeting started with Grady very much in charge, although he didn't say much. No one was leading the discussion, which had no agenda.

"We'll represent ourselves and explain our motivation to a jury, if the judge will let us," a Jesuit priest from New York said early on, "and put the Vietnam War and the government that's waging it on trial. You know, jury nullification. If the judge won't let us, he may face some nonviolent resistance."

Several others nodded in agreement, but one defendant asked, "What do you mean 'nullification'?"

"We ask the jury to acquit because raiding the draft board, though it technically is a crime, was the right thing to do in the circumstances. Juries can acquit for any reason, and they don't have to explain why they do it."

"That's fine," a short, young man without a collar said. "We'll try that, as movement folks usually do, and hopefully we'll get some jurors to reconsider the war, get some media coverage, and raise some consciousness. But let's be realistic. Even if the judge allows us to explain anything we want, we're going to do some time."

"Yeah," one of the women said, "we all knew we'd be caught in one or another of these actions. For me, it's time to think about how to put my life in order and prepare for jail."

That seemed to be the sentiment of most, although some saw going to prison in a more positive light. "When your country is napalming villages," Father Doyle said, "jail is the honorable place to be."

At one point someone turned to me and asked what I thought, which I was wondering about myself. "You each have to decide how you approach this," I said. "Judges are generally allowing more motivation evidence these days, mostly to avoid the scene that Judge Julius Hoffman created at the Chicago 7 trial—you know, Bobby Seale, the Black Panther leader, bound and gagged in the courtroom. It made the court look ridiculous and created sympathy for the defendants. It'll depend on the particular judge, but you'll probably get some leeway to talk about the war and your principled commitment to end it."

"Has that gotten anybody an acquittal? I know we were caught in the act, but I for one don't want to go to jail." Buckalew said, to some laughter.

"There have been some hung juries, but acquittal requires all 12 jurors to agree to it. They can do it for any reason they want, and the government can't appeal a not-guilty verdict. It's called 'nullification' because they're nullifying the effect of a law in a particular case, but that term makes it sound negative and lawless, when it's a great tradition connected to the right to a jury trial. Anyway, there haven't been any acquittals in major antiwar cases, at least not without some other credible defense. Some have won when the charges stem from a demonstration that's at least arguably protected by free speech or when they credibly argue that they didn't do what's charged. Sometimes minor civil disobedience charges stemming from actions done in public view have been thrown out, usually by judges—trespassing or blocking a doorway."

I paused for a moment, looking around the room. I was tempted by their intense focus on me to hold out more hope than I thought realistic, but I knew I had to avoid that, whether or not they liked my message. "I honestly don't think anything like that is available to you. This was, as you heard the prosecutor say at the bail hearings in his every other sentence, a wartime, middle-of-the-night burglary of a federal building that resulted in the destruction of war-related documents. Sentiments have shifted against the war, and a hung jury is possible, at least as to some of you. But I wouldn't hold out hope that, if that's all you have, all 12 of your jurors can be so convinced that was the right thing to do that they acquit you."

"I don't need false hopes," Buckalew said, "but I still don't want to go to prison." A few laughed, but most sat silently.

§§§

After the meeting, Grady asked me to take a walk with him and Cookie. We slowly strolled along a dirt path next to some woods.

"What do you think of the meeting?" Grady asked.

"It's an impressive group of people. I like the energy, the commitment to press the war issue in court, and the realism about jail time."

"How about self-representation? Have you dealt with that before?"

"Yeah, a number of times. It humanizes defendants. You talk and you have a personality and character that the jury experiences for themselves rather than the usual trial in which everybody talks about the defendants. I've found it effective—movement defendants are usually best at expressing their views."

"Would you want to work with us, back us up as we represent ourselves?"

I thought he might suggest something like this, and I wasn't sure how I'd respond. "I would like to do that, John, and, regardless, I'd set up a training session for you that would help everybody understand the basics of the trial process. But backup in court isn't a good use of what would turn out to be an awful lot of my time. This trial will take months, particularly if there are fireworks with the judge over what you can or cannot say. You should have a movement lawyer there, but I don't think I can justify devoting that kind of time to it unless I'm an active participant in the trial, if that's what you want. I've got a law firm we started just six months ago, and I have to be out there taking in new cases and making some money. Cookie saw—"

"Yeah," Cookie said, smiling, "they got a little room way in the back of an office. Ya gotta walk a mile or so before you can even see them."

"Yeah, I've got to make some money so we can get a grown-up office."

We all laughed, then Grady stopped walking and looked straight at me. "What if one or a few of the defendants wanted to make you their lawyer, so you'd participate as a lawyer alongside the rest of us representing ourselves?"

"I'd think seriously about that. If I did it, I'd want to work on possible ways to beat this, even though that looks unlikely."

"What could you do?"

"I'd look at all the possibilities, including technical challenges that could be made to the charges and procedures the government used. Right now, without diggin' into it or thinking about it much, it sounds like there was a point at which you may have legally abandoned the conspiracy—given up on it and quit. That could provide at least a partial defense."

"You mean after the FBI showed up at our meeting at Hi-Nella?"

"Yeah, I've heard a little about that. The other possibility from what I've heard is the role Hardy played. It sounds like he did a lot more than inform on you."

"Hardy? Nah, he was nothing. He's a blowhard. You know, hundreds of draft boards have been raided. We didn't need him."

"Anyway, I'd be trying to find a way to win, while respecting the politics of the action and what we just heard in there—for many of you, it seems the time to prepare for prison. No one is interested in false hopes."

"Thinkin' about defenses is fine. We could cover your expenses and get you some money, but, realistically, not much. I'd also want you to head up a team of lawyers, take the lead. You all could file pretrial motions and write briefs on issues like that, and you and maybe some other lawyers would participate with us at the trial."

"I'd need enough money to live on. Let me think about all this and talk to my partner."

"Call me when you're ready to talk more, or call Cookie; she's easier to reach."

I nodded to Grady and to Cookie, who was oddly silent in his presence.

§§§

I am not sure why they picked me. I was a young lawyer who understood what they did and liked the Catholic Left tradition of self-representation. I had one other obvious attribute: I came cheap. Segal had submitted a fee estimate to them that was not unreasonable for the amount of work involved, but it was beyond their ability to pay or raise money. They also wanted someone more movement oriented than Segal, and Grady and I hit it off pretty well. Cookie told me Grady was impressed with my intervention at the bail hearing when the prosecutor was cross-examining the priest.

I had some doubts myself. Grady seemed too dominant and communicated right away that he was in charge and would maintain control. Privately, most of the defendants talked a lot about Hardy, but Grady didn't, and they didn't either around him. Cookie and other defendants seemed to defer and become passive around him. And the Jesuit priests from New York had a strong idealistic bent that wasn't shared by everyone. Some defendants wanted to confront the government, no matter what the price; others wanted to minimize their prison terms; some wanted acquittal on any ground available. The large, unexpectedly diverse group of defendants, some of whom would have to get to know each other, and the variety of goals for the trial could make things difficult. But Grady proposed my participating alongside the self-representation and liked my interest in looking for defenses.

This was a decision Rudy and I had to make together. The case would take up a lot of my time, require some reshuffling of other cases, and likely put a dent in our income. But this was the kind of case we had in mind when we started the office. We decided Rudy would take over the primary role in *Resistance v. Mitchell,* which we had been doing together, and I would take the Camden 28 case.

§§§

Assembling a team of lawyers was easy. Two other lawyers I knew by reputation and had briefly met through the National Lawyers Guild were brought into the case by other defendants, Marty Stolar from New York and Carl Broege from northern New Jersey. The Guild began as an alternative bar association in 1937, when the American Bar Association still didn't admit African Americans. It fell on hard times during the red-baiting 1950s. But early in the 1960s the Guild sent civil rights lawyers to the South and had a revival among progressive lawyers of my generation, providing us a national base to meet and discuss our work with like-minded lawyers. Marty and Carl were skilled movement lawyers about my age, and I knew we'd work well together. A group of lawyers based at Georgetown Law School who had done pretrial motions in several political criminal cases volunteered to assist us. Their motions and supporting briefs requested government documents on the case and challenged searches, wiretapping, and other FBI actions.[2]

I knew the basics and the leading cases on jury nullification, but I wanted a thorough legal memorandum and some new research focused on the New Jersey area. Nullification, like the jury trial itself, was a British export. The leading British case came in the late 17th century, when a jury refused to convict William Penn for preaching before an unlawful assembly. The judge sent the jury to jail for ignoring his instructions, but that was overturned on appeal on the ground that the jury can disregard the instructions of the judge and decide according to their consciences. The early American experience with nullification came with rebellion against British rule. In 1735, the printer John Peter Zenger published books not approved by the British mayor of New York, but a jury refused to go along with the prosecution or the established laws, as Alexander Hamilton urged in his famous closing argument, in "the cause of liberty."

Some of the oldest American nullification cases grew out of the Boston Tea Party. Dumping tea belonging to someone else into a harbor was certainly criminal, but Boston grand juries refused to indict the tea-tax activists, and trial juries refused to convict them. I remembered reading somewhere that there were also tea parties in the mid-Atlantic area. I asked Dick Lavine, a law student working in my office, to look into tea party cases in the Camden area and to research and prepare a complete legal memo on nullification that could be used by all the defendants and lawyers.[3]

With the legal work under way, I scheduled talks with the defendants who were in the Philadelphia area, to understand them and the raid. Lots of activists I knew were outraged by the war and committed to do what they could to end it, but raiding a draft board was a different level of action and risk. I particularly wanted to understand the religious aspects of it, the Catholic in Catholic Left.

§§§

It didn't take long. Father Michael Doyle called and wanted to talk. I was aware of the FBI's penchant for snooping and thought it would likely be directed at us, so I suggested he take the short trip on the Lindenwald Line from Camden to a stop a couple blocks from my office. We talked while walking around downtown because my office might be bugged. His Lindenwald Line trips and our walks became our mode of doing business. We never talked about the case on the phone or in my office.

"Bob Hardy talked to me yesterday, after the Sunday service," Michael said.

"What did he say?"

"Not much, but the way he looked at me said volumes. I think he's feeling really guilty."

"That seems appropriate."

"Yes, it does. But I didn't think I'd see him one on one like that so soon after the arrests."

"He's a member of your church?"

"Yes, I brought him into the church."

"Into Sacred Heart?"

"Yes and Catholicism."

"You converted him to Catholicism?"

"I did."

"He turned in to the FBI the priest who converted him to Catholicism?"

"He did." Michael stopped walking and looked up with an impish, almost devilish smile, although I know I should avoid allusions to the devil in descriptions of him. "How do you think I should deal with him?"

I thought a moment as we resumed walking. "Encourage further contact, but be careful not to push too hard or to forgive too easily or quickly. I'd like to get him to help us. From what everyone has said, he went way beyond informing. He was a provocateur. He could tell us a lot, or maybe he would repudiate them or even testify for us. We could find a way to relieve his guilt."

"I don't know if that's possible, but I'll try."

We walked quietly for a while. "What brought you to Camden?" I asked.

"Well, I knew my whole life that my older brother, Patrick, would inherit the family farm. It wasn't much. It provided five children and our parents enough to eat but no money. The common path for a second son is the priesthood. There weren't any positions at home for someone like me. I had attended a two-room school in a barn that was in the tradition of underground 'hedge' schools from the time not too long gone when educating Irish people was illegal. I was for export."

"The United States and Camden must have been quite a shock."

"I'll say. I left the farm in central Ireland only once before. I was 25 and knew a lot about rural poverty but little of the world.

"They sent me to teach in a Catholic high school in Cape May. I saw the Vietnamese efforts to forge their liberation as Moses leading his people nonviolently from oppression to liberty and as the Irish republicans so influential in my youth, although their path, like the Vietnamese, was not nonviolent. I spoke out in opposition, so I was sent, against my will, to a church in the inner city. I found my mission because of my opposition to the Vietnam War."

"But many oppose the war," I said. "Few risk all that is dear to them."

"I had to explain that to my mother, Roseta, back in Ireland. I wrote her from jail, told her a story told to me by Seamus MacEoin, a local republican leader. Fifty years before, two British soldiers were ambushed and killed by Irish republicans not far from our family farm. MacEoin told me he and another republican shot the soldiers. 'He was 22, and I was 22,' MacEoin said. 'We could have gone into Argah and had a drink together, but he was dead in the yard.'"

Michael paused, looking down at the sidewalk, then up to me. "Dead in the yard. It changed my illusions about the glory of the fight. This is what Jesus said in the Sermon on the Mount, although Christians have been slow to embrace it. You can't square the Vietnam War with the Sermon on the Mount."

"So how did you wind up ransacking a draft board in the middle of the night?"

"I favored the Berrigan style of open acts of resistance, but I accepted the group's decision to avoid detection and arrest. Still, I'm not sorry I was arrested."

§§§

Not long after, Michael called again. His voice was different. "David," he said slowly, "a terrible thing has happened. Bob Hardy's son, Billy, was in an accident. He climbed a tree and fell on some pointed metal fence posts. They went right through him. He's dying."

Michael came to my office, and we went for a walk. "I saw Bob and Peg, his wife, at the hospital," he said. "Bob can hardly speak. The strangest part of it is Billy was supposed to go out somewhere with Bob, but that morning Bob got a call from Sandy Grady, the columnist at the *Philadelphia Bulletin*, who came to Bob's house for an interview about our case. Bob told Billy they'd go out after the interview, and Billy went outside and climbed the tree."

Neither of us spoke for a moment. With all the religious talk and people around me in that period, I couldn't help but see a glimmer of fate or a vengeful God at work. "Does God operate like this, Michael?"

"I think Bob believes he does. He asked me to do the service if Billy dies."

"What did you say?"

"I said I would, of course. It's my job, and this is a time of need for Bob and Peg."

"Is it hard for you, being around him?"

"Yes, I can't fully tell him what I think of what he's done."

Billy died a few days later. We spoke frequently and got in a lot of walking time over the next several days and weeks, strategizing how Michael could move Hardy along.

"When you think he's ready," I told Michael, "get him talking and pick up on any regrets he has. Go slow. See if you can get him to meet with me. Maybe tell him your lawyer has an idea how he can make it right."

In the late fall, Michael came over the river very excited. "I mentioned you said you could make it right. He heard of you from some case you did that got on TV. He said he doesn't like lawyers but he would meet with you. He seemed willing but afraid."

"I'll have to go slow. Can you set up a meeting at a secure place? Tell him we'll just talk, no recordings, not even any notes."

§§§

"Dave, I'm very glad to meet you," Hardy said as Michael led him from the outside entrance into the room where Michael and I had waited anxiously.

I had driven in circles for an hour around Philadelphia and South Jersey to make sure I wasn't followed. I was excited and relieved that I was finally in a room with Hardy. "Glad to meet you, too, Bob."

"Let's sit here in the den," Michael said, pulling a stuffed chair for Bob closer to the sofa we sat on. "The O'Donnells, from my church, have let us use their home and this room that can't be seen from the street. They've gone away for the day, so we're alone. David and I came a half hour ago, so no one would see us all together."

We sat, somewhat uncomfortably looking at each other. "Well, Bob," I said, "Michael has told me how you and he have reconnected and how upset you are with the FBI about what happened."

"Yes, Dave. I want you to understand that from the beginning all I wanted to do was stop the raid. My friend Mike Giocondo and my priest here, Father Doyle, were headed on a dangerous path that I couldn't support. I wanted them stopped, not sent to jail for the rest of their lives."

"The FBI said they would stop it?"

"Yes, and I trusted them. I thought of them as upstanding guys."

Hardy sounded sincere. He saw his role as benevolent, and the breach of trust was by the FBI. He seemed to be deluding himself, but it also sounded like the FBI used him and that way of seeing it was important to him. I was listening carefully, trying to figure out what made him tick and how best to bring him to where he would publicly take our side. "Did they tell you particular times they would stop it?"

"Yes. I thought they would right away, but instead they told me to get into the group, and I wound up making the whole thing possible. The one time they definitely told me was at the dry run, a week or so before the raid. At the dry run, we did everything we planned except actually go in the building. I was furious when they didn't make the arrests, and I told them so."

"That's important, Bob, but I'd like to go back to the beginning. How did you get into it?"

"Mike Giocondo came to me one night, troubled. He told me about the plan to raid the draft board and their discovery by the FBI that day."

"This was at that meeting at Hi-Nella?"

"Yes. I told Mike those raids don't accomplish anything. The next afternoon, I went to the FBI office."

"Had you worked with the FBI before?"

"I gave them anonymous tips, but nothing like this. They said I should keep them posted."

"Had they discovered the plot?"

"Not really. An agent lived in the same apartment complex, saw them, and was suspicious. But I found that out later. They didn't give me any information in the beginning. They're very professional, and I'm very unprofessional. I always say what's on my mind."

"You're honest."

"Yeah, I have nothing to hide. The only thing dishonest about the whole thing is that I didn't tell my friends who I was. But they never asked me."

I wanted to know more about how he perceived himself and honesty, but I thought it best to let go of that line of thought. "What happened next?"

"I saw Mike later that day and went with him that night to pick up Grady at the bus station. I was part of the group from then on. Grady and the others are the finest group of Christian people I have ever been associated with."

"Did you get right into working on the raid?"

"Yeah. They had been working on it for a while and didn't even have a plan. Grady went on about all the draft boards that have been raided. But I could tell the problem right away. The other draft boards were much easier. They were inside jobs—they'd hide in the bathroom 'til after closing, or once I heard they waited in hammocks above a drop ceiling. But this one was on the fifth floor of a major building in downtown Camden—a serious burglary. They had no idea how to get into the draft board. If they did what they planned so far, they'd have gotten caught before they got into the building. They were incompetent when it came to this kind of job. I work construction, paint, do all sorts of jobs. I wouldn't let any of them work on a job for me."

"What had they planned so far?"

"Soon after meeting Grady, I went with Gene Dixon to check out the building. He took me to the fire escape and told me they would pull down the hanging bottom ladder and go up, but he said they didn't have a plan for getting in the fifth floor from the fire escape. I took one look at the fire escape and saw an alarm wire attached to the bottom ladder. If anyone pulled it down, an alarm would go off and police would be there in minutes."

"What did you suggest?"

"After that visit, I told them we'd make a tripod that would hold the bottom ladder up while we climbed onto it. Later, I decided to use ladders to go right to the lowest landing. That's what we did. Then I checked out the inside of the draft board—Dixon was amazed that I just walked into the office and started chatting with folks working there—and came out with enough rough measurements to draw a schematic of it. They were scared shitless to do something like that. The schematic was a big morale boost for the crowd."

I could see how this would boost morale, but he seemed to have no understanding that his romp in the building was hardly courageous, since he was working for the FBI. "So did you plan more of it?"

"Yeah. I figured we could get in from the fire escape with a portable drill and a glass bit. You tape the glass nearest the inside lock and then drill a semicircle of holes big enough for a hand. Put a block of wood on it and hit it with a mallet so the glass breaks. The glass sticks to the tape. You pull the tape out with the glass and reach in and unlock the door."

"And I got the tools and equipment—the ladders, walkie-talkies, portable drill. They were going to drill out the locks on the file cabinets, which would take a long time. I told them to use pry bars 'cause there wasn't much to those cabinets, and I got the pry bars for them. I trained them to climb the ladders quickly and safely, like my days in marine boot camp. I was afraid they'd hurt themselves if I didn't teach 'em. I also brought a couple bags of groceries to the group each week."

"You fed them?"

"Yup."

"Did the FBI know all this?"

"Sure. It wouldn't have happened without me, and I told my FBI guys that all the time. I reported regularly to my FBI control agents, Mike Ryman and Terry Neist, often in daily meetings at a diner early in the morning. They understood it's difficult for a guy like me not to assume leadership."

"Were you reimbursed for money you spent on the raid?"

"They paid for it all and gave me my usual working rate for my time. I'd tell them what I'd bought and how much time I'd spent, and they'd give it to me in cash once a week or so. I'd sign some FBI receipt for the cash."

"You told them you were taking a leadership role?"

"Yeah. That wasn't a problem. They wanted me to do it, and they wanted to know everything I could find out, particularly about Grady. He was their main target. They thought he did that Media raid, but I don't think so from what he said. I told them there was a constant battle beneath the surface between John and me for leadership. Neither of us is the submissive type. After a few weeks, I was in command or at least equal to John."

"They paid for the groceries, too?"

"Every last potato chip."

§§§

We met several more times, always at private places arranged by Michael and preceded by an hour riding in circles to avoid detection by the FBI. Hardy was increasingly at ease and didn't mind my taking notes and then recording some sessions. I had everything we needed if he testified at trial to what he told me, but I felt it was all vulnerable.

Hardy was with us now, but I could imagine swings back and forth. He wanted to be respected and liked by both sides. I came to like him, and I didn't doubt his sincerity about feeling guilty and wanting to do something to make it right or his courage in doing so. No doubt that finding meaning in Billy's death pushed him our way as well. But he was an insecure guy who tended to place himself at the center of every story he told and to exaggerate his role and status. He didn't understand the enormity of what he'd done and had strange rationales for it. His need to see himself as powerful and a leader was a major factor in everything that had happened, including his swing our way. My thoughts regularly came back to his turning in his priest who converted him to Catholicism. If he really just wanted to stop the raid, he could have told Michael and his good friend Mike Giocondo that if they continued he would go to the FBI. He sure didn't need to make the raid happen.

I worried that the longer this went on, the more likely the FBI would find out. They weren't keeping close contact with him, which seemed stupid on their part, but they did call him once in a while, and they visited when Billy was in the hospital and came to the funeral service. The service looked like a joint FBI-Camden 28 affair. Hardy liked to talk and viewed them as his friends. It might come out that way, or someone might see us or overhear something.

If the FBI found out, they would at least pressure him to water down his testimony about his role. Then there was the dark side of the FBI's history with movements and whistle-blowers to consider—the "counter-intelligence" and the "black bag jobs" that included phony documents, shootings, and anything else necessary to discredit or eliminate opponents. The FBI's COINTELPRO included provoking a street gang in Chicago to go after the Black Panthers by forwarding phony threats to gang members that purported to come from the Panthers. In the mid-1970s the leading whistle-blower against the nuclear power industry, Karen Silkwood, drove off a road and died in suspicious circumstances while on her way to meet an investigative reporter for the *New York Times*. Hardy might be institutionalized with phony claims about his mental stability or worse. The scenarios swirled through my imagination. Hardy and our defense looked good but were at risk.

"Bob," I said as we sat down for a meeting in a house in Woodbury, New Jersey, "I've been thinking about the trial, and I'm concerned because it's so far away. The FBI could find out about our meetings, and they'd put a lot of pressure on you. Anyway, you know how fragile and unpredictable life is. You could be in an accident or get ill. The best way to make sure that you have set things right like you want to do is to put your story in a sworn affidavit. Then it's there, preserved. I'll hold on to it. If anything happens, I can use it to make sure Michael and Mike don't spend the rest of their lives in jail."

"I guess that's alright. You know, this is a matter of spirit to me. It's Billy living on. So I want to do what's right."

His connection of this to Billy was helpful. I was personally uneasy about it, but this wasn't the time or occasion for discussing what God does or doesn't do. "So let's go through it all again and set out what we want in the affidavit. Then I'll write it up, and I'll use almost all your words from what I have on tape and in my notes and what I remember from these meetings."

"That's good."

It was easier than I thought to convince him; it seemed to make him more comfortable. I typed out a draft and then edited it and made some more changes after showing it to Hardy. I destroyed the typewriter's carbon ribbons because they contained everything I wrote, strung out like the lines in a telegram. I did it all myself. No one in the office but Rudy knew, and I wanted to keep it that way.

But I needed the affidavit notarized, and the notary had to be present when Hardy actually signed. The result was the midnight meeting under the Walt Whitman Bridge recounted in the introduction. We made three signed and notarized copies. Hardy took one; I kept one hidden in another case file in the office; hid the other inside a wallboard wall I was building on the third floor of our house; and sent a Xerox of it to a friend in another state to hold in a sealed envelope.

About a week later, we met with Hardy again. "We're filing pretrial motions in the case in the next week or so, Bob, and I've thought of a motion we can file now to ask the judge to throw out the case based on your affidavit. There wouldn't have to be a trial or any more delay for Michael or you."

"I thought the affidavit was in case I die or something."

"That was what we had in mind. But I researched the possibility of a motion to dismiss the indictment on the ground that the government made the action happen, through you. It's unusual to hear it pretrial, but there's a basis for it in the legal research I've done."

"Wouldn't that be public, if you file it?"

"Yeah. There would be publicity, but you could just say you are going to testify in court, not in the media. You don't have to say anything to them. And this way, not only would the affidavit preserve your vital testimony, but it would be a matter of official record, since it would be filed in the court with the motion. Press stories that quote the affidavit would solidify that and make it harder for the FBI to repudiate your testimony or you personally."

"I guess so."

"It could be over sooner rather than later, Bob."

"Okay, go ahead."

I didn't want to use the affidavit this way unless Hardy knew and agreed, although from the beginning I wanted to file the affidavit as soon as possible to insulate Hardy and his testimony from challenge. Once it was filed and public, there was little the FBI could do about it, and Hardy would be committed to its content. He was tentative, but he agreed.

I gave an advance copy to the *New York Times* reporter in the Philadelphia area, who agreed to hold the story until the affidavit was actually filed. His story ran on the front page of the *Times:* "The FBI Is Accused of Aiding a Crime, 'Camden 28' Informer Says He Acted as 'Provocateur.'"[4]

§§§

After I filed the Hardy affidavit, the case got a lot of national publicity but then slowed down. It didn't look like it could go to trial before 1973. I kept in regular touch with Hardy—I wasn't going to make the same mistake the FBI did—but otherwise I was able to return to other work. In the fall of 1972, Rudy and I were talking about our cases, as we did constantly, when he asked, "Did you see the Supremes granted cert. in that case you're using in Camden, *Russell v. United States*?"

"No, I haven't looked at *Law Week* this week." "Cert." was short for certiorari. The Supreme Court decided which cases they would review, and lawyers asked them to review a case by filing a petition for writ of certiorari.

"Yeah, *Russell* should get the Court into some of those issues you've been dealing with."

"It will, but that probably won't help us."

"Which one is *Russell*?"

"It's out of Washington State, the Ninth Circuit. A government agent supplied a necessary and hard-to-get chemical the defendants needed to make an illegal drug, and then the government busted the defendants for possessing and manufacturing the drug."

"Good entrapment defense, but they had that predisposition problem."

"Yeah, you know, there isn't any opening in the Supreme Court cases—the entrapment defense is available only to a defendant who is 'otherwise innocent,' not one 'predisposed' to commit the crime, which usually means in practice one who has an earlier conviction for a similar offense. In every case entrapment is raised, the defendants have not walked away—they're all predisposed in the sense that, given the government's enticement, they went along. It's almost like saying the government is allowed to entrap defendants who did something similar before."

"And your folks did it before," Rudy said, smiling.

"Some of them did. I wasn't worried about this because the last Supreme Court case on it was in 1958, and in between there has been a tendency to downplay predisposition, like Justice Frankfurter spelled out in dissents in the early cases. Several lower courts have dropped predisposition or adopted another defense and given it another name—'creative' or 'overreaching' government activity. I can easily say there is a recent trend in the law, unless the Court overrules *Russell* and the rest of the trend and goes back to 1958. That's the way things are going with Rehnquist et al. these days."[5]

"Yeah. Maybe it won't be decided 'til after Camden is done."

"But it could be, even if the trial starts in early 1973. Maybe I should try to affect the *Russell* decision."

"How?"

"I don't know. Maybe an amicus brief, if I could put together one with enough clout that the Supremes would pay attention. You know how we've wanted to get our NECLC and the ACLU more cooperative. This could be an occasion and could draw attention coming from both."

"It seems a long shot, and it's a lot of work."

"I'd like to write a brief on predisposition anyway, and I could argue that, even if they stick with predisposition, there should be some exception for the worst government provoked or manufactured crimes."

§§§

"This entrapment nonsense is demeaning to us and the whole movement," said Ed McGowan, one of the Jesuits from New York, "and the lawyers are taking over."

"I don't think so, Ed," said Mel Madden, a former priest who ran a state drug rehab program in New Jersey. "We've got a way to possibly win, and it's a political defense, like nullification. This is what governments do when they want to sustain a brutal, unnecessary war built on deception."

"I'll have none of it," Grady said. "We didn't need Hardy. It's built on a lie, and it'll undercut nullification."

They went back and forth in a heated discussion at this last big meeting of defendants and lawyers before the trial, as they had in discussions since the Hardy affidavit. I was feeling like the sizable elephant in the room. I didn't set out or anticipate this role for me in the group or the trial. But I had come up with a defense that could actually win for a group of defendants whose most outspoken and forceful members opposed it.

Most of the defendants saw the overreaching defense as a political defense that could win and didn't want a conviction or jail time. But they weren't used to challenging their leaders, particularly angry leaders. I had also gotten into heated discussions with some of them, so I thought a lot and talked over strategies with some defendants before this meeting about how we could minimize the confrontation and establish some ground rules for the trial.

"I think it's obvious now that we have two different ways to see the trial among the defendants," I said, "and we're not going to change that, no matter how much we talk about it. More of this discussion would only cement more disunity. What I suggest is that either you make an agreement among yourselves that nobody will do anything to undercut anybody else's defense or we move to sever some defendants, who would be tried later in a separate trial if the judge allows a severance. Mel, if you want to use the overreaching defense in addition to nullification, but John, you say in the trial that Hardy's affidavit and major role in making it happen are a lie, you'll both lose and undercut the principles and movement that got you all here. What I suggest is that we go around the room and each defendant say whether he or she agrees not to undermine the defenses of the others. If you all agree to that, fine, but it has to be everybody. If not, we should consider a motion to sever some defendants for a separate trial."

There was silence for a moment. "I want us to stay in this together," Michael said. "That's so important. I hope we can agree not to undercut each other. I want to try the overreaching defense, but I also want all of us to go on trial together."

"Let's stick together. If we divide, the government wins," said Joan Reilly, who was a college student and hitchhiked to Camden to help the day of the raid. Several others agreed.

I thought I better not say anything more. I noticed, as I'm sure a lot of the others did, that no one spoke against the proposal. After awhile, Mel Madden spoke again. "Instead of going around the room, what I'd like to do is just ask, is any defendant going to undercut either of the two defenses?"

No one spoke. Several, including me, looked toward Grady and the Jesuits, all of whom sat quietly. We were ready to go.

§§§

"My wife and I were assured by the FBI," Hardy said from the witness box of the packed large courtroom on the third floor of the U.S. courthouse, the same building the Camden 28 broke into, "that they would stop the raid, our friends would be charged only with a conspiracy, and our friends would not go to jail."

"Your FBI control agents told you they would not go to jail?" I asked.

"Yes, my friends would not receive any jail time."

"If you thought this was not so, that they would spend over a week in jail after the arrest and that the Justice Department would seriously seek to imprison them for 47 years, would you have continued your involvement?"

"I would not."

"I object to the question," John Barry said in a huff. "It calls for speculation." Barry, tall and solidly built with dark hair and an often angry, sometimes beady-eyed look, headed the team of five prosecutors from the New Jersey U.S. attorney's office who were trying the Camden 28 case.

"He answered it," Judge Fisher said. Clarkson Fisher was the second judge assigned to the case. The first was known as among the more liberal on the federal bench in New Jersey, but he disqualified himself for reasons I never understood. Fisher was known as a tough, proprosecution judge who often handed out long sentences, but he was also fair and respectful to all in the courtroom.

Fisher made it clear early on that he wanted no confrontations with the defense. He had ruled for the government on almost all of the pretrial motions, refusing to give us even reports on Hardy's meetings with his FBI control agents. But then he granted some of our unusual motions about the conduct of the trial, hoping, I thought, this would make confrontation unlikely. He allowed defendants and lawyers to be "cocounsel," so both could be actively representing the defense in the trial. There is a right to self-representation, but the cocounsel arrangement was unusual if not unique. I started as counsel for Michael and Mel Madden, but after this ruling I became cocounsel to them and three other defendants, and the trial proceeded as if I and the other lawyers were cocounsel to all the defendants. A month or so into the trial, Fisher also appointed Marty, Carl, and me to represent defendants who could not afford to pay an attorney. I had been getting only $75 a week to live on from the Camden 28 Defense Committee; this meant I'd get a real fee.

One of the defendants made a motion that the jurors be allowed to ask questions since they are the ones who have to make the decision. Fisher granted it although there was no precedent for it. I thought he was appeasing us on something he didn't imagine would have much significance. If you're used to jurors being silent and passive in trials, it could easily appear they would play the same role if told they could ask questions. But they didn't. Once unleashed, they asked some good questions, and Fisher had to institute a procedure for juror questions that would allow for objections out of the hearing of the jury. We said we wouldn't object to any juror question.

The trial started on February 5, 1973, but it wasn't until April 10 that Hardy took the stand. The prosecution didn't call him as a witness. They spent over two months proving what the Camden 28 openly and proudly announced—they raided the draft board and destroyed draft records. I said in my opening argument to the jury that the prosecution case was going to be "a waste of time." The jurors looked at me skeptically then, but by the end of the prosecution's case they looked bored.

Hardy was the second defense witness. Our first witness got the jury's attention: Michael beautifully testified about his beloved Ireland, his view of the war, and his reasons for raiding the draft board.

Hardy started with the events that got him into the Camden 28 group and the next day into the FBI office. He detailed his role—the plans used to pull off the raid, the tools and equipment, schematic drawings of the draft board office, the training, the morale boost that revived a dead or dying plot, the groceries. Barry interrupted him several times with objections that seemed mostly aimed at interfering with the flow of the testimony and jarring Hardy. The judge denied all the objections, and Hardy was straightforward and believable.

I had thought a lot about how I could most convincingly bring home to the jurors what Hardy and the FBI had done. Now it was time. "Mr. Hardy, I have in front of me all of the tools that the defendants were caught with inside the draft board. These are the burglary tools the FBI agents testified were used to break into the draft board office in the middle of the night. I'm going to show you each one and ask you where it came from and who paid for it. Then I'm going to make two piles with these items on the floor directly in front of the jury. One pile will be items you or the FBI provided or paid for; the other will be items the defen-

dants provided or paid for. Include in the second pile—the defendants'
pile—items that you are uncertain about or that you can't say for sure
were provided by you or the FBI."

"Okay."

"One thing before we start. Your own personal tools that you gave to
the defendants, were you reimbursed for them?"

"Yes, I was reimbursed for anything at all that I provided."

"So if you say an item was from your shop and you provided it to the
defendants, that also means the FBI reimbursed you and paid for it?"

"That's right."

"Okay. Exhibit G-11. What is this?"

"These are bolt cutters. I bought them."

"You bought them for the defendants to use, and the FBI reimbursed
you, so these go in the FBI pile?"

"Right."

"How about these three screwdrivers, Exhibits G-608, 609, and 604?"

"The black-handled one, 604, is my own personal screwdriver. The
other two were bought."

"So the FBI pile. How about G-615?"

"These are utility knives, several of them. One was mine, and the others were bought."

"And this, G-610?"

"It's a plumb hammer. That was bought."

"G-659?"

"This is duct tape that we used from the fifth-floor fire escape to tape
over the glass before we drilled it and broke it out. This is my personal
tape."

"G-707, 102, and 104?"

"Walkie-talkies. These I purchased, and the FBI paid me."

"Okay. D-101?"

"A prying tool. Purchased."

"D-111?"

"Two drill bits for glass. I didn't buy these. I told them what to get and
where to get it, but I think they paid."

"D-103?"

"A portable drill. That isn't mine, but I gave it to them."

"How about D-100?"

"This is my rope, a long rope."

I went through all the items with Hardy until the piles on the floor were complete. The FBI pile had a large number and variety of tools and equipment, covering a lot of the rug in front of the jury. The defendants' pile had two drill bits, a small flat piece of metal, and a small V-8 juice can.

I walked to the piles on the floor and picked up Exhibit D-103. "Mr. Hardy, this portable drill you had me put in the FBI pile, whose is it?"

"That drill belongs to an FBI agent."

"An FBI agent. How did it get here?"

"My plan required one of those new kind of drills, portable, run by battery, but I couldn't find one in stores around here. The group had waited for me to get them one. A few days before the raid, I called my FBI guys and told them I had to have a portable drill right away or the action would be called off. They told me to meet later that day at a parking lot we used in Merchantville. My lead control agent, Mike Ryman, met me there. I asked him where he got the portable drill. He said one of the FBI agents in the office had one in his personal shop. That agent went home to get it so Agent Ryman could give it to me and I could give it to the defendants."

§§§

"Mr. Hardy," said John Barry, who started his cross-examination with an intense, disbelieving tone and look, "during the course of your direct examination you corrected certain statements you made in your affidavit, did you not?"

"That's correct," Hardy replied.

"Was the significance of making a statement under oath explained to you?"

"Not really. David didn't go into that explicitly, I don't think, but I know what it means."

"What do you understand a sworn statement in an affidavit to mean?"

"To tell the truth as you know it and as you can recall it," Hardy replied. "No intentional lies. If there is a mistake, it's because I am only human and I can only remember so much."

"In the affidavit you say you were given a 'small cash amount' by the FBI in addition to payments for your time and expenses."

"Yes."

"In point of fact you received $5,000."

"That's true."

"In the discussions about the affidavit, did Mr. Kairys or Father Doyle say what they believed the key points were?"

"They did at times, but I disagreed with them."

"But you say it is 'almost all written in my words.'"

"It is. That's how David did it. There are some terms that aren't quite my normal vocabulary."

"How about 'civil disobedience'?"

"I knew what that was. I'm against it, 'cause it's breaking the law."

"How about 'provocateur'?"

"That's my word. I read it in *Time* or *Newsweek*; that's what they called me. It's French. It stuck with me 'cause I didn't like it. But that's what I unknowingly became, like the affidavit says."

"But the magazine articles were after the affidavit. They reported on the affidavit being filed."

"You're right. I can't say one way or the other who first used that word."

Barry went on like this, also pointing out that things were provided by others, but they were minor and mostly not among the tools used to get inside the draft board. My piles weren't dented.

I was mostly concerned about the questions he would ask about one of the defendants shoplifting to get things they needed. This could undercut our high moral plane. So I requested that the judge hear argument on it out of the presence of the jury.

"Judge, we have discussed and you have partially ruled on evidence of prior crimes. We understand your ruling that since we have raised entrapment and that defense isn't available to a defendant who is 'predisposed,' Mr. Barry can introduce evidence of participation in prior draft board raids to show predisposition. But he wants to ask Mr. Hardy questions about a defendant shoplifting. We should first find out if Mr. Barry intends to ask questions about that."

"I do," Barry said.

"Hardy is the sole support for the defendants and action," Judge Fisher said, "according to him."

"He didn't say he was the sole support," I said.

"Just about as much. Mr. Barry is entitled to inquire into that. Do you have proof of it, Mr. Barry?"

"I have proof."

"Proof," Grady said, "or hearsay?"

Judge Fisher leaned back in his chair and paused for a moment. "Hardy has given the inference to the jury that he is the sole support."

"He didn't say sole support," I said.

"Forty bucks a week for food according to Hardy," Grady said, smiling. "I couldn't feed my family on 40 bucks a week."

"I know I can't," Fisher said, "the way those boys eat. Hardy opened the door way wide."

Ed McGowan, a Jesuit priest from New York, rose. "But, Judge, that's beside the point. I'm amazed that Barry would bring this up." He glared at Barry.

"Well, I'm amazed at you. I'm amazed—"

"You must be desperate," McGowan said, shaking his head.

Barry silently looked down at the prosecution table in front of him, perhaps realizing that he had just gotten into a high school–level debate with McGowan about who is more amazed. "Your Honor, I'm entitled to bring out the whole truth, which is what the defendants say they want. They think that means only their truth about the war. Certain defendants call this an antiwar trial. In fact, it has been an anti-FBI, anti–Justice Department trial."

"That's pretty good," Grady said. "They are part of the military."

"Judge, if I may," I said. "It is relevant that other people provided resources. It is not important or relevant how they got those resources, particularly if, as the Third Circuit rulings make clear, that introduces prejudicial evidence. As I understand it, Mr. Barry wants to make a big deal of one incident where some defendant allegedly was caught shoplifting camping equipment. You have to weigh the prejudice against the probative value that some resource not only was provided, which is not objectionable, but also may have been acquired by shoplifting."

"All that has to be said is that food was taken from another source," McGowan said.

Barry continued going through Hardy's expenses "to clarify what was supplied to the defendants." He questioned details like Hardy's reimbursed expenses for damage to his truck and gas to run it, to which defendant Bob Good interjected, "He supplied the truck and the gas for that. I would say that fell into that category." When Barry again tried to get Hardy to testify about what he had heard about shoplifting, Fisher sustained our objections. This is how it went for more than a day of Barry's cross-examination of Hardy, with all the defendants and lawyers arguing most everything, and how it went generally for the four-month trial.

§§§

Judge Fisher allowed us to explain to the jury what the defendants thought of the war and why they chose to resist it by raiding a draft board. This was consistent with the trend in antiwar cases and included testimony by experts and others that showed the background for the defendants' beliefs and motivations, or their "state of mind." He allowed more than most, but in his charge to the jury at the end of the trial, Fisher, like other judges, told them that the defendants' motivations or beliefs were not an allowable defense and the jurors should not acquit on that basis.

It was quite a show. After Hardy's affidavit and with public sentiments shifting against the war, the case drew national media attention. The defendants' testimony was moving, and we recruited an impressive array of other witnesses on the war and the FBI's role in making the raid happen. Robert J. Lifton, a well-known Yale professor of psychology, testified about the plight of Vietnam veterans. Frank Donner, a friend of mine, was a leading authority on informers and law enforcement. Clement St. Martin, a former head of the New Jersey Induction Center, to whom the Camden Draft Board sent its inductees, testified that he would not send any soldier to the Vietnam War.

The most moving testimony was by defendant Bob Good's mother, Betty, who passed away during the writing of this book. She told the jury about being informed that Bob's brother, Paul, had died in Vietnam, and she reacted angrily to hearing, by chance, the witness before her testifying about the purposes of the war as revealed in the Pentagon Papers. Cookie asked historian Howard Zinn to testify about civil disobedience and the leaked secret government study on the war. Betty, looking directly at the jury with a mother's grief about one son, concern and support for another on trial, and pride in both, said it was horrible to hear that her son had died not to stop communism or to bring about freedom but to secure "tin, rubber and oil."[6]

§§§

In the fourth month of the trial, which spanned midwinter to mid-May, we finally got to the jury instructions. The judge's charge to the jury is regularly hotly contested ground in criminal and civil jury trials. Much of it is routine and set out in boilerplate instructions, like the elements of the crime of breaking into a federal building. But a lot depends on the evidence that has been presented and on the issues in a case, about which the parties usually differ. Jury instructions were particularly important in the Camden 28 case.

By the end of the prosecution's case and Hardy's testimony, we had stripped away prosecutors' usual bedrock advantage. Jurors come to trials with the assumption that the authorities have acted, as the jurors intend to act, in good faith and with the purpose of fairly enforcing the law. While they are usually aware that criminal defendants are presumed innocent until proven guilty—and know how a good juror responds when asked about the presumption of innocence during jury voir dire—jurors also assume or suspect that a person charged with a crime probably did something wrong. Jurors' assumptions of regularity and guilt are the first and often foremost challenge to any criminal defense. We deprived this prosecution of both and of its pretensions to legitimacy. Our cross-examination of the FBI witnesses, Hardy's testimony, and the failure of the prosecutors to come back with any evidence to rebut Hardy established that the government wanted this crime to happen and did everything it could to make the crime happen. This case was about a government attempt to imprison and publicly undermine its political opponents rather than to enforce the law.

The hurdle that remained was the jurors' perception of what the defendants had done. They didn't just picket or circulate petitions—this was hardly free speech, although it said a lot. The defendants broke into a federal building in the middle of the night, during wartime and with the goal of impeding the war effort. A hung jury or maybe a jury compromise that acquitted at least some of the defendants, most likely the local ones, seemed within reach. But acquittal of all of the defendants on all counts required that all 12 jurors agree to the ultimate not-guilty verdict. Some jurors were probably there already, but getting them all there required a basis for acquittal that was convincing and they could live with. Particularly in widely publicized cases, this can have a lot to do with how jurors perceive the reactions of their families and communities to an unusual verdict. The more a ground for acquittal was familiar and easily understood, the better.

"Judge Fisher," I said, "I've informed you and kept you posted about a pending Supreme Court case on entrapment and overreaching government activity, *United States v. Russell*. As you know, the Supreme Court decided *Russell* just a few weeks ago. They rejected the recent trend in the lower courts away from the predisposition rule and reaffirmed the old Supreme Court cases from the 1950s and earlier.

"But they also said there could be an exception, that predisposition could be irrelevant in an extraordinary case if the government goes too far. Justice Rehnquist put it this way in the majority opinion: '[W]e may some day be presented with a situation in which the conduct of law enforcement is so outrageous that [it] would absolutely bar the government from invoking judicial processes to obtain a conviction.' Rehnquist went on to characterize the kind of law enforcement conduct that might fall into this exception as 'violating fundamental fairness [and] shocking to the universal sense of justice.'[7]

"You also know that the ACLU and the National Emergency Civil Liberties Committee filed an amicus brief in the *Russell* case for the precise reason that, if the Court should reject the recent trend away from predisposition, there should at least be an exception stated. You have seen this brief, which I wrote with an ACLU attorney. It stresses that predisposition would be least appropriate and an exception would be most appropriate in political cases where the defendants are political opponents of the government prosecuting them. The clearest example of this—the amicus brief says—is this case. The brief sets out what Mr. Hardy swore to in his affidavit, with long quotes from the affidavit. And this is the first time in any of the Supreme Court cases in this area that the Court held that there is any exception to the predisposition rule.

"The facts presented to the Supreme Court from the affidavit are the same as the testimony here, and it's unrebutted. Mr. Barry hasn't rebutted any of those facts. In *Russell,* the Supreme Court was worried that cases like the Camden 28 were coming along, and they did not want to close off the possibility of an exception. This is the case, this is the exception."

"The exception, as Mr. Kairys calls it," Barry said, "is not in the terms proposed by the ACLU and is about extreme measures like torture, not this case at all." The exception was not in the terms we proposed, and the "shocking to the conscience" language was from older cases dealing with extreme measures, although not limited to torture. This was a problem, but Fisher was more concerned about another aspect of it.

"Even if I accept your view of the exception, Mr. Kairys," Fisher said, "there is still the question of whether Rehnquist meant the issue would be decided by the jury or the court."

Barry said, accurately, "No adherent in the courts of the 'creative or overreaching activity' approach has suggested that a jury should grapple with this issue. In the dissents in the older Supreme Court cases that favored that approach, they discussed it as a question to be resolved by judges."

This was a hard question for our side. Barry, and Fisher, stated the usual understanding on such issues. Whether the government conduct was "shocking to the universal sense of justice" was something judges decided based on what was called their "supervisory" powers over the courts. I couldn't cite any contrary precedent. And I knew, as Barry knew, that Fisher wouldn't decide this issue our way. Even if Fisher thought the FBI overreached, I doubted that he'd throw out the case. He had protected the FBI from what I thought would be its greatest embarrassment by refusing to give us access to Hardy's reports made to his FBI control agents, although such reports were regularly provided in criminal cases. He wouldn't personally repudiate the FBI or the Nixon administration that way, and even if he thought they deserved it, he wouldn't take such a bold action that would undoubtedly become big national news. I thought the best way of arguing it was to tap into what he and I both knew—since he wouldn't or couldn't do it no matter how strong the evidence, he should at least allow the jury to decide.

"The whole defense is a new one," I said. "It is a case of first instance. But it is pretty clear what you should do. I think the people should decide this issue. If you are not going to throw this case out, as I think it should be, then I think those 12 people in that box have to be given the right."

After much argument and apparently agonizing thought, Fisher announced his rulings on the jury instructions. He did so in advance of closing arguments, as judges usually do, so everyone could frame their closings to take into account what he would tell the jury at the end. It was mostly standard instructions that didn't help us.

"The defendants' motives," Fisher told the jury, "in no way provide a defense or a justification for any acts that you find were committed by them. The law does not recognize religious or moral motives or higher law for the commission of a crime, no matter how noble. I charge you that you may not treat the defendants' beliefs with respect to the war in Vietnam, or other possible injustices to which you have heard references, as a possible negation of criminal intent. The motivations, the fact that defendants were engaged in a protest in the sincere belief that they acted in a good cause, are not an acceptable legal defense or justification."

Fisher admitted to making a mistaken statement late in the trial to the effect that the jury doesn't have the power to nullify, but what he said was muddled, and he didn't explain its significance. He did rule that we could openly address nullification in our closing arguments, which was un-usual and significant. Nullification was generally treated as the big truth about jury trials that no one is permitted to mention.

Fisher defined entrapment in the usual way and told the jury it was not available as a defense if they find the defendants were predisposed, which everyone knew they were. But then he said this: "There is another defense. You have heard the terms *creative activity* and *overreaching governmental participation*. The evidence focused to a great extent on the ac-tivities of Robert Hardy. You must determine what role Hardy played. If you find that overreaching participation by government agents or in-formers was fundamentally unfair and shocking to the universal sense of justice, then you may acquit the defendants. And under this particular defense you need not consider the predisposition of any defendant."

There it was, right out of the *Russell* exception.

§§§

I was in front of the jury, focused on the 24 eyes looking straight at me, with the two piles of tools on the rug between us as they had been during Hardy's testimony. "I guess you could tell it was my turn," I began. "You had to step over all the tools and all my toys."[8]

"We have set some records in this case, with both the number and va-riety of witnesses. I've been told that I set my own personal record by wearing a white shirt each one of the 59 days of the trial. I just want to assure you that it wasn't the same shirt."

It felt good to see smiles on their faces. I set out the two defenses, then said, "The question is who went too far. Did the government of the United States go too far in the war in Vietnam? Did the defendants go too far in their resistance to that war? Did the FBI go too far in manufacturing and provoking a crime?"

I went through the testimony of the FBI agents in detail, looking for an answer to another basic question: Why would the FBI wait while people enter a government building and destroy files in a draft board? The explanations offered by the FBI—that it was all driven by concerns for safety and locating the defendants—were belied by their own and Hardy's unrebutted testimony. The FBI had sufficient evidence and many opportunities when all the defendants were gathered at one place.

I had cross-examined all of the FBI agents along these lines. I asked Agent Ziel, who some on the defense side nicknamed "Overzeal," "Did you do anything to stop the destruction of files or the entrance into the board?"

"Nothing," he answered. Ziel and the other agents testified that decisions to arrest or not to arrest were made by higher-ups in the FBI or government. And the prosecution did not call any witnesses for rebuttal, which was their opportunity to dispute anything we presented in the defense, including Hardy's testimony.

I then turned to the "legally recognized" defense of overreaching government participation, which Judge Fisher would recognize in his jury charge. "No one has argued that Mr. Hardy overcame anybody's will or became a leader in a moral or political sense," I said. Nor did we contest that the defendants were "predisposed," which was the issue on which Barry was allowed to bring in evidence of prior draft raids. I reviewed Hardy's testimony and Barry's cross-exmination of Hardy in detail.

"Would the crimes likely have happened without the FBI and without the informer? The nature of the assistance provided is important. Was it incidental, or did it include major strategies, planning, overcoming obstacles, boosting morale, training? How intense was the government participation, and was the same assistance available from other sources? Had the defendants abandoned the plan, out of frustration with the lack of strategies and plans and their discovery by the FBI during one of their meetings, and how and by whom was it revived?

"You should remember, when the prosecution decries violations of law or destruction of property, or coming in secret in the middle of the night, that they could have stopped every single violation of the law or destruction of property that occurred in this case. When Hardy came to them, the plot was over. All they had to do was nothing. It was over.

"Neither the FBI nor the defendants placed any value on those pieces of paper in the draft board office. To the defendants, they were nonliving matter that had no right to exist. To the FBI, they were part of the machinery of war but a part of that machinery that was expendable to discredit antiwar movements.

"For the American people and for yourselves, I hope you won't rubber-stamp what the FBI did in this case. That's what Mr. Barry is going to be asking you to do.

"Let me move on to the second reason these defendants should be acquitted, 'nullification,' although that is too negative a term for what it stands for—the power of a jury to acquit if they believe a particular law is oppressive or if they believe that a law is fair but to apply it in certain circumstances would be oppressive.

"The second situation, where the application could be oppressive, is something like the Boston Tea Party. No one would say that breaking into a ship or destroying tea shouldn't be criminal. But should those defendants, who captured the spirit of their new nation, be convicted of any crime?

"This power that juries have is the reason why we have you jurors sitting there instead of computers. You are supposed to be the conscience of the community. You are supposed to decide if the law, as the judge explains it to you, should or should not be applied in these circumstances. Nothing the judge will say to you is inconsistent with this power.

"This is not a request on our part that you show any disrespect for the law. It's an essential part of the law. It's as essential as reasonable doubt. You decide what to do with the law the judge explains. You decide, considering the circumstances of the case, whether you should brand the defendants as criminal. You are only required to say 'guilty' or 'not guilty'; you don't decide that they did it or they didn't do it. You don't have to give reasons or justifications, and if it's 'not guilty,' it can't be reviewed by any court.

"Are they criminals or not? Are they deserving of the community's scorn—you being the community? That's the question.

"The defendants violated the law and destroyed property. They explained to you that they did this to preserve life and to preserve liberty.

That may sound radical, but I submit that it's in the best American tradition. It starts, of course, with George Washington, Thomas Jefferson, and Ben Franklin, all of whom violated the law to preserve life and liberty.

"The Boston Tea Party was a violation of the law to preserve life and liberty. There's that statue I've discussed in a town square in Cumberland County, New Jersey, for a participant in a New Jersey tea party who was elected governor after juries refused to indict or convict him.

"The underground railroad violated the Fugitive Slave Act, which required the return of escaped slaves. It was also done in darkness, in the middle of the night. They did not stand up and say 'arrest me for it.'

"Rosa Parks violated the law by sitting in the front of a bus. It was the beginning of the civil rights movement. Martin Luther King, Jr., and Daniel Ellsberg, who released the Pentagon Papers, violated laws to preserve life and liberty. All were called radical and condemned, particularly in their own time.

"Think about the philosophies, morals, and principles of living you heard expressed by these defendants, from their own mouths. Nonviolence, thou shalt not kill, life being more important than property, the liberty all peoples deserve, having the courage of your convictions. We've all heard these things from people we hold dear, and those of you who have children have probably said the same things to your children. The main difference between the people on trial here and the rest of us—and I include myself—is that they risked acting on these things we all believe.

"They explained the careful, sometimes painful process of change that brought them here. It involved no disrespect for law. They saw a conflict between law and morality, between law and life. They believed the Declaration of Independence when it says: 'Governments and laws are a means to an end, not an end in themselves.' They made the same choices we would want people to make throughout history, the same choices that we would want German people to make when Jews were being killed, the same choices we would want Americans to make when black people were in slavery.

"The Vietnamese are not less deserving of our concern. And acquittal in this case will not lead to chaos or undermine society. It will enrich it, just as we all feel our society was enriched by those American jurors who refused to convict people for violating the Fugitive Slave Act. I think everybody in this room can say, 'I'm proud that American jurors did that.'

"If this society cannot tolerate the tearing up of papers or the violation of law, how can it tolerate the napalming of a child? How can we reconcile that? Last Christmas we heard our government proclaim peace on earth while they were bombing Bach Mai Hospital in Hanoi.

"It's in the best tradition of this country, of every country, to resist this nonviolently, not to stand by. And that's what these defendants did.

"You must decide who went too far. Did the government go too far in prosecuting the war? Did the defendants go too far? Did the FBI go too far? Those kinds of judgments really require you to look at and in some sense judge yourselves. The prosecution is asking you to brand these people as criminals. If that's done, it will be done in your name. No one else's.

"I urge you to say no to the prosecution, say no to this horrible war, say no to the FBI's manufacture of a crime, and say yes to some hope for the future. Say yes for life. Thank you."

§§§

The fourth day of jury deliberations was under way, and I wasn't sure what to expect. Jury deliberations were the hardest time for me and for trial lawyers generally. I tried not to think about it too much. We had done what we could, and the jury would do their thing, whatever that might be.

Juries are notorious compromisers. Sometimes they arrive at compromises that they think favor one side or the other, but the thought isn't shared by one or both of the parties. There were some bad compromises to worry about: they could single out the "ring leaders" from outside the Camden area for guilty verdicts, or they could convict everyone on just the conspiracy count, one of the risks to our side of emphasizing that the FBI could have arrested them for conspiracy rather than let the raid happen. They could also be unable to agree unanimously—a hung jury on some or all of the counts or defendants. Many variations or combinations of all of these were possible.

On the second day of deliberations, they asked the judge to read back to them portions of the testimony and the jury charge. They wanted to hear Hardy's testimony, testimony from some of the FBI agents, and the charges on conspiracy and overreaching. The request to hear the conspiracy charge was worrisome. Fisher had all of it read back to them, and

I looked at them while they listened. They seemed intensely focused but almost grim, like folks who have been arguing among themselves.

On the third day, the jury sent out a message to the judge saying they needed to speak to him. Fisher talked to them privately and then told the prosecutors and us that juror Groverline Bartlett had received an upsetting phone call from a member of her family. She wanted to be relieved of being the foreperson, which she was because she happened to be seated in the number one position. Fisher said he would accommodate her, and James Lomax was made foreperson.

We got a call at noon on the fourth day saying the jury had reached a verdict. It took a few hours for everyone to get to the courtroom. I sat in the seat I had gotten so used to—it was where I worked for four months—looking at the jurors for some sign. Some made eye contact with me, which is usually a good sign, but they mostly looked wiped out.

"Members of the jury, have you agreed upon a verdict?" the clerk asked.

"Yes," Lomax said, as he stood up.

"How say you? How do you find the defendant, Terry Edward Buckalew, on count one of the indictment?"

"We, Your Honor, find him not guilty."

Asked about the other six counts as to Buckalew, Lomax responded the same, not guilty.

"Mr. Lomax," Fisher asked, "do you have any different verdicts than that on any count for any defendant?"

Lomax looked over at us briefly, then back to the judge. "None different, Your Honor."

The packed courtroom broke into pandemonium, followed after awhile by all of us, and many in the courtroom, singing "Amazing Grace." That wonderful song, written by a repentant former captain of a slave ship, never sounded the same since.

§§§

I talked to almost all of the jurors after the trial—and reporters and Anthony Giacchino, the filmmaker of the award-winning documentary *The Camden 28*, interviewed many of them—about what had happened in the jury room. The accounts of what happened are consistent. They took a first vote that was purposely tentative to avoid hardening of positions. About half were for acquittal; the others were undecided or leaning or at least open to guilty verdicts. In sometimes heated deliberations, the jurors for acquittal convinced the others to go along based on the overreaching defense, emphasizing the overreaching charge and Hardy's testimony they asked Fisher to read back. The holdouts, as one juror put it in a *Philadelphia Inquirer* article, "didn't like the idea of breaking and entering, but when we brought in the FBI participation that changed their minds." Mrs. Bartlett resigned as foreperson after a family member's call about the trial so upset her that she had to spend a night during deliberations in the hospital. That was late in the deliberations, when it looked like the jury would acquit, and she didn't want to have to announce an acquittal.[9]

Among the initial jurors voting to acquit, two, Samuel Braithwaite and Anna Bertino, would have acquitted on the war issue alone. Braithwaite, a middle-aged black man who drove a jitney (a mix between a taxi and a bus) in Atlantic City, most often took advantage of Fisher's ruling that jurors could ask questions. Bertino was a widow who ran the family's manufacturing business. I would like to believe, as some commentators seem to, that we convinced all of the jurors to acquit based on opposition to the war. But the two defenses, and the defendants and lawyers, wound up working like a charm together, and overreaching provided a basis for acquittal all 12 jurors could embrace and live with.

Supreme Court justice William Brennan called the trial of the Camden 28 "one of the great trials of the twentieth century." I still get calls from lawyers, usually in drug cases, asking how we got the overreaching jury charge. I tell them it's a long story and won't help their clients. No other defendant has gotten an overreaching jury instruction, before or after the Camden 28 case. The Supreme Court and lower courts later greatly limited, if not eliminated, the exception, and judges didn't treat it as an issue that should be decided by juries. My closing argument has been featured in books and articles on jury nullification.[10]

I have kept in touch with many of the defendants. Jayma Abdoo worked in our law office for many years on police misconduct and other issues and as an administrator. Joan Reilly has found a variety of ways to make Philadelphia a better place to live and is a good friend. Cookie Ridolfi became a lawyer. Father Michael Doyle, whose mother and mine were excited to meet at the closing arguments, continued speaking and acting on behalf of the poorest in a poor city, for which he was profiled on *60 Minutes*, praised by elected officials and business and community leaders, and criticized by some of the same leaders when they were the objects of his ire. Camden, one of the bleakest of our urban landscapes, has been the better for it. I don't see Michael often enough, but we have a connection that feels like it could outlive us both.

CHAPTER EIGHT

Free Speech and the Baby Doctor

AVID, YOU HAVE A CALL ON THREE," Linda Backiel said. Linda, a poet and activist, worked for us for several years and later went to law school and practiced in Puerto Rico. Her voice came through the new phone system that had an intercom built in. It gave me the same satisfaction as wiring batteries and small lights on most every door in our house when I was a kid. I never could explain why it helped us to have a little light go on when a door closed, but it felt right, and my parents seemed to think it showed talent, along with an odd streak.

"Thanks, Linda," I said into the phone, which she could hear through the intercom and from my mouth about 15 feet away from her. I pushed the button for line three. "Hello, this is David Kairys."

"David, excellent. I think you're just who I want to speak to. This is Ben Spock. Leonard Boudin suggested I call you."

"Ben Spock?" I said, shook by the name.

The voice was familiar from TV news reports. He was Dr. Benjamin Spock, the pediatrician known worldwide for his pathbreaking, best-selling book on raising children, *Baby and Child Care*, which my parents used. He thought children grow best if supported and encouraged to communicate rather than forced into submission by physical discipline. His approach came to be called "permissiveness" by people who opposed it. In recent years, he had become one of the most prominent opponents of the Vietnam War.

"Hello, Dr. Spock," I said, collecting myself.

"I've got a free speech case, and I need a lawyer."

"What's it about?"

"You know I'm running for president in November 1972 on the People's Party ticket. I'm particularly concerned about these young men going off to fight a war that has no legitimate purpose. I've gone to the open, public areas of Fort Dix in southern New Jersey, areas that are like any other open town but are frequented by young soldiers in training— that's mostly what they do at Fort Dix. But the authorities won't let me talk to them or give an address there."

"You mean the town and area that is technically on the base, with a state road running through it? I drove through there just a few months ago."

"That's it. I can't remember the name."

"There is a general principle that the government's open, public streets, sidewalks, and parks are available for appropriate free speech activities. Which agency of government controls them goes to the scope of the activities, but if the military does it, that shouldn't foreclose all rights as long as you honor their determination of which areas are open." I felt the principle was important to defend, though the campaign speech was pushing the envelope.

"I'd like to challenge this in court. Leonard thought you'd know how to proceed."

"There are two basic ways to challenge it, and I think you're familiar with both. You could go there, deliver your address, and get arrested, and we'd defend you against criminal charges. It would yield a lot of publicity but also take a lot of time, effort, and funds. The alternative is to write to them based on what's already happened and see if we can get a written response that clearly denies your right to speak there, which we could then take to federal court."

"I'd prefer the latter route. Leonard said the NECLC would cover the expenses. Shall I have our people get in touch with you? The candidates of the Socialist Workers Party, Linda Jenness for president and Andrew Pulley for vice president, want to speak there as well, and we can all do this together."

§§§

I hung up the phone and turned off the intercom, thinking about Eugene Debs, a labor leader and prominent socialist who ran for president a few times in the early 1900s. He opposed U.S. entry into World War I, which socialists generally saw as a contest between European monarchs and elites aiming to expand their borders. Working people in the various countries were killing each other instead of struggling together to change oppressive conditions and regimes. This and the domestic program of the socialists were quite popular in that period.

Debs articulated these ideas at a Socialist Party political convention in 1918, for which he was prosecuted for violation of federal Espionage Act provisions on obstructing recruiting and causing insubordination or disloyalty in the armed services. His sentence: 10 years in prison. The government imprisoned a prominent political opponent for disagreeing with government policy. Debs got more votes for president from prison than he ever got before. In law school, I was surprised to discover that the Supreme Court had affirmed Debs's conviction.[1]

Debs was a favorite of some in my mother's family. My grandfather Hyman Lovett and uncle David Lovett were active socialists and knew Debs, who had been a guest at the Lovett home. I was named after David Lovett, the first of the family to go to college, who got a PhD in English and became a Shakespearean scholar. He got Parkinson's disease in his mid-20s and slowly deteriorated until his death in 1950. It's unusual in a Jewish family to name someone for a person who is still alive, because it tends to be viewed as taking his spirit. I was always honored to be given his legacy, but it also was a little spooky and carried a heavy burden—to live, and maybe die, as he had.[2]

Sometime around the middle of law school, in 1967, I was eager to try out my new legal research skills, so I set out to find the earliest Supreme Court case on free speech. I chose free speech because of my long-standing interest in it and because my civil rights course and constitutional law casebook skipped the early history and started with the famous dissents of Justices Oliver Wendell Holmes, Jr., and Louis Brandeis in the early 1900s.

The Holmes-Brandeis dissents are stirring and inspiring statements of the social and constitutional importance of free speech. Justice Brandeis spoke in a 1927 opinion of the value of liberty "both as an end and as a means," the "tyrannies of governing majorities" that seek "silence coerced by law," and the "futil[ity]" of discussion "without free speech and assembly." He acknowledged the risks of disorder and rebellion but found the alternative far worse: "[T]he greatest menace to freedom is an inert people. . . . [O]rder cannot be secured merely by fear of punishment for its infraction; . . . fear breeds repression [and] menaces stable government; . . . the path of safety lies in the opportunity to discuss freely supposed grievances and proposed remedies."[3]

But I was bothered by something that didn't seem to bother anybody else: why did they have to dissent? Free speech is a bedrock principle—the foundation of our country, I thought. Why wouldn't the other justices join them? And how could Debs's conviction be affirmed?

My civil rights professor, Louis Lusky, was a prominent constitutional scholar, but he didn't know much about the earlier history of free speech. I assumed the great Holmes and Brandeis dissents came in a period of judicial gloom, of which we've had quite a few. The majority was out of step with American law and tradition. I thought I'd discover an early case in which the Court reprimanded some local sheriff for failing to allow someone to speak their mind.

Legal research seldom, if ever, yields actual discoveries, although lawyers like to think of it that way. It gives a sense of quest and uniqueness to a pursuit that is tedious in its execution. Most of what you find is useless, and the significant cases you find are already known to others, of course. But I was surprised by the results of this research. None of the leading books, casebooks, or articles cited or said much about early cases. Freedom of speech was described in the most glorious terms and attributed to the Founding Fathers, but its history in the United States, if mentioned at all, started with the Holmes and Brandeis dissents. After a day of trudging through probably more than 50 cases, I found the first one—a short opinion reviewing the 1894 conviction of a Reverend William F. Davis.

Davis had spoken about social responsibility and corruption in high places, including the city administration, and handed out leaflets that contained tracts from the Bible on Boston Common, a big, open, public park. He appealed first to the Massachusetts Supreme Judicial Court and then to the Supreme Court of the United States. This seemed the most elementary, protected free speech, but both courts unanimously affirmed his conviction.[4]

A Boston ordinance prohibited "any public address" on public grounds without a permit from the mayor. While we allow licensing of drivers, marriages, dogs, and much else, the essence of free speech has been a refusal to allow the government to prejudge, screen, or license speech. There are many cases striking down such permit schemes. This would be an easy case under current interpretations of the First Amendment. But in Davis's case in 1897 the Supreme Court of the United States said the Constitution "does not have the effect of creating a particular and personal right in the citizen to use public property." The mayor could deny permission to speak selectively or for any reason.

The reasoning, drawn from the Massachusetts opinion, turned on property rights: the mayor was simply exercising the rights of the city as owner of the streets, sidewalks, and parks. "That such an ordinance is constitutional," the Massachusetts Supreme Court had said, "does not appear to us open to doubt. . . . [F]orbid[ding] public speaking in a highway or public park is no more an infringement of the rights of a member of the public than for the owner of a private house to forbid it in his house." In other words, the public streets, sidewalks, and parks were the mayor's living room!

I was disappointed and confused. Worse yet—in one of the strange twists of history—the author of the Massachusetts Supreme Court opinion was none other than Oliver Wendell Holmes, Jr., who 20 years later became America's hero of free speech when he wrote those famous dissents as a justice of the U.S. Supreme Court. In between Holmes also managed to write the awful majority opinion for the U.S. Supreme Court in the *Debs* case.

I went back to the cases we had read in class that followed the great dissents. In the mid-1930s, the majority opinions rejected the reasoning and result of the *Davis* decision and sounded like the Holmes and Brandeis dissents. In one of the leading cases, 40 years after *Davis*, labor organizers sought to speak and distribute literature to workers about unions and their rights under the new National Labor Relations Act of 1935. They got a hostile reaction in Jersey City, New Jersey, the turf of political boss Frank Hague. He promised local businesses they didn't have to worry about unions, prohibited distribution of literature on the streets or sidewalks and all outdoor meetings, and very publicly kicked some labor organizers out of town. His response to doubters, covered in newspapers around the country: "I am the law."

The majority in *Hague v. CIO* (1939)[5] upheld the free speech rights of labor organizers and everyone else. The Court repudiated the underlying theory of *Davis:* "Wherever the title of streets and parks may rest, they [are] held in trust for the use of the public." I didn't do a thorough search at that time, but I couldn't find any Supreme Court case before the mid-1930s upholding the basic rights we call free speech.

§§§

I won the first round for Dr. Spock at the federal Court of Appeals for the Third Circuit. He and the socialist candidates spoke to a sizable gathering of soldiers before the 1972 election at an agreed upon place on the base. I smoked my usual pipe and listened to the baby doctor and Judy Collins with great satisfaction. But the government appealed, and I found myself in front of the Supreme Court of the United States in 1975.

"We will hear argument next in Greer against Spock," Chief Justice Warren Burger said. "Mr. Solicitor General, you may proceed." Burger was square-jawed with a mane of white hair. He looked like a chief justice, particularly larger than life so close up and elevated behind the bench at the center of the row of seats occupied by the nine justices. I sat only about a dozen feet in front of him.

"Mr. Chief Justice, may it please the Court," Robert Bork began in the usual way with a deep baritone voice. Bork was the stocky, serious, favorite lawyer and legal theorist of a new breed of conservatives gaining a foothold in politics and law. His nomination to the Supreme Court a decade later was narrowly defeated after he disapproved of privacy protections against the government in widely watched Senate Judiciary Committee hearings.

"I have no trouble agreeing," Bork said, "that if this were about civilians within a city, an ordinance like the commander's rules here would be unconstitutional. But we're dealing here with a military base, devoted to the training of soldiers. The commander of Fort Dix has the lawful power to exclude all civilians from the base."

"Well," Justice William Brennan asked, "that was true in *Flower,* too, wasn't it?" It was common for the justices to ask questions throughout an argument. Justice Brennan was referring to a recent Supreme Court case, *Flower v. United States* (1972), invalidating a conviction for handing out a leaflet on the similarly open areas of another base.[6]

"*Flower* is a different case and does not govern this case," said Bork. "That street was indistinguishable from any civilian street, indeed continued straight through from the city."

"If I recall correctly," Brennan continued, "*Flower* was a public street; in fact, that was part of the base."

"The military had abandoned control over that street. In Fort Dix that is not true. The commander retains lawful power."

"But didn't he retain that power in *Flower,* too?" Justice William Rehnquist asked.

"This Court thought that street had been abandoned," Bork responded, "and 10 days after *Flower,* this Court discussed in *Lloyd v. Tanner* the fact that a shopping center that allowed civilians or shoppers to enter freely nevertheless did not extend its invitation to speakers or leafleters."

"Well, can't you argue just the opposite, since the shopping center is private, it may be able to limit speech in a way the government can't?"

"*Hague v. CIO* speaks of streets 'from time immemorial' being used as places for discussion in the exchange of political ideas; that makes them a public forum. Campaign speeches have never been allowed on military bases."

"How about," Justice Byron White asked, "a referendum matter in a city?"

"You mean an issue speech as opposed to a candidate?" Bork replied. "It would be a political speech. It would be constitutionally prohibited."

"But you are justifying the regulation on the grounds that particular kinds of speech just don't fit in the military."

"If it were discriminatory among different kinds of political speech, I wouldn't be here. The reasoning that allowed the only campaign speech on a military base, as far as I know, in our history, rests on two propositions, both of which I think are demonstrably false. The first is 'if the base is open to all the rest of the public, there is no basis for holding that it may be closed selectively to political candidates or to distributors of unapproved literature.'"

"Well, wouldn't you concede that if the commander allows access in certain areas to the public," Justice Potter Stewart asked, "he has to allow access to Dr. Spock?"

"The court below seems to be saying if he allows access for any purpose, it has to be for all purposes. This Court allows access, but not for all purposes. That's also for shopping centers in *Lloyd v. Tanner.* The other point is that there are a wide range of media allowed on the base with campaign speeches, and minor party candidates can't afford those media. The court of appeals's remarkable analysis used this to refer to the Fort Dix policy as 'a feigned neutrality that serves no discernable military purpose.' The policy is the separation of the military establishment from our political processes."

"Mr. Solicitor, I have a little problem with that point," Justice Thurgood Marshall, who had argued *Brown v. Board of Education*, said. "If the leaflets Dr. Spock wants to hand out were mailed to each soldier on the base, there's no restriction."

"Right."

"But you can't hand them out?"

"You can if you get prior approval."

"You don't need prior approval for the mailing."

"They have not censored the mail."

"Could the base forbid soldiers from attending political meetings off the base?"

"I don't believe so. They can't attend in uniform. The military is establishing a clear line between military and political activity."

"So their worry is how the military would look to the public rather than any danger to the soldier?"

"I think not."

"Well, they're going to let him go off base and attend any political meeting he wants to attend?" Justice White asked.

"That's right. This is not an attempt to prevent him from hearing any ideas."

"And they let him listen to the radio all he wants?"

"Yes."

"What is the reason, then, for the regulation?"

"I think it's simply this: There is a separation between the military and the political process. When you come to a base as part of your military life, you are a citizen but you leave partisan political activity behind. It's largely a symbolic difference, but it's a crucial symbolic difference."

"But while they are sitting there on the base," Justice Louis Powell interrupted, "they're free to listen to political speeches on the radio or TV, in their uniforms."

"That is true. Differences of degree at some point become so large that they are differences in kind."

"You've been addressing yourself to the speeches. How about the leafleting?" Justice Stewart asked.

"The argument on the leafleting regulation is close to that on the speeches. But I want to say one other thing about the 'feigned neutrality' statement. It is a real neutrality. The Constitution does not require the commander at Fort Dix to make his troops available as compensation for a candidate's inability to buy ads. Leaflets have to be presented to the commander, and he can ban them if he finds a clear danger to morale and discipline."

"Has he made such findings?"

"I believe there are instances."

"Very well, Mr. Solicitor General," Chief Justice Burger said. "Mr. Kairys."

He looked at me directly as I quickly went from my side's table to the lectern in front of the justices. They were close, and the whole scene was intimidating, but finally getting up there and having my chance seemed mostly a relief.

"Mr. Chief Justice, and may it please the Court. I'd like to start with a few facts about the base. First, the solicitor general hasn't distinguished the areas of this base in which First Amendment rights were granted from the areas involved in *Flower* or from the usual kinds of civilian streets. There are highways and state and county roads that go completely across the base. The area involved in this case, pictured in Appendix Volume II, at page E-2, on Wrightstown Road, is certainly indistinguishable from a city. You can't even figure out on that picture where the base starts and the city ends."

"You mean," Rehnquist asked, "because it looks like a company town of an older case, it is a company town?"

"No. The road goes right through the city, Wrightstown, and right through the base, exactly as in *Flower*. It is indistinguishable from a city street."

"On this picture, which side is the base and which side is Wrightstown?" Rehnquist asked.

"The photographer is standing on the base. Do you see the railroad crossing, the crossed white pieces of wood at the top of a post?"

"Yes."

"That's where a railroad comes through, and right next to that there are two small mounds on either side of the street that indicate you are entering the base."

"Where's the 'Cleaner and Laundry'"?

"That's in Wrightstown. There is also another laundry on the base open to the public. It's maybe five feet from the commercial district of Wrightstown to the beginning of the base. This picture was taken when two of the plaintiffs were stopped from handing out leaflets. They were arrested, as the leafleter was in *Flower.* In both, the military was in control and hadn't abandoned any part of the bases."

"There are state roads that go through the base that are not under the control of the military?" Brennan asked.

"Absolutely. The state retained easements over those roads when the land was ceded to the military."

"I've been over this base many times, and there are countless streets like that," said Brennan, who was from New Jersey.

"Colonel Olsen, the provost marshal, testified that there were 10 such open entrances, similar to this, wholly open to the public, merely marked that you are entering the base," I said. "Exhibit E-4 was taken on New Jersey Route 68. The sign shown on the photo marking entry into the base says 'Visitors Welcome.'"

"Who has jurisdiction of the roads for traffic violations?" Powell asked.

"They are patrolled by the military."

"Whatever property right the state has is subject to military requirements?"

"That's correct."

"Mr. Kairys, who maintains the roads?"

"The military does."

"If Dr. Spock were to run a parade down one of the state roads on the base, is it your view that the commander can't refuse?"

"Parades and demonstrations are not part of this case, but they are a protected form of speech. That would have to undergo the same kind of analysis that we have urged the Court to make in this case. We'd have to look at the government's interest involved, under the test that this Court has prescribed over and over again. That's what the solicitor general fails to do in this case. The government doesn't point to any specific or concrete interest but has created a false dichotomy that has emotional appeal. They say it's a military base rather than streets, sidewalks, and parks. These are streets, sidewalks, and parks. They are open to the public; anyone can go there for any reason they please or for no reason at all. The government entity that operates them this way is the military, which has relevance but doesn't make them any less public streets, sidewalks, and parks or automatically resolve the issue."

"Do you agree that the commander of the base could exclude them all for all purposes?" asked Rehnquist.

"I do. Certainly. It's central to the difference between *Davis v. Massachusetts* and *Hague v. CIO* that the power to exclude all no longer includes the power to exclude some or to exclude based on the content of the messages. What the solicitor general is urging is that we go back to *Davis v. Massachusetts,* where the only question is property rights, who owns the property. That was overruled in *Hague v. CIO* and other cases, for over 40 years now. The provost marshal testified that no one questions what anyone, including civilians, is saying on the open areas of the base. Once the government places an area open like that, it can't exclude certain messages."

"Well, the United States' position is that they ought to be able to exclude political speeches generally?" asked Powell.

"That gets to the neutrality point. The only kind of favoritism that makes any difference to the government is favoritism as to who speaks person to person. They want to eliminate favoritism as to that one form of speech. That's not the relevant concern."

"That's neutral as to people," Rehnquist said.

"As to people exercising just that one form of speech. But they aren't actually neutral even as to that. They are wrong when they say Dr. Spock is the first one who gave a political speech. Former vice president Spiro Agnew gave a political speech at Quonset Naval Base not long ago."

"That speaker was the incumbent vice president, wasn't he?" Stewart asked.

"Yes."

"And one remembers a great many occasions when an incumbent president spoke only at—almost only at—military bases, for the last year or so of his incumbency."

"Yes. Neutrality obviously doesn't mean much to the Department of Defense."

"But there are two different neutrality arguments. One is that neutrality really hasn't been maintained; it's just a kind of screen. But it's quite another thing to say that, if maintained, neutrality is not a legitimate or compelling interest that would justify what the army is trying to do here."

"We're saying both. Putting aside what they did at Quonset, they are trying to maintain a kind of neutrality around one form of speech, face-to-face speech. It means that the only candidates who can get information to the voters—there are 22,000 voters at Fort Dix—are the ones who can afford to pay the mass media to get their messages across. We also stressed in our brief that there is not neutrality even among various visitors or face-to-face speakers on the base. There is a striking admission in the trial record from the questioning of the commanding officer, Colonel Johnson. Quoting from the transcript:

Q (Mr. Kairys). If a proposed visitor to the open areas says, for instance, 'I intend to urge the soldiers not to use drugs,' that, from what you have said, would be something that the base might favorably look on?
A (Col. Johnson). That would further our mission, yes.
Q. But if they are to speak against the war in Vietnam—
A. That certainly wouldn't forward our mission, would it?
Q. So the content of what they are to say, that is the basis of whether or not they are approved?
A. Yes, to a great extent."

"Could you help me with one point?" Justice White asked. "This isn't a general army regulation, it's a regulation of Fort Dix we're talking about?"

"That's correct."

"So where does Quonset come into this?"

"I was responding to the statement by the solicitor general that Dr. Spock was the first."

"Do you agree with neutrality of the military?"

"I wholly agree with neutrality of the military. That's extremely important. But I don't think they are neutral when they allow one group of candidates to have this total barrage of access with some forms of speech and then deny these candidates access, since it's an open base and there is no countervailing military interest. Colonel Olsen testified that he saw no problem with soldiers talking about the election campaign; it happened all the time. Groups of soldiers talk about the campaign, and they have events that draw 5,000 civilians. There is an ad for President Nixon's reelection in *Army Times,* the predominant newspaper on the base. It's a feigned neutrality. The real question of neutrality is overall."

"Your argument, I take it," Justice Powell asked, "is that nobody can hold this type of rally and that isn't fair to candidates who can't afford the media?"

"No, regardless of whether they can afford the media, it simply isn't neutrality. If one or a group of candidates gets exposure on the base, it's not neutral to exclude other candidates from exposure in ways consistent with the usual openness and city-like environment of portions of the base."

"But the Court has always treated rallies and parades differently, with rigorous time and place restrictions. They're not treated like magazines at a newsstand."

"That's right, but that's not what I'm saying. If civilians generally have the right to exercise some First Amendment rights on these areas of the base, which I believe they do because these areas are open and there is no specific or concrete military interest that competes with it, there is no reason to exclude exposure of other candidates at appropriate times and places."

"Dr. Spock wants to appeal to soldiers as soldiers?" Rehnquist asked. "Yes."

"That's one thing the other candidates that have access through the media are not doing. They're making a general appeal."

"Well, if you read President Nixon's ad, it's pitched toward soldiers."

"You're talking about poor candidates not being able to buy an ad."

"They can't buy an ad in *Army Times* because it's censored. They could in other media, and they could mail the same leaflets they want to hand out."

"Why not hold the rally next to the base? Any military man is completely free to attend if he wants," said Justice Powell.

"But they're not. Most of them are restricted to the base, according to the testimony of the provost marshal."

"You mean you want a captive audience."

"They're hardly captive. The base covers 55 square miles. They can come or not. The rally was held, after negotiations with the army, on a parking lot adjacent to a movie theater. It's called Theater V, one of six different open movie theaters on the base."

"Some could feel compelled, raising the same problems as under the Hatch Act."

"I think it would go the other way—many would feel hesitant to attend. And I don't consider attending a rally as 'participation' in electoral politics under the Hatch Act."

I paused. The barrage of questions skipped from topic to topic, some of them unanticipated in my preparation for the argument. It felt something like being in a swarm of bees and trying to swat at each that attacked. I liked it but worried about losing the edge and focus of the argument. I glanced down at my watch, which I had put on the lectern, and I was just about out of time.

"I would like to come back to the central issues, if I can. I think the case hinges, in addition to this neutrality question, on whether civilians generally have the right to exercise First Amendment rights on these open, city-like portions of the base. I would subject that question to the Court's usual free speech analysis. Assertions or observations that views might be expressed that could undermine, without a specific or concrete basis or government interest, are hardly sufficient as a government interest to override freedom of speech. If the Court holds that sufficient to impose a prior restraint, we've created a problem for speech law generally. I'd like to—"

"Mr. Kairys," Burger said, "the order you won below limits restriction of speech rights in unrestricted areas of the base. Does the record define what those areas are?"

"It defines them in a negative sense as any area not marked 'Restricted.' We accepted the army's definition of restricted."

"Thank you, gentlemen, the case is submitted."

§§§

That's what they always say. It was November 5, 1975, and *submitted* meant you'll get the result and opinions sometime before the Supreme Court's yearly session ended late the next June. That's a long time to wait if you don't like waiting.

The decision came down in March. We lost six to two.[7]

Supreme Court opinions came on bound book-sized, soft paper with no cover, looking like a chunk of book that fell out. Justice Stewart had written a majority opinion that I didn't want to read. Burger and Powell wrote concurring opinions, meaning they voted with the majority—against me—but wanted to set out some reasons of their own. Brennan and Marshall each wrote dissenting opinions.

In his majority opinion, Stewart stressed the long-standing constitutional importance of speech on "open streets, sidewalks, and parks," quoting *Hague v. CIO*. But he qualified it with a new concept and term: streets, sidewalks, and parks held by the government and maintained open to anyone's coming and going and speaking are not subject to First Amendment protections unless they constitute a "public forum." The government can reserve its property for what it is "dedicated," "no less than a private owner of property." This was an unexpected return to the pre-1930s *Davis* decision.

He said *Flower* dealt with an open part of a base that had been "abandoned" and emphasized the "neutrality" of the military, without explaining what he meant by either. Messages about candidates were all over the base, but if Dr. Spock spoke where the public is welcome and regularly speaks, the military would become "the handmaiden for partisan political causes."

I was prepared to be disappointed, and angry, but the surprise was how little the loss had to do with the military's involvement. I thought I would lose, in my more honest moments anyway, because these open streets, sidewalks, and parks were on a military base. But the reasoning was broadly applicable, not just to speech on open portions of military bases, and it established a new, potentially major hurdle for free speech rights.

Brennan found the majority's distinction of *Flower* "wholly unconvincing" and noted our evidence that the areas of Fort Dix at issue were "so open as to create a danger of muggings after paydays and a problem with prostitution." Free speech should not "evaporate with the mere intonation of interests such as national defense, military necessity, or domestic security."

Much of his dissent was a critique of the majority's new public forum analysis, which has since this decision been used to limit the areas and range of speech rights. "The notion of 'public forum' has never been the touchstone of public expression," and the focus on such a "rigid characterization blinds [the analysis] to proper regard for First Amendment interests. . . . Unrestricted admission of the public to certain areas of the fort indicated that an exercise of public expression in those areas, such as distributing pamphlets, would not interfere with any military interests."

"Neutrality," he said, was the majority's "final retreat." The government's "permitting public expression" is not "sanctioning" the views expressed. "If there is any risk of partisan involvement, real or apparent, it derives from the exercise of choice, in this case." Marshall added, in his dissent, that "the Constitution . . . applies to the military," and there was no good reason for the majority's "unblinking deference."

It was a lot to take in. I noticed how easy it was to see the value judgments in every line and phrase of an opinion that announced my defeat, compared to how uncritically a winning opinion can seem obvious and valueless. Something hit me clearly that day that had been brewing for some time. Legal opinions are written in a style that emphasizes objectivity and requires results. But there is broad, though usually hidden, discretion, choices made based on values nowhere specified or required in the law.

What struck me that I hadn't heard or thought of before was the regularity of value judgments in legal decision making. It wasn't unusual to find criticism of particular decisions or judges for applying values. That was considered wrong, a deviation from what is normal and right. But maybe values were always involved, although all legal decisions have a theme that emphatically rejects values or discretion: the law made me do it. It reminded me of something I'd heard comedian Flip Wilson say. He had a routine delivered in a woman's dress called "The devil made me buy this dress." She excused her misdeeds with "the devil made me do it." No other explanation or justification was offered or necessary.

CHAPTER NINE

Celebrating Freedom, Free Speech, and a Book to Speak About

I TRIED NOT TO LOOK DOWN. That's what I'd heard you should do if you're afraid of heights, but it wasn't working. I was hanging on to a ladder almost four stories above the ground in North Philadelphia, fairly terrified. It was July 4, 1976—the bicentennial of American independence—and I was sort of litigating a free speech case. I tried not to think about where I was as I slowly crept up the last 10 feet so I could peer over the top of all the houses and see their roofs.

The bicentennial Fourth of July brought hundreds of thousands of people and dignitaries from around the country and world to Philadelphia. The main events were downtown at the Liberty Bell and Independence Mall. I represented several thousand protesters who felt the spread of freedom hadn't quite been completed. They had come from around the country and the world for a peaceful march through African American and Puerto Rican areas of North Philadelphia with poverty and deprivation everywhere you looked. No one downtown or at the protest march was particularly focused on roofs, although from the ladder I saw quite a few in need of repair.

The march was about to begin in an area of Fairmont Park in the Strawberry Mansion neighborhood, when someone from a Puerto Rican contingent at the front suddenly stopped it. He frantically called the leaders of several of the major groups and me to the starting point. "There are snipers on the buildings along the march route with scope rifles aimed at us! Look up there." He pointed to the top of a row of houses across the street from the park. "I knew Rizzo was going to make trouble. We can't march. I'm in charge of Juan Marie Bras's security detail, and we're not marching into the range of the snipers." Bras was a leading figure in Puerto Rico and one of the featured speakers at a rally at the end of the march.

"I thought we had this worked out," said Mohammad Kenyatta, a prominent activist and friend. "Didn't we, Dave?"

They all turned to me. I looked up at the roofs of the buildings along the beginning of the march route and saw some men with what looked like rifles.

"Let me find out what's going on," I said. "It would be best if we don't spread word about it. People could panic. Maybe announce a short delay of the start." I had talked to Lt. George Fencl, head of the police Civil Disobedience Unit, earlier in the day, and we arranged to be where we could reach each other if there was trouble. I ran to his location a block away as someone announced the delay over a loudspeaker.

§§§

Weeks before July 4, Mayor Frank Rizzo publicly accused the marchers of planning violence, saying there would be "disruption and violence by leftist radicals." He claimed to have "extensive documentation which indicates the magnitude of the existing threat" and asked President Gerald Ford to send 15,000 troops to protect the Philadelphia bicentennial celebration.

"[I]t is heartbreaking to me to think that we should be compelled to put federal troops in our city," Rizzo wrote in a letter to President Ford. "[But that] must be weighed against the risk to human lives and safety that now exist. The soldiers could be made part of the bicentennial scenery. Just as the British use military force in dress for security, I believe that if the troops were deployed quietly and ostensibly as part of the pageantry of the day, that we could accomplish our objectives. I recommend that the troops be equipped with sidearms, rather than rifles."

This was Rizzo's typical game—he'd stir up fear and hostility and pose himself as the only one bold and strong enough to protect the public. He didn't share any documentation with the public or media, and it didn't convince President Ford or Pennsylvania governor Milton Shapp, perhaps because the protest was planned and designed to be completely peaceful. When it became clear that the federal government would not send troops, Rizzo said, "the blood is on their hands." His fearmongering substantially reduced the numbers of folks who came to Philadelphia to celebrate or protest.[1]

With Rizzo sounding off on the local and national stage, I thought I would have to go to court to get a parade permit. I started with a letter accompanying the permit application that explained what was planned and who was expected to participate. My letter said that we would negotiate and compromise on some of the details but not on the right to have a large, visible protest march. I usually started with such a letter to facilitate discussions, although I thought that futile in this situation, and to be able to show a judge once in court that we were reasonable and tried to resolve the issues without litigation.

I got a call in response, not from the city solicitor's office, as I expected, but from the city's managing director, Hillel Levinson. In Philadelphia's legal structure, the managing director has substantial duties and power, although he is chosen by and responsible to the mayor.

"David," said Levinson, an ardent Rizzo supporter, "can we talk about this permit? I don't know you, but I've heard good things about you, and I'm hopeful you and I can resolve this."

"I'll be glad to talk to you, but what about the big scare the mayor is stirring?"

"Don't worry about that."

"The mayor is talking Armageddon. Are you saying you'll agree to a permit anyway, and he'll allow you to do that?"

"I'm saying, don't listen to what the mayor is saying. Listen to me and you'll have a permit."

I was surprised at Levinson's dismissal of Rizzo. "I will certainly listen to you, but I'm sure you'll understand that my listening will be combined with some skepticism. I don't want to waste time talking, only to find us rushing or too late to bring a lawsuit. Let's set a deadline. I'll take you up on your offer to negotiate in good faith but only if we have a permit agreed to by you and by the mayor at least three weeks before July 4."

"That's fair. Let's start talking tomorrow."

He came through. We negotiated a march route and all the details before the three-week deadline, and Rizzo signed off on it. No one mentioned snipers.

§§§

"George, we've got a major problem," I said, out of breath as I ran up to Fencl as the start of the July 4 march was delayed. "There are some fellows with rifles on some of the rooftops. Are they with you?"

"Yeah. The Secret Service thought it a good idea, and the mayor concurred. They are just there to protect life and property should there be a disturbance."

"Snipers with scopes and long rifles trained down on a peaceful demonstration? I don't know whose life or property you're talking about, but we are going to have some trouble if you don't remove them now. If those thousands ready to march hear that snipers' rifles are pointed at them, there could easily be a panic. A federal judge will find this outrageous and hold you responsible for whatever happens."

"Alright, let's not go to court yet. Lemme see what I can do."

He walked several feet away and talked into a portable radio. I could not tell if he was talking to the mayor or someone from the Secret Service.

"Alright, Dave, I've gotten clearance to remove them, and I've ordered them to stand down."

"And get off the roofs?"

"Okay, I'll tell them to get off the roofs."

"How long will it take?"

"Maybe 10 minutes. I'll tell you when they're gone."

I ran back to the gathered march leaders. "The snipers are being removed. The police say it was the Secret Service's idea. I don't know, but they will tell me when it's done."

"Dave," Mo Kenyatta said, "this is Juan Marie Bras." He gestured toward a distinguished-looking man of medium height dressed in a formal suit, who smiled as he held out his hand to shake mine.

"I'm glad to meet you," I said, "but sorry about the circumstances. We had no warning about this."

Bras nodded and smiled as he spoke calmly in Spanish to me and the others. "He wants the removal of the snipers confirmed, and he won't take the word of the police," someone translated. "He wants you to go up there and see them gone for yourself, and then he'll accept that it's safe to march."

"Me?" I said.

"Yeah."

"Okay. There must be some stairway to the top. Tell him I'll look for myself and tell him what I see."

I ran back to Fencl and told him I had to personally see the roofs empty of snipers.

"Look, you're the one worried about a panic, and I'm telling you the snipers are gone," he said. "I don't have keys to these buildings. We ordered people to vacate the buildings along the first block of the march."

"How'd the snipers get up there?"

"We pulled up a fire ladder behind the buildings, and our guys climbed up. The ladders go up over four stories." He pointed down the street. About a block away I could see one of those long, red fire trucks with a rear steering wheel at the end of a huge ladder. The ladder was extended up, leaning on the top of one of the buildings. "I'll have a fireman go up and tell you they're gone."

"A fireman's not good enough at this point, George. I have to go up."

"You? I don't know about that. It's dangerous."

"I'll be careful, but the march leaders need to get confirmation from me."

"I think I'm going to need you to sign something saying you take responsibility. I'll get the guy from the city solicitor's office on the radio."

"I'll sign it. But let's not lose any time."

The guy from the city solicitor's office was satisfied by my telling him I accept responsibility over the radio. I walked to the fire truck and looked up, way up.

I was never sensitive to heights as a kid. I first felt it as an adult when skiing at Stowe, Vermont, in the 1960s. The last part of one of the ski lifts took me high over steep slopes. I was gripping the seat and my ski poles so tightly that it was hard to get off at the top. Since then, I've usually avoided heights, particularly if there isn't much under me.

I went quickly up the big red ladder at first, thinking speed would get it over with, but then I was too worried about not getting a good grip with my hands or foothold with my feet. I settled on a steady but slower rate, my eyes focused only on the rungs right in front of me. The bricks of the building wall drew closer as the leaning ladder took me up. At the top, I gazed over, but the view across the roof, which was why I was there, felt terrifying. By then, I was used to the bricks. I wanted to climb over the top and onto the roof, but I didn't think I could get back on the ladder—I'd have to dangle my legs over the top to get back on. I pressed myself to look around and as far as I could so I wouldn't miss any snipers, but my main thought at that moment was how I'd get down and how quickly I'd be able to find a place to pee.

I used the same steady rate to climb down, almost holding my breath until I got pretty close to our usual altitude on earth. "They're gone," I announced to the march leaders. The march started as I stood by the side of the road, feeling oddly elated, as one probably feels after reaching a mountaintop or surviving a near-death experience. I hadn't quite done either, but that's how it felt.

The march and rally proceeded without any trouble. The next day an article in the *Philadelphia Inquirer,* a very conservative newspaper at that time, said, "the chief permit negotiator is lawyer David Kairys. Quite apart from his liberal convictions, Kairys is considered, in legal circles, to be one of the sharpest lawyers in town." I remember liking that comment, although it seemed to say liberal and sharp normally don't go together easily. They might also have said I wasn't too bad under pressure on a big ladder.

§§§

Most of my free speech cases were less stressful, but it was never easy to predict which would require extended litigation and which could be resolved with a phone call or letter. In the late 1970s I undertook what looked like a difficult challenge to the conditions for applying for parade permits when a local activist raised a question about a ban on black flags.

Several conditions were printed at the top of the parade permit form, most of which were not a problem. But the conditions included a ban on carrying black or red flags and on parading in blackface. The history of these bans was that red flags were carried by communists and black flags by anarchists. The blackface restriction came because Philadelphia's Mummers Parade every New Year's Day, one of the city's biggest events, used to be performed with black makeup.

The Philadelphia Mummers were all white, mostly of Italian ancestry, and did not allow blacks or women in their macho, heavy beer-drinking event, which included many men dressed as women. It was a day for white men to be black and in drag. Something deep was going on, but I was never sure what.

The Mummers Parade presented and mocked black stereotypes and was particularly insulting since whites dressed up as blacks while excluding them. Parading in blackface was banned by the city in the 1960s. Women were voluntarily included in the Mummers Parade in the 1970s. Philadelphia was surely better off without a yearly parade racially mocking its most oppressed, but the ban on blackface parades—and on black and red flags—presented a free speech problem.

I sent a letter to the city solicitor explaining that the ban on the content of flags displayed by paraders was a clear violation of the First Amendment and that I was preparing a lawsuit to invalidate it. I didn't mention the blackface issue, because I had no client or circumstance related to it and because I was ambivalent about it. Free speech rights have never been absolute. You can't shout "fire" in a theater (if there isn't one), falsely accuse someone of adultery, obtain someone else's money by fraudulent speech, and so forth, and racial mocking seemed as worthy an exception as any.

About a month later, I got a response from the city solicitor. He ordered all of the conditions removed from the parade permit form and instructed city agencies not to enforce any of them.

§§§

On the other hand, many free speech cases I thought would be easily resolvable turned into extended battles and appellate court decisions. Professor W. T. M. Johnson—Bill to his many friends—was the chairman of the Chemistry Department at Lincoln University, one of the nation's earliest and most prestigious black colleges. Johnson was a quiet, soft-spoken man who had risen to the top among chemists at Dupont before becoming a professor and was the unlikely leader among the faculty at Lincoln in a dispute with the administration and university president, Herman Branson.

Branson was a highly regarded scholar, but as an administrator and leader, he tended to lash out rather than to talk or compromise when the faculty opposed some of his policies and plans. In a series of conflicts, the most intense over Branson's proposal to greatly reduce the size of the faculty, Branson became increasingly repressive and the faculty became more vehement in its opposition. Branson threatened faculty members with punishment if they continued to speak out, and he removed Bill Johnson as chair of the Chemistry Department. The administration arrested some faculty in classrooms; forced respected English professor Edward Groff to "retire" after undergoing surgery; and fired a promising, outspoken young English professor, James Trotman, without a legitimate reason.

Some of the faculty's actions were provocative and arguably disruptive, but most of the problem, and the legal case, was traceable to Branson's attempts to shut up his critics. Some of his threats were in writing. He sent one professor who made a motion at a faculty meeting that upset Branson a registered letter saying "treat this as a warning" not to make the motion again or he would face "termination." When President Gerald Ford was scheduled to visit the campus, some faculty planned a small, peaceful picket to inform him of the problems at Lincoln. Several faculty members got telegrams at their homes saying "any faculty picketing" would be "a cause for discipline up to dismissal."

I thought negotiation would be productive, until I met Branson's and Lincoln's attorney, J. Freedley Hunsicker, Jr., who worked at one of the major corporate firms in town. I thought such a name was only to be found in novels. The name triggered a range of stereotypes in my mind— he had to belong to a club or two that wouldn't allow blacks or Jews, at least not until very recently. When we met, he introduced himself as Freedley, a name I never could quite say easily, but he turned out to be smart, friendly enough, and an easy fellow to deal with one on one.

Freedley, however, saw nothing wrong or actionable about Branson's conduct, and the more I looked into things, the more he seemed personally involved in much of it. The telegram threatening dismissal if faculty picketed when President Ford came was signed "J. Freedley Hunsicker, Jr."

In 1978, I brought a lawsuit based on the First Amendment on behalf of over a quarter of the Lincoln faculty. Federal judge Joseph McGlynn ruled for Lincoln on all the issues. He found "a reasonable basis for every action complained of here, which was totally unrelated to the exercise by the plaintiffs of their constitutionally protected rights." Later, however, the Third Circuit Court of Appeals reversed his decision.

"That much of the activity engaged in by plaintiffs falls within the protection of the First Amendment seems too evident to require any discussion," wrote Judge Doris Sloviter in a unanimous opinion. The lower court "appears to have fashioned or accepted two defenses to free speech restraints, one based on the defendant's good faith and the other based on the plaintiffs' persistence. Neither defense has any support." We got an injunction against further threats and denials of speech rights, the discipline was revoked, Trotman got his job back, and I got a counsel fee paid by Lincoln.[2]

§§§

My earlier interest in the history of free speech and the plight of Reverend Davis and Eugene Debs came in handy in all these cases, but it had taken a backseat since I'd finished law school.

One of my best friends in law school, Bob Cover, immediately started an academic career when the Columbia faculty, for only the second time in its history, hired one of its students right after graduation. Bob had been a civil rights worker in the South, and he and I were among a handful of first-year students who in 1965 organized that open letter in the *New York Times* opposing the Vietnam War that led Leonard Boudin to first contact me.

I noticed Bob during law school orientation because we both wore jeans, which in those days meant something. In a hallway during one of the early sessions, I saw a hole in the stuffed seat of Bob's jeans that showed his underwear, and I knew we'd be friends. The lecture rooms and hallways were awash in suits and ties or an occasional casual sweater and tie. I don't remember what the women wore since there were only a few among the 300 in the first-year class.

Bob wanted to research, understand, and write about justice, history, and law, which he did wonderfully before dying way too soon in 1986, becoming, even with such a short career, one of the leading legal scholars of our generation. (One of my deepest feelings of loss is the visit Bob and I planned for the fall of 1986 that would never happen.) I was also focused on justice, history, and law, but I wanted to sue.

Free speech issues became a staple of my practice, but I didn't get to systematically research the history of free speech until my interest in writing reemerged in the late 1970s. By then I had done enough research to reach a startling conclusion: The *Davis* case was not an aberration, and the system of free speech we usually ascribe to the Founding Fathers actually was not established until the mid-1930s. This left me puzzled. What about the First Amendment and all those Fourth of July speeches? Could it all be myth? And what led to the change in the 1930s?

The opportunity to figure it out came in the late 1970s, when I went to an early conference at the University of Wisconsin of a group that became known as Critical Legal Studies. They were mostly law professors who focused on the nature, functioning, and social role of law and the ways law can legitimate injustice by making it appear rational and natural.[3]

I was invited to an organizing meeting in 1979 at the Cambridge, Massachusetts, home of Duncan Kennedy, who taught at Harvard Law School and was the leader, although he had no official role or office. This progressive movement, like so many in this period, found it difficult to deal with leadership. Privilege and elitism were to be defeated, including any signs of them in progressive organizations.

The room was full of young legal scholars whose names I had seen in print. They all knew each other, many from their student days at Yale Law School.

"I'm really glad to see David here," Duncan said as he introduced me. We had never met but knew of each other by reputation. He was tall and thin, with a big smile and long blondish hair, more the look of the lead guitarist than the lead legal theorist.

"Maybe we should recruit more practitioners," someone whom I didn't know said. "We don't want this organizing committee to get too big, but maybe we need to reach out and include folks doing it in the trenches."

They discussed it for a little while and decided that I and Michael Avery, the other practitioner there, were enough. Mike was an accomplished civil rights lawyer from Connecticut whom I knew through the National Lawyers Guild. He knew some of them as a law student at Yale.

"Did we get some kind of affirmative action?" I asked Mike later.

"It felt a little like that, didn't it? They're sensitive about teaching and writing rather than litigating progressive cases."

"Yeah. I hadn't thought of myself as an oppressed minority, certainly not because I try cases."

"We make them a little uneasy."

"They make us a little uneasy, too. They write and think all the time, and they may be smarter than us. It's also hard to like a law professor after experiencing law school."

"These guys are different in the classroom than our profs were."

"I'm sure. Maybe there's a love-hate thing going both ways. They're good folks, and we could all do a lot together if we get beyond it."

"Maybe," Mike said. "It's fun talking theories, but I'm not sure there's much to be gained by theorizing and writing now. There's too much work to do representing folks and building organizations like the Guild."

"But the articles they write often help us as litigators. Alan Freeman's model for understanding race cases is good theory and helps sort out issues and arguments in litigation. Besides, they've got a name for something that's bothered me for a long time."

"What name?"

"Indeterminacy. Everybody else talks about judges' discretion as minimal or as sometimes necessary but to be avoided. The law should be followed, and courts shouldn't make things up."

"But they do make things up."

"Yeah. We want to take some credit when we win and often feel guilty when we lose. What we do matters, but ultimately judges, or once in a while juries, decide, and the results and reasoning aren't required by the law."

"Yeah, but aren't a lot of or some things required? Isn't it sometimes determinate?"

"That's what I'm trying to understand."

§§§

The "Crits," as folks involved with Critical Legal Studies became known, were controversial in academia. Their criticism was not limited to the established ways in which courts operate or law is perceived but also encompassed how it was taught and how law faculties operated. There was also a rebelliousness against the elders that reminded me of the 1960s; and, like the 1960s, established institutions predictably overreacted. Many law faculties developed pro- and anti-Crit camps, and policies and practices about most everything—hiring, tenure, course assignment, use of faculty lounges—became controversial. Though much of what my friend Bob Cover wrote and said had a lot in common with the Crits, he sometimes spoke of it like I had gotten in with a bad crowd.

In 1980, I started to think about some kind of publication that would explain this new trend and present it alongside other progressive approaches to law. I wasn't interested in a very abstract work but in something that could appeal to non-law-trained readers and law students while still having significance as a work of theory. I thought the new trend and the range of theoretical issues would be best explained, instead of abstractly, by a range of academics and practitioners each taking on an area or field of law and explaining how the law has worked in that concrete area. Done this way, each chapter would also provide a substantive and historical overview of a particular area of law. And we would take on not only the usual areas of "public" law, like constitutional and criminal law, but also "private" law areas that were less visible parts of everyday life, like contracts and torts.

An obvious question is why, as it turned out, I would initiate, organize, and edit what became a very successful book, *The Politics of Law: A Progressive Critique.* I was not among the initial or most prominent Crits, and I had a very active law practice and pressure from the law office to take more cases rather than write books. I just started asking several people—Mort Horwitz, Karl Klare, Bob Gordon—to write particular chapters, and they all said yes. After a short while, when I looked at the list of topics and authors, I realized it was a significant book.

I decided to contact some major trade publishers. It took only one call. I called Pantheon, a Random House division, because I had noticed that a lot of books I liked were published by them. I asked the receptionist at Pantheon who dealt with law-related books, got put through to editor Phil Pochoda, and within two weeks had a contract.

The toughest moment in the publication process was meeting André Schiffrin, the head of Pantheon and a publishing icon who would make the final decision. Phil took me to a top-notch Japanese restaurant, where André joined us. I'd never had Japanese food and was thoroughly enjoying the sushi when André appeared. He was a small, soft-spoken man who said little but then looked up slowly from his miso soup. "Collections with lots of authors and topics are difficult to pull off and sell to a general trade audience, David," he said. "I can easily see sales on the academic side, but it'll need a trade audience. Tell me why I should believe this will work and you can pull it off."

Raw tuna was dangling midair from chopsticks I didn't know how to use. "A fair question, André. It's a new progressive approach to law presented alongside older progressive approaches in bite-sized pieces that present a concrete overview of an important area of law. The theory comes out of discussions of law and social reality about crime, car accidents, free speech, corporations, and so on. The authors are good writers who have agreed to write for the non-law-trained trade audience. I haven't done anything like this before, but I've regularly innovated and made things happen, in litigation, starting a successful law firm—"

"Your practice has been impressive," André said. "I've heard of several of the civil rights cases on your résumé. I also like the inclusion of practitioners among the authors."

"I'm taking off several months from my practice, and I've told the authors they have tight deadlines, and I'll hand in the manuscript in a year because that's all the time I have for it."

André perked up at the last comment. I couldn't read him otherwise, but Phil called a couple days later saying he would put a contract in the mail, and I handed in the manuscript in a year.

The Politics of Law was published by Pantheon in 1982 and is now in its third edition (Basic Books, 1998). André was pushed out of Pantheon, in the process of media concentration that has become so controversial, and then founded a nonprofit publishing house, the New Press, which in 1993 published my book *With Liberty and Justice for Some: A Critique of the Conservative Supreme Court.* I returned to Phil with this memoir.

§§§

One of the chapters I reserved for myself in *The Politics of Law* was on freedom of speech. I dug into every court decision I could find. I wanted to test my earlier conclusion that the system of free speech, as we know it, didn't develop until the mid-1930s and to find the legal rulings and follow the progress of legal reasoning that would lead from *Commonwealth v. Davis* to *Hague v. CIO.*[4]

But I was not only focused on legal rulings and courts. I wanted to understand what happened in various times and places when Americans tried to express dissident views, which I often found in historical accounts of particular periods. The lack of a legally enforced right to speak, experienced by Reverend Davis as a Supreme Court decision, would have had an enormous effect on our history, political process, and culture beyond the small number of cases actually decided by courts and retrievable so many years later. The lack of legally recognized free speech rights must have been a background assumption for most of our history. Yet, there was spirited debate in many times and places. I wanted to understand this and, most of all, to explain how and why the law of free speech changed in the mid-1930s and, if possible, to understand the retrenchment of legally recognized speech rights in the McCarthyism of the 1950s and their expansion in the civil rights years of the 1960s.

The constitutional period, with its First Amendment and rhetoric of freedom, was puzzling. There were seditious libel laws in every state that essentially made criticism of the government or government officials—now one of our favorite pastimes—a crime. These go back to English laws based on the notion of a king as divine, above reproach.

In 1798, the Federalists, the country's first majority party, controlled Congress and the presidency. They passed the Sedition Act, which made it a federal crime to "write, print, utter or publish . . . against the government [or government officials] . . . with the intent to defame [or] bring them into contempt or disrepute." Unlike the English common law of seditious libel, truth was a defense, and a jury determined if the message was seditious. But Federalist judges negated these reforms by refusing to distinguish between fact and opinion, requiring proof of the truth of every minute detail and manipulating the composition of juries so they were almost all Federalists. They treated the First Amendment as if it simply codified preexisting law rather than making any significant change, prohibiting only censorship prior to publication (for example, stopping a newspaper from running a particular article), "prior restraints" that had been prohibited in England since 1695 and in the colonies since 1725.

One Matthew Lyon, a member of Congress critical of the Federalists, was convicted and imprisoned, and his house had to be sold to pay his fine. A laborer who erected a sign on a post that said "No Stamp Act, No Sedition . . . Downfall to the Tyrants of America, Peace and Retirement to the President" got the longest prison term, two years. All of the states also criminalized seditious libel by statute or common law decisions by courts.[5]

I arrived at a surprising summary of the law of speech in the constitutional and early period of our history: First, the courts, federal and state, criminalized dissent with seditious libel laws.

Second, the courts accepted what has become known as the "bad tendency" doctrine, which rendered speech unprotected if it could have some bad effect, or tendency, some time in the future. The courts ruled, for example, that one could not advocate abolition of slavery because some slave at some point might be encouraged by it, which might contribute to a slave revolt. The causal connection is so weak and distant in time and place as to be meaningless. This justified repression of criticism and made it impossible to have real debate about the major issues of the day. A corollary, the "constructive intent" doctrine, assumed that the speaker or writer had the intent to cause the bad tendency, effectively negating the protective requirement in criminal law that a defendant must be shown to act intentionally.

Third, use of public spaces for expression was under the control of local authorities, who could selectively or completely prohibit speech they didn't like. The *Davis* decision wasn't a fluke; it repeated long-accepted law.

Fourth, the courts disfavored and sometimes invalidated prior restraints, particularly of the press.

This is not a summary befitting Fourth of July rhetoric. Free speech as we know it was not a founding principle of the republic. The only aspect of the law protective of speech in our early history, prohibition of prior restraints, developed long before the First Amendment or the Constitution. But this summary is not surprising or unusual if we look at the rules in other Western democracies. England, France, Germany—all still have seditious libel laws today, long after they were banned in American law.

American free speech is unique; it was not, however, established by the Constitution or the First Amendment. Leading historian Leonard Levy views the First Amendment, which specifically limits only Congress, not as a change in existing law but as a reservation to the states of the power to regulate speech, which we know the states were doing and continued to do after the First Amendment in ways that contradict what later became basic notions of free speech.[6]

From the early constitutional period to the mid-1930s, many organizations, individuals, and leaders sought broader speech rights and advocated change on the issue, which was regularly controversial. In the early 1900s, for example, Margaret Sanger and Emma Goldman were regularly arrested for speaking and distributing leaflets on birth control. In 1909, Goldman, who was also a literary critic, gave a lecture in a packed private hall in New York City entitled "Henrik Ibsen as the Pioneer of Modern Drama." Police said she could talk as long as she stuck to the nonpolitical topic. However, when she first mentioned Ibsen, a sergeant stopped the lecture. The police apparently thought Ibsen was some European anarchist or communist. Goldman tried to explain, but the large crowd was roughly cleared from the hall with clubs.

Denials of free speech were directly challenged by groups like the Industrial Workers of the World, a labor organization known as the "Wobblies," who used "free speech fights" in the early 20th century in a "struggle for the use of the streets for free speech and the right to organize workers." In 1908 the Wobblies and others won the repeal of a ban on street speaking in Los Angeles by repeatedly violating the ban until they filled the city's jails. Each speaker would mount a soapbox and start speaking with the usual Wobbly greeting, "Fellow workers and friends." This was enough to result in arrest, after which the next person rose on the soapbox. The jails were filled, and then schools were used for the overflow. Wobbly free speech fights were successful in Missoula, Spokane, Cleveland, Denver, Detroit, Philadelphia, Omaha, Kansas City, and Des Moines.

World War I brought a range of free speech issues to the public and the Supreme Court. Many opposed our participation in the war, like Eugene Debs and my uncle and grandfather, David and Hyman Lovett. But the Espionage Acts of 1917 and 1918 made almost any expression of opposition a federal crime. Debs's conviction was affirmed by the Supreme Court in 1918. In 1917 a federal court approved the postmaster's refusal to deliver a newspaper to subscribers because it questioned the purposes and conduct of the war.[7]

There were hundreds of Espionage Act convictions and hundreds more similarly repressive decisions based on other laws, none of which were reversed by the Supreme Court. Justices Brandeis's and Holmes's dissents became famous only after the basic change that occurred in mid- to late 1930s decisions like *Hague v. CIO*.

I wanted to understand and explain this fundamental change in an area of law that was commonly viewed as defining American freedom. I looked for historical works that addressed the problem. Some recognized that free speech as we know it was not adopted or accepted in the early constitutional period, but hardly any even acknowledged that speech as we know it was the result of a transformation of speech law in the 1930s rather than the wisdom of the framers. Legal scholars who noticed the change tended to focus on the development of legal theory and doctrine and to stop their analyses when the "right" or seemingly inevitable theory and rules were articulated in the Holmes and Brandeis dissents. Historians hadn't addressed the issue.[8]

My history would easily show that until the 1930s the law pretty consistently sided with repressive government officials and against dissenters. The practical reality—the ability to express oppositional views—was spotty and depended on the discretion of local and sometimes federal officials, who could legally repress dissent if they so chose but didn't always do so. Attempts to secure freedom of speech were frequent and often drew popular support, going back to the widespread opposition to the Sedition Acts in the 1790s.

The question was, Why did it change into a legal regime of broadly protected speech rights enforceable in courts, and why did that change occur in the mid-1930s? The more I read and thought and talked to scholars and participants in events and legal cases, the more the labor movement loomed large in this history. The 1930s was the first time free speech as we know it was persistently demanded by a powerful movement with broad popular support that was having its way in all three branches of the federal and most state governments. Labor saw basic free speech rights as necessary to and inseparable from the right to organize unions.

One example of the role of labor was a reorganization of a free speech group called the National Civil Liberties Bureau in 1920. Roger Baldwin, a World War I draft resister whose ancestors came on the *Mayflower*—"I am a graduate of Harvard, but a year in jail cured me of it," he said after getting out of prison—led the reorganization. He formed an alliance with the labor movement; took on a prolabor board; adopted the Wobbly tactic of free speech fights; and gave his group a new name, the American Civil Liberties Union.

I was fortunate to speak with Baldwin in 1981. Candace Falk, who scared off-campus military recruiters during the Vietnam War (see chap. 7), took me along when she got an interview of Baldwin for a book she was writing about Emma Goldman.

Baldwin said the free speech issue was primarily political and only secondarily legal and was inseparable from the rights of workers to organize and bargain collectively. He sought to form a coalition of labor, leftists, and others at all levels of society and of all political persuasions who supported free speech.

"Organization was the basis of our service in the ACLU," he told me. "We as an organization were powerless and therefore had to attach ourselves to the defense of movements that had power. . . . If we had been a legal aid society helping people get their constitutional rights, as such agencies do their personal rights, we would have behaved quite differently. We would have stuck to constitutional lawyers and arguments in courts. We would not have surrounded ourselves with popular persons. We attached ourselves to the movements we defended. We identified ourselves with their demands . . . and depended on them for money and support."

I presented my historical analysis in considerable detail in the chapter, focusing on the choices the justices had in the 1930s and explaining the ways a powerful movement could affect public attitudes, culture, and Supreme Court rulings.

I felt confident that I had figured it out, but to be certain I consulted a leading free speech scholar and a leading labor historian. Thomas Emerson, at Yale Law School, said with some excitement, "You're right in the details and the overall point, but I haven't heard anything like it before!" Labor historian David Montgomery, also at Yale, agreed. A political process in which the labor movement played a major role changed American society and culture and persuaded or moved enough of the people and the government, including the courts, to establish this very American idea of freedom as the law of the land. There is something here to be proud of, although it isn't the founders or the original text: the American people, through a political process, established this new conception of freedom of speech. I'm glad to be as well known for this and *The Politics of Law* as for anything else I've done.[9]

§§§

On May 25, 1987, Philadelphia hosted another celebration, the bicentennial of the Constitution. Vice President George H. W. Bush and other of the nation's highest officials were scheduled to speak. The Pledge of Resistance, a leading group opposed to U.S. intervention in Latin America, wanted to draw attention to events there, including the Iran-Contra scandal involving the Reagan administration's illegal funding of the Contras in Nicaragua. They planned to march to an open area of Independence Mall, where a "soapbox" had been erected as part of the official celebration to symbolize the history of free speech. The Lesbian and Gay Taskforce and several other groups had approved plans to engage in similar activities.

I had negotiated march routes with federal and local officials and with the organization officially presiding over the celebrations, "We the People 200." But on the day of the bicentennial celebration, the soapbox had been moved next to a row of port-a-potties far away from the events, and police and federal law enforcement wouldn't let anybody with a protest sign or button in any of the open, public areas near the events.

The protestors publicly denounced the denial of speech rights, most vociferously and effectively Rita Addessa, the executive director of the Lesbian and Gay Taskforce. Local and national media picked up on the theme of repression as a form of constitutional celebration—"What in the world did the security people think the bicentennial was celebrating?" a *Chicago Tribune* editorial asked.

Philadelphia police commissioner Kevin Tucker, a former Secret Service agent brought in to reform the department, which he generally did quite well, responded to the criticism. He said the police had infiltrated the Pledge of Resistance and uncovered a plot to "kidnap" federal officials. I knew this had to be wrong, but I worried that Tucker may have had some basis for such a serious charge.

We found out after I brought, with Stefan Presser of the ACLU, a lawsuit in federal court on behalf of 15 organizations and some individuals challenging the free speech violations and the police infiltration of groups that express dissenting views. Captain Francis Friel, who was head of the police intelligence unit and known for his work on organized crime cases, testified that at a meeting the Pledge "decided on such a kidnap if the United States invaded Nicaragua or El Salvador." He knew this because Louis Zayon, a police officer who infiltrated the group, was at a meeting where the plans were made.

I called Zayon to the stand. He testified that the meeting included a "brainstorming" session about what they might do if the U.S. intervention escalated to an invasion of Nicaragua or El Salvador. Someone "suggested" that they might make a "citizen's arrest" of some federal official. That was enough for me to guess who made the suggestion and just what had happened.

It was my friend Joe Miller, the investment banker who helped us establish Kairys & Rudovsky. Joe often told the story of how in the 1970s he was among a small group of opponents of the Vietnam War who went to the draft board on Broad Street north of city hall and made a citizen's arrest. They went in the draft board office, announced that everyone working there was violating international law because the Vietnam War was illegal, and called the police to arrest them. The police came, to everyone's surprise, along with some reporters, and the press carried the story the next day of the debate that ensued about whom, if anybody, to arrest. I had heard Joe reminisce about and propose the citizen's arrest tactic a number of times.

Zayon, to his credit, was measured and precise in the paperwork he submitted to Friel. He never said it was a plan or plot and never considered it a proposal to kidnap. No one responded to Joe's brainstorm, and there was no decision of the group to pursue it.

After hearing testimony for a long day, Judge John Fullam, one of the smartest and more liberal local federal judges, granted our request for a preliminary injunction. He prohibited federal and local authorities from "preventing individuals or groups from distributing literature, assembling or soliciting signatures in Independence National Historical Park or on streets, sidewalks, parks or other areas open to the public, so long as such activities do not involve breach of the peace, and do not actually interfere with similar activities by others, or with public events then in progress."

On the police infiltration, I argued that police needed probable cause or at least some substantial basis to suspect a crime before they could send a covert infiltrator into a group that was simply exercising its free speech and associational rights. I suggested, as others had, that the judge adopt the warrant requirement from the Fourth Amendment. It was puzzling that police can't enter a home without probable cause and a warrant, but they need no cause or warrant if they come in to attend a meeting of a protest group. The law was not good on the issue, resting the lack of minimal protection on the participants' "consent" to allow the police to be part of the meeting, even if no one knew the infiltrator was a police officer. The police were allowed to gather information and maintain files on participants, as long as they didn't gather or use the information illegally.

Fullam was sympathetic to my position, but he'd get quickly reversed on appeal if he ordered the police to stop infiltrations unless they obtain a warrant. He denied our request for an injunction on infiltration because the police had testified that the Pledge and the other groups were no longer being infiltrated.

But he didn't stop there. "The undercover officer accurately reported what had occurred," Fullam said in his opinion, "but this has now been described by his superiors as proof that the plaintiff Pledge of Resistance 'planned' to 'kidnap' a federal official and hold him/her 'hostage.' A dispassionate observer might well conclude that there never has been any genuine justification for undercover surveillance of Pledge of Resistance—an organization which apparently goes to great lengths to eschew violence in any form." "It remains," he concluded, "a close question whether what has thus far occurred violated anyone's constitutional rights. A more fully developed evidentiary record might lead to a different conclusion."

Calling it a "close question" was a stretch I liked, and it suggested that Fullam might rule for us on the issue if the case continued through discovery and further evidence were found. We had settlement discussions that easily resolved most of the issues. The preliminary injunction would be made permanent, and the feds and city would pay agreed-upon damages for the plaintiffs and counsel fees and costs. The sticky point was what to do about the police infiltration.

I knew they wouldn't agree to a warrant requirement, and it wouldn't last long even if adopted. I proposed an analogous solution: no police infiltration unless it is formally approved by the mayor and the city's managing director. The city's highest officials would adopt guidelines, and they would be responsible for any infiltration they approved. To my surprise, the city agreed. Philadelphia's civilian responsibility and control of police infiltration of protest groups got national attention, which resurfaced when state police infiltrated groups protesting at the 2000 Republican National Convention in Philadelphia.[10]

James Jiles (*right*) with David Kairys in 1969 after the governor of Pennsylvania refused to return Jiles to a Georgia chain gang.

Some graduates of Tony Amsterdam's program at Penn Law School gather around Tony (*from back left*: Aurelio Munoz, Ben Lerner, George Johnson, Louis Natali; *front left*: Don Stern, Tony Amsterdam, David Kairys, David Rudovsky).

Dr. Benjamin Spock
with David Kairys
in 1972 just before
Dr. Spock delivered
his campaign address
at Fort Dix, New
Jersey.

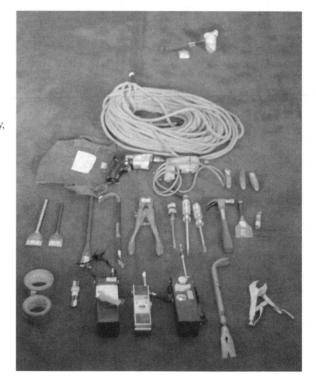

Tools used in the
break-in of the
Camden, New Jersey,
draft board arrayed
on the floor in front
of the jury box dur-
ing the Camden 28
trial in 1973. Tools
supplied by the FBI
are in the fore-
ground; beyond the
rope are three small
items supplied by
the defendants.

Camden 28 news conference after the jury acquitted them in 1973 (*from left:* Father Ned Murphy, Father Michael Doyle, Cookie Ridolfi, David Kairys).

COURT TRIAL SUBPOENA (Duces Tecum)

IN THE NAME OF THE PEOPLE OF THE STATE OF NEW YORK:

To Crucian Messina, Jury Commissioner of Erie County, N.Y.

You are commanded to appear before the Supreme Court of the County of Erie, at the Erie County Hall, in the City of Buffalo, New York, on the 3rd day of June, 19 74, at 10:00 o'clock in the fore noon of that day, as a witness in a criminal action prosecuted by the people of the State of New York, against Attica Brothers, Ernest Bixby, et al.

and you are required also to bring with you the following: The questionnaires from the qualified file listed by number in Attachment A, attached hereto and incorporated herein.

Dated in the City of Buffalo, N.Y., the 31st day of May, 19 74

_____ Clerk

F7-24 2-69

Subpoena of jury records in the Attica Prison rebellion challenge to the jury system in 1974.

The family of scientist Frank Olson, who was unwittingly drugged with LSD by the CIA and later died, outside the White House before going in to see President Gerald Ford in 1975 (*from left:* Alice Olson, David Kairys, Lisa Olson Hayward, Eric Olson, Greg Hayward).

David Kairys at his desk in 1976.

PART THREE

After the Movement

CHAPTER TEN

Sins of the CIA

I N THE MID-1970s, the political landscape began a steady conservative shift that has lasted three decades. It may be drawing to an end as I write in 2007 with President George W. Bush wearing out his welcome, but one consequence was the deterioration of progressive activism and organizations. Many never stopped working and struggling for progressive change, but we lost the moral and political edge that was so effective in the 1960s and early 1970s. I continued to litigate interesting and important issues, but the practice felt less grounded, more like, as with these concluding chapters, a string of unconnected cases.

§§§

The stereo on the first floor of my house in Powelton was blaring Joe Cocker as several of us hung out on a hot, Philadelphia-summer Friday night in 1975. I was enjoying sharp cheddar cheese somebody brought over, with potato chips and my usual Coca-Cola. I could smell pot smoke wafting out of the kitchen, and I remember feeling particularly relaxed and content that evening.

"David, phone for you," one of the guys shouted from the kitchen. "Sounds very official." He and others laughed that marijuana laugh that finds anything funny.

I picked up the phone in the hallway. "Hello."

"Hello, is this Mr. Kairys?"

"Yes."

"I'm Rod Hills, counsel to—"

"Sorry, I can't hear you with the music going. Can you hold while I go upstairs?"

"Sure."

I went to my second-floor area, where I had a bedroom, bathroom, and living room. "Hello, I'm sorry I didn't catch your name?"

"I'm Rod Hills, counsel to the president. You are the attorney for Alice Olson?"

"Yeah. Did you say counsel to the president?" I almost added "of the United States."

"Yes. President Ford asked me to call you to extend an invitation to Mrs. Olson."

I tried to quickly shift into lawyer mode and to figure out if this was real or some prank. Maybe a friend who saw my name in the national media outpouring on the Olson case had someone make a joke call. The only counsel to the president I had heard of was John Dean, who turned on President Nixon in the Watergate scandal that had just brought Gerald Ford to the presidency.

"What kind of invitation?"

"President Ford would like to meet with Mrs. Olson confidentially at the White House on Monday."

"This Monday, three days from today?"

"Yes."

"Can you tell me the purpose and subject matter of this meeting so I can explain it to the Olson family?"

"The president will not discuss the legal claims you have asserted but as I understand not yet filed. The president has turned that over to the attorney general to discuss with you. President Ford feels strongly and personally about what occurred and is outraged by what our government did, and he wants to express sympathy and apologize to Mrs. Olson."

"Do you literally mean just Mrs. Olson or the Olson family, which includes two sons and a daughter?"

"The whole family is fine. That won't be a problem. Since it won't be about the legal issues, it's limited to the family and won't include you or me."

I started to believe and became concerned. The apology would be nice—the Olsons sure deserved it—and could help our claims, but a get-together like this usually happens when the issues are resolved. The meeting could convey that the matter is over, resolved, and the fickle media could lose interest. "When you say *confidential,* do you anticipate a press conference or press coverage?" I asked.

"No press conference."

"A news release or some communication to the press?"

"There would be a statement saying briefly there was a meeting, who was there, and what was discussed, and maybe a photo op for the press."

"You mean they would be in front of TV and photographers for pictures?"

"Yes, a photo opportunity for a few moments after the meeting."

"Does there have to be a photo op or a statement?"

"We have an obligation to do that. It happens anytime someone meets with the president. The president doesn't want to be secretive, and people watch who comes in and out of the White House."

"I'll contact the Olsons right away. How can I reach you over the weekend?"

"I'll give you my home phone and a central White House number where they can reach me and patch you through at any time."

I took down Hills's numbers. "I'll get back to you tomorrow sometime."

§§§

The Olson case began in June 1975, about a month before Hills's call, when a presidential commission investigating the CIA issued a report. The CIA had been widely criticized for wrongdoing and deception mostly related to the Vietnam War and a range of misdeeds that included overthrow of the democratically elected, left-leaning government of Chile and the death of its leader, Salvador Allende. Congressional hearings and investigations were spearheaded by Senator Frank Church, whose committee issued scathing reports. Former vice president and New York governor Nelson Rockefeller was appointed to head a presidential commission to investigate the CIA. The Rockefeller Commission identified some abuses but generally played down any serious or systemic problems. It did mention that some of the CIA's activities had hurt individual Americans, including one unidentified person who died in CIA drug experiments when he was unwittingly given LSD.

The dates and sketchy circumstances about that death announced in the Rockefeller Commission report fit the death of Dr. Frank Olson, a biochemist who worked on high-level military research projects. A CIA researcher gave Olson and a few other scientists gathered at a retreat large doses of LSD secretly mixed in an after-dinner liquor. He died about a week later. Vincent Ruwet, one of Frank's former research colleagues who still lived down the street from Frank's wife, Alice, in Frederick, Maryland, confirmed that Frank was the person discussed in the Rockefeller Commission report.

Alice had been told that Frank committed suicide by jumping out a tenth-floor window of the Statler Hotel in New York on November 28, 1953. No one mentioned to her that he had been unwittingly drugged or that drugs were involved at all. All she knew was that he returned from the retreat depressed and acting strangely. He told her, before going to New York, that he had "made a mistake" and would leave his job. She and her three children, Eric, Lisa, and Nils—9, 7, and 5 years old when Frank died—had tried to cope for over 20 years with what they thought was Frank's inexplicable suicide. Ruwet was among several of Frank's colleagues and family friends who watched the family suffer without revealing the circumstances of his death.

Eric Olson shared an apartment with Rudy when we were in Tony's program, and Eric was a graduate student. I got to know him through Rudy. When Eric later taught at an experimental school for kids from Mantua, a poor black community near Powelton, I took off a month to teach and help build classrooms there with him, and we took a couple of the kids on a skiing trip.

Eric asked Rudy if we were interested in the case, which of course we were. Eric also knew and approached Harry Huge at Arnold & Porter, one of the most prestigious law firms in Washington. Huge won a big case for the victims of the Buffalo Creek mine disaster with help on establishing the types and extent of the harm done from Robert Jay Lifton, a leading psychologist at Yale. Eric worked with Lifton, and they co-authored some important works.[1]

Huge was interested in the Olsons' case, and his firm had deep connections in government and unlimited resources. We had independence from Washington and a habit of questioning and challenging government and could probably get the expenses covered by NECLC. It seemed a close call for them made easier because Arnold & Porter's connections created conflict of interest problems.

This was one of the few cases that Rudy and I decided to do together. We always talked out our cases—sometimes it seemed that's what we mostly did—but one of us would take each case. The Olson case would require a lot of work and time, and we were both busy on other cases. We decided to do it together, but as it turned out, I took the lead and did most of the work. I particularly liked the investigative side of it, trying to figure out what happened to Frank Olson, which Rudy was less interested in.

The Olsons held a news conference on Alice's lawn to announce that they were the family of the deceased man described in the Rockefeller Commission report and that they intended to take legal action. Eric, reading the family's statement, said, "Suddenly we learn that Alice Olson's being left in adulthood to raise a family alone, her children left to grow up without a father—we learn that these deprivations were not necessary. And we suddenly learn that for 22 years we were lied to."

"It never occurred to me," Alice said, "that there was foul play."

"When friends would ask, 'How did your daddy die?'—that's always been a tough one," Lisa said. "I used to say he died of a concussion," Nils added.

They struck a chord with the national media and with the nation, perhaps because they were a tall, mostly light-haired, handsome family in a country setting and with obvious integrity who had suffered a great deal. News of every move and development in the case was widely covered.[2]

§§§

While the party continued downstairs at my house, I called Alice Olson. "I'm sorry to call in the late evening, but President Ford's counsel just called to invite you all to the White House, Alice," I told her. "He wants to apologize to you." It took a little while to get used to calling her Alice instead of Mrs. Olson. I was only 32, and I admired the way she got through Frank's death and raised the children with an unnecessary, false cloud over all of them.

"No kidding. I didn't expect that."

"I didn't either. Government and large institutions often settle cases, but they rarely apologize. He wants you to come to the White House on Monday."

"This Monday?" Her voice trailed off and she paused.

"Are you okay?"

"Yeah, it's okay. I feel like I'm going through all this again and don't know what comes next. But this is nice. They should apologize."

"It's fitting that it come from the president."

"Yes. "

"If you don't mind, I'd like to raise some issues with them before we go down there on Monday. Apologies and a public meeting where the parties come together usually happen at the end of the process. I don't want the government or the media to get the idea that this ends it or diminishes what is yet to happen. I'd like to link the Monday meeting with a commitment on their part to provide us documents and to discuss the claims, and I want to discuss with them how the meeting is presented to the public so we can have a role in defining the story. I think we have some leverage since they want this public apology to happen Monday."

"Sure. I really would like to hear this apology."

Hills balked at some of my demands but, after checking with "our folks here," accepted all of them. The White House would issue a joint statement following the meeting that consisted of a first part written by them and a second part written by the Olson family. They agreed that we could see their part in advance and suggest changes and that the Olsons' part would be up to them with no advance look or suggestions. There would be photos taken by the White House photographer but no media access to the visit.

The White House part of the statement, which included all of our suggested changes, emphasized Ford's apology. "The president met with the family of Dr. Frank Olson," it said. "He expressed the sympathy of the American people and apologized on behalf of the U.S. government for the circumstances of Dr. Frank Olson's death. The Olson family asked that they be told of all the facts about Dr. Olson's death. The president told the family that he had instructed his counsel's office to make information available to them at the earliest possible date. He also informed the Olson family that the attorney general has been asked to meet with their legal representatives to discuss the claims they wish to assert against the CIA."

The part written by the Olsons, mainly Eric, emphasized the importance of finding out what happened and resolving the legal claims. "We deeply appreciate President Ford's expression of sympathy and apology to our family. His concern and his invitation to meet with him are of great value to us. We hope that this will be a part of a continuing effort to ensure that the CIA is accountable for its actions and that people in all parts of the world are safe from abuses of power by American intelligence agencies."

§§§

The White House followed through on its commitments. Rudy and I were invited to meet with Attorney General Edward Levi to discuss the Olsons' claims a few days later. The next day we went to CIA headquarters in Langley, Virginia, to see CIA director William Colby, who wanted to extend the CIA's apology and provide us with documents about Frank Olson's death. Alice refused to go to the CIA and didn't want their apology. "Colby was there when Frank died," she told me. "I got the apology that means something to me."

At the CIA, Eric, Nils, Lisa and her husband Greg Hayward, Rudy, and I were ushered up an elevator to the seventh floor, which was the hub of CIA operations throughout the world. We walked through corridors and open areas that mostly looked like ordinary workplaces. There were desks in open areas and private offices. But some desks had large glass bowls on them. If it were anywhere else, I'd have thought they were fish enthusiasts. But the bowls were there for burning documents. And the drawers on file cabinets had thick metal fronts with combination locks. Handling documents was no simple matter there.

We were surprised to be met and hosted by Mitchell Rogovin, who introduced himself as "special counsel to the director." Rogovin was a well-known partner at Arnold & Porter, who was brought in to help the CIA during this period of widespread public criticism.

I had read enough about the CIA to know that it had complicated and sometimes contradictory political tendencies. The CIA covertly aided foreign governments that supported narrow U.S. economic or political interests and covertly disrupted—or overthrew—governments that did not. But it also welcomed into its ranks many who had been removed from jobs at the Defense Department or the military as suspected communists during the "red-baiting" McCarthyism of the 1950s. It was often liberal on social and domestic issues, though the typical CIA employee had elite WASP origins and often went to the best schools. There were very few Jews or African Americans. Arnold & Porter fit this complex mold as a liberal corporate law firm, so its sending a major partner to help the CIA wasn't as strange as it could seem.

Rogovin greeted us all warmly and acted, then and throughout our dealings, as if he was one of us. I returned his friendliness but didn't trust him. I told him we preferred that Colby's apology and the Olsons' responses were private. He agreed and assured me that we would not be recorded or photographed while at the CIA.

Rogovin led us into Colby's office, and Colby came in another door just after we sat down. He was a thin man of medium height with brown hair. He avoided eye contact and seemed wooden, perhaps worried that one of the Olsons might lash out.

"Please extend my apology to Mrs. Olson," he said. "I want to apologize on behalf of the CIA, myself, and everyone here. I can't explain why we didn't tell your mother the truth about Dr. Frank Olson's death. I can assure you that we are changing. Under our current regulations, this could not happen again. Our activities regarding Allende in Chile constitute an abuse, as Congress has said. It was initiated and ordered from the White House, but it's still an abuse."

I was surprised by his candor on issues beyond Olson's death and by his dull, emotionless tone as he detailed a series of abuses that cost lives and overthrew governments. None of us responded.

"I want to give this to you and your attorneys," Colby continued. "This is the entire file concerning the death of Dr. Olson." He handed us a folder of documents about an inch thick.

"Does this include," I asked, "all of the information and materials available to the CIA and the whole government?"

"Yes, it does," Colby said.

"It's everything we have," Rogovin added.

After an uncomfortable silence, Rogovin said, "If you'll come with me, I'll go over these documents with you."

Colby nodded to us and quickly exited as if he had something important to do, and we went down the hall to a small room with Rogovin.

"There are some excised portions of the documents that refer to other matters, and I can let you skim unexcised versions of documents on these other matters briefly to see that they don't mention Dr. Olson. I can't give you copies of them."

He pointed to two thick stacks of documents, which I looked

through. Most referred to projects called "MK/ULTRA," "Bluebird," and "Artichoke," which I knew nothing about and couldn't figure out with such a quick skim. I could see that it had a lot to do with drugs, but why and how was not clear.

Rudy and I looked through the stacks for maybe a half hour. "It's hard for us to get anything from these with a short skim," I said. " We'll have to talk about this further."

"That's fine. Would you all care to join me for lunch?"

Lunch hadn't been mentioned; I was surprised by the invitation. "What do you think, Eric?" I asked.

"I suppose, since we've got to get lunch soon anyway."

Rogovin led us into a nearby small dining room on the seventh floor. It was very fancy and formal, with tablecloths, formal silverware and china settings, and drapes on the windows. This had to be the director's private dining room. We sat at a long table, Eric at one end and Rogovin at the other. A waiter poured us each a glass of water and put butter patties on our small plates.

"Is this the official CIA china?" I asked the waiter, the first black person I had seen. The plates had a distinctive maroon design with a CIA logo.

He had a formal waiter outfit on with a large security identification badge on one of his lapels. "Yes, that's official."

"Do they sell them at the gift shop? It's impressive."

"I don't think there is a gift shop." He smiled.

Then Colby entered the room and sat next to Rogovin. He was joining us for lunch.

I wanted to leave, but this was the Olsons' visit, not mine. Maybe everyone on our side felt the same, but it was hard to tell. There wasn't any opportunity to discuss it, and I was hesitant to do it on my own. But as it turned out, I'm glad we stayed. Colby's coming to lunch removed the formality of the visit and its limit to the Olson case.

"Eric, if I may call you by your first name, what are you doing now?" Colby asked, less stiff but still cold.

"I'm working on new ways of testing that involve responses to collages. We're finding that they can be most revealing. What kind of testing do you use at the CIA?"

"We use the polygraph, and with great success. Agents are polygraphed before hiring and periodically thereafter."

"What is it you want to find out about them with the polygraph?"

"Trustworthiness, loyalty, things like that."

"Do you have political criteria you get at with the polygraph or else-wise?"

"No, no political criteria, as long as you can do the job."

"Do you have any socialists or serious critics of government policy?" I asked.

"Sure, that's possible. There was a lot of discontent about the incursion into Cambodia, particularly among the younger CIA people. Those people are still here."

"You mean they haven't been allowed to leave the building?"

Eric laughed. Colby looked up from his soup and directly at me, then cracked a smile. Rogovin kept his head down in his soup, which was quite delicious. Colby had a gourmet chef somewhere in the building.

"Yes, very funny," Colby said. "You know, the CIA was realistic about the strength of the enemy in Vietnam, and we saw the struggle as political, not really military. We regularly differed with presidents and the military on the political nature of the war."

"But politically," Eric said, "the people favored the Vietcong and North Vietnamese, not our propped-up Theiu regime."

"That's not so. The people had swung over to the Theiu regime, but by then we stopped the military aid and lost the will to continue. The Tet Offensive of 1968 was carried out by guerillas, but the offensives against us in the 1970s had to be carried out by North Vietnamese regular units. The guerillas had come over to the Theiu regime."

"On what do you base that? We and the Theiu regime were widely despised by all accounts."

"Look, I gave a half million guns to the people, and they didn't use them on us. I could ride around freely without getting shot, and I talked to a lot of people who expressed widespread support for the Theiu regime."

"What makes you think," I said, "that the Vietnamese people would or could tell you what they really think? Your Phoenix program resulted in widespread assassinations and fear." Colby was most known for the controversial Phoenix program, which armed locals loyal to Theiu and told them to weed out locals believed to be opposed.

"The support was there; the military aid wasn't."

"If the people were so supportive of Theiu, why did the South Vietnamese army fold in two weeks?"

"Because we didn't give them the needed support anymore."

"Weren't there good political reasons why the people would be for the National Liberation Front, the Vietcong, and against the Theiu regime?"

"There were issues to exploit."

There was a long silence, then we returned to more mundane matters. I was struck by his emphasis on the politics of the conflict but resort to miliary considerations to explain our loss. His explanations and arguments were weaker and less articulate than I would have thought, and he wasn't used to being questioned.

§§§

"Please extend my deepest regrets to the Olson family," Attorney General Edward Levi said after greeting Rudy and me at his office at the Justice Department in Washington. "This was a horrible series of events." President Ford selected Levi, a law professor, law school dean, and president of the University of Chicago, to restore public trust in the Justice Department after the "Saturday Night Massacre." President Nixon had ordered Attorney General Elliot Richardson to fire the special prosecutor investigating the Watergate scandal, Archibald Cox. Richardson refused and instead resigned; the next in line at the DOJ, Donald Ruckelshaus, did the same. The third in line, Solicitor General Robert Bork, fired Cox. It was an ugly scene. Levi brought integrity and unusual ability to the DOJ, along with a lot of bow ties and cigars.

"Thank you, and we will," I said.

"President Ford has asked me to give this matter some priority, so we have looked into it and want to begin discussions with you today. You've made a claim under the Federal Tort Claims Act."

"Yes," Rudy said, "and we set out the relief we seek in some detail, including the maximum allowable damages."

"I've asked Rex Lee, from the DOJ Civil Division, to attend and explain the problem we've uncovered."

We knew Lee from earlier cases. He was very conservative but a straight shooter. "The difficulty as we see it is that Mrs. Olson received benefits under FECA, the Federal Employee Compensation Act. That's an exclusive remedy and forecloses any other claims."

Employee compensation schemes usually had such provisions. They set up a trade-off. Limited benefits were relatively easy to obtain by filing an administrative claim, but much larger damages that might be obtained through a lawsuit were prohibited.

"We understand that argument," I said, "and in the typical case, it would have considerable merit, but the circumstances here are quite unusual. The CIA made the decision to deceive Mrs. Olson and to cover up what had occurred, regardless of the impact on her and her children. The FECA benefits were part of the deception and cover-up. They told her she would be paid a monthly sum, which made it less likely she'd ask questions or hire a lawyer."

"But once she got and accepted those benefits, we have a statutory defense to any claims you may raise."

"She never should have gotten FECA benefits. It covers injuries 'in the performance of his duties.' A drug experiment—or being an unwitting guinea pig in an experiment—was not part of Dr. Olson's duties. There is also an explicit exclusion of coverage in the FECA for suicide. The government cannot commit such a fraud and then benefit from it by using it as a defense to these claims."[3]

Levi paused. "What concerns me is we'd have to raise the defense; you'd make those arguments, which have considerable merit; and a judge would rule. It might get sent back to the secretary of labor to look into the circumstances and determine if Mrs. Olson was due FECA benefits."

"You'd raise the defense if we file the suit, but you can settle it before then. Cases are settled all the time when there is some defense that might be raised. This doesn't seem a hard or unusual case to settle. The alternative is to litigate it, which from our perspective provides a formal discovery process that will enable us to fully explore what happened."

"You are right, but these are, as you know, strange times. I do not want any public perception that we paid compensation in spite of a statutory defense. You've got the CIA documents, and we'll cooperate fully on getting the facts."

"We're not satisfied that we got all the documents or yet know what happened, and that's a predicate to any resolution of the case."

"I understand. On compensation, we have an alternative to propose—a private bill adopted by Congress to compensate the Olson family."

"I don't know a lot about private bills, but they're rarely passed and difficult to even get Congress to vote on."

"That's true, but this one would have the full support of the White House."

§§§

"I enjoyed your spirited questioning of Bill Colby at lunch," Rogovin wrote in a letter to me the day after the CIA visit. "I have assured others at the agency that we have an agreement," he added, "that the documents are for the sole purpose of prosecuting any claim. When you get a moment, simply send me a note confirming that."

Documents provided in litigation or anticipation of litigation were not made confidential by law or court rule. A lawyer wanting confidentiality had to say so and negotiate confidentiality terms or get a court to require confidentiality before providing documents. Rogovin had neglected to do this and was trying to cover his tracks. The Olsons wanted to make all the documents and everything we could find out public, so I paid careful attention to any hint of a request or expressed assumption of confidentiality by Rogovin or Colby, and there was none. The documents that were previously classified had been declassified before they were given to us, so I saw no limit on our use of them. I told Rogovin that we would make them all public, and we did in January 1976.

The documents, which we started calling the "Colby documents," were obviously incomplete and raised more questions than they answered. There were a variety of statements, memos, letters, and other writings but no overview, no discussions of policy or strategy, no medical or psychiatric opinions or details, no blood tests, no coherent or credible account of how or why Frank died, nor any credible investigation of what happened. The materials from the New York police and medical examiner were sketchy and had little content. The unwitting drugging was described as part of an experiment, but there were no details or discussion of the design of the experiment, what they sought to find out, how it was conducted, or what results they expected or obtained. Rogovin and the Justice Department added another handful of documents, and we asked for and got an affidavit from them saying under oath that we had everything there was, but the gaps and problems raised by the Colby documents weren't resolved.

I spent most of my time for weeks looking for witnesses, additional documents, books and studies, experts—anything or anyone who could help me understand what the government had been up to and what happened to Frank. I shared a lot of information and leads with an investigative reporter at the *New York Times,* Joe Treaster, and to a lesser extent with Bill Richards at the *Washington Post.* They had useful resources, including offices and reporters around the world; came up with significant information and evidence; and kept the story alive. Treaster was able to find one of the main characters identified in the documents in India.

Using the Colby documents and everything else I could find out reliably, I began to piece together some details of the CIA operation and Frank's death. The retreat at which Frank and others were unwittingly drugged was a gathering at Deep Creek Lake, in a remote area of western Maryland, of scientists who worked at Camp Detrick. Though innocuous in appearance and located in a beautiful rural area near Frederick, Maryland, Camp Detrick was the nation's primary facility for chemical and biological warfare. Frank worked there for many years as a biochemist and had held some midlevel managerial positions. He and his colleagues were funded or employed by military and intelligence agencies, including the army and CIA.

LSD emerged as a pop culture drug in the 1960s. Onetime Harvard professor Timothy Leary became the guru of LSD, and the Beatles sang "Lucy in the Sky with Diamonds." Its hallucinogenic effects and altered state of consciousness fit the times. But in 1953 LSD was unheard of publicly. It was often dangerous in the 1960s, though taken voluntarily with some knowledge of its effects. Receiving it unknowingly and without any understanding of what it was—or that the effects usually go away— would be terrifying.

My research on LSD led to episodes in Europe going back centuries in which whole villages were suddenly overcome with some mass hysteria. People went raving mad. Many died, and more never recovered. It was usually seen as the wrath of God—the name given it was St. Anthony's fire—but the most likely culprit was a form of ergot in bread that in some circumstances spontaneously formed lysergic acid diethylamide, LSD. Bread was picked up from bakers each day, so a whole village unwittingly got LSD-tainted bread at the same time. Well-known author John Fuller wrote about the common symptoms in these episodes and in the "bad trips" of the 1960s: "the distortion of time and space, hallucinations, the feeling that the walls and ceiling are closing in, the trembling, the profuse and chilled sweating, the insomnia, the compulsion to commit suicide, the compulsion to jump out of windows, including the conviction that one could fly."[4]

At the retreat, LSD was added to an after-dinner liqueur by Sidney Gottlieb, an organic chemist who was Frank's boss at Camp Detrick; chief of the CIA's chemical branch; and a central figure in the CIA's research and use of drugs, chemicals, and biological agents. Gottlieb's assistant, Robert Lashbrook, also participated in the unexplained "experiment."

The CIA looked into and developed a variety of substances for use in assassinations, interrogations, and localized or general incapacitation or killing of large populations. This work was used, for example, in the 1961 assassination of Patrice Lamumba, prime minister of the Congo, and in attempts to assassinate Fidel Castro. I didn't know the range of substances or uses until much later—including the assassinations and unwitting doses of LSD to hundreds, if not thousands, mostly soldiers. The Colby documents and other materials showed CIA use of drugs, wittingly and unwittingly, in programs like MK/ULTRA, Artichoke, and Bluebird with a cavalier irresponsibility that was chilling.[5]

Gottlieb may have wanted to watch the immediate impact of unwittingly administered LSD on his colleagues and friends and to hear their descriptions of it later; he may have wanted them to learn what it felt like; or he may have used it as an interrogative tool, a use the CIA was making of LSD though it wasn't suggested in the Colby documents, in an effort to gain information. It may have been Gottlieb's idea of a joke, a Camp Detrick sense of humor run amok. It wasn't clear and, as discussed in the Colby documents, didn't make sense. CIA director Allen Dulles reprimanded Gottlieb for "poor judgment" in unwittingly administering the drug, but no further explanation was offered.

The Colby documents' account of Frank's fall from a 10th-floor window at the Statler Hotel and the circumstances leading to it was bizarre. According to statements from mainly CIA personnel, Frank was out of it and delusional for days after he was unwittingly drugged with LSD. They described him as agitated, somewhat paranoid, unable to sleep, and generally confused. They decided that he needed help, so they took him to an allergist.

Dr. Harold A. Abramson was a well-known New York allergist and, covertly, a leading CIA researcher on LSD. He had no training or expertise in therapy and no therapeutic association with hospitals or mental institutions that might help Frank. His statements and memos showed he was unfamiliar with the common negative effects that LSD had on many people. The documents sometimes suggest that Abramson was helping or treating Frank, but his primary if not exclusive role, as someone familiar with LSD research who had top security clearances, was to evaluate the situation for the CIA. Frank saw Abramson a few times, was then taken back to Frederick for Thanksgiving dinner with his family, and then returned to New York to see Abramson again. He stayed with Robert Lashbrook, assistant chief of the CIA chemical branch, in a 10th-floor room at the Statler.

In the middle of the night, the statements said, Frank suddenly got up, ran across the room, and dived through a closed window with the blinds drawn, falling to his death on Seventh Avenue across from Pennsylvania Station. Lashbrook said he awoke when he heard glass break. He stayed in the room, without going to the ground floor to see how Frank was or calling for any emergency assistance. He telephoned CIA folks in Maryland and Dr. Abramson. The hotel night manager ran outside and found Frank on the ground, still alive and trying to speak but unable to say anything understandable before he died.

Experts on suicide I contacted found this scenario implausible. Someone intent on killing himself, particularly if able to precisely run and dive, would open the blinds, open the window, and jump.

The Colby documents sometimes described the presence of CIA people with Frank as protective of him, but they sounded more like a security detail. Hotels routinely placed anyone they were informed was having a mental problem on a low floor, and the Statler had such a policy. There were no medical or psychiatric reports, no consultations with any therapist, no results of blood tests, and the like. They shunted Frank around for a considerable period without helping or seeming to want to help him. Security, secrecy, and containment—rather than the well-being of Frank Olson—seemed the driving force for the government.

§§§

"Alice," I said, "we're at the point of making a decision on the case. Rudy and I are on the phone." We were on extensions at our office; Alice was at home in Frederick.

"Okay."

"We've been talking about this for a while, but I think we should review it all now. The government is offering to push through a private bill for the amount we've discussed, $1,250,000. We got somewhere with damages spread out on that table I showed you that highlights the different categories, pecuniary losses, pain and suffering to you and the children, additional pain and suffering due to the deception, loss of his companionship as a husband and parent, and the pain and suffering Frank experienced."

"I like the table."

"Thanks. This is much more than the actuarial calculation of Frank's expected lost income, about $300,000, but it's not gigantic."

"Just so you're clear, Alice," Rudy said, "if we did litigate, we can only sue under the Federal Tort Claims Act, and that doesn't allow any recovery for the deception or any punitive damages. A lawsuit would take at least a year, and we could lose, although we think that's unlikely. Also, you keep the employee compensation benefits already paid to you, about $150,000, and it's all exempt from taxes. Your total recovery would be $1,400,000."

"It's a lot of money, and I don't know how much more of this I can take."

"The decision we need from you," I said, "is whether to go the private bill route or litigate or do whatever it takes to find out what happened, why and how Frank died."

"What do you think now? I know you, David K., have thought we should go on."

I looked up and across the room at Rudy. "We both see good reasons for either decision, Alice, but there is some difference of opinion on our end. I don't like ending it without a credible account of what happened and why it happened. The Colby documents say Frank gave away his identification and security cards and talked to strangers about his work, and he mentioned resigning to you. This could be delusional or the actions of someone greatly mistreated who was doubting his work and his government. Either way, he may have become what they regarded as a security risk or a risk of revealing something they wanted kept secret. There is the look and feel of a cover-up, but what they were covering up isn't clear. That's where Rudy and I have some difference."

"Alice," Rudy said, "I don't find the Colby documents satisfying either, but there's no motive to kill him. We can't find anything that would rise to that level."

"Rudy and I agree on that. From the Colby documents and from what we've been able to piece together so far, there doesn't seem to be a strong motive to kill him or to facilitate his suicide. The LSD stuff was potentially embarrassing, but if Frank talked about it publicly, they could say he had a breakdown or contain it with national security explanations. There wasn't much questioning of military and intelligence agencies back then, particularly so soon after World War II.

"Pushing ahead, with litigation if need be, might uncover a motive as well as the details of what actually happened to Frank. We'd exhume Frank's body, and I've got that prominent pathologist we discussed. We'd depose Gottlieb, Abramson, Lashbrook, all of them, and get more documents."

"Maybe I should go on," Alice said. "I don't know what Frank would want me to do. I guess I can't imagine that what they did was even worse than we already know. I don't know if I could handle it if they murdered him, and I don't like bringing him up from the grave. I think we know enough. I've talked it out with all three of my children, and we're ready to go with the private bill."

"I understand, Alice," I said. "You did miraculously well through all this, and you fought back for Frank and the whole family."

The Olsons issued a statement about the settlement by private bill that closed with this: "For our family this agreement represents vindication of the claims we have made. The government has acknowledged the illegality of the CIA's actions; we will be compensated in a reasonable amount; and the public will be provided with the facts concerning the circumstances surrounding Frank Olson's death. Nothing more could be accomplished by a lawsuit."

§§§

Only a handful of private bills were enacted each year. Congress's usual work was on public bills directed at the future, which apply to everyone. Private bills granted something, usually money from the treasury, to a particular person based on something that occurred in the past. This made them ripe for abuse, which probably explains the congressional rules that make them so difficult to pass.

The bill was introduced by Marylanders, since that was Frank Olson's home state, Senator Charles Mathias and Representative Goodloe Byron. It was taken up initially by the Senate Judiciary Committee and the Subcommittee on Administrative Law and Government Relations of the House Committee on the Judiciary. We prepared memos on several issues for the committees. Letters in support were sent from the White House and the CIA to the chairs of both committees. The CIA letters were signed by the new director, George H. W. Bush.

Almost all private bills failed to make it out of the committees. It was unusual for one to come to a committee vote because any objection could foreclose a vote and the committees were usually occupied with other matters. Members of Congress often used the gesture of proposing a private bill to satisfy constituents though they knew it went to the dead-end committees. This was so common that members had to tell the committee members when they really meant a private bill to pass.

Even with White House and CIA backing, it took months and secret CIA briefings to finally get quorums, votes, and no objections in the committees. It mattered just how each committee member was approached. When a House committee member was balking, one of the White House liaisons told me, "They like to be asked—they will want a post office in their district or something else later."

The Senate wasn't a problem. But when the bill came to a vote in the House in late September 1976, three members moved that it be "passed over." They could have been overwhelmingly outvoted, but that was unusual on private bills. "It's risky to call for a vote to override the objectors," the White House liaison said. "Many might vote against us to uphold the tradition on private bills." A small number of objectors could kill a private bill.

I went to Washington early the next morning and met with the White House, DOJ, and CIA liaisons and House staff and members. The three objecting House members were led by Republicans John Rousselot of California and Robert Baumann of Maryland. There was a range of ideas about why they opposed the bill. Rousselot had expressed opposition to all private bills and regularly objected to them. He was well known in Congress as an injured war veteran who was a leader of the extreme right-wing John Birch Society. He had written an article in 1964 entitled "Civil Rights: Communist Betrayal of a Good Cause."

The liaisons and staff and favorable members of the House had spoken to Rousselot to no avail. Rousselot said that when he spoke to CIA director Bush about the bill, Bush said, "I don't give a damn one way or the other." When they offered to have the president call him, Rousselot said, "Fuck the president." Some of them had heard that the Justice Department was undermining our effort by saying the bill should be for a maximum of $500,000, which was their proposed settlement amount and the most agreed to in Federal Tort Claims Act cases. Others said Representative Byron had told Rousselot that it wasn't a priority for him. They were all embarrassed and seemed to blame each other. They thought we should agree to accept $500,000, which might secure passage immediately.

I asked to talk to Rousselot, so they set up a meeting in the Republican cloakroom on the floor of the House. I was led through checkpoints and security barriers to the back of the chamber, just beyond the rows of chairs for members. The House was in session; members walked every which way, and many were talking or hanging out in the cloakroom. I was asked to sit at a table while Rousselot was summoned. He approached, stern-faced with a pronounced limp, probably from his war injuries, I thought.

"We don't have much time," he said. "I am opposed, I suppose you've heard, to private bills in principle."

"I have heard that, and I can understand it. But some do pass, and none is more compelling than this."

"The government shouldn't be handing out money to individual people."

"This is a man whose work was dedicated to his nation and his military, who was drugged and struck down by that military. We wouldn't be here except the same government officials who did this covered it up by giving the widow paltry employee compensation benefits. That's a legal barrier to the usual sort of legal claim. This is a legitimate, compelling use of a private bill. The CIA and the military fully support it." I left out the president, who wasn't much help with Rousselot.

"It's extremely large for a private bill. I don't think the CIA or military really want it. They're bowing to media pressure. This family should take $500,000. They've got Ford on his knees apologizing. Isn't that enough?"

"That would barely cover the lost income of this well-educated scientist. They've lived close to the edge since all this and had to deal with the lies about some inexplicable suicide."

"There are always sacrifices. You get me a private letter from the CIA director exclusively to me, not for public consumption, saying unequivocally that he wants this, and I'll go a little higher, maybe $600,000."

"We'll get you that letter, but I can't in all conscience recommend that figure to the Olsons. We'd take our chances with a lawsuit, and this would be all over the media and an embarrassment for the military and intelligence agencies for years to come."

"Seven hundred and fifty thousand, and you get me that letter. I'll go that far, more than I ever have before."

I talked to the Olsons, and they talked among themselves. They agreed to accept $750,000. Rousselot got an unequivocal, personal letter from Bush, and the private bill passed at $750,000.

President Ford issued a statement when he signed the private bill. "My administration is opposed to the use of drugs, chemicals, or other substances without the prior knowledge and consent of the individual affected," he said. "At the request of the family of Dr. Olson, I take this opportunity to highlight this continuing policy."

§§§

But it wasn't over. More investigations of the CIA yielded more victims of drugs, biological agents, and assassinations. And there was more tragedy for the Olsons. In 1978, Lisa; her husband, Greg Hayward; and their son, Jonathan, were killed in a small-airplane crash. Alice died in 1993 from a relapse of cancer that had first appeared when we were debating the private bill.

Eric moved to Sweden. He never really accepted the CIA's explanations, and in the 1980s he came back to the United States, where he and his brother, Nils, continued their pursuit of the truth of their father's death. After Alice's death, they exhumed Frank's body under the supervision of well-known pathologist James Starrs. His findings contradicted the CIA account with forensic evidence and a computer simulation of the fall. He found some evidence of a blunt-force blow to the head inflicted before the fall from the hotel window. A "homicide, deft, deliberate, and diabolical," Starrs concluded.

In the mid-1990s, New York district attorney Robert Morganthau opened a grand jury investigation, but no charges were brought. More details about the work at Camp Detrick emerged, including Frank's work on airborne biological agents and on aggressive interrogation techniques that killed some subjects. The latest revelations focus on Anthrax research and allegations of the use of germ warfare by our forces in the Korean War. These theories provide both a more substantial motive to silence Frank and more reason to believe he was discontented with his work and may have become a whistle-blower.

Frank Olson's death and the CIA's mischief are now the subject of many books, articles, films, TV exposés, and talk shows, with many theories of how and why the CIA may have murdered Frank Olson. There are reports of Israel's Mossad's studying the Olson case as an effective example of "deniable assassination." Some tie Colby's firing to the case or suggest that Colby's death in 1996 might be related. Others emphasize the behind-the-scenes work in the Ford administration to avoid further revelations with a settlement by none other than Dick Cheney and Donald Rumsfeld. Internal memos surfaced about CIA and White House concern that I disbelieved the Colby documents explanations and was pushing for full disclosure, which they didn't want. The best information is available on a Web site maintained by Eric and in the work and forthcoming book of author Hank Albarelli, Jr.[6]

I have not been actively involved in the Olson case since the private bill. I still don't know with certainty what happened to Frank Olson.

CHAPTER ELEVEN

More Juries, Less Peers

H ELLO, DAVID," I heard as I picked up the phone, in a deep voice that could only be Jay Schulman's.

"Jay, how are you doing?"

"Fair to middlin', I guess, but look, I got something big, and I want you in."

"Okay, what is it?" Jay sometimes had little time for small talk but often had things brewing that I liked.

"Attica."

"What about Attica?" A couple years earlier, in September 1971, inmates at New York's Attica Prison seized parts of the prison and took hostages in a protest of notoriously harsh prison conditions. Prisoners and hostages stayed in an open yard for a few days while a team of journalists and activists tried to facilitate negotiations. On the fourth day, Governor Nelson Rockefeller ordered state police to storm the yard and other parts of the prison held by inmates, although there still seemed room for talking. Ten prison employees and 29 prisoners died, and twice that number were wounded in a hale of police gunfire.[1]

"You know, we won the change of venue motion using our survey of attitudes on the Attica defendants," Jay said. "Three-quarters of the public believe the inmates killed the hostages, and most believe what the assistant warden said about inmates 'slitting throats' and 'castrating guards,' although none of it was true. Anyway, the case got moved to Buffalo, so we checked out the juries there. They're all old white men that're bigger than me, like that Philadelphia jury challenge you did. When they gather for jury duty, it looks like a reunion of Notre Dame linemen. We need you to challenge the jury system."

Jay often looked like a mountain man who occasionally came down to town for supplies and a jury consultation. He was big, particularly his chest and shoulders, a lineman on his college football team. His sandy brown hair was long and usually all over the place, and he had a narrow ribbon of a beard, similar to the Amish style.

Jay had originated and developed innovative jury selection techniques that are now often used by the wealthiest litigants, but he used them in political cases and for indigent defendants.[2] He was a middle-aged sociologist who had been denied tenure at some of the best universities in the nation. He was outspoken and could never seem to fit in long enough to hold down an academic job. I enjoyed plotting and hanging out with Jay from our first meeting, when he helped us pick the jury in the Camden 28 case. We became good friends but also got into strange conflicts I didn't understand until much later.

"What do the stats show?" I asked.

"For Erie County, the jury pool is less than 10 percent black and the population is about twice that. Women are way underrepresented."

A few days later, Beth Bonora, who was running all the jury operations for the Attica case, called. She was putting together a team of lawyers for the jury challenge, which eventually included Neal Bush from Detroit, Paul Chevigny from the ACLU in New York, and me.

"Jay said something about women as well as race."

"Yeah. They're only 15 or 20 percent of the pool. There's a voluntary exemption for women. They can opt out if they want to by checking a box on the questionnaire."

"Does that explain it all? Fifteen to 20 percent is awful low."

"I don't know; we'll look into it if you think it might matter. There are also very few young people, which I think has a lot to do with how they maintain the jury pool."

"How is that?"

"They have a permanent pool instead of making a new pool each year like everybody else seems to do. The pool gets older, and they add few young people. Can I count you in?"

More than a year later, I flew into the Buffalo airport, and Beth was there to meet me. "Good to meet you in person, after all those phone calls," she said. She was thin and medium in height with short dark hair, smaller than I pictured from her strong voice and leading role. She drove me from the Buffalo airport to a house the jury project was working and living in.

"Yeah, it looks like we're ready to go."

§§§

"Mr. 'Carey,' or however you say it, I don't understand why it takes three outside lawyers to litigate one minor motion, but I'll admit you for purposes of this jury motion," said Judge Gilbert King, who was hearing pretrial motions in the Attica cases. A lawyer had to get court approval to practice in another state, but usually it was routine. With Judge King, nothing our side asked for was routine.

We proved the racial disparity with expert statisticians and social scientists who designed and supervised a survey of the race of several hundred people randomly chosen from the jury pool. The responses of each in phone interviews were handwritten on forms stapled to copies of their jury questionnaires. When the prosecutor objected to the methods used to do the survey, we promised to introduce the actual survey forms and copies of questionnaires later in the hearing, which satisfied the judge. This seemed straightforward, until we were all called to an urgent evening meeting several days into the hearing.

"We've got a problem," Beth said. She looked worried and angry. "The survey forms and questionnaires were stapled together and put in boxes after the survey was done, over six months ago. But the basement was flooded in one of the endless winter storms around here. We knew some of the boxes might have gotten wet, but it looks like somebody threw them out with other wet stuff."

"You mean," Bill, one of the underpaid staff, yelled at Beth, "we don't have the forms we promised the judge?"

"Yeah, that's what I mean."

"Well, who the fuck did this? We're in deep shit." He got up and glared at Beth.

"I don't know who or when or why, but we have to deal with it," Beth said, looking sternly at Bill and the whole group.

"Now look, Beth, you know how this is going to go down with the judge—and the prosecutor and cops," Bill said, pointing at Beth. "They raided the Defense Committee office awhile back based on nothing, and on the streets they pull us over and hassle us any chance they get."

"We're looking at lawyer trouble, too," one of the lawyers said. "I could see disbarment proceedings. We told the judge we have it and will introduce it as evidence. King will come down heavy on us." He looked at Beth, then over at me. I wasn't worried about disbarment, but "deep shit" said it about right.

"Look," Beth said, "maybe we have to go in and apologize and explain it, or I don't know what, but let's get some ideas. Now, tonight. We probably have to do something in court tomorrow."

"I want to know who did this, let them take the fall," Bill said, still yelling. "I'm not gettin' in this kind of trouble because some ass threw the boxes away." He stormed out of the room, but others expressed the same fears.

There was a level of panic I hadn't seen from a legal team, but then again we were defending the inmates who took over Attica Prison, the most hated and feared people of the time in Buffalo, New York State, and probably the whole country. I wasn't that concerned, although I wondered if I should be since almost everybody else was. There had to be some way to deal with this, and I wanted to get to that, but it was hard to think with all the fear and yelling.

"Beth," I said, in the lowest-decibel, calmest voice I had, "do you have any doubt that the data on those thrown away forms add up to the numbers we presented in court?"

"No question. It was done by a guy experienced with surveys, then checked by me, and one of the experts had his graduate student add it up and recalculate everything again to be sure."

"So we haven't presented incorrect data or bad evidence, we just can't produce the underlying survey data, the recorded answers that each member of the jury pool in the sample gave to our callers?"

"That's it. Are we screwed?"

"We may have to drop the race issue in the case, which would be a shame, but whatever happened was not intentional on our part—no one knowingly presented false evidence or knowingly promised to bring in evidence that doesn't exist. They can make a big deal if they want, but we have a good explanation. I just want to save the race issue."

§§§

"Alright, let's resume the hearing on the defendants' jury motion," Judge King said the next morning. "But before we start, I received a message that the jury commissioner wants to address an issue in the case that has arisen. Crucian, what is it? Come up here now."

"Your Honor," Erie County jury commissioner Crucian Messina said as he almost ran up to the bench, "it's about a subpoena related to this case that I got this morning. It asks—"

"Maybe we should address this in chambers," King said. "Let's do that; I'll see all counsel and Mr. Messina in chambers."

We all took seats around the front of King's desk. "What is it, Crucian?" he said.

"Your Honor, I got this subpoena that gives me just a few days to bring a long list of juror questionnaires, hundreds listed by questionnaire numbers, to court for this proceeding. I assume you know about it, Your Honor, but it would take my whole office doing nothing else to comply." He handed the subpoena to the judge.

"I don't know anything about it," King said, turning to us, "What is this?"

"Judge," I said, "you remember we said we would introduce the questionnaires from the survey sample during the expert testimony. The best evidence rule says we should prefer, and maybe you should only accept, originals of documents when they are available. So we've given Mr. Messina the list of the questionnaire numbers that were in the random sample and asked that he produce the originals of those questionnaires to be entered as exhibits in the case."

"Your Honor," Messina said, "we'll do it if that's what you need, but it's a ton of work."

"Can we stipulate or something to get around this?" the prosecutor said. A stipulation is an agreement about facts or issues in a case that is formally presented on the record so neither side has to present evidence on the matter.

"That's a good idea," I said. "Maybe there's a way to do this that could avoid the burden on Mr. Messina's office, which is not our intention. We could all agree to a stipulation that the questionnaires listed by number in the subpoena are evidence in the case to be held by Mr. Messina as they are now, with the other questionnaires in numbered drawers in the Jury Commission office and to be available to counsel or Judge King or any appellate judges that may hear the case. Mr. Messina, you could just leave them all right where they are."

"That sounds good to me, Your Honor," Messina said.

"Do we have a stipulation then?" King said, looking toward me.
"Sure."

§§§

As we walked back into the courtroom, Neal Bush took me aside. "I can't believe that worked. They never asked about the survey forms." He was shaking his head. "How did you think of that best evidence crap that doesn't really apply in this situation?"

"I don't know. I was trying to figure out a way to make them want us not to bring in the lost stuff rather than us asking for mercy. Subpoenaing the questionnaires used in the survey and waiting for them to ask us to make the burden lighter seemed to do it, and the best evidence rationale seemed a way to explain the subpoena. If they asked for the survey materials we promised, I was going to tell them exactly what happened."

"I like it."

"Thanks. You're up now with several of the clerks from the Jury Commission office."

"Yeah. I'll go through the systematic selection stuff we talked about."

Neal was going to question the clerks about their role in the process for selecting jurors. I asked him to include some detail about the way they picked names from the voter list to be sent questionnaires. I had noticed an odd pattern in the way they did it, and we couldn't figure out why they did it that way or what, if any, significance it had.

Systematic selection was an easy way to randomly select names from a long list. Software for random selection is now available at Radio Shack, but back then it was difficult to do. IBM published long books full of random numbers that were used for manual random selection. Systematic selection also did it manually by first calculating the "interval," which is the gap between selections you would need to go through the list and get the desired number selected. If you wanted 1,000 randomly selected names from a list of 25,000 names, you'd pick every 25th name; the interval is 25. It's random as long as you randomly pick a "starting number" from 1 to 25 or 1 to the interval number. For example, if the starting number randomly picked, often by drawing numbers on pieces of paper from a hat, was 5, you'd select the 5th name, the 30th, the 55th, and so on through the whole list.

Erie County used this method, but the intervals were often off. We looked at one printout of the voter list they used with an interval of 356, but when we counted to check, we found that they frequently picked the 357th, 355th, or 354th names, within a few of the interval but not exactly the interval.

"Mrs. Clardy," Neal asked one of the clerks, "so you used the systematic selection method to draw names from the voter lists, and on this occasion, the one in which you used the list I've handed you and marked as an exhibit, your interval was 356?"

"Yes, that's right."

"Well, we counted the intervals, and by our count, the second one was 357 and the third was 355.

"Do you want me to recount now, in court?"

"You can, but we've done it several times."

"Alright, I'll accept that. We must have made a mistake."

"Well, let's look at the second one. If you count down 356 names, you'd have picked Marcia Abrams, but you actually picked Thomas Abrams, the 357th."

"Well, I see what you mean now. I would have gotten to the 356th name, Marcia, and noticed that she and the next name were a man and woman at the same address, so they're married. See here, it's the same address." She pointed to the addresses on the exhibit.

"Yes, I see, so they're married. What does that mean?" Neal asked.

"We wouldn't bother picking Marcia, since she would just ask for an exemption or excuse. Thomas would be her husband, and he would likely serve. It's really the man's duty anyway."

"So you rejected Marcia, because she is a women, in favor of her husband?"

"Yeah, I guess. We don't think about it that way. We don't reject, but that's what we did. We picked the husband."

"Do all the clerks do it this way?"

"Yeah, that's how we done it as far back as I can remember."

That was it, the whole case. It explained the huge underrepresentation of women, and the judge couldn't avoid an admission on the witness stand of deliberate discrimination against women. He invalidated the system, and someone was hired to help them get a more representative pool of jurors.

The prosecutors had indicted over 50 inmates separately, which would result in that many trials, for "felony murder," an old form of mur-

der we got from the British. If someone dies during the course of commission of a felony, anyone committing the felony can be charged with
murder, although they didn't actually kill or mean to kill anyone. After
the jury challenge, the newly constituted juries acquitted inmates
charged in the early felony murder trials, then the prosecutors dropped
the rest. The juries were able to separate the hostage taking, the racial divide, and the community's understandable outrage from the deaths of
hostages and inmates killed by police bullets. The diversity of the jurors
played a significant role. Jury challenges could integrate an important institution from which minorities and women had been excluded not long
before—discrimination against women as jurors was upheld by the
Supreme Court as late as 1961—and provide justice to litigants.[3]

§§§

It didn't take much or long for a lawyer to be regarded as a leader in a
field. After the Attica and Philadelphia jury challenges, I got calls from
lawyers around the country who wanted me to litigate or advise them on
their jury challenges. After the Attica case, I joined an effort led by Jay
and Beth to create a national organization that would deal with the range
of jury issues—representativeness, juror questioning (voir dire), selection techniques, change of venue because of prejudice, and protection of
the jury as an institution from attempts afoot to limit or eliminate it. We
and others, including another lawyer who became a close friend, Rhonda
Copelon at the Center for Constitutional Rights, founded the National
Jury Project (NJP) in 1974. The next year, we published a short how-to
book on jury issues aimed at lawyers and social scientists, *The Jury System: New Methods for Reducing Prejudice,* which I edited. We went on tour
throughout the country giving talks and selling books.

In April 1975, a few days after my 32nd birthday, I stood before a
crowd of a couple hundred people, mostly lawyers, at UCLA, ready, or almost ready, to begin a tour event. I was used to speaking to judges, juries,
and small gatherings, but the sight of all those faces and the sound of
their noisy chatter were daunting. I steadied myself by remembering that
law practice had been unfamiliar and daunting every step of the way and
realizing I should just do it my way without trying to be Perry Mason or
anybody else.

"Most criminal lawyers pay little or no attention to jury selection," I said. "A trial is usually viewed as won or lost by evidence and arguments, and the common assumption is that jury selection can be done well by any decent trial lawyer.

"There are exceptions. Federal prosecutors routinely use juror investigations conducted by FBI agents, files in government and private data banks, and records of prior jury service. The prior jury service information is often used to remove anyone who has previously been on a jury that acquitted, since they likely believe in reasonable doubt. Local prosecutors use some or all of the same methods.

"In the Harrisburg 8 case, the prosecutor introduced into the record information on a juror's participation in an antiwar demonstration overseas. In the Minnesota trial of Indian activists Dennis Banks and Russell Means, the prosecutor had deputy sheriffs 'check out' potential jurors. In the Camden 28 case, the prosecutor struck a juror who seemed favorable to the government but had served on a jury that found an accused bank robber not guilty.

"The defense doesn't get any access to this information. But we can do our own investigations, and other new techniques we're going to talk about today are available.

"These techniques originated in 1971 when sociologist Jay Schulman was asked to help the defense figure out how to select jurors in the Harrisburg 8 case. John Mitchell's and J. Edgar Hoover's Justice Department could have chosen to bring that case in many places, since a conspiracy is chargeable anywhere any minor part of it occurred. They chose Harrisburg, Pennsylvania, because its population is very conservative and pro-prosecution.

"Schulman asked local defense lawyers how they selected jurors, and a common response was, 'We like college graduates and folks who read the *New York Times*. They're more liberal and more open to reasonable doubt.' He decided to test this out with a survey of eligible jurors. What he found surprised everyone: college graduates and readers of the *New York Times* were among the most proprosecution jurors.

"Schulman then sought an explanation by talking to a range of local people who might have some insight about it—social scientists at local colleges, survey outfits, political party operatives, taxicab drivers, and lunch counter servers, just plain folks who might know something and want to talk. An explanation emerged: Most 'liberal'-leaning locals who go to college leave Harrisburg and don't come back, since there isn't much opportunity for them there. Local readers of the *New York Times* aren't attracted by all the news that's fit to print but by the financial pages, which aren't available in the local newspapers. In Harrisburg, college graduates and *Times* readers tend to be better for the prosecution."

I paused and looked out at the crowd. "Do I have your attention?"

"Yes!" came booming back. That did in the last of my jitters.

"Alright. What Schulman, Beth Bonora, and others in NJP have developed since the Harrisburg 8 case is a sophisticated use of survey data that looks for correlations like I just mentioned. We're looking for characteristics that correlate with attitudes about trials generally, such as belief in the presumption of innocence and reasonable doubt, and about particular issues in a case. But it's not only a numbers game. We look for, as to particular jurors, reasons they might not fit a general tendency—a recent divorce, for example, can lead to a reexamination of and change in one's life. We try to figure out who will be leaders in the group of some segment of jurors. Sometimes what a person believes is less important than who else on a jury they will tend to follow. Finally, we look at the group as a whole and try to figure out how the group dynamics might work out. There are surveys, numbers, correlations, but it's ultimately an art as much as a science."

§§§

Not long after the jury tour, I found myself seated in an NBC studio at Rockefeller Center in New York City next to Assistant Attorney General Dick Thornburgh, later attorney general and governor of Pennsylvania, and Tom Brokaw, on the set of the *Today* show. We debated investigation of jurors by prosecutors and defense lawyers. But the jury issues that most interested me then had more to do with voting patterns and statistical methods used in jury challenges.

In the Philadelphia and Attica challenges, and in data from many others, the underrepresentation of blacks and other minorities was mostly caused by the use of voter lists as the starting source of names for selecting jurors. Voter lists were an improvement over the "key man" systems but not a good place to start if one wanted a cross-section of the community. Almost half of eligible Americans didn't vote, and the proportions of nonvoters were much higher among minorities and poor and young people.

Use of voter lists was sometimes justified as providing better jurors, but juries are supposed to represent everybody, not anybody's notion of who is "best." The laws in most states, and the federal laws, treated the voter lists as a means to an end—representativeness—rather than an end in themselves, but many jury challenges were decided by judges on the ground that voter lists were an allowable source, avoiding consideration of how well they provided representativeness. There was also a practical rationale that was harder to challenge: we don't have lists of our citizens, which almost every other country does, because of conservative and liberal fears of big-brother government, and combining the voter list with additional lists was technically difficult and expensive.

I developed some ways to challenge the use of unrepresentative lists as unconstitutional and, often, violative of the statutes that establish jury systems. It was obvious that to get a cross-section you'd want to include lists rich in names not on the voter lists, such as drivers, unemployment, and welfare lists. But I had no idea of how to deal with the technical difficulty of using multiple lists—including the problem that some names are on more than one of the lists—until an unexpected phone call from Jay Kadane at Carnegie Mellon University in Pittsburgh. He and a colleague had developed a cleverly easy, inexpensive way to randomly draw names from long lists.

Jay visited soon after, and we began discussing other jury issues. "Did you notice in the materials I sent you," I asked him, "what I've been doing in terms of standards of representativeness? Most courts and statisticians assume that the traditional statistical significance test is the way to go, but I prefer the comparative disparity."

"I did notice that, and you've gotten yourself into a big debate in statistics. By 'comparative disparity' you mean the relative underrepresentation. If blacks are 30 percent of the population but 20 percent of the jury pool, it would be 30 minus 20 divided by 30, or one-third."

"That's it. That gives you a good measure of the extent of underrepresentation. The statistical significance method 'tests' whether the jury pool was randomly selected from the population by calculating the probability of randomly drawing a jury pool that's 20 percent black from a population that's 30 percent black. If that probability is low, less than 5 percent, you conclude it wasn't. But we already know that—it was picked from the unrepresentative voter lists. If the number drawn randomly is large—like maybe 5,000 for a year's worth of jurors—a small difference comes out significant. I calculated that if the draw or sample is over a couple thousand, a pool that's 28 percent black when the population is 30 percent comes out statistically significant. I want the courts to adopt a standard, but this has bothered me."

"You're a Bayesian."

"Is that bad?" Bayesian could be some low-life group in Pittsburgh.

"Not at all. Bayes was a cleric several centuries ago who came up with some amazing ideas about math and statistics. Bayesians think the statistical significance test is overused and 5 percent has become a mantra without much meaning. Your comparative disparity is, mathematically, the reduced probability of serving. A comparative disparity of one-third means that blacks' chances of being selected are reduced by one-third."

We went on like that, sometimes for hours, as we eventually worked together on a range of issues and became friends. Our law review article on representativeness, which has been widely cited by courts and scholars, appeared just in time for me to use it in my testimony before the Senate Judiciary Committee opposing an attempt to amend the federal jury selection law to make it harder to challenge use of voter lists.[4]

§§§

"Wasn't that case on TV?" I asked Ruben Sandoval, a well-known lawyer calling from Texas in 1978.

"Yeah, *60 Minutes*," he said. "They played it up as some major ripoff of the government, the worst example of Medicaid fraud, but it's nothing like that. Anyway, we want you to come down to San Antonio and challenge this jury system for us. Hispanics are over half of the population here but only 30 percent to 35 percent of the jury pool."

I looked into the case. Some media accounts depicted the defendant, Dr. Raul Gaona, as a Robin Hood. He treated the poor without regard to payment and at all hours of the night, which made him popular in the Hispanic community. The implication was that he also overcharged the federal government to pay for it. It sounded interesting, but the underlying case didn't really matter. If the jury system is not representative, it should be fixed for all defendants. They also offered me a good hourly rate, so it wasn't Robin Hood for me.

A judge from Louisiana was brought in to hear the jury challenge, since the local federal judges were involved in the jury selection process.

He took the issue seriously and agreed that such a large racial disparity wasn't acceptable, but he didn't accept our evidence on the proportion of the population that is Hispanic. Our main expert was a demographer who served as a consultant to the Census Bureau. Figuring out the Hispanic percentage was complicated. He did it the way the Census Bureau does, using official lists of Hispanic surnames and accounting for a range of factors, including the Census Bureau's acknowledged undercounting, particularly of minorities. The judge denied the jury challenge but said in his opinion that "efforts directed toward improvements will be made."

Then a strange thing happened. The panel of jurors for the Gaona trial was almost all Hispanic, the apparent result of some quick changes made by jury selection clerks in light of the widely publicized jury challenge. The resulting jury had only one non-Hispanic. Dr. Gaona was acquitted, in what some saw as the kind of jury nullification the Camden 28 sought. Since an unrepresentative jury system undermined the integrity and legitimacy of the legal system, this was an area of law in which you could win by losing.[5]

§§§

In the late 1970s, an accountant in a cubbyhole office at Coca-Cola's headquarters in Atlanta noticed that Coke was paying a lot of money for garbage disposal. They looked into it and discovered that the major garbage disposal companies in the Atlanta area were all charging the same, very high price. Coke reported this to the federal prosecutor in Atlanta—who, like most everyone around there, listened when Coke called. The garbage disposal firms were indicted for price fixing, based on evidence that reportedly included detailed minutes of their meeting to fix prices.

The defendants hired the best lawyers in Atlanta and beyond, who sought all possible ways to defeat or derail the prosecution, including hiring me to launch a jury challenge. I had two requests. I wanted to include in the jury challenge all of the clients of the public defender and the same hourly rate as the highest paid lawyer on the defense team.

They agreed. The first day of the two-week hearing in January 1981 looked like an American Bar Association convention. There was at least one lawyer, and usually two or three, for each of the over 30 garbage defendants; several public defenders; and several public defender clients in prison garb brought to court for the hearing. I sat in front of this assemblage, facing Judge William Keady.

Keady was a federal judge in Mississippi brought in for the jury challenge because all of the Atlanta judges disqualified themselves. We wound up focusing on the grand jury and the selection of its forepersons, which recent cases ruled had to be representative, because the underrepresentation was glaring. Blacks were 19.1 percent of the population but 4.7 percent of the forepersons, and only the same proportion, 4.7 percent, were women. Women were underrepresented by 90 percent and blacks by 75 percent.

Some associates at the big firms were assigned to me, available to find a case or research an issue any time of the day or night. I was also put in a nice room in one of the new atrium-style hotels, with nothing in the middle and elevators hanging off inside and outside walls, and fed anything I wanted. I enjoyed it but knew I shouldn't get too used to it.

Most of the witnesses were experts for us or the government testifying on the racial and gender underrepresentation, but I had noticed another problem in their jury selection process. I waited until we called the jury clerk, Angela Turner, to testify about how the process worked. After going through the process, I said, "Let's go back to the process used for picking jurors from the jury pool, the pool of people who have been sent questionnaires and determined to be qualified. You said you use a systematic selection technique?"

"Yes, sir. We calculate the interval based on the number in the pool and the number we need, then we select the starting number. Those numbers are entered into the computer, and it does the rest."

"And you testified that you pick the starting numbers out of a 'drum or box,' in the words of the formal rules of the court, that has cards with every number from one to the interval?"

"Yes, sir."

"Do you understand why it's important to do it that way?"

"Yes, sir. It has to be random, and that makes it random."

"Alright, Mrs. Turner. I want to ask you again so we are completely sure about this. You actually pick the starting numbers the way you've described so far, from a box or drum the way it's set out in the rules?"

"Objection," the prosecutor said.

Keady looked over to me. "If she's already said it, why again?"

"That will become clear very soon, Judge, if you will allow me to proceed."

"Very well, go on."

"Mrs. Turner?"

"Yes, sir, I'm sure that's how I did it."

"Alright. Mrs. Turner, I've looked at the starting numbers you selected for the last three years. The interval is usually from about 300 to as high as 500, but the starting numbers are mostly less than 100."

"Well, that may be. It's just chance."

"Just chance. The highest starting number was 288. None were between 288 and 500?"

"If you say so."

"Of 59 starting numbers that are supposed to range from 1 to about 500, you picked 18 numbers, almost a third of them, twice?"

"Okay."

"Eight, 12, and 16 got picked three times each. Doesn't that seem unlikely?"

"I don't know."

"Twenty-one got picked four times. Four times out of 59, with numbers that are supposed to range up to 500. Did you pick them from the box, randomly?"

"I don't know how it came out this way."

"Mrs. Turner, 78 was picked six times and so was 89. Six times. Those 2 numbers alone, out of a total of 500 numbers, were picked in one-fifth of the selections. You picked these numbers out of your head, didn't you?"

"I, I guess. . . . I don't know." She looked down, and her hands came to her face. She sobbed, then lurched out of the witness chair and ran out of the courtroom.

That's about as close as I've gotten to a Perry Mason moment, but it wasn't as satisfying as I had thought it would be. I felt a little sorry for her. It was a silly shortcut, she should have followed the rules, and I gave her many chances to fess up. But a shaming in open court seemed a bit much.

Keady wasn't feeling sorry for her. In a long opinion that was sharply critical of Mrs. Turner, he dismissed the indictments in the garbage and public defender cases. He adopted our arguments that the error was not merely technical because randomness assures that everyone has the same chances of being selected and is central to the whole jury system. She also ignored the requirement in the rules to post a public notice of starting number drawings, and the clerk's office ignored earlier challenges that should have at least alerted them to improprieties in jury selection. An administrator should not have the power to select this way and could, in theory, use it to place any particular person in the pool on a panel for a particular case.

On appeal, the Fifth Circuit didn't see it that way, but the Atlanta federal court had already established a new, more representative jury system, and the garbage defendants got a long delay, and some got off with a small fine.[6]

§§§

Tony Amsterdam, who brought me to the Penn program and Philadelphia, led a decade-long halt of executions throughout the United States. When executions resumed after the Supreme Court rejected all challenges to the death penalty, some states significantly changed the way death penalty cases were handled. New Jersey was a leader in requiring and funding new protections for defendants charged with capital offenses. One of those protections was a funded effort to make sure that juries in capital cases were representative. In the mid-1980s New Jersey's statewide public defender hired me to examine the jury systems in each county and challenge any that were insufficiently representative. I challenged the jury systems in Newark (Essex County), Atlantic City (Atlantic County), and Woodbury (Gloucester County).

Each of the three had a substantial racial underrepresentation, but I also investigated their systems thoroughly. Woodbury was using voters and drivers lists, which was much better than voters alone, but they botched the merging of the lists. A computer eliminated a duplicate only if they were exactly the same. The judge explained in his opinion that "William Legal" on one list would not be considered to duplicate "William L. Legal" on the other. They also excluded drivers from eight zip codes, amounting to about a quarter of the drivers, because parts of those zip codes were not in the county. The judge invalidated the system on those grounds, not because blacks were 4.6 percent of the jury pool but 8.6 percent of the population.

In Newark, the population was 35.9 percent black, but the jury pool was 21.8 percent black. The source list, which was 21.3 percent black, was the problem. The prosecutor's expert, who taught sociology at Princeton, criticized the methods our experts used to arrive at those figures. I decided to take advantage of my science studies in college. I read all the articles and books the Princeton expert had written and found among them an example of his use of each of the methods he criticized our experts for using. The judge accepted the figures, but he ruled that the underrepresentation was not substantial enough.

The New Jersey Supreme Court found the underrepresentation of blacks "significant enough to alert us to a possible constitutional violation," "far from optimal," and "straddl[ing] the borderline of substantial underrepresentation." They reviewed the various standards of representativeness and prior cases in considerable detail, citing my article with Jay Kadane. In the end, they instructed jury officials to "undertake improvements" but approved the execution. I have never understood how judges live with such decisions, particularly in death penalty cases. A black man was executed by a decision of a jury that was "borderline" unconstitutional because it underrepresented blacks.

In Atlantic City, I was plowing through mounds of jury system paperwork with one of the public defenders, Barry Cooper, when I noticed something strange about some of the lists of jurors on panels. The panels were randomly drawn from the pool of qualified jurors, so panels should have been representative.

"Barry," I said, "look at the names on this panel and tell me if you see anything out of the ordinary."

He looked down the list of about 30 names. "Well, they have some kind of similarity, but I can't put my finger on it."

"That's how it struck me, and when I thought about it, it looks like a Jewish panel."

"What do you mean?"

"I recognize a lot of Jewish names, and this panel has more of them than the other panels. There's another panel in the pile that felt Italian. Maybe I've looked at all this paper too long."

"What could cause that?"

"I can't imagine anything that would cause that."

The selection of panels from the jury pool was done by the county's computer expert, Harold Simms, who had performed most all of the county's computer tasks since the late 1960s. I interviewed him prior to the hearing about the panel selection process.

"We use this system I devised before it became easy to make random selections from a list. If I were designing it now, I'd just have them use random selection software. But that wasn't available back then, so I improvised a program to get randomness, a little oddball maybe but random."

"How does it work?"

"Well, the old computers could alphabetize a list, so I had them alphabetize the jury pool by the fifth letter of the last name, then the sixth letter, and so on."

"Fifth letter of the last name?"

"Yeah, I know, it's arbitrary, and that was the idea."

"What if someone had a three-letter last name?"

"I programmed it to go to the last name, then the first name, and consider blanks as the letter following z."

"So what did your program do when it was picking a panel to be sent to a particular case for a trial?"

"It just takes the number of names needed in order alphabetically by the fifth letter of the last names, then it realphabetizes in the usual way and prints them out."

"Give me an example."

"If the first one was last-named Jones, the next might be Carlson. It would be in the s's of the fifth letters. It's so arbitrary and meaningless that it comes out random."

"That's ingenious. You were one of the early programmers, weren't you?"

"I guess so; nobody appreciates seat-of-the-pants programming anymore."

I liked Simms. I understood his system but not how it might have affected the panels, until I went back to that Jewish panel. There it was: Fishman, Goldman, Kaufman. . . . Simms's system was selecting at the fifth, sixth, and seventh letters "man." They weren't all Jewish names, but Jewish last names often had as their fifth, sixth, and seven letters "man." I then figured out similar ethnic last name patterns that explained the Italian panel. Many panels had no distinct ethnicity I could determine, but some of them did.

Spelling patterns have ethnicity, and arbitrariness is not the same as randomness. True randomness means that any person in the jury pool would have the same probability as any other to be selected for a given panel. The judge threw out this system, putting an end to over 25 years of seriously skewed criminal and civil jury panels in Atlantic City and the rest of the county.[7]

§§§

I wound up winning most of the jury challenges that were won over a few decades, using my no-stone-unturned approach. Recently, I was part of a team that traced a sizable underrepresentation of blacks in Indiana to a computer program that went through names alphabetically town by town but had been set many years earlier to quit after it went through 10,000 names. It never got to towns at the bottom of the alphabet, including Wayne Township, which was where a lot of the blacks in the county happened to live. The Indiana Supreme Court invalidated the system, reversing a death penalty.

But even when I lost a challenge, the result was almost always a new and much improved jury system. Jay Schulman, who died in 1987, suffered from manic depression before it was a well-known affliction. I wish I had known what he was going through. The NJP has had offices around the country and is doing well. Beth Bonora is a jury consultant in California. Jay Kadane and I have worked on several projects together.[8]

CHAPTER TWELVE

Going to School at the Electric Company

I WAS AT A PARTY IN POWELTON in 1978 doing my best jerky, feet-not-moving, trance-inducing dance that looked a lot like one of my favorites, Joe Cocker, with nobody in particular, or with everybody, when Bill Moyer walked up with a serious face and asked to talk to me outside about PECO, the Philadelphia Electric Company. The Stones blared so loud from a big stereo that it was hard to think—"You can't always get what you want, but if you try sometime, you get what you need." I wasn't into drugs, even in those druggy days, in part because I was able to drift away to good music or a mountain stream without them, so it took some effort to think about an electric company.

Bill grew up in poverty in Holmsburg, the white working-class section of Philadelphia where that prison is. In the 1960s he worked closely with Martin Luther King, Jr., and later wrote a significant book on how movements work. I knew him as a leader of Movement for a New Society, a part Quaker, part civil rights activist organization based in West Philadelphia, and as a leading opponent of nuclear power.[1]

"PECO's following us and taking our pictures," Bill said, "and they write down the license plate numbers of cars at antinuclear demonstrations and meetings. It has some folks scared to participate. And we got ahold of some odd flyers they're distributing to teachers, inviting them to meetings with free dinners."

"Anything else?"

"We heard some grumbling from reporters about how they're treated by PECO."

I could still hear the Stones but tried not to pay attention to them or the dancing inside. "Do you know what they're doing with the information they gather?"

"No, but everybody assumes that they've got files and lists of participants that they could use against folks."

I explained to Bill that privacy rights against the government are more limited than most of us assume and they're even more limited against private individuals or entities. They can observe, write down what they see, and photograph people in public places. The limits on them mainly go to how they use the files and information. Ralph Nader had an extreme case awhile back. After his book *Unsafe at Any Speed,* General Motors hired women who looked like playmates of the month to entice him into embarrassing liaisons and followed him so closely and persistently it looked like physical intimidation. Even then, the courts didn't help much, but he was able to get a settlement with GM.

I asked Bill to find out as much as he could about what PECO was doing, and I would see if there was anything we could do through the Public Utility Commission (PUC), which regulated PECO. I knew who to call from my brief stint at Community Legal Services, Steve Hershey, who litigated utility issues on behalf of consumers. He explained that the PUC doesn't stop or allow much of anything. They set utility rates, which are based on whatever legitimate costs there are plus a percentage for the utility's profit. They determine which expenditures can be counted as costs the ratepayers have to bear or as costs the utility or its shareholders must pay. We could claim these costs were not properly charged to the ratepayers.

The surveillance issues were familiar, but utility regulation was an odd, arcane area of law I knew nothing about. I decided to dive in because it would draw attention to the company's surveillance of its outspoken opponents and, as it developed, to modern techniques of propaganda. PECO produced science materials for schools and trained 6,000 science teachers how to teach science, in a ratepayer-funded pronuclear campaign disguised as science education.

An assortment of groups joined as complainants, including Keystone Alliance, the leading antinuclear group in Pennsylvania; American Friends Service Committee, the Quaker national service organization;

and the Consumer Education and Protective Association (CEPA), an innovative consumer group.[2] I filed the complaint in August 1978.

§§§

We took over the whole law office space in 1977 after Segal, Apple & Natali left. Rudy and I moved to the big room in the front with a large window onto Walnut Street and a view of the front door and of who came in and out of the office. A few weeks after the *Keystone Alliance* complaint was filed, someone called about a new incident with PECO. I vaguely recognized her voice. When I saw her come into the office I remembered.

"Hi, you're Antje?"

"Yes."

"Come in and have a seat. Did I say your name right?"

"Sort of. It's pronounced like it was spelled A-n-t-y-a."

She was tall with light, almost blond hair and very strong, pretty features. Her accent wasn't heavy but a little confusing, a bit German, where she had told me she grew up, and a bit British, because that was the way English was taught in her schools.

"Didn't we meet at the United Farmworkers Union house a few years ago?"

"Yes, I lived there and worked for the Farmworkers, and you were our lawyer on something I don't remember."

"I don't either." We laughed, though it wasn't that funny. "Weren't you brought to the United States by some agency in Germany?"

"Yes. Action Reconciliation Service for Peace. We work as volunteers with people who were victims of the Holocaust or who are now unfairly treated, like farmworkers in the United States."

"It sounds like the Peace Corps. Most Americans would never guess that Germany is sending a Peace Corps here. Anyway, what happened with PECO?"

"I was at one of our many Keystone Alliance demonstrations at the site of the Limerick nuclear plant construction."

"Bill said you founded Keystone Alliance with him and a couple others."

"I did. On the way home, I was driving and other demonstrators were in the car when we were pulled over by the state police. I rolled down the window, and the state trooper called me by my first name.

"He knew your name? I'll look into this and see if you have a case."

§§§

"Alright, is everybody ready?" PUC administrative law judge Isador Kranzel asked in his quiet voice. We were in what looked like a small classroom in the state office building at Broad and Spring Garden Streets for the first of what turned out to be over 40 days of hearings spread out over two years. "Mr. Kairys for the complainants?"[3]

"Yes, Judge, we're ready."

"Mr. Weinstein for PECO?"

"We're ready."

"Alright, then, let's go on the record. It's April 27, 1981, and we're here for the hearing in *Keystone Alliance et al. v. Philadelphia Electric Company.* I've denied Mr. Weinstein's motions to dismiss the complaint and to remove the promotion of nuclear power issue from the case and allowed Mr. Kairys to amend the complaint on the promotion issue. Mr. Weinstein has appealed some rulings to the full PUC, which upheld my decisions. We've had a lot of difficulty in the discovery phase, with PECO refusing to disclose any information or documents on the promotion issue and either or both of you calling me about disagreements and asking me to make rulings. I've decided to grant Mr. Kairys' request that we conduct the discovery and the hearing at the same time so I can rule as we go."

Kranzel was knowledgeable and serious about utility law and informal and friendly to everybody. He disliked the frequent disagreements and antagonism that had erupted between Weinstein and me.

Weinstein was about my age, medium height, slender, and annoyingly well dressed and groomed. Suits always felt like a uniform to me; he seemed born in one. His curly black hair was cropped close to his dark complexion and, like everything else about him, always right in place. He wrote detailed notes on long lawyer pads with a thin mechanical pencil that looked like the drafting pencils we used in engineering.

Weinstein and I got off to a bad start when he stressed from the beginning a defense that would not have occurred to me—that PECO had, as he said many times, an "absolute" First Amendment free speech right to promote whatever PECO wanted and "to charge the ratepayers." He argued that we were trying to censor PECO.

Weinstein worked at Kohn, Savett, Klein & Graf, a firm known for plaintiffs' class actions and for its very public representation of the *Philadelphia Inquirer* on freedom of speech and press issues, which gave him some credibility. I responded throughout the case that PECO could say and promote whatever it wanted but that, unless it was directly related to providing electric service, it was speech on behalf of the company and its shareholders that the ratepayers should not pay for. The Supreme Court had never said that anyone has to pay for the speech of someone else, an issue that had been more appealingly raised by rejected claims that government should support the speech of people of limited resources.

More of a challenge, but less annoying, was his argument that what I saw as promotion of nuclear power was nothing more than PECO's providing information to the ratepayers and public about electric power and service. He distinguished messages that were "informational" from "advocacy" and resisted any attempts to portray PECO as promoting nuclear power. PECO officials and teachers working with the Energy Education Advisory Council (EEAC) depicted PECO's communications as neutral, balanced, scientific, and unrelated to the nuclear power issue.

§§§

Michael McCormick, executive director of the EEAC since its inception, was also PECO's full-time manager of energy information and education and the national chairman of the public information committee of the American Nuclear Society. His early testimony described the EEAC as independent and focused on science and education, not nuclear power or energy policy.

But McCormick had to concede that all of the "members" of EEAC, the teachers, were selected by Clifford Brenner, PECO's vice president in charge of corporate communications; the staff was entirely made up of PECO employees assigned by Brenner and McCormick; and EEAC had no independent corporate or other existence, financial statements or books, office, or bank account. PECO made all the expenditures and supplied all the funding.

EEAC produced Our World of Energy curriculum for elementary school science classes and Energy in Our Society for high school classes. McCormick testified that they produced 4,200 sets of materials, with enough for 30 students in each set, and trained 4,000 elementary school and 2,000 high school teachers. Kindergarten and middle school programs were in development, so EEAC would soon cover the whole K through 12 science curriculum.

"You testified that PECO personnel play no substantive role," I asked, "in the writing or development of EEAC materials, that they don't even make 'suggestions' about 'content' or 'format.'"

"Yes."

"Then at a later point in this hearing you acknowledged 'some substantive input' but said it was very limited and occasional?"

"Yes."

"EEAC and PECO paperwork, which we just got, and the teachers' testimony have shown that all EEAC materials are submitted to PECO for approval and you sometimes express 'strong disapproval.'"

"That's their opinion."

"It's not just an opinion. I'm handing you Complainant's Exhibit 153. Do you recognize that?"

"It's a memo on my stationery from me to several of the EEAC teachers working on Energy in Our Society."

"It says, 'I am suggesting changes to the narration of the filmstrips.' Dr. Fred Hofkin, a science teacher at Overbrook High School whom you and Mr. Brenner made EEAC's first president, testified that your changes made the filmstrip more strongly pronuclear. You added, for example, a long paragraph to the narration that minimized the danger of nuclear materials getting outside a plant, as happened at Three Mile Island."

§§§

I summarized Our World of Energy, for elementary schools, in my cross-examination of Dr. Hofkin. "There are three units: 'Energy—What Is It?' 'Energy—Where Does It Come From?' and 'The Energy Crisis.' The 'What Is It?' unit starts with a description and definition of work and energy. Then 'forms' of energy are introduced: light, heat, sound, and 'atomic,' including some details on atomic structure. Unlike the other forms, atomic is associated with 'electrical energy.' Of the concluding 10 frames of the unit, half are visuals associated with nuclear power. First, do you agree with this summary?" I was aware that this case got me asking unusually long questions but found it unavoidable.

"Yes," he replied.

"Alright. Isn't atomic energy one of many ways used to obtain heat rather than being another 'form' of energy?" My many years of science and engineering studies came in handy.

"Yes, I suppose that's right."

"Isn't it confusing if not misleading to suggest that atomic power and electrical energy are connected because both have something to do with the motion of atomic particles? Atomic power uses the heat generated from an atomic reaction used to boil water, which generates electricity when the very hot steam is run through turbines."

"Yes."

"And doesn't the sun also 'release a great deal of energy'?"

"Sure."

"Couldn't electricity be derived from any of the three forms of energy—light, heat, and sound?"

"Yes."

"Can you see any good reason the filmstrip goes into atomic structure in detail but not molecular structure, which could be used to explain how heat works by the action of molecules?"

"Molecular structure is more complicated for young students."

"Dr. Hofkin, didn't you say just the opposite earlier? Quoting your testimony from page 3517 of the transcript: 'We have got to begin with either a very small particle or a very large particle, and generally most people begin with molecular structure and go from there to atomic structure.'"

"I guess I did."

"The second unit, 'Where Does It Come From?' focuses on the importance of electricity and the need to use the limited resource of fossil fuels for other products and purposes. A variety of sources of energy are discussed, and at the end it asks which of the sources is 'best,' which is addressed by the third unit, 'The Energy Crisis.' The narration of the first frame says to the children, 'Suppose your parents were unable to get gasoline for their cars.' The next several frames tell how it happened in the early 1970s and show some very confused-looking children as the narration asks: 'What are our energy alternatives?' Doesn't that scare the children and then set them up for a big solution?"

"Perhaps."

"A series of frames and narrations then raise and criticize a variety of alternatives. Solar is 'expensive' and can't be used on cloudy days; geothermal yields only 'small amounts' of 'localized' energy; tidal is 'very expensive'; synthetic coal is 'costly.' Then a question for the children: 'Can you think of some problems in using wind or trash as a source of energy?'

Conservation is not mentioned. Then a frame shows an atom and a chunk of coal, and the narration says: 'Two of the more practical energy resources are coal and nuclear energy.' But coal doesn't survive for long: 'burning coal can produce air pollution and may be dangerous to your health.' At last, there is an answer, described in several frames as if it were the choice of environmentalists:

> Can you suggest a way to obtain clean energy? What is the role of the environmentalist? Electricity can be generated through the fission of atoms in a nuclear reactor. Does some of our electricity come from a nuclear power plant? The energy produced from one kilogram of uranium is about equal to the amount of energy contained in 2,500,000 kilograms of coal.

Balanced?"

"I could see changes that could be made."

"Educationally, is there any significance to asking the children to think about some issues and sometimes specifically asking them to think about problems?"

"Yes. Open-ended and fill-in-the-blank questions and anything that provokes participation is most effective for learning and absorption of materials."

"But it's used very selectively here. The show doesn't mention any problem with nuclear and doesn't ask the children to think about any. Are there any problems related to nuclear?"

"Of course there are."

"Why aren't there any questions like 'What are the problems with nuclear?'"

"Perhaps there should have been."

"Do you agree there should have been?"

"Yes."

"So as it is, you find it somewhat unbalanced?"

"Perhaps."

"There are also environmental problems; how about the waste issue around nuclear power?"

"Yes."

"In the workbook that each student gets, nuclear safety and environmental issues are addressed as follows:

Another non-fossil fuel is nuclear energy. Nuclear reactors are built to produce electricity we can use. Some environmentalists fear that nuclear energy may cause too much radiation. Radioactive materials can be dangerous to our health. Nuclear physicists have worked hard to control the radiation given off during the production of nuclear energy and they feel that it is as safe or safer than other forms of producing energy.

'Some environmentalists' is counterposed to 'nuclear physicists' and 'they'—meaning all of them. Nuclear physicists seems an odd slice of expertise to single out so heavily, since they've chosen to go into the nuclear specialty, but anyway, do all nuclear physicists agree on this?"

"No. That should have 'generally' or 'most' before 'nuclear physicists.'"

"Are environmentalists and nuclear physicists, the latter of which sounds like a harder science, the only scientific disciplines that would be of concern here?"

"No."

"The workbook has a table with blanks for the children to fill in. Various sources of energy for electricity are listed down the left side, and two columns with blanks to be filled in are headed 'Where does it originate?' and 'What are some of the problems in using this source?' Nuclear is not included in this invitation to the children to think creatively. Conservation isn't mentioned. Below the table, it says: 'For the near future, scientists'—again, apparently all of them—'believe that the available supply of our energy will have to come from two sources—coal and nuclear fission power.' Balanced?"

"Nuclear should be included."

"The workbook says it was prepared by the EEAC and shows the copyright as to EEAC. PECO isn't mentioned except as part of the address of EEAC, which could easily look like PECO only donated space or a mailing address. The teacher's guide has on the title page just what teachers would look for: a long list of teachers with their affiliations. Isn't this misleading about PECO's role?"

"The teachers who work for EEAC have raised this. They've asked PECO to acknowledge sponsorship."

"But PECO hasn't done that?"

"No, not yet."

"Should it also note that whatever generosity is involved should be ascribed to PECO's customers, who are involuntarily footing the bills?"

"Objection," Weinstein said.

"I'll withdraw the question."

I argued that PECO's "informational" campaign fit recent trends explained best by Christopher Lasch: "The master propagandist, like the advertising expert, avoids obvious emotional appeals and strives for a tone that is consistent with the prosaic quality of modern life—a dry, bland matter-of-factness. . . . [P]artial truths serve as more effective instruments of deception than lies. . . . By using accurate details to imply a misleading picture of the whole, the artful propagandist makes truth the principal form of falsehood."[4]

§§§

"Mr. Chernow, in early 1975 you wrote the article in the *Sunday Philadelphia Inquirer Magazine* entitled 'Atomic Power: The Light That Failed?'"

"Yes, I did." Ron Chernow was a young freelance journalist in the Philadelphia area, who has recently become a best-selling author of biographies of the giants of industry and finance.

"Was that article critical of nuclear power in some respects?"

"Yes, it was."

"What happened after the article appeared?"

"Someone from PECO called the magazine's editor and asked for a meeting about the article. I went to the meeting with the editor. I was surprised that PECO brought four or five high executives. James Everett, PECO president, did the talking, saying the article was one-sided. He mentioned that there were 92 errors in the article. I asked for them and said I would look into each, but they said they didn't want to get into details. Everett said that the company was willing to 'underwrite'—and that was his exact word—the cost of a follow-up piece that would give the other side. He added that the company would get a suitable author. They wanted to take out an ad that would be masquerading as an article by an independent reporter, and their hard-sell approach left me flabbergasted."

"Was that the end of it?"

"No, the magazine rejected their request. I had been commissioned to write another piece that was a profile of Dr. Ernest Sternglass, a major critic of the atomic power industry. The piece had been written, revised, edited, and marked 'final.' The magazine killed the piece, a rare occurrence for an article that far along in the process."

"Did you write about nuclear power for other publications?"

"Yes. I wrote a four-part series on the economics of PECO and nuclear power for the weekly *New Paper*. After the first part was published, the *New Paper* editor, Howard Coffin, and the publisher were asked to meet with Mr. Brenner of PECO."

Howard Coffin took the stand next. "Mr. Brenner was incensed. He took out copies of Ron Chernow's electric bills and threw them on a table, saying Ron paid so little he didn't understand why Ron would be so antielectric or anti–Philadelphia Electric. The publisher told me to kill the rest of the articles. Not long after that, I was fired, and PECO and nuclear power were raised as reasons."

§§§

In September 1983, Judge Kranzel issued a 275-page opinion ruling that PECO's customers should not pay for PECO's "unreasonable, overdone and imprudent" campaign to promote nuclear power. He recommended that the PUC lower PECO's pending rate increase by $4 million per year. The *Inquirer* described the ruling as "the first in the nation to shed light on practices that other states have never taken the time to investigate."[5]

The PUC had for years before this case been moving toward a standard for utility public communications that PECO liked—allowing the customers to be charged if the message was "informational." But they accepted Judge Kranzel's decision. PECO appealed through the courts, to no avail. The case got a lot of media attention, including a segment on NBC's *Monitor*, a predecessor to *Dateline*.

After all the appeals, in 1989—11 years after the case started—I discovered that there was an unusual provision of a federal statute on public utilities that provided for counsel fees for an attorney representing consumers who successfully urges a state utility commission to adopt certain recommended standards. One of the standards was on advertising by utilities. I had done that, so I sent a letter to Weinstein requesting that PECO pay me counsel fees, from the shareholders' money, of course. He refused, I sued PECO, and PECO later settled.[6]

The incident involving Antje Mattheus, whose name a state trooper knew when he pulled her over after a Keystone Alliance demonstration, didn't have much impact on the case. But she called me the day after I talked to her in my office to invite me to take a bike ride. We have been together since; have raised two now-grown daughters, Marah and Hannah Mattheus-Kairys; and still live with our bikes in Philadelphia. PECO's pronuclear fanaticism brought me an interesting case, a good fee, and my wife and family.

CHAPTER THIRTEEN

Round Up the Usual Suspects

PHILADELPHIA POLICE COMMISSIONER Gregore Sambor—the same commissioner who would later preside over the nationally publicized eviction by bomb of the group MOVE that resulted in 11 deaths and the destruction of a full residential city block—initiated "an all-out coordinated effort to eradicate serious narcotics activities in the City of Philadelphia" on March 27, 1985. Using the latest computerized police equipment, Sambor had located the 50 street corners where the most drug arrests were made. His plan, called Operation Cold Turkey, was to send massive police "strike teams" simultaneously to each location. The teams would detain and search everybody they found, "clearing" the corners and surrounding areas and maintaining a continued police presence. This would cut off the drug trade, so users would have to go "cold turkey."

Local media were invited to attend Sambor's roundups in the black and Hispanic neighborhoods. Mayor Wilson Goode, the city's first black mayor, and district attorney Ed Rendell approved.

Sambor announced the operation publicly with much fanfare. I saw the local TV coverage that night. The visuals showed black and Hispanic people being herded into police wagons, looking embarrassed and guilty, while TV anchors and city officials talked about stopping drugs. Sambor and various politicians said we were all safer for it.

The next morning I got a call from Stefan Presser, the relatively new legal director of the Philadelphia ACLU. "David, it's time for us to do a big one together. Did you see what Sambor did yesterday?"

"Yeah, I caught some of it on local news. There's a certain logic to it, and computerized police tactics are all over prime-time police shows, but people also live there. Most black and Hispanic folks aren't dealing drugs, and dealers and addicts will go somewhere else when they see the police on the corners."

"Precisely. There's no basis to search or detain them. We've got to get on it right away."

"We did a case in 1972, *Farber v. Rizzo,* where the police picked up anyone with a protest sign near President Nixon's signing a bill at Independence Hall."

"I heard of that one. That involved First Amendment free speech rights and baseless detentions, searches, and arrests."

"Right," I said. "This is purely a detention, search, and arrest issue, Fourth Amendment rights. How many were arrested?"

"I don't know, hundreds possibly. It'll be a class action; we'll go in for everyone detained, searched, or arrested. I've been wanting to work with you, David. The ACLU board will surely approve, so our expenses will be covered. What do you say?"

"Sure, let's do it."[1]

Stefan was a thin, wiry guy, smart, dedicated, and very intense. He'd come to Philadelphia from Austin, Texas, where he worked on death penalty cases. We'd gotten to know each other, including a Friday night dinner at his loft downtown that included far more Sabbath ceremonies in Hebrew than I could handle. Jewish ceremonies were boring and annoying to me, probably from my experience with them for all-Hebrew hours as a child. We became good friends.

When we filed a class action lawsuit less than a week later, over 1,200 people had been detained, searched, arrested, or charged. This was an ideal case for a class action. There were many plaintiffs, and all had been harmed by the same explicit operation and policy.

Among all these people, only a few were found with small quantities of drugs. There were no dealers, no serious offenses, no felony charges. One plaintiff, Sidney Cliett, Jr., was a young black man held at Thirty-eighth and Haverford Streets in West Philadelphia, near his home. "I stopped to chat with a friend," he explained to a reporter. "Next thing I knew the corner was being besieged by police in marked cars, unmarked cars, and two lady police officers in those jeeps they drive."

"Do you go to school or work?"

"Yeah. I got a job in one of the Penn dining halls, and I'm tryin' to learn photography."

We referred to another plaintiff as "John Doe II" to protect his identity. He was picked up while waiting for a bus near his home to go to a kidney dialysis treatment at a hospital. He was held and refused medical treatment for almost a full day.

The city caved in quicker than I thought. There was a lot of criticism in the media, and Goode and Rendell soon expressed doubts about the effectiveness and legality of the operation. Within two weeks we negotiated a "consent decree"—an injunction agreed to by both sides and approved by the judge—that the police "shall not stop, frisk, question, search, interrogate, detain, or arrest any person" based "on a person's presence in a high-crime location" or with less basis or cause than provided by the Fourth Amendment.

Then we negotiated a settlement for damages and counsel fees. People who were stopped and searched but not taken into custody each got $100. The criminal charges arising from Operation Cold Turkey were dropped, and the small number charged with crimes got $882 if charged with summary offenses and $1,250 if charged with misdemeanors. The city paid a total of $500,000 to 1,444 plaintiffs in the class action. We also got counsel fees, and the ACLU was reimbursed for the expenses.[2]

§§§

The scene was very different a few months later when the police swept a predominantly Puerto Rican area in the Spring Garden neighborhood.

A police officer, Thomas Trench, had been found dead in his patrol car at Seventeenth and Spring Garden Streets, shot twice in the head. The story was all over the news, and there was an outpouring of sympathy for Trench and his family. I got a call that day from someone in the nearby Puerto Rican area of Spring Garden, who said police had picked up his friends and family from their stoop in front of their house. He said this was happening all over Spring Garden and asked me to come to a meeting of the Spring Garden United Neighbors (SGUN) to discuss it. Soon after, Stefan was on the phone. The ACLU had gotten similar complaints.

The next evening, I went to the office of SGUN at Eighteenth and Mt. Vernon. SGUN was an established community group working on a range of issues, including opposition to gentrification and the renovation of abandoned buildings for use as homes for low-income elderly. A large room with maybe 50 chairs was packed, with many standing in aisles and at the back of the room.

Stefan and I talked briefly to Raul Serrano, Willie Martinez, and Wilfredo Rojas, who had organized the meeting. When we were ready to start, I looked out at the crowd. The only non-Hispanics in the room were Stefan; me; and, sitting in a chair way at the back of the room, Spencer Coxe, the retired former director of the ACLU. There weren't any representatives of the community or any civil rights and political groups who opposed Operation Cold Turkey and usually rallied on such occasions. Spencer was, as usual, undeterred, but others were hesitant to offer support or be present because a police officer had been killed.

Raul, president of SGUN, introduced us and spelled out what he knew from complaints he received, first in Spanish, then translated into English. "After Trench was killed, police from the Ninth District spread through the Puerto Rican community and took into custody every Puerto Rican man they found. Some of them were kids, maybe 13 or 14, others, like my father, were older."

"It's the culture around here to hang out on the streets and socialize," Willie, who had gone to Yale, said. "Now everyone is afraid to go outside."

Several others in the crowd told what had happened to them. Ramon Rivera had been picked up three times. Luis Galbon and Rolland Vargas were teenagers pushed into police vans packed with men. Some were held as long as 10 hours. All were released, often without being questioned at all. A few said they knew Trench; and Raul and Willie later told me that Trench, though an Anglo and a cop, was widely respected and liked in the community he patrolled. Margarro Serrano, Raul's 65-year-old father, said, "They knocked on my door Monday morning, asking for me with their badges out in their hands. I was scared. Why would they ask for me?"

"I'm afraid it was because I spoke out against the sweep," Raul said.

"One of them said something smelled. I was cooking a pork shoulder. My wife is ill, bedridden, so I do the cooking and cleaning. They told me to get dressed. I was going with them, and it wouldn't take long. 'Can I tell my wife who's sick upstairs?' I asked. 'Can I call my son?' 'No, just get going.' They wouldn't even let me turn off the oven. I was held for seven hours, no food and just a little water. They asked me what I know about Trench, who did it. I told them many times I don't know nothing about it. They asked about Raul, who he works for, how he gets money.'"

"I appreciate your openness and your willingness to tell us what happened to you," I said after the eyewitness accounts. "We're going to follow up on this and prepare a lawsuit to restore your rights. We have the backing of civil rights groups that will pay the expenses, and Stefan and I will act as your lawyers without you having to pay us. I ask you to do two things. First, if you have been stopped, searched, or taken into custody or saw someone else treated that way, talk to Stefan or me tonight or make an appointment with one of us to talk in the next couple days. The second thing is, if you have information about Trench's murder, let us know privately, and we will find a lawyer to accompany you personally as you tell the police what you know. We're not here to discourage anyone from cooperating with the legitimate investigation of the murder."

§§§

A week later, Stefan and I were seated at a counsel table in the federal courtroom of Judge Clarence Newcomer arguing that our class plaintiffs, estimated at over 100 men of Puerto Rican ancestry, should be granted an injunction ordering the police to stop the Spring Garden sweeps. Trench's murderer had not been caught.

Newcomer was a former prosecutor appointed by Richard Nixon. That gave me two reasons to worry. I thought our only chance lay in the small details of stories of people like Margarro Serrano and the big picture of how counterproductive, offensive, and wrong the racial sweeps were. The sweeps lost the cooperation of a community that liked Trench, and if the federal court didn't stop them, the police would be encouraged to use sweeps. If Newcomer wasn't deeply moved on both scores, we would lose.

"Good morning, everybody," Newcomer said. "This is *Spring Garden United Neighbors et al. versus City of Philadelphia et al.*, and we're here for a hearing on plaintiffs' request for a preliminary injunction. At counsel table for the plaintiffs are David Kairys, Esquire, and Stefan Presser, Esquire, and at the defense table is Armando Pandola, Jr., Esquire, chief deputy city solicitor."

"Before we begin, Your Honor," Pandola said, "I have a brief motion. Taking testimony about actions that occurred a couple of weeks ago will not do any good. There must be an ongoing problem or a likelihood that it will continue into the future. That is not so here. Plaintiffs should be limited to more recent proof."

"Would you care to respond?"

"Yes," I said, "the cases are clear that, when an unconstitutional pattern or practice has been engaged in, the fact that the defendants called it off in response to a lawsuit is not a ground to deny a preliminary injunction. In addition, it did continue after it was purportedly called off, and there is a substantial basis to believe it will continue to continue. The leading case I think is closest to the facts is *Lankford v. Gelston,* a Fourth Circuit case cited in our memo."

"I see it," Newcomer said. "A 1966 Fourth Circuit case."

"Yes." The date, 1966, meant it may be of limited authority for him, since it came from the liberal 1960s. "Also, we have in Philadelphia a history of police use of sweeps in minority communities. We've submitted to you materials on the *Cliett* case, dealing with Operation Cold Turkey."[3]

"That had to do with a drug sweep."

"Yes, sir, but the point is that the police in this city are basically out of control and believe they have the right and the authority to make sweep arrests."

"All right. We'll hear argument on that later."

Stefan started with several of our plaintiffs. The first was David Velasquez. "After the officer's death, would you tell the court what if any trouble you have had with the police in your community?" Stefan asked.

"Objection, Your Honor," Pandola said. "I thought we're going to have witnesses with specific individual incidents."

Newcomer looked turned to Stefan. "I will sustain the objection and ask that you rephrase the question."

"Mr. Velasquez, I am asking you for your own experience. Have you had any trouble with the police?"

"Only they picked me up on the street, and they asked me questions."

"When?"

"Last Wednesday, 11:00 o'clock, in the evening."

"Where?"

"I was with my friends on the steps next door to my friend's house."

"What were you doing?"

"We were standing down hearing the radio and talking. They drove by, stopped, and came back. They got out the car and walked toward us. They asked us do we got any weapons on us."

"What did you say to the police?"

"I said, 'No, I don't.'"

"And what did the police do?"

"They started talking, then they told us put our hands up and searched everybody. They started pulling out their handcuffs, and they cuffed us. They walked us toward the paddy wagon, and they put us inside."

"Did they take everybody?"

"Well, they looked at the girls that was standing with us and told the girls, 'You are lucky we don't got enough room for you.'"

"Where were you taken?"

"To the Ninth District, second floor, homicide, in a little room with other guys."

"How long were you held there?"

"An hour and a half."

"Did they question you?"

"They took us out one by one and asked us about the Trench murder."

"What did you say?"

"I told them I was sleeping. The only way I found out was in the newspaper the next morning."

"We will pass the witness at this time, Your Honor." Stefan used *pass* that way a lot, probably picking it up from Texas or someplace else he'd practiced. Legal customs varied, and that one always sounded strange to me.

"Would you tell me your age?" Pandola asked on cross-examination.

"Sixteen."

"Were you aware of the curfew that exists in the city of Philadelphia for people who are under 17 years old?"

"Yeah, but I wasn't charged with that."

"Would you have preferred him to charge you with a curfew violation?"

"Counsel," Newcomer said, "we have a lot of witnesses coming. It doesn't sound very relevant to me."

"Okay, Your Honor. I'm just trying to establish, Your Honor, that there was a basis to pick up the witness. How far away from the place where Officer Trench was found murdered in his car do you live?"

"Two blocks."

When Pandola was done, Stefan said, "Just one or two more questions."

"Let's try to get the questions in and not have a redirect."

"Yes, Your Honor. When the police approached you, did they ask any of the questions they asked when you were taken in?"

"They ain't asked us nothing. They just searched us, cuffed us, and put us in the paddy wagon."

"Would you have been willing to tell them then what you knew or didn't know?"

"I would cooperate with them."

Stefan presented four more witnesses with essentially the same story, who also testified that they were afraid to go out on the street because of the sweeps. Then I called Yale-educated Willie Martinez, who was the executive director of SGUN.

"Please tell us what Spring Garden United Neighbors is and very briefly what it does."

"The Spring Garden area has experienced a substantial socioeconomic change. With perhaps the city's most valuable land, there has been a displacement of the long-time, low-income residents, who are predominantly black and Hispanic. The purpose of United Neighbors is to offset any negative impact from the gentrification by assuming the characteristics of a community development corporation. We are rehabilitating the former Darrah School into a 32- unit low- and moderate-income cooperative. We are developing a shared home for the elderly and a large-scale Acme-type supermarket cooperative."

"How did Spring Garden United Neighbors get involved in the police actions following the death of Officer Trench?"

"A number of community residents, members as well as nonmembers, came into the office and stopped Raul Serrano, who is president, or me on the street. They expressed concern that the police were picking everyone off the streets."

"Objection and move to strike," Pandola said emphatically.

"Overruled and denied," Newcomer responded.

"Did Spring Garden United Neighbors determine that it should speak out about this problem?"

"Yes, sir."

"Objection, Your Honor."

"Overruled. This man is the executive director. He should be able to speak for the corporation."

"I am questioning the relevancy of this testimony at this point."

"Overruled."

"That means," I said to Willie, "you may answer."

"Yes, we held a number of press conferences opposing the police actions. Way before that, we approached city councilman Angel Ortiz and asked him to come out and survey the neighborhood so he could know what is going on for himself."

"Did Spring Garden United Neighbors say anything about the death of Officer Trench?"

"Although I didn't know him, a lot of people in the community were saddened and expressed deep regret that this happened to such a good person."

"Did you meet with Captain Margolis, commander of the Ninth District, about the problem with the police?"

"Yes. The pastor of the Lutheran church, Edward Neiderhiser, asked us and Captain Margolis to meet at the church to open some lines of communication between the community and the police department."

"What happened?"

"The captain said there was tension over the murder of a fellow officer. He said that he had attempted to help our community in the past, but his efforts never got anywhere. He said we needed to get our act together. Our youth are out on the street selling drugs. When we eat chicken, we throw the bones out on the streets in front of the faces of the police. Then he went into something about filth, and later he stated that we were pigs."

"I have no further questions."

On cross-examination, after some preliminaries Pandola asked, "When Captain Margolis mentioned the word *pigs*, as you refer to it, he was referring to the people who were throwing the bones?"

"I don't believe so, no."

"Well, what was he talking about at the time?"

"He was talking about the community."

Our next witness was Reverend Edward Neiderhiser. "I called Captain Margolis and asked if he or someone could come over to the church and discuss the situation with various representatives of the community," Neiderhiser said.

"What happened at the meeting?"

"I expressed sympathies to the captain for the loss of an officer, which was echoed by the other gentlemen present from the United Neighbors. I also expressed our concern on behalf of the neighborhood that there was some rough treatment and asked the captain if that was necessary. I suggested that we discuss the whole issue with him."

"What did the captain say?"

"The captain was not as responsive or sensitive to the concerns of the community as I had hoped that he would be."

"Objection and move to strike," Pandola said.

"Sustained and granted."

"Just limit yourself to what he said," I said.

"The captain said there was a murder investigation going on and he wasn't going to do anything about that to change the course of the investigation. Then he made some statements about the neighborhood. He said he attempted to do some work among the residents, but he felt that members of the community lived like pigs. He made reference to people eating chicken and throwing bones into the street."

"I have no further questions."

Pandola stayed mostly away from what was becoming a major chicken-bone issue, but Newcomer asked, "Was the captain incorrect about the chicken bones and the appearance of the neighborhood?"

"I have never witnessed anybody throwing chicken bones in the street."

"My question was a little broader than that."

"Yes. There is trash on the street, but members of the neighborhood in my experience are rather perpetually trying to keep that clean."

Stefan called a couple more people taken in by sweeps, and then I called city councilman Angel Ortiz, an attorney at Community Legal Services who became the first Hispanic council member and the chair of council's public safety committee.

Ortiz contacted Mayor Goode to complain about the sweeps. "He told me he would inform the police of our conversation and that, if there was harassment or undue detainment or presence, that would be stopped. I met the next day with deputy police commissioners Crudup and Armstrong and informed them that the situation was dangerous. When there is such fear and people do not feel secure, either the police in their zealousness or a community person might lead to something tragic happening. They said they would proceed with their investigation in another manner. I also told them this had impeded the investigation of the actual murderer. Nevertheless, for at least a few days later, there were more arrests and detentions."

"Mr. Ortiz, what do you think would be the effect on the community if this court fails to issue an injunction in this case?"

"Objection," Pandola said.

"Sustained."

"May I argue, Judge, briefly?" I asked because usually courts don't want to hear arguments on evidentiary objections, particularly after the court has ruled.

"I don't think so."

"Well, may I just make, for the record, a brief argument as to why that is relevant?"

"All right."

"Judge, the defendants have taken the position that the injunction shouldn't issue because—and this is an element of the established law—it is not in the public interest or, as you phrased it, the balancing of equities, according to them. They leave out of the public this particular community when they say something like that. This particular witness I think more than anyone in this city is the appropriate person to assess the effect of such an action on this particular segment of our community."

"Because of his being chairman of the public safety committee?"

"And the first member of council from the Hispanic community, Judge, ever in the history of councils, as far as I am aware."

"All right. I will allow it."

"Well," Ortiz said, "I think the community is looking for some reassurances that they are safe in their own neighborhood and safe from harassment. The relationship between the police and the community has been strained after many years of trying to build up good community relations. They would be afraid when that squad car is coming up the street. I am afraid that what happens in a community when fear like that takes hold is it can eat away at a certain fabric of the neighborhood."

"No further questions."

Our last witness was Margarro Serrano. "I was cooking a pork shoulder in the oven. My wife is sick, and I have to do everything; she can't walk, and I have to clean and cook and wash the dishes and everything myself."

"The police came to your door?" I asked.

"They knocked at the door. I was in the kitchen cooking. I opened the door, and they said, 'detectives,' with a badge. I said, 'Come in, sit down.' And he said, 'Put on your shirt and shoes, we are going to take you with us.' They took me to Eighth and Race."

"What did they do with you there?"

"They locked me up in a room and asked me questions. If I knew the policeman. I said, 'No.' If I had been around at that time. I said, 'No, I go to bed at eight, the latest nine.'"

"How long did they hold you?"

"From about 9:00 in the morning 'til 4:00 in the afternoon."

"Were you given anything to eat?"

"They took me out for a drink of water. That's all."

"At your house, did you ask them to let you tell your wife you were going?"

"Yes, but they didn't let me tell her or my son, who was across the street. I had to leave the pork in the lit oven, and it was burned when I got back."

Newcomer didn't reveal much in court, but I thought I saw a look of anger and disgust during Margarro's testimony.

I was ready to cross-examine the police the city might call to testify, but Pandola stood when we were done with our case and said, "Regarding the preliminary injunction, Your Honor, the city of Philadelphia will offer no testimony and rests."

"Is the testimony then closed?" Newcomer asked.

"Yes, sir," I said.

"I will give you my decision on this tomorrow morning at 9:30."

I thought this a bad sign. If we were going to win, he'd want more time to write a full opinion grounding his decision in the details of the testimony; a short opinion rejecting our case wouldn't take long to write.

§§§

The next morning, Newcomer presented his decision as a "bench opinion," speaking from the bench and into the transcribed record.[4] He began with a summary of Trench's murder, our claims, and the evidence. "The evidence adduced by the plaintiffs at yesterday's hearing demonstrates that this police investigation included a persistent and ongoing practice of stopping, searching, detaining, frisking, handcuffing, and questioning plaintiffs without probable cause, reasonable suspicion, or warrants. There were no charges levied against any of the plaintiffs who testified. This practice can only be described as a 'sweep' of the Spring Garden neighborhood.

"All of those picked up were of Puerto Rican origin, none were charged with a crime at any time, none had any material information bearing on Officer Trench's death, and all were eventually released. No explanation by the police officers was given when the persons were picked up. No requests were made for the individual voluntarily to come to the police headquarters, although nearly all testified that they would have.

"No evidence was produced showing that any of the individuals even fitted a profile that was being investigated. No evidence was offered to show that the police believed the suspect is of Puerto Rican origin or that he or she is from the Spring Garden neighborhood.

"These 'sweeps' affected the entire community. A couple of instances were unbearably egregious: Sixty-five-year-old Margarro Serrano was ordered out of his house at 9 a.m. while cooking for himself and his invalid wife. The police officers refused to let him turn off the oven, inform his wife of his hasty departure, or even notify his son across the street. No explanation was given and no charges brought against Mr. Serrano, who had no information on Officer Trench's death.

"Jose Rosario was walking with a bag of groceries, when he was picked up and he was forced to leave the bag on the sidewalk. He was cuffed, frisked, and taken to the police station for two hours, questioned, and released, after police determined he had no information on the Trench death.

"A city councilman, Angel Ortiz, met with police and got assurances that the 'sweep' would stop, but it continued.

"In order for plaintiffs to sustain their burden of proof on the request for a preliminary injunction, the plaintiffs must show, first, a reasonable likelihood of success on the merits; and secondly, irreparable injury and the inadequacy of the legal remedies. In addition, I must consider and balance the equities involved.

"The city solicitor argues that whatever occurred is over and moot, so an injunction is not appropriate. Any cessation of this 'sweep' was either, one, as a result of filing this suit; or two, it was a natural petering out, based on the police officers' completion of the 'sweep.' It appeared that the 'sweep' was a waste of time and effort, since residents either did not know anything or were not cooperating as a result of the fear instilled by the 'sweep.'

"In addition, the city has, in recent history, conducted other 'sweeps,' notably a drug 'sweep' known as 'Operation Cold Turkey.'

"Apparently the city and the Philadelphia Police Department continue under the misapprehension that they can randomly 'sweep' certain racial and ethnic groups with impunity, provided the goals sought are laudable. This 'sweep' following so closely on the heels of Operation Cold Turkey makes it clear to me that the defendants would conduct a 'sweep' again if they believed they could escape unscathed. To permit that would make a mockery of our constitutional right to be free from undue restraint in our daily lives, on the street, in front of our homes, and inside our homes.

"The defendants claim that any injunction will impede their investigation, but it will, of course, permit all lawful means of investigation. It is actually in the interests of the police department to provide reassurance to the citizens of Spring Garden. It is also a sign to the Spring Garden community that their rights as citizens have meaning and that they will be protected.

"I must remark in closing that this case sadly brought to mind a famous line from the well-known movie *Casablanca:* 'Major Strasser's been shot! . . . Round up the usual suspects.' However, in the movie the farce is humorous and draws chuckles. In this case, I believe the line is devoid of humor.

"I have therefore issued the following preliminary injunction: Police officers shall not stop, frisk, question, threaten, search the person or property of, detain, take into custody, arrest, or use physical force against any person in the Spring Garden community without meeting the requirement of the Constitution of the United States or take any such action against any person based only on his Puerto Rican or Hispanic ancestry and/or his presence in the Spring Garden community."

The city decided to settle after that and transferred Captain Margolis out of the Ninth District. The injunction was made permanent, and each person taken into custody got $548. Stefan and I got counsel fees and reimbursement for expenses. Judge Newcomer described me as "one of the preeminent civil rights lawyers in the country" in his opinion granting counsel fees.[5] The case got national publicity and, most importantly, stopped the sweeps.

§§§

Police misconduct was a staple of my and the firm's practice from the beginning. After the Spring Garden case, Spencer Coxe and I thought that, in addition to more lawsuits, it was time to revive the Philadelphia tradition of community organization and activism on police issues. That tradition was so strong that, when Ed Rendell first won election as district attorney in 1977, both he and his Republican opponent made firm campaign pledges to create a separate unit in the DA's office to prosecute police. Rendell followed through, hiring a former federal prosecutor, George Parry, to head the unit and for the first time prosecuting a police officer for mistreatment of a civilian. The media, probably driven by community interest and activism, often covered police issues; in 1978, the *Philadelphia Inquirer* won a Pulitzer prize for a series by Jonathan Neumann and William Marimow on the systematic beating of homicide suspects. For many years, the Council of Organizations on Philadelphia Police Accountability and Responsibility and the Coalition Against Police Abuse played this role, since the mid-1970s with the tireless leadership and efforts of Jayma Abdoo, the Camden 28 defendant who worked in my office, and Spencer, among many others.

After the sweeps, the disastrous confrontation with the MOVE organization, and a series of police corruption scandals, Spencer and I thought a new, broadly based group should form to take on the array of police reform issues. We established the Coalition for Police Accountability, and a range of community, religious, civil rights, and public interest groups eagerly joined, including some of the most influential in the city—the Urban League; the Fellowship Commission; American Friends Service Committee; Women Organized Against Rape; the Tenant Action Group; and the Guardian Civic League, the organization of minority police officers.

I was asked to chair the coalition and to take the lead on the first order of business—a thorough report that explained and documented the
array of police problems and made specific recommendations, which the
coalition would release publicly and then work to get implemented. This
took some time but provided the opportunity to systematically look at
the issues and set out specific proposals. We were operating like an
official commission but without any authority, staff, or funding. After
months of research, discussion, and writing, we released the "Report and
Recommendations of the Coalition for Police Accountability" in April
1986.

The report started with the recent problems and placed them in the
history of police misconduct going back to the 1960s. "Routine abuse
and harassment by the police has been increasing and becoming more violent in recent years."

"In the face of all this, the Department has, as in the Rizzo era, failed
to discipline officers for abuse of citizens. During the 1970s, despite
numerous complaints of police abuse, documented by investigations of
the U.S. Civil Rights Commission, by a committee of the State House of
Representatives and by the U.S. Justice Department, the Police Department did not, to the best of our knowledge, discipline a single officer
for use of excessive force. . . . Police use of excessive and unnecessary
force is viewed by some as necessary to combat crime or maintain order.
Without detailing the other obvious shortcomings of this approach, it
simply poses a false choice: the police, who are not to blame for and
cannot alone be expected to deal with the social problem of crime,
would be *more* effective if brutality were curbed and law enforcement,
public accountability, command control, and competence were encouraged. We already have more police per resident than any other city except Washington, D.C., and probably as much abuse per resident as
anywhere in the United States. We need better police work and less
abuse."

We made 13 specific recommendations in three general areas—policy
and procedure, personnel, and remedial procedures and discipline. Included were the following recommendations: a stress program should be
available to all officers without charge or recrimination; a fair complaint
procedure should be established and followed; a finding of police misconduct in any civil or criminal case, including settlement of a civil case,
should trigger an inquiry to determine whether discipline should be im-

posed and should be noted in the officer's personnel file; there should be a ban on sweeps; all policies should be public; and the mayor and police commissioner should prepare a yearly report on all aspects of police operations, including claims of abuse and discipline. The coalition played a significant role over many years, and many of its recommendations were adopted.

CHAPTER FOURTEEN

The Cities Shoot Back

T HIRTY OR SO OF US WERE crowded around a long table in the conference room at the Recreation Department headquarters near city hall. Around the table were former street gang members; clergy known for work in poor neighborhoods; a range of activists; some academics; and several city, state, and federal officials. Michael DiBerardinis, the recreation commissioner under Mayor Ed Rendell, had brought us together in mid-1996. Mike was one of the few people in government who could have gotten this unusual assortment of folks together or who would have thought to. Best known as the leader of the Kensington Joint Action Council, a successful multiracial coalition in a working-class area of the city, Mike got things done with unusual ease and integrity, including serving up great pasta at halftime of Philadelphia Eagles football games. I had known Mike for over two decades as an effective antiwar activist and leader, and he and his wife, Joan Reilly, a Camden 28 defendant, were good friends. Rendell tapped Mike to revive a dormant city department and then broadened his duties so much that I used to call him vice mayor.[1]

Mike, looking his usual dapper, De Niro–like self with neatly combed dark hair and a stylish suit, had us going around the room to introduce ourselves. "Special Agent Cliff Waldron, Philadelphia FBI office," an FBI-looking fellow sitting across from me said as he smiled self-consciously, probably because he wasn't used to being in such company. I smiled back and thought, the FBI, I sued them.

"Marian Davis, from the mayor's office. I will participate fully and assure you that this effort has the mayor's complete support." I sued several Philadelphia mayors.

"Deputy Police Commissioner Richard Zappile," said the also dapper, plainclothes second in command at the police department. "We're behind this as well and will help however we can."

I sued them a lot. But we all got to know each other over the course of several months. In one of the early meetings, Deputy Commissioner Zappile said as we broke for lunch, "Dave, you gonna serve papers on us when we get back?"

"Depends what you do over the lunch break."

We became Philadelphia's Handgun Violence Reduction Taskforce. Our mandate was to do something about the problem of youth violence and guns. This sounded like the kind of effort that ends up with a report no one reads. But Mike was pushing hard for fresh, concrete ideas. He said that's why he wanted me on the task force, and I'd worked with him enough to know I wouldn't waste my time.

§§§

I knew little about guns and only slightly more about youth violence. I'd been cochair of the board of an innovative gang-control agency, the Crisis Intervention Network (CIN). CIN was created in the 1970s by Bennie Swans, a decorated Vietnam vet, and by mothers like Blanche Nixon, who organized against gang violence in their communities.

When I came to Philadelphia in 1968 there was an average of a gang death every week. By the mid-1980s, there were a few each year, and some years there were none (the average increased again not long after in a new form focused on crack and drug gangs). CIN reduced gang violence by respecting gang members and kids drawn to gangs, negotiating agreements between gangs, maintaining a network to pick up gang problems before they got to a fight, and patrolling the city with quick-response gang-control teams that included former members.

Bennie was known for fearlessly standing between armed gang enemies with a message of black pride and a plea to work out differences and work together to make things better. One of his early successes came out of his simply listening to gang members. Bennie sought out a gang member who was frequently going into the territory of a rival gang. When the rival gang spotted him, there were fights, reprisals by his gang, and reprisals to the reprisals. If it kept up, someone could die. Bennie asked him why he kept going into the rival gang's territory. He said he went to his invalid grandmother's house there to buy her groceries every week or so. Bennie called the leaders of the two gangs together and negotiated a written agreement between them—the rival gang granted him permission to visit his grandmother and buy groceries once a week.

I got to know Bennie when my wife, Antje, worked at CIN on a project and then as a manager. Bennie asked me to be cochair with Blanche, who called us a "salt-and-pepper team."

§§§

The gun death and injury statistics, presented to us in studies and talks by experts, had a depressingly familiar ring: about 50 handgun deaths each day in the United States and three or four times that many injuries. In most large cities, armed criminal violence was the biggest threat to public health and safety. Yet the toll taken by handguns had an aura of regrettable normalcy that Mike and I found hard to understand or accept.

Handguns were commonly thought to bestow protection from harm by others, although research had shown that bringing a gun into your home increased the probability that someone in the home will be the victim of a gun homicide by three times. It also increased the probability of a suicide in your home by five times. If you had a teenager in the household, the suicide increase went up to ten times.

We all knew handguns were easily available in and around Philadelphia. We weren't sure how cheap, readily concealed, new handguns found their way to city streets. Most of us assumed—if we had thought about it at all—that something illegal must be going on. Yet as we listened to experts and each other on the task force and researched and read about gun violence and prevention efforts, much of what I thought I knew about guns turned out to be wrong—starting with the common belief that it's mostly stolen guns that get used for crimes.

A former gang member told us of a corner not too far from our meeting place in downtown Philadelphia where we could buy as many new handguns as we wanted. Studies tracked several channels from factory to street: gun shows, mail orders, and straw purchases—someone buying for someone else who can't legally buy or purchasing sometimes large quantities for resale on the streets.

Anyone who could pass the record check prescribed by the Brady Act could walk out of a gun store with as many handguns as they pleased. The limit would be the limit on the buyer's credit card. Ten, a hundred, whatever he or she wanted and could pay for. There were reporting requirements on the dealer who sold a lot of guns to one person. In certain circumstances, a dealer was supposed to send a notice of multiple purchases to the federal Bureau of Alcohol, Tobacco and Firearms (ATF). But little or nothing could be done about that because the purchase was not illegal. The purchaser legally owned those guns and had no legal duty to report or explain what he did with them.

Under federal and most state laws, it was also legal for private owners to resell handguns without running a record check on the subsequent buyer and without reporting or recording the transaction. Purchases from a nondealer, common at gun shows and on the streets, were not subject to a record check, because the Brady Act only applied to licensed dealers.

The bottom line: Under federal law and the laws of most states, a person so inclined could buy handguns—huge quantities of, say, easily concealed, cheap handguns—and sell them to others indiscriminately often without violating any law and usually without having to worry much about getting arrested, prosecuted, or convicted.

If the person buying was a felon, it was illegal for him or her to possess a handgun. But the process, the market structure up to that point, was largely legal. And the person who sold a handgun to a person with a felony conviction had no meaningful or enforceable responsibility.

§§§

"The research and the literature don't say much about the handgun market," I said at one of our meetings.

"No," said ATF agent Tom Stoner, "it's usually about public health, deaths, whether guns make you safer or unsafe, things like that."

"And the manufacturers are pretty invisible. It's not like tobacco or lead paint, where the research and public debate focus on the manufacturers."

"I don't know about that. What do you mean, what would they say?"

"Well, I'm starting to see the manufacturers, and the whole industry, as much more responsible for the slaughter than I did before we started. If a lot of new handguns are getting to criminals and youth in significant numbers, doesn't that mean the manufacturers are making more than they know they can sell to lawful, well-intentioned buyers? I assume they know their markets and they don't make more than they think they're going to sell."

"I'm not sure. Part of our job at ATF is keeping the industry functioning well. We know that areas with weak handgun controls, like the I-95 corridor in the south and states like Pennsylvania, are oversupplied so they can funnel handguns to stricter states, like New Jersey."

"Yeah, we heard a lot about that. That's consciously done, isn't it?"

"I don't know about that. There are some gun manufacturers I'd rather not talk about, but most are honest, upstanding businessmen."

"Seems it would have to be consciously done by someone," Mike said. "And some handguns have features that facilitate criminal use. They even advertise it. That brochure we saw the other day is mind-boggling—touting, what was it, a line of Navegar, TEC-9 handguns as having a coating that yields 'excellent resistance to finger prints.' And that average time to crime, you know, from purchase from a retail dealer to recovery at a crime scene, is pretty short, according to the research we've seen. Something is going on there."

"Those studies we got copies of the other day," I said, "say that a very small number of distributors and dealers are responsible for the majority of handguns used in crime. It looks to me like the government regularly tells the manufacturers which distributors supply these rogue dealers."[2]

"How so?" Mike asked.

"Tom, explain again how ATF traces of crime guns work."

"Sure. The police get ahold of a gun used in a crime, say at a crime scene, and if it has an intact serial number, we call the manufacturer and ask who they sold that gun to. It's usually a distributor; then we ask the distributor who he sold it to, on down the line, to the point of a retail sale. The person using the gun in a crime is usually not the first retail, nondealer purchaser. Manufacturers, distributors, and dealers have to keep records of who they sell to, but after that, there's no record, which makes tracing much less effective."

"I understand the trace problem, Tom, but let's put that aside for now.

When you guys call the manufacturer, who do you talk to and what do you say?"

"We've got a number and sometimes a person to contact. We tell them we are tracing a gun they manufactured, give them the serial number, and ask who they sold it to."

"Do you tell them anything about the crime?"

"No."

"So it could be any crime, a murder or just someone carrying a gun without a permit someplace where a permit is required?"

"That's right."

"How many traces does ATF do, say, in a year?"

"About 200,000 guns used in crimes get traced each year."

"That's a lot of traces. It seems to me that, over time, these trace requests to the manufacturers give them a clear picture of which distributors are putting guns into the hands of criminals."

"What do you mean?"

"Well, if the studies are right, manufacturers would get a lot of trace calls about some distributors or dealers and few or none about others. They're warned, put on notice, however it's characterized, about who, among the people they sell to, is feeding the crime trade. We can get some idea about the quantity of this information the manufacturers get from ATF. I brought my calculator." I scrambled through my briefcase. "To get an order of magnitude, we could assume the traces and calls are proportional to market share, although I have no idea if that's true. If a manufacturer who has 5 percent of the handgun market got 5 percent of these trace calls, they'd get a trace call from ATF, let's see, about every 15 minutes of every work day. At 10 percent, the biggest market share, Smith & Wesson's, you'd get a trace call every 7 or 8 minutes."

"That's a lot of calls and data," Mike said.

"Yeah, particularly for manufacturers whose proportion of crime gun traces exceeds their market share. Tom, you guys at ATF, while trying to trace guns and solve crimes, are informing the manufacturers not only that one of their products was used in a crime but also which distribution channel resulted in the use of the product in a crime."

"I see your point, but what if they don't tabulate it or it stays with whomever they assign to receive our trace ATF calls?"

"I don't think that matters. You give them the information. They know the harm associated with their products; they could easily monitor the distribution system they created and control, which as I understand it is common in most American industries. They could drop or restrict distributors and dealers who feed the crime market."

§§§

One aspect of the market puzzled me from the beginning. The handguns that wind up being used in crimes were not a large proportion of the total number of handguns sold; the best estimate was in the range of 10 to 15 percent. Why would manufacturers continue to conduct their businesses as they do for an additional small profit when they could seriously reduce the supply to criminals and youth? People sometimes do awful things to make money and often find strange ways to justify themselves. But gun manufacturers were already the object of public criticism and wanted to avoid governmental regulation.

I wound up concluding that a lot more than the visible 10 to 15 percent was at stake when you consider how the market functions and is structured. In the eyes of the public health community, gun deaths and injuries constitute an epidemic. But this epidemic is spread not by a bacteria or a virus but by fear. Fear is the engine of demand for this industry's products.

Anything that increases fear is great for gun sales. The worst things that could happen for the country are the best things for the handgun industry. In between the big scares and spikes in handgun sales, the usual level of fear that generates the bulk of handgun sales is provided by crime, particularly crimes with guns and all manner of shootings. The gun industry needs the daily local news accounts of shootings and murders—fed by easy access to handguns for criminals and youth—to maintain its high level of new handgun sales.

§§§

The bigger question was why this market in handguns was allowed to thrive when the consequences were clear day after day, gloomy statistic after gloomy statistic. I was confused and bothered by this, particularly since the usual and most obvious answers didn't explain it.

The gun lobby, which includes the National Rifle Association (NRA), the gun industry, and other gun-focused groups, is well funded and very influential, especially with politicians. Congress has done pretty much whatever the gun lobby asks.

After Bobby Kennedy was killed with a small handgun in 1968, Congress was moved to ban small, inexpensive handguns, called "Saturday night specials." At the last minute before the bill's passage, however, the gun lobby got an amendment that exempted Saturday night specials manufactured in the United States. We got made-in-America mayhem rather than foreign-made mayhem.

In 1976, Congress exempted anything to do with guns or ammunition from the jurisdiction of the Consumer Products Safety Commission (CPSC). If defective ammunition is blowing up in the hands of hunters, they can't go to the CPSC.

In the early 1990s, Congress reacted to the public health studies showing the danger of handguns in the home by barring the Center for Disease Control (CDC), which had funded the studies, from conducting or funding any research on public health "to advocate or promote gun control." The next year, Congress removed from the CDC budget the exact amount of the grant that had funded the studies.

Recently, Congress has let the ban on assault weapons expire; restricted ATF from providing important data and information on guns used in crime to the public, scholars, or law enforcement; and granted a broad immunity to the gun industry in response to the city handgun lawsuits.

A lobby this strong operates on many levels. The gun lobby is politically active, visible, and flush with campaign funds. The gun lobby also gains strength from the implicit threat of violence to anyone who opposes the unregulated flow of guns, when, for example, Charlton Heston, as head of the NRA, often held a rifle in the air and said menacingly, "From my cold dead hands."

But there are a lot of well-funded, well-connected, powerful, and sometimes intimidating lobbies that do not succeed to this extent. Lead paint and PCBs were banned despite rich, powerful lobbies representing those industries. Guns touch a deep nerve in American society.

The cultural and political dimensions of public opposition to gun control are often ignored by those who believe that there are too many handguns and want to do something about the problem. The widespread identification of guns with our highest ideals—freedom; liberty; and, for some, God and country—affects the politics of guns and of proposals for government regulation.

Some Americans think and feel on a gut level that guns and the constitutional provision on guns in the Second Amendment are central to everything that they hold dear about America and that any attempt to put limits on them is a terrible threat. Their thinking is similar to that of many more Americans about the protection of freedom of speech in the First Amendment. So I can disagree with what you say but defend your right to say it, even if what you say is deplorable or disgusting to me. Similarly, one can deplore what some do with guns but defend the unregulated right to them—sometimes accompanied by tortured denials of any connection between the two.

The most extreme form of this cultural and political identification of guns with freedom, the NRA version, leads to opposition to restrictions on Teflon-coated bullets called "cop killers" because they can pierce bulletproof vests. Any government regulation of guns or ammunition, even if favored by law enforcement, is seen as a threat to fundamental American ideals.

Less extreme versions have more widespread and significant effects on American society and politics. Sometimes even the wildest arguments against regulation strike a chord with a broad segment of Americans, who think the NRA goes too far but still see guns as linked with freedom. They may accept that something should be done about the slaughter but feel deeply uneasy with gun restrictions.

The moderate version of this cultural and political identification contributes to the gun lobby's success with the strategy of supporting and proposing meaningless laws and then arguing that all that is needed is enforcement of existing laws.

§§§

The task force was interested in the manufacturers' role in marketing handguns, but the group mostly focused on other things, like a program to identify likely young gun toters and their victims and to intervene before shots are fired. None of us, including me, began with thoughts of suing the manufacturers or anyone else. The courts had turned so conservative that progressive law reform by courts seemed outmoded, and gun manufacturers hadn't been sued successfully except when a particular weapon was defective. Most handguns worked all too well.

But when I started thinking about the handgun market, the public health perspective, and the role of the manufacturers, the prospect of a very different kind of lawsuit began to take shape. The way the manufacturers knowingly marketed handguns—not the design or any defect in the products—made them easily available to criminals and youth and thereby endangered public health and safety. The public health and safety focus drew me to a tort hardly mentioned in law school: public nuisance, a chestnut of common law developed over centuries to protect the public from danger. I didn't remember anything specific about the tort except that I had run across discussions of it in cases that defined it in terms of "unreasonable interference" with public health or safety.

I went to the *Restatement of the Law of Torts*, the widely recognized text that set out the accepted definitions and elements of tort law, expecting that there would be some features of public nuisance law unknown to me that made it less useful than it seemed. Public nuisance had easier than usual burdens of proof. The defendant's duty, often a problem in cases against manufacturers, was to the public at large, so it didn't require proof of a duty to particular people harmed. Causation was formulated as "creating or contributing to" the nuisance rather than the usual "proximate cause," which was often hard to prove. A city or state was the usual plaintiff.

The available remedies were unusual, more focused on stopping the interference with an injunction and cleaning up the mess—"abatement"—than on monetary recovery for the harm done, which made sense in light of the relaxed requirements of proof. The point of the tort was to give city and state officials a quick remedy for stopping conduct that was endangering the public and for recovering the costs of removing the danger and cleaning it up.

Public nuisance suits were often against a licensed or regulated business and worked even if a business had done nothing illegal. A blacksmith shop could be a public nuisance if it was located near a residential neighborhood, even if it were operated properly and there before the houses. Since public danger comes in many forms and from many kinds of conduct, courts had adopted a case-by-case approach. It all looked very promising.

The legal theory relied on existing law—no reform or change of the law was necessary. I wondered why the state tobacco lawsuits, then at their early stages, didn't focus on public nuisance. A city, county, or state could sue handgun manufacturers for creating a public nuisance by showing that the companies made it easy for criminals to get handguns, even though they knew the deadly consequences. The case wouldn't be about how guns are made or about their defects but rather about how they're distributed. It wouldn't sever the link between guns and violent crime, but a court could make handguns harder for criminals to get by barring some forms of distribution and thereby, in some measure, reduce handgun deaths and crimes. And the manufacturers might have to pay back cities for the costs of cleaning up the handgun mess, which might include the costs of emergency healthcare, 911 calls, police, perhaps the washing of blood off the streets. A public nuisance suit could also help educate the public about how guns get to the street. Since the suit wouldn't seek to restrict who could buy or own handguns, the Second Amendment didn't pose a plausible problem.

The theory met my toughest test for a novel legal claim: it made intuitive sense. How hard would it be to convince juries, judges, and the public that knowingly opening the door for criminals to buy handguns is dangerous and wrong?

§§§

Mike was excited and set up a meeting for us to propose a Philadelphia lawsuit to Rendell. As good as the theory was, I doubted that Ed would bring the suit, but he was often unpredictable.

He surprised me the last time I had contact with him, while he was still the district attorney. I was asked to help the leaders of People for the Ethical Treatment of Animals (PETA), who were under long-standing subpoenas to appear at a grand jury investigating a break-in at a Penn lab using monkeys in experiments on head injuries. The subpoenas kept the leaders of PETA from speaking engagements in Philadelphia. When Ed balked at withdrawing them, I asked him if he'd watch the lab video for 10 minutes. Just a few minutes of monkeys with their heads screwed into a vicelike grip being hit with a skull-crushing blow was enough. He withdrew the subpoenas.

Buzz Bissinger's book on Rendell, *A Prayer for the City,* captures the smart, likeable, sometimes volatile guy with a short attention span that I remembered. As mayor, Rendell reminded me of President Bill Clinton. He spoke movingly about Philadelphia's problems and lifted the city's morale yet was cautious when it came to making significant changes beyond large budget cuts, and he was a favorite of the city's business establishment.

But Rendell was enthusiastic when Mike and I pitched the lawsuit. He was disturbed by the easy availability of handguns in Philadelphia. He liked the suit's focus on distribution—he used the prosecutor's term, *trafficking*—and its distance from the Second Amendment. He also relished the opportunity to take the lead nationally on a major issue. I asked if he wanted to be on the cover of *Time* or *Newsweek*. He said either was fine, smiling, and we reminisced about the old days when he and I were very young lawyers in the courtrooms of city hall. Ed hired me to gather evidence and prepare a case against handgun manufacturers as counsel for the city of Philadelphia.

§§§

I started by reading every public nuisance case I could find. Most of them dated from the 1950s or 1960s; some were from before World War II. I also investigated the local gun market, visiting or calling stores in and around Philadelphia. They carried the small semiautomatics most frequently used by criminals, often for under $100. I could legally buy as many as I could pay for. At Lou's Loans in Upper Darby, just outside Philadelphia, I picked out five cheap handguns. The salesman told me the store would have to file the form with ATF if I bought five. I asked what that would mean. "Don't worry about it," he said. "They won't bother with you, and if they contact you, tell them you're a collector."

With the help of several other lawyers and city staff members, I collected crime data from the Philadelphia police to illustrate the human toll exacted by easy access to handguns. The fire, police, welfare, and streets departments figured out how much money they spent dealing with handgun crime so we could quantify the city's costs. We used data about the handguns that were frequently used in deaths to single out the manufacturers we wanted to sue.

We tried to fill in the big gaps in the literature about handgun marketing ourselves. There wasn't much research that detailed how frequently people legally bought more than one handgun from a dealer or how many they bought. We were able to do our own study when we gained access to a state police printout of all handgun sales by dealers in Pennsylvania over a 15-month period.

About half the handguns sold over the 15-month period were purchased by buyers who bought at least 1 other handgun. Thirty percent were purchased by someone who bought 3 or more. Nearly a fifth of all handgun purchases were made by the industry's best customers—people without a dealer license who bought 5 or more handguns, some of whom bought over 100 handguns. That's why proposals to limit buyers to 1 gun a month were cast as reforms—though it's hard to think of a legitimate reason for buying 12 small, inexpensive handguns in a year.

When I had a handle on the law and basic facts, I started asking others in the field for help. Stephen Teret and Jon Vernick at the Johns Hopkins Center for Gun Policy and Research and Josh Horwitz at the Education Fund to Stop Gun Violence knew the research on guns and violence and prior litigation. Elissa Barnes, a lawyer who'd sued the manufacturers on behalf of victims of gun violence in New York, knew a lot about the marketing tactics of the industry, and her case had already yielded revealing testimony. "The industry's position has consistently been to take no independent action to ensure responsible distribution practices," Robert Hass, Smith & Wesson's former vice president for marketing, stated in an affidavit—even though the industry is "fully aware" of "the seepage of guns into the illicit market."

The other leading gun control groups—the Brady Center to Prevent Gun Violence and the Violence Policy Center—helped too, although they had their own long-standing agendas. The Brady Center liked the idea of city lawsuits and wanted to be included in any lawsuit we filed, although they didn't like the focus on distribution and marketing and were resistant to the new legal theory. We didn't have to resolve these differences because Rendell liked the approach and theory and didn't want any gun control groups involved in the case. The suit was to be about Philadelphia's response to a public danger, not about gun control.

§§§

By the summer of 1997, we had a solid, well-researched case. I couldn't predict the outcome, but I thought a reasonable judge should deny a gun manufacturer's motion to dismiss our complaint. That was how I assessed our prospects for Rendell. Surmounting this initial legal hurdle allows a plaintiff to build a case by asking a defendant for documents and testimony. I'd brought a lot of novel lawsuits, and surviving a motion to dismiss was my regular standard.

I contacted a producer at *Nightline* and explained, off the record, what we were about to do. I told him we would give *Nightline* an exclusive national TV interview with Rendell if they wanted to break the story. Another producer I knew put me in contact with a regular reporter for *Newsweek,* to whom I offered a print magazine exclusive.

"It's *Newsweek,* not *Time,* Ed," I told Rendell, "and they said there's a good chance you'll be on the cover. The day we file, you'll be live on *Nightline.*"

"Who's Koppel gonna have against me, Charlton Heston?" he said, smiling.

But 10 days before we planned to file the suit we got a different kind of publicity. Our plans were leaked to a local television station, and Rendell was immediately attacked. State senator Vincent Fumo, a powerful Philadelphia Democrat with close ties to the NRA, questioned Ed's sanity and said that if he brought the suit he'd never win statewide office. Ed made no secret of wanting to be governor.

For weeks and then months, the suit was in the local and national news. While Rendell stressed that we were relying on settled law, the public nuisance theory and marketing facts behind it went largely unexplained, and when he tried to explain, he often got it wrong. I was quoted occasionally, but the media was really interested in one question: Would Rendell sue the gun industry?

I began to ask myself the same question. Ed used the publicity effectively to talk about the issues, but he seemed to be losing his nerve, looking for a safe middle ground. He tried to negotiate a settlement of the unfiled lawsuit, but the companies didn't take that seriously. Then, to my great surprise, he made an alliance with Charlton Heston and the NRA to step up enforcement of existing gun laws. The point of the lawsuit was that those laws didn't address the easy availability of handguns.

Six months after the news leak, Rendell told the *Philadelphia Inquirer* that he "very much wants to file the suit because I believe with every ounce of feeling that I have that there are far too many guns." That had been his reaction from the beginning, and I thought he still meant it. But the press widely reported that Rendell and his close advisers and supporters were worried about the fallout that Fumo had threatened.

Ed's closest advisers and friends were David Cohen and Arthur Makadon at the prominent corporate law firm Ballard, Spahr, Andrews & Ingersol. Cohen was a wunderkind in the Philadelphia legal world who served as Ed's chief of staff and left to take over as chair of the firm. Makadon was known as an effective litigator who was often hard to get along with. I knew them both, though not very well, and I knew and thought well of a lot of lawyers at the firm. Many of them had done impressive pro bono work, although they also did what corporate firms usually do. The firm's biggest moneymaker for many years was the defense of asbestos manufacturers, and Makadon was most known for his role in originating the strategy of profitable companies' exploiting loopholes in the bankruptcy laws that allowed them to avoid or postpone their liability to people dying from exposure to asbestos by declaring bankruptcy.

Cohen and Makadon brought the firm on board, which I favored since we would need a lot of high-quality legal work. But they never seemed enthusiastic about the lawsuit, although others at the firm were. Cohen was strategizing about Ed's run for governor and had close ties to the NRA's Senator Fumo. There was a generic sort of conflict of interest because we would be advocating a new theory for corporate liability that some of their regular clients could face. Makadon was, true to his reputation, hard to figure. He pushed hard for a contingent fee for Ballard Spahr, which meant that Ballard Spahr would make a lot of money if we won. He reviewed the complaint and told me he had no changes to suggest and was ready to go, while sending a letter to Ed, which Ed showed me, saying he didn't like the complaint and didn't want me working on the case.[3]

At a news conference in January 1998, Rendell was asked whether he hadn't sued because of the "political damage" to his gubernatorial aspirations. He launched into an angry tirade about the pressures and difficulties of his job. "I'm tired of the crap you have to put up with," he said, "like everybody threatening and extorting you."

I wondered about the political calculus behind not filing. Since Rendell was already closely identified with suing gun manufacturers and with gun control—not popular in much of Pennsylvania, with its large NRA membership—I couldn't see how holding back would help him. No Philadelphia Democrat had an easy time running statewide in Pennsylvania; no Jew from New York had yet tried. But I was hardly surprised that bringing an untried high-profile lawsuit would involve political calculations.

The problem for me was that Ed wouldn't say that he wasn't going to sue, even though it was clear to me that was what he'd decided. For months, Ed and his staff and advisers said publicly they were "thinking." That positioned him at the forefront of the national gun control debate. But as the city's lawyer, I couldn't share the work I'd done with other mayors, whose lawsuits would have shifted the media spotlight away from Ed. They were exploiting the gun control guru status the lawsuit idea had bestowed on Ed, while keeping the lawsuit, its pro-gun Pennsylvania fallout, and me contained.

Ed would probably be a good governor, and I understood the strategy that made the lawsuit too risky politically. But he was keeping other cities from pursuing it. So I came up with a plan to get out from under Ed, Cohen, and Makadon.

On January 9, 1998, I sent a confidential letter to Ed, with copies to Cohen and Makadon, withdrawing as counsel for Philadelphia. I explained the circumstances that led to my withdrawal in some detail and asked Ed to release me from the obligation of client confidentiality to the extent necessary to fully explain the case I'd developed. I got, as I expected, no response from any of them to the request to release me from confidentiality or to my suggestion that we discuss how to present my withdrawal publicly.

My next step involved some risk. There were two ways to go public with the basis and theory of the lawsuit. I could negotiate with them and try to arrive at an agreement that would release me from confidentiality, or I could go public to the extent allowable without breaching confidentiality. I consulted a law professor whose field is professional responsibility, since I wanted to be sure that I understood the nuances of the law on this. The recommendation was that I negotiate with them, which made sense, except that I knew Cohen and Makadon would, at best, drag out negotiations so Ed could continue to straddle the issue and get the publicity. I was done waiting. I chose the alternative course of going public while being very careful not to breach confidentiality. This was made considerably easier by the main constraint being specific confidences of my client and by Ed's already setting out publicly most of the important basis and theory in his many media interviews on the subject.

In a press release on January 20, I praised Ed for his efforts to deal with gun violence while announcing that I'd withdrawn as counsel, and simultaneously I released a paper (later an article for the *Temple Law Review*) laying out my theory that gun manufacturers were marketing their products in a way that created a public nuisance. I was careful not to reveal any confidences and heavily relied on Ed's public statements. Still, Cohen and Makadon were furious. Cohen blustered ridicule and questioned my sanity in an interview with a local magazine. Ed told the *Philadelphia Inquirer,* "We are sorry he's not going to be a part of it any longer. He did a very good job."[4]

§§§

I was inundated with requests for information from cities, scholars, researchers, and groups on all sides of the gun control debate. I faxed the paper setting out the theory and basis so many times it wore out and had to be printed out again a few times. Soon after the release, I started working with Larry Rosenthal, a lawyer for the city of Chicago, and then other city lawyers.

In the fall of 1998, New Orleans and Chicago brought the first city suits against handgun manufacturers. By 2000, more than 40 cities and counties brought lawsuits, including Los Angeles, San Francisco, Detroit, St. Louis, Atlanta, and New York City. Some of the cases, led by the Brady Center, which wound up playing a major role, emphasized gun safety and defects rather than marketing and public nuisance. Almost all raised the public nuisance theory based on the marketing facts, and that became the primary focus of the city lawsuits.

I wound up on most of the legal teams, including on the team of the one state that brought the lawsuit, New York. And shortly after taking office, the mayor who succeeded Rendell, John Street, brought me back to file the long-contemplated suit for Philadelphia. Ed, Mike, and I appeared on *Nightline,* and I was profiled in the *Wall Street Journal,* the *Philadelphia Inquirer Magazine,* and the *Chronicle of Higher Education.*[5]

Almost half of the cities' cases against the manufacturers were halted by statutes barring them, which the NRA lobbied for after the suits began. These legislatures decided to exempt the handgun industry from public nuisance rules that protect the public and had applied to everyone for hundreds of years. In about half of the cases not barred by statute, the manufacturers' motions to dismiss the cases were denied. They got further than the state tobacco suits at a comparably early stage.

Many of the decisions dismissing the cases did so by changing or distorting public nuisance law. In one case I argued for Camden County,

New Jersey, the federal Third Circuit Court of Appeals dismissed the case because "no New Jersey court has ever allowed a public nuisance claim to proceed against manufacturers for lawful products that are lawfully placed in the stream of commerce." Historically, companies and individuals doing business lawfully or acting lawfully were commonly held liable if their conduct created a public nuisance. Public nuisance, like other torts, doesn't require that the conduct be unlawful. One can be driving within the speed limit but be negligent for going too fast in particular circumstances. The traditional process is for courts to apply the established elements of any tort to the facts presented rather than creating immunities for manufacturers or other categories of defendants. This opinion was the not unusual handiwork of Judge Samuel Alito, who now sits on the Supreme Court.[6]

In 1999 Smith & Wesson, the largest handgun manufacturer, agreed to a settlement with several of the cities that required S&W to restrict and monitor its distributors responsibly. In 2003, a major gun industry whistle-blower broke ranks. Robert A. Ricker, former executive director of the leading industry trade group and a former NRA official, filed an affidavit in the cases brought by 12 California cities and counties. Ricker accused the major gun manufacturers of playing "see no evil, hear no evil." The companies had fostered "a culture of evasion of firearms laws and regulations," he said, even though they'd "long known that greater industry action to prevent illegal transactions is possible."

Then Congress stepped in. In 2005, Congress enacted and President Bush signed a law granting the gun industry a broad immunity from a broad range of lawsuits in response to the city cases. Like the state legislative immunities, Congress exempted the industry from laws and rules established to protect the public to which all other industries and individuals are subject.[7]

So the handgun industry, and only the handgun industry, is allowed to create a public nuisance. I suppose this is a testament to the strength of my approach—it could only be stopped by an unprincipled exemption from the rules that apply to everyone else. The congressional immunity and the lack of public attention or concern about it are also another triumph for that moderate version of the identification of guns with freedom and our highest principles, which still pervades much of our politics.

Ed is in his second term as governor of Pennsylvania, and my good friend Mike is his innovative secretary of conservation and natural re-sources. During the first, 2002, campaign, the NRA and gun enthusiasts attacked Ed relentlessly. His Republican opponent often said that Rendell "just doesn't want people to have guns." In response, Ed often noted his "cooperation with the NRA."

My public nuisance approach has had an effect beyond guns. In 2004, a leading publication for corporate lawyers ran an article that detailed how the theory is now prominent in the range of litigation against man-ufacturers for endangering public health or safety, such as the suits against lead paint manufacturers for poisoning children.[8]

CHAPTER FIFTEEN

Hoover's Legacy

"LAW OFFICES," I said, answering the phone one morning in the summer of 1986.

"David Kairys, please."

"Speaking."

"Okay." There seemed to be disappointment in his voice, perhaps because lawyers, or maybe good lawyers, usually don't answer their own phones. We had decided that, since almost all the calls were for Rudy and me, we might as well answer the phones, unless we're doing something else that's important. I got so used to it that I sometimes said "law offices" when I picked up my home phone.

"This is Special Agent Donald Rochon at the Philadelphia FBI office."

"Okay." I tried to figure out what the FBI had in store for one of my clients or me but couldn't think of anything current.

"I've been having a problem in the bureau, and I think I need a lawyer," he said. "Can I speak to you in confidence?"

"Absolutely. Let's find a time for you to come in rather than talking on the phone."

"Is today possible?"

"Sure."

When I got back from court a few hours later, he was seated in our conference room, looking nervous as I came in.

"Mr. Rochon, I'm David Kairys."

"Glad to meet you," he said, rising to shake my hand. He was a light-skinned black man with a friendly smile, about six feet tall, trim, in a nicely pressed gray suit. His hair was well groomed, dark, medium length, and he had a small dark mustache.

"What's brought you in to see me?"

"Am I right that anything we say is covered by attorney-client privilege?"

"That's right. I can reveal it only if you want me to."

He was hesitant, as if he wasn't sure he should talk to me. I had my own doubts. He looked and talked like an FBI agent, but I wondered about a possible FBI setup for something illegal or embarrassing. It was just that trust and the FBI didn't jibe in my experience. Asking to see his FBI identification would make him more nervous. I thought it best to listen to his story and see where it went.

"Okay," he continued after a pause. "I was a detective in L.A. and grew up there. I never thought race played much of a role in work or socializing. I got into the FBI in 1981, a big career move, and was in training and at the L.A. office 'til 1983, when they sent me to Omaha."

"Nebraska?"

"Yeah. It's a small office, and the scene was dominated by a few white guys who were on me almost from the beginning. I'm not a confrontational guy; I get along with everyone, 'til this anyway. I saw there was a problem, so I thought the best thing to do was be friendly, talk to them one on one when I had the chance. I hoped it would stop."

He spoke slowly and softly. "What were they doing that was racial?"

"It started out with some juvenile stuff, like fraternity hazing but often with a racial side. I got bogus phone messages, and when I called back it would be recorded sermons by black preachers or gospel singers. Or it would be the numbers of some unsuspecting black folks upset by a call from the FBI. They put stuff in my office mail slot. An African in native dress, a picture of a black man and a white woman, a picture of a badly beaten black man. Invitations to office events had 'Don't come' handwritten on them.

"Then it started to escalate. A picture of two black scuba divers swimming in a dump with a photo of my face from my personnel file pasted on one of them was put on the office bulletin board. When my wife and I went to an office party, two of them had a 'fart contest' right in front of her while I went to get us drinks. We left right away, and I never took her to another office social event."

"Is your wife white?"

"Yes. They made comments about her being white and blond and attractive. One day I came back to my desk and there was a big bowl of water there, and a battery-operated toy scuba doll with the flesh areas painted black was swimming around in it. They all stood around and laughed. Someone said something like, 'Blacks can't swim.' I looked at the scuba toy and at them in disbelief."

"What's going on with the scuba theme?"

"I took scuba lessons. I swim regularly, and there was a local class. Not much else to do in Omaha, so I thought I'd learn something and have some fun with it. They thought a black person doing scuba or swimming at all was very funny. I never ran into anything like this before."

"Did it go further?"

"Oh yeah." He hesitated. "The next thing was they pasted a photo of the face of a monkey over the faces of my kids on a picture I had on my desk."

"A monkey?"

"Yeah. They got a photo of a monkey or ape out of a magazine and cut it out."

"And they thought that was funny, too?"

"The whole scene was regularly filled with bigotry to blacks and other minorities. They'd talk among themselves and in public about Martin Luther King and Jesse Jackson being 'Russian spies' and 'commies.' Jews were referred to as 'cheap Jews' or 'kikes.' President Jimmy Carter was a 'communist sympathizer.' They often criticized the director, FBI director William Webster. They were Hoover men. Do you know what I mean?"

"I do. How did you react to all this?"

"I tried to ignore the initial stuff, hoping it would go away when they got to know me. When it didn't, I asked them to stop it. That didn't work, so I told them if it continued, I'd report it to the supervisors."

"Did you report it?"

"Yes. I told my supervisor, Mike Santimauro, and I told the EEO officer, you know, each office has an equal employment opportunity officer, a black agent named Charles Wiley. Later I complained to the special agent in charge (SAC) at Omaha, Herbert Hawkins."

"So there were other blacks there?"

"Yeah, but they put the first black agent out in a resident office off by himself, and they converted a closet for Wiley, put his desk in there, and had him do checks on applicants for federal jobs. I was the first black agent in the 'bull pen,' the main office area for agents with many desks in a big open room, and was getting regular criminal case assignments."

"Did you talk to Wiley about his experiences?"

"Yeah. He thought they were a bunch of racists. He called them 'peckerheads' when he and I talked privately. He told me to ignore it, the way he and other blacks had. He said the worst thing you could do is complain."

"Who were the agents doing this?"

"The ringleader was Tom Dillon, who grew up in Chicago, and the others regularly included Charles Kempf, Larry McGee, and Jerry Webb. The whole thing continued when I was transferred to Chicago against my wishes several months after Dillon was transferred there. It got much worse. Look at this."

He reached into his briefcase and pulled out several packets of papers clipped together. That removed my doubts—he was an FBI agent. Each packet was held together with a brown backer, a stiff piece of folderlike paper with two prongs a few inches apart at the top sticking through the papers. Other lawyers and law enforcement still used backers, but these were unmistakably FBI backers.

Rochon unclipped one of the packets and handed me three sheets of paper from the top. One had a picture of a mutilated black man, with a typewritten message:

ASSHOLE, LOOK AT YOUR FUTURE REWARD FOR YOUR DEEDS. YOU MADE YOURSELF A NIGGER AND SHALL PAY THE PRICE. WE ARE GOING TO CUT OFF YOUR NIGGERASS LIPS AND BALLS. YOU ARE SHIT AND SHOULD BE FLUSH. YOUR WIFE IS A CHEAP WHORE AND WE CAN FUCK HER ANYTIME IN YOUR SECRET NIGGERVILLE HOUSE. WE ARE GOING TO FUCK HER IN THE ASS AND THEN IN HER MOUTH. YOU ARE ALWAYS IN OUR SIGHTS AND CAN NOT ESCAPE. LOOK OUT!

The second sheet showed a bull's-eye with the head of a black man with devil's horns in the middle and typewriting that said: "JACKOFF BEFORE WE SHOOT IT OFF. WE ARE WAITING FOR YOU. CUM NOW." The third sheet, on Allstate Life Insurance stationery, was an insurance policy in Rochon's name for death and dismemberment coverage.

I looked up at Rochon. "Who sent these?"

"They all came in the mail to the office. I don't know exactly which agents did it, but it's part of the office harassment led by Dillon. See the reference to 'secret niggerville house.' I asked the agent in charge to keep my home address secret to avoid harassment at home. We lived in Napierville, outside Chicago—that's the 'Niggerville house'—and the only people it was kept secret from was these agents. We told our friends and the kids' day care center."

"What did Dillon and the others say about all this?"

"In Omaha, they said it was just pranks. They denied any of it has anything to do with race. In Chicago, Dillon denied he did anything, denied even that he got others there on me, though everybody knows he did. They say I can't take a joke, I'm incompetent, and I do ridiculous things. They say everybody gets pranks but I got more because I do such silly things."

"Like you caused all this. What silly things?"

"They told stories all the time in the bull pen. They didn't get much work done. One was I let an FBI car engine run all night to keep it warm and the engine burned out and was ruined. They said when it rains I jog with a lightning rod. I supposedly tried to remove snow from my driveway in freezing weather by hosing it down, making a sheet of ice. They said I kept my service revolver under the washer in the basement, causing it to rust. I supposedly slept in the backseat of a car during a surveillance mission. You get the idea. They'd say all this nonsense and laugh it up in the bull pen, sometimes in my presence."

His flat FBI demeanor broke. He was upset and angry; who wouldn't be? "Where'd they get these stories?" I asked. "Was it all just made up?"

"Sometimes they related to something that happened, with all the nonsense added."

"Give me an example."

"I had an FBI car with a dead battery, so if you turned it off, it wouldn't start. I left it running outside the office for a short time while I went in to get maintenance personnel to deal with it. It all took less than an hour, and no engine burned out. One of them saw me leave the car running; the rest is office bullshit."

"How were your performance ratings?"

"Fine, always very positive. I never had any negative performance evaluations."

"What did the supervisors and management do about the race harassment?"

"Nothing. In Omaha, there were no investigations, no discipline of any white agent, nothing. The special agents in charge at Omaha and Chicago and management at headquarters in Washington always sided with the white agents. They punished me, retaliated, with a censure in Omaha and the transfer to Chicago."

"They censured you?"

"Yeah. I filed formal EEO complaints about the race harassment and my transfer to Chicago. They needed more agents in L.A., where I particularly wanted to go since my father was seriously ill there. The Chicago transfer was management sending me right to where Dillon was—all the other agents at Omaha got the transfer to the major offices or areas they requested. Anyway, when they interviewed me on my EEO complaints, we talked about different kinds of discrimination and how sometimes it's hard to know if it's discrimination. I mentioned that my wife and I thought a realtor in Omaha steered us away from houses in white areas, but we weren't sure. Hawkins started an investigation of whether I had failed to report race discrimination in housing. I was censured for that, with the approval of high-level management at headquarters, just below the director, including Assistant Director Groover and Deputy Assistant Director Edwin Sharp."

"Have you filed timely complaints with the Equal Employment Opportunity Commission on all this?"

"Yeah. I've got four pending EEOC complaints and an evidentiary hearing coming up soon in Omaha on all the claims arising there. That's why I think I need a lawyer."

He handed me the packets containing each complaint, which I quickly browsed. "These complaints are very well done. Did you have a lawyer?"

"No. I went to law school at night while I was an L.A. detective, but I never practiced."

"What brought you to me?"

"You were quoted in a *Philadelphia Inquirer* article a few months ago about trends in race discrimination. I liked what you said." He hesitated and then said, "Look, I want to be up-front about finances. I'm in no position to pay a fee. Can you do this on a contingent fee basis?"

"I can, and I'm pretty sure the National Emergency Civil Liberties Committee will cover the out-of-pocket expenses. I want to be up-front about something, also. I've done several cases that challenged the FBI. My opinion of them is not high. I know that they were very slow to integrate and that the first black agents, after undergoing training at Quantico, were assigned as valets and chauffeurs. But I wouldn't have thought even they could do what they did to you. Anyway, is my litigating major cases against them a problem?"[1]

"What cases have you done?"

"You heard of the Camden 28, the antiwar draft board raiders who were acquitted after an FBI informer became a defense witness? In *Resistance v. Mitchell,* my partner and I challenged the FBI's tactics in the search for whoever did the Media FBI office burglary. The FBI settled."

"I've heard of both of those cases. No, that's fine with me and may help get them to take this seriously."

§§§

"I declare this hearing to be open. This is the discrimination complaint of Donald Rochon," Bernard Steinberg, the EEOC complaints examiner hearing Rochon's Omaha complaints, said emphatically. He was thin, weather worn, or maybe trial worn. He seemed to be trying to create a trial-like environment in this small conference room in the Omaha federal building with scattered chairs and three beat-up tables arranged to form a tee. A stenographer shared his table at the top of the tee. Two lawyers from FBI headquarters, John Oscadal and Bernard Thompson, sat at one of two tables pushed together to form the stem, and Don and I sat at the other.

The complaints examiner would issue an opinion after the hearing, but a federal agency accused of discrimination could "accept, reject, or modify" his decision. This was an obvious problem for us, though the DOJ, the parent agency of the FBI, would make the decision. I liked the opportunity for a full hearing and cross-examination of FBI witnesses, which wasn't available in the usual, private employer EEOC procedure. In any event, there was a right to go to court if we lost.

The procedure and substantive rules were statutory, set out in the Equal Employment Opportunity Act, usually called Title VII. I had litigated a lot of constitutional discrimination cases before, based on the

Fourteenth and Fifth Amendments, but this was my first EEOC case. It was also my first race harassment case. My research revealed, surprisingly, almost a complete lack of prior decisions on race harassment in Title VII and constitutional cases. I relied mostly on sex harassment cases, which I had litigated for some time.[2]

Our first witness was Don. I started with his education, work history, and performance evaluations and introduced as an exhibit a packet that contained all of the performance evaluations. They were uniformly very positive.

"In your employment with the FBI," I asked Don, "what was the first incident or event that you thought raised a racial problem?"

"The first time was when I was in training at Quantico, Virginia. A couple of my classmates were using the word *nigger* in classes and in the dorms."

"Objection," Thompson said, "I don't see how this relates." Oscadal had done the opening statement and all of the preliminaries for the FBI. He was white; Thompson was black.

"Mr. Kairys, what is the relevance?" Steinberg asked.

"We intend to show that Mr. Rochon does his job extremely well and works extremely well with others, white and black. He grew up in an overwhelmingly white neighborhood in L.A. and had many close white friends. He's not a troublemaker or complainer. But when he's confronted with overt racism, he doesn't let it pass but responds calmly and rationally. This is what happened at Quantico and later at Omaha."

"If you can connect it, I'll listen and consider it."

"Mr. Rochon, who was it that you heard use that language?"

"My classmate, Patrick Gray."

"Is he related to the former director of the FBI with the same name?"

"His son."

"When you got to Omaha, did you observe anything unusual regarding racial matters?"

"There seemed a lack of sensitivity that I saw elsewhere toward minorities. They joked about Hispanics, Asians, Jews, blacks. A lot of it was about politics or sex lives. Martin Luther King was a big subject there, particularly his sex life. They thought Hoover was right to go after King. Supervisors would sit in, Hawkins or Santimauro, and listen and laugh, sometimes make a comment."

"Give us an example."

"I object," Thompson said. "That question assumes there are other examples. It's leading, and you're coaching him."

"Mr. Rochon, are there other examples of derogatory comments against other minorities other than blacks?"

"Oh, yes. We were sitting at a bar with Hawkins, having a drink. Dillon said to Hawkins, about a white technician with us who was married to an Asian woman, 'He's been eating slanted pussy.' Another time, Kempf was complaining about a Jewish tenant who had rented his condo in Chicago when he left for his Omaha assignment. Kempf was going back to Chicago, but the tenant didn't want to give up the lease. Kempf said he would never do business with a Jew again. Hawkins said, 'Those kind of people will sue you in a minute.'"

"Were comments directed toward other blacks?"

"Yes. For example, one day in the bull pen just before Charles Wiley was to move out of his closet office, Dillon, Kempf, McGee, and Webb were mimicking him as a submissive black man, saying things like, 'Yes'm, boss, I do that.' Webb made a sign that said 'Uncle Chuck's Cabin.' One said, 'Please, boss, don't call me a nigger.' They roared with laughter at each comment."

Don then testified to the events directed at him that started a few weeks after his arrival in Omaha in February 1983. He had kept a lot of the written materials and objects like the scuba toy, which were made exhibits, and detailed his attempts to convince the white agents to stop the racial harassment.

Don didn't keep the picture of his children with the monkey cutout pasted over their faces. It was too upsetting; he threw it away. We reconstructed it by printing another copy of the children's picture from the same negative and Don's finding a similar monkey picture to cut out from a magazine. Thompson objected.

"It's unduly prejudicial," he said. "The best evidence rule would apply, too. He should produce that evidence, as he's done meticulously with other exhibits, so we'd have a clear representation of what was shown."

"Do you wish to respond?" Steinberg asked me.

"Well, it is prejudicial. It shows a virulent form of racism. It's at the heart of this case, and it happened. At least one other agency employee saw it and described it as 'disgusting' in a statement that's included in the materials in the case file."

"The agency's objections will be overruled."

"Mr. Rochon," I continued, "what effect did this have on you, the picture of your kids with the monkey pasted over them?"

"It was degrading. In law enforcement, there's usually a certain level of pranks and sometimes conflicts, but you don't attack a family member. I was in a real state of shock. Wiley told me, 'Your wife is young; she is attractive. These are all macho guys, and they can't handle that. They can't handle a black man having children that look white.' Then he told me I should have known better and not put the picture on my desk, like it was my fault. Agents frequently had family pictures on their desks, and there's no reason why black agents shouldn't."

This brought us to the hardest issue in the case for our side. The FBI's defense, set out in documents and statements we got prior to the hearing, was that these events were just "office pranks" that occurred because Don did such ridiculous things. Some of the pranks in response to Don's "funny" actions may seem racial, they said, but they simply identified Don, like the blackened skin on the scuba diver, and weren't meant as racial. Their defense was to blame Don.

The usual legal strategy in such situations is to direct the hearing and evidence as much as possible away from the stories about Don that circulated in the office and to keep the focus on the harassment. Often, this makes sense, but I wanted to take an unusual tact, and after we talked it out, Don agreed. The stories were false, distorted, or exaggerated and depicted Don in racially stereotyped ways—lacking common sense, afraid of the elements, lazy, and stupid. Their circulation in the office, with the knowledge and complicity of management, created a racially hostile environment in the Omaha FBI office and made it impossible for Don to effectively perform his duties. The stories were not only an insufficient defense; they constituted or were an integral part of an independent violation of Title VII. The risk was that this strategy required us to emphasize the stories rather than turn attention away from them.

"Mr. Rochon," I said, "the statements of a number of FBI personnel in the Omaha office contain stories about you that place you in a negative light. I'm going to ask you about each of these stories or stereotypes, whatever we call them, and ask you what truth, if any, there is or if it's related at all, but exaggerated or distorted, to something that did occur. First, it is said that when it rains you jog holding a lightning rod. Is that true?"

"Absolutely false."

"Do you jog?"

"Yes, regularly."

"How do you dress for jogging?"

"When the weather is bad, I jog in a silver Gore-Tex jogging suit."

"For what purpose?"

"To protect me from cold, dampness, and rain."

"Does your jogging suit have anything on it resembling a rod or stick?"

"No."

"To your knowledge, did this story circulate outside of as well as inside the FBI?"

"Yes, it did. An Omaha police officer told me Kempf told a group of them there was an FBI agent who jogged with a lightning rod. Others told me they heard the driveway hosing story about me. They talked like I came from L.A. and didn't know what to do in snow, so I froze my whole driveway."

"Did this undercut your ability to work with them?"

"I think it did. I couldn't tell who believed all this stuff."

We went through each of the stories this way, pinpointing incidents and times when Don knew Hawkins or other management had knowledge or was present, and we called some witnesses to corroborate Don's testimony. Then we called Tom Dillon.

§§§

"Mr. Dillon, I'm David Kairys, counsel for Mr. Rochon. Do you remember during your time in the Omaha office being called in to speak to supervisors about a complaint by Special Agent Rochon?"

"Yes, sir. They called in Jerry Webb, Larry McGee, Chuck Kempf, and myself and told us to stop playing pranks on Rochon. We were some of the office practical jokers. I didn't believe we did anything that should have upset Mr. Rochon."

Dillon looked younger and less menacing than I expected. He was short, with a friendly, informal demeanor. "Did they say the pranks or the complaint was racial?"

"No. I don't remember racial being made mention at all."

"Did they ask any specifics, who did what?"

"No. It was quick. They told us to stop the practical jokes. We were never blamed."

"You were never blamed?"

"No, sir. We were told, if we were doing anything to him, to stop. I thought he was using these factors to explain why he may be performing poorly. I considered Don Rochon a friend. I didn't think he was the victim of any racial pranks or any other pranks other than the normal pranks we did to everybody else in the office. I thought it was funny."

"Why would that make it funny?"

"Because it was just the opposite. I had more practical jokes played on me than anybody. And I was never offended."

"Did anybody ever paste a picture of an animal over a picture of your kids?"

"Me? No, sir."

"Would you find that funny?"

"No, sir. Well, you know, it depends on the context. I'm familiar with the incident you're talking about, and I would not find what Don Rochon went through on that funny at all."

"Would the monkey in that incident have particular meaning to you if it was done to a black agent?"

"Yes, sir. I think it would be a racial slur."

"Were you questioned or interviewed by Omaha supervisors about that incident?"

"No, sir."

"Were you present when a scuba toy in a bowl of water was placed on Rochon's desk?"

"I saw it on the desk. Yes, sir."

"Did you notice anything unusual about the diver toy? That's Complainant's Exhibit B I'm handing you."

"I see now it has a black face and black hands. I don't consider that unusual if it was meant as a joke to Don Rochon since he's a black man and was taking scuba lessons."

"Why is that a joke or funny?"

"I don't think it was meant as anything but good humor for Don."

"Isn't it funny because, according to many people, blacks have difficulty swimming? Haven't you said that?"

"I was a swimming instructor. I don't remember saying it myself, but I believe that their bone density is thicker than the white people."

"You believe it's physiological?"

"Yes, sir."

"Isn't that what makes this funny?"

"No, sir."

"Do you remember another incident where a picture of a scuba diver had a photo of Mr. Rochon's face from his personnel file pasted over it?"

"Yes, sir."

"Did you have anything to do with that?"

"Not with putting the photograph on it or anything. I remember seeing it and laughing about it."

"We have the original of that preserved in a plastic container, Mr. Dillon. Would we find your fingerprints on it?"

"Sure, I handled it. But it was on the wall. I laughed about it and touched it."

"Why did you handle it?"

"Because it was on the wall, and I was laughing at it. I took it down to show it to people."

"To laugh at it, you didn't have to touch it or take it off the board, did you?"

"No, sir."

"So why did you do that?"

"I thought—"

"Objection," Oscadal said. "That question has been asked and answered at least three times."

"I don't think that it has been," Steinberg said. "Why did you have to take it off?"

"Because I thought it was funny, showing it to people, making sure everybody saw it. I didn't think that it showed anything but people liking Don Rochon."

"You had heard about Agent Rochon before he came to Omaha, hadn't you?"

"I had heard that he was very upset that he wasn't going to go to Los Angeles and that caused him to have an attitude problem and made his work performance not as good as most other agents."

"Who did you hear that from?"

"Someone in his training class."

"Wouldn't performance ratings be the best gauge of that?"

"I don't think we would have access to that, sir."

"Was he described by his race before he came?"

"I don't recall. But I would assume that I was aware that Mr. Rochon was a black male before he came there."

"And you said in your sworn affidavit you also heard he was lazy?"

"Poor work performance. Lazy would be a word for that, yes, sir."

"Do you know of anything to back any of that up?"

"Again, I liked Mr. Rochon all the way through his Omaha days. But I thought there were numerous instances where he was shown to be a poor worker and lazy, yes, sir."

"Then you purposely saw to it that he would sit next to you and your friend, Agent Kempf?"

"I thought Don would be an okay guy. I had nothing against him just because I heard he wasn't a great worker."

"You thought he would be an okay guy? You heard he was a poor performer and lazy, and you knew nothing positive about him. How does that make sense?"

"I saw Don when he came in. I liked what I saw. I saw a guy that looked strong; he liked to work out. He was an attorney. I talked to him, and personally I liked him."

"In Mr. Rochon's time at the Omaha office, you've said he got a bad reputation for performance. What is your basis for that, and what did that reputation specifically consist of?"

"I didn't work with Don much. There was an extortion case in Coon Rapids, Iowa, where we had some differences when I asked him to go to the back of the truck we were in to take some photos while we rode by certain scenes."

"Did you report anything about that?"

"No, sir."

"Why not?"

"I liked Don Rochon."

"Because you liked him, you would cover up poor performance?"

"It's just not my style to talk to a supervisor about an agent's performance."

"What other things did you hear about him in the way of bad performance?"

"I heard he fell asleep in the back of a car on a surveillance. His reputation was not a very good agent workwise, not real good work habits. And we heard stories of him doing a number of things that we felt showed a lack of common sense."

"What stories?"

"Mr. Rochon told me—I thought it was so funny at the time—that he had trouble starting his car because it was 20 below zero. He was going to leave it run all night long so that it would start in the morning. I told him that it will ruin the engine. I know that conversation took place because it was with me. The next day I heard from our mechanic, Gary, that Mr. Rochon had a breakdown on the way to work that everybody felt was due to the car being left running all night long."

"Do you know, in fact, whether he left the car running all night long?"

"No, sir, I do not know that for a fact."

"You know that the car had a problem because you heard that from Gary?"

"And I know that Mr. Rochon told me he was going to leave it run all night long."

"Then you put those two together and thought probably he had let it run all night long and that's why it burned out?"

"Yes, sir."

"Did you tell that to other people?"

"I probably would have told people. I would have laughed and told people, Jesus, you can't leave a car run all night long."

"What other stories did you hear or start?"

"I heard he took a garden hose, during winter—being from California he wouldn't understand the way our winters were—and was trying to hose snow off his driveway, not realizing that this would ice up. I also recall Mr. Rochon saying he had a weapon that had been left by his wife underneath a washing machine in the basement to keep away from the kids, that had gotten rusted."

"You never saw the weapon?"

"No, sir."

"You said in your affidavit that when you'd hear stories or criticisms of Mr. Rochon, you would defend him; is that right?"

"I have on occasion, yes, sir."

"I'm having trouble understanding that. He starts off with a reputation for being lazy and a bad performer."

"Uh-humm."

"He proves that reputation to you, according to your account, in situations where you're personally involved."

"Uh-humm."

"He's doing all these nonsensical things."

"Uh-humm."

"Why would you be defending him?"

"Because I liked him. There's other agents that don't do a good job either that you can still work with and are good people."

"Are you aware that his supervisors always rated him 'fully successful'?"

"No, sir."

"And none of these stories appear in his files or were ever reported except in the responses you and others made in this case?"

"I wouldn't have reported them."

"Have you ever suggested that an animal picture be placed over any other agent's face on a picture?"

"I play practical jokes all the time. I know the incident you're talking about."

"With animals?"

"I don't remember. I've seen so many practical jokes in my bureau career with animals' faces put on agents."

"Didn't you suggest that it might be fun to put a picture of the face of a bulldog over a picture of Assistant Agent in Charge Johnny Evans because that bulldog symbolized something about his personality?"

"I don't definitively recall, but it's certainly possible. Certainly I could have made comments like that."

"It's not just a comment. It's a specific way of making whatever point you're making."

"I don't recall."

"In your affidavit, page five, on the sixth line up from the bottom, you said, 'I might even have suggested placing a bulldog photo over his photo.'"

"Uh-humm."

"Placing a monkey over a picture of Mr. Rochon's children sounds like the kind of jokes you played?"

"No, sir. It was a terrible thing to do. I'm sorry if it did happen. I know Don has a lot of hatred for me, but even through Chicago, I never did any racial stuff to you."

§§§

Thompson questioned Barry Mawn, the FBI official assigned by the Office of Professional Responsibility to investigate and determine SAC

Hawkins's formal charge against Don for failing to report race discrimination in housing against Don and his wife. Don and his wife suspected but were not sure there was discrimination and had decided not to pursue the matter. Mawn and his supervisors agreed with Hawkins, and Don was censured.

"Mr. Mawn," I asked, "what complaints about housing discrimination weren't reported?"

"Mr. Rochon believed he was a victim of racial housing discrimination."

"That's different than a complaint, isn't it?"

"If there was a complaint and they believed that they had been victims of discrimination in housing, then it would be reported and investigated."

"That policy makes sense. If someone makes a complaint of a violation of the law to relevant law enforcement, it should be considered and reported. But that didn't happen here, did it?"

"No."

"The FBI policy and the exclusive source for this supposed violation is in the MIOG, the Manual of Investigative Operating Guidelines, Section 177–5?"

"Yes."

"Well, that policy and section clearly wasn't violated. It says 'upon receipt of a complaint alleging violation.' Was there any complaint that wasn't reported?"

"Correct, he didn't receive a complaint. You could make that interpretation."

"You tell me how any other interpretation could possibly make sense."

"Well, it's in the MIOG."

"Do you know of any policy or law that compels victims of housing discrimination or anything else to complain?"

"No."

"Is there anything in the policies or regulations that requires an FBI agent to complain when he is a victim?"

"Not in the strict sense, no."

"So what is it he violated? What was he censured for, sir?"

"You have to report violations of law."

"Were you told in your training that an agent must report violations where he or she is the victim?"

"No."

"Have you been told that since training?"

"No."

"Are you aware of any other agent or employee of the FBI or Department of Justice who has been disciplined or even investigated for not reporting housing discrimination where that person was the victim?"

"No, not off the top of my head."

"For not reporting any violation of civil rights or any federal law?"

"No."

"Prior to the hearing, we asked the agency, with the approval of the complaints examiner, to provide information about any such instance, and they gave us none. Does that surprise you?"

"Am I surprised of that? No."

"Now if an agent who is the office EEO counselor or a special agent in charge of an office receives a complaint from another agent in the office of a civil rights violation committed against him, would failure to report the complaint be a violation of the FBI policy and regulations?"

"Potentially, yes."

"Did you or were you called upon to investigate any such matter in connection with the civil rights complaints Mr. Rochon actually made?"

"No."

§§§

Herbert Hawkins, Jr., the SAC at Omaha and by the time of the hearing the SAC at Phoenix, appeared in a nice suit; a nice tan; and, for some of his testimony, with eyeglasses dangling from one of the ear hooks placed in his mouth. I couldn't figure out if he was making a statement about the lack of significance of the hearing or just weird. It was tempting (but unfair) to connect his style and what he had done to the stench that wafted through downtown Omaha that morning. I expected cornfields, flat terrain, and the midwestern feel of Omaha, but the slaughterhouses were a surprise. The odor only occasionally came downtown, and the upside was good, inexpensive steak dinners.

Oscadal's direct questioning of Hawkins yielded few surprises, except at the beginning he volunteered, "I was very impressed with Mr. Rochon. He walked in the door bright and bushy tailed, and he was an attorney. He was well spoken, and I never had a problem in terms of his work."

"Mr. Hawkins, I'm David Kairys. I'm counsel for Mr. Rochon."

"How do you do, sir?"

"Fine. How are you?"

"Good."

"Of the 13 agents who came up for transfer from Omaha in the same period that Mr. Rochon did, is it correct that 12, all of whom were white, got either their exact office of preference or the region of the country that they wanted?"

"I don't know."

"And Mr. Rochon had, in addition to his preference, a hardship request that you said you supported to go as close to Los Angeles as possible, because his father was gravely ill?"

"Yes, he did, and I did support that."

"Mr. Hawkins, you testified earlier that around June 1983 Supervisory Special Agent (SSA) Santimauro told you that Mr. Rochon had complained to him. When Mr. Oscadal called it a 'race harassment' complaint, you agreed. Then later you were sure that race was never mentioned. You're sure that race was never mentioned?"

"Yes, I'm positive of that. Had it been mentioned, I would have taken a very serious view of that type of complaint."

"Do you remember giving a statement in this case on July 1, 1985?"

"Yes, I remember giving a statement. During the time I gave that statement, I was trying to recall facts that were sometimes two years old. I did not have the benefit of FBI communications to refresh my memory. So that statement may have inaccuracies."

"Well, sir, if it was stale by two years, then it would be staler today, at four years."

"That's correct."

"Is there any reason to believe that you remember better now than you did then?"

"No."

"I've placed the investigative file, item 10, in front of you. The last paragraph beginning on page four says, 'based on his color.'"

"Then it was raised, yes."

"Don't you have a duty, sir, to report that?"

"Absolutely, as I have written it."

"Did you report it to headquarters?"

"No, I did not."

"Did you investigate it?"

"I didn't conceive of it as an accusation of racial harassment."

"You're back to the issue of whether it's as you said in your affidavit and as you said the first time today."

"It was an informal conversation, with Mr. Santimauro and Mr. Rochon."

"Is there any reason you would so clearly state in your statement that it was an allegation of racial harassment, if that's not so?"

"No, I would not make that up."

"Complainant's Exhibit P is from FBI regulations, called the MAOP. Please read Section 13–2(1) on page 153."

"Yes, sir. It says 'All allegations of employees' misconduct must be reported to the administrative services division.'"

"Did you do that, sir, about these allegations of racial harassment by an employee?"

"I didn't receive an allegation of racial harassment."

"Even if it wasn't racial, wasn't it an allegation of misconduct?"

"Bull pen–type joking is probably the most common in-office thing in any FBI office."

"You did make a report to headquarters on April 16, 1984—that's my birthday—concerning your recommendation that Agent Rochon be censured. It's tab 93, page four, the 15th line down."

"I don't recall—well, okay, I wrote that 'SSA Santimauro, at that time, indicated his concern that SA Rochon may interpret some of this as racist.' Right. Okay."

"That's about the same meeting with Santimauro?"

"Yes."

"So on the two occasions you've written documents about that, both of the documents say that you were informed that there was some racial overtones to this."

"Technically, the way you put it, yes."

"Well, let's be untechnical."

"That's how SSA Santimauro interpreted it. I did not interpret it as being racist."

"So your only explanation is—though you responded positively to

Mr. Oscadal's characterization of it as a complaint of racial harassment, and the two times you have earlier put your recollection of it in writing both say it was racial—you're still saying you were unaware of any racial allegation?"

"I was unaware. It was not my interpretation."

"The MAOP regulation doesn't depend on your interpretation. You were presented with allegations of racial harassment, and you failed to report them or to do any investigation."

"I did not believe then nor do I believe now that I was actually made aware of allegations."

"Okay. Getting back to your July 1, 1985, statement, you say there, 'I explained to Rochon I was sure no racial discrimination was involved.' How could you be sure? You didn't investigate it at all."

"Based on my conversations with SSA Santimauro, SSA Wiley, and the ASAC."

"What 'pranks' were you made aware of in these conversations?"

"Someone had put a scuba diver in a fish bowl, and someone had left a message for Mr. Rochon to call a number that was a dial-a-prayer, just to name a couple. Things like that. I didn't attach racial discrimination to things like that."

"Did they tell you the scuba diver had the face blackened in and was accompanied by jokes about how blacks can't swim?"

"No, sir, not at all."

"Were you aware that a picture of Mr. Rochon's two children had a cut-out face of a monkey pasted over them, as in Exhibits D and E I'm handing you?"

"I was not aware of any of this."

"What significance would you place on a monkey face being pasted over the kids' faces?"

"I wouldn't appreciate it; it's a defacement of his children's picture. I'm not too sure I'd interpret that as racial."

"Doesn't that monkey have any symbolism to you?"

"It doesn't have any symbolic meaning to me."

"You see no connection of a racist persuasion between monkeys and black people?"

"Absolutely not."

"You've never heard that?"

"Never."

"Would it be employee misconduct to do this, to, in your words, deface the picture of an agent's children on his desk?"

"I would have to say yes."

"At the time you made allegations against Mr. Rochon for not reporting housing discrimination against him and his wife, although they were unsure if it was discrimination and decided not to pursue it, weren't you aware that he had made racial civil rights allegations that could implicate you personally?"

"Certainly not."

"Were you ever concerned about gossip around the office about Agent Rochon?"

"I never heard any gossip about Agent Rochon, except the stuff he complained about and something about him leaving an automobile running all night and the engine conked out. Later I looked into it and determined it was not true."

"But the story was going around the office?"

"Yeah."

"Did you do anything to stop it from going around the office?"

"It was just inconceivable that Agent Rochon could have done such a thing."

§§§

We didn't hear anything for months after the hearing. Then in early August 1987, I got a heavy box from the Department of Justice that contained a 65-page opinion by Complaints Examiner Steinberg, a 14-page "Final Decision of the Department of Justice," and a full copy of the transcript of the hearing.

Steinberg concluded that Donald Rochon was the victim of race discrimination when the FBI transferred him to Chicago while 13 other agents transferred from Omaha in the same period, all white, got transfers to their office or region of preference. He found that the censure of Don by management at FBI headquarters for not reporting possible race discrimination in housing against him and his wife was also racially discriminatory, emphasizing the lack of any duty of agents under the regulations and policies to report suspected violations when they are the victims. The transfer and the censure were also acts of retaliation because Don filed EEO complaints, which made them also independent violations of Title VII.

Steinberg concluded that each of 10 major incidents of race harassment occurred as we alleged, that Don reported them to his supervisors as violations of Title VII, and that Hawkins and the FBI failed to investigate or take it seriously and retaliated against Don because he made these complaints. He also concluded that the harassment included the "creation and circulation of demeaning stories or rumors," which Hawkins did nothing to stop. However, Steinberg concluded that Don "did not pursue formal EEO processes" on the race harassment claims, so he denied them based on what he considered a procedural flaw. This seemed unwarranted and strange, but he had gone our way on most everything and rejected all of the FBI's explanations and defenses.

I was anxious as I picked up the DOJ decision, written by DOJ complaint adjudication officer Mark L. Gross. They could simply reject it all.

It began by accepting most of the facts as found by Steinberg. Then they disagreed with some of Steinberg's legal analysis, and I felt a hammer about to fall. But the conclusions they reached were the same—we won on discrimination and retaliation based on both the transfer and the letter of censure.

The section on race harassment began, "a working environment infected by racial antagonism constitutes a Title VII violation." The examiner, they said, considered the race harassment allegations "only as the factual and legal foundation for a subsequent complaint of retaliation." They continued: "This evidence should also have been evaluated in order to determine whether the race harassment amounted to an independent violation of Title VII." They found that Don sufficiently alleged race harassment in his EEO complaints and consistently raised it to his supervisors.

Then they analyzed the race harassment claims. "The complainant must prove more than a few isolated incidents of racial enmity. It must be sufficiently pervasive to create an abusive working environment." The "ten racially obnoxious pranks followed by the unrestrained proliferation of rumors directed at Complainant painted a clear picture of blatant racial harassment." The "supervisors should have been alert to any additional elements of unfair treatment, such as the ridiculous rumors circulating in the office." None of the supervisors took "any actions at all to curb the rumors."[3]

They found a pattern of race harassment that included the stories. The number three man in the FBI, Assistant Director Edwin Sharp, was found to have discriminated and retaliated. The transfer and the censure of Don were invalidated, he was granted a transfer anywhere he wanted, and all of the agents involved in the race harassment were ordered to undergo special training. I got a nice counsel fee. We won it all.

§§§

The ringing victory on the Omaha portion of Don's case—it is still the leading and strongest race harassment decision on the books—didn't resolve the remaining claims from his time at the FBI office in Chicago. But I thought the FBI would be eager to settle the Chicago claims. Omaha had a lot of subtle and difficult issues, including the racial "overtones" and those stories. In Chicago, along with more of what he went through in Omaha, it was "cut off your niggerass balls" and "your secret niggerville house," and Don got a bill from the *Chicago Tribune* for an ad that said "Mr. EEO, We thank you and your wife for visiting us. You will be missed." Dillon had gone to Chicago before Don, and the Omaha decision provided unquestionable proof of a pattern of race harassment, discrimination, and retaliation led by Dillon. The supervisors at Chicago, SAC Edward Hegerty and ASACs Milt Ahlerich and Michael Wilson, and the same high-level managers at headquarters again fully backed the white agents and retaliated against Don.

We didn't know who among the Chicago agents wrote and sent the worst racist threats, but we had a good start. The FBI had to open an investigation of the explicit racist threats and the death and dismemberment insurance. Don's forged signature on the application for the death and dismemberment insurance, which has the same theme as the explicit threats, matched the handwriting of SA Gary Miller. Miller confessed to this and to checking a box on the insurance application so it included Don's wife and kids. He also confessed to following Don home after work to find out where he lived. Miller was suspended for 14 days for conduct that is hard not to interpret as a threat on the life of another agent. White agents at the Chicago office responded by pitching in to make up his lost salary.

My assumption was that Dillon was infuriated by Don's EEO claims and stirred up white Chicago agents to go after Don. They continued the race harassment, and one or more of them sent the racist threat letters.

There might have been crazed racists among them, or I easily imagined Dillon or some of the others thinking something like, "If Rochon wants to complain about race harassment, we'll give him the real thing," and then writing the letters as if they came from a crazed racist. But if you effectively pretend to be a crazed racist, you become a crazed racist. The distinction resides in one's mind, or sense of humor, but matters little.

The FBI and DOJ had another good reason to settle. The whole federal EEO process, including the Omaha opinions, was confidential. If they settled the Chicago claims, none of the events or the Omaha decisions would be public; if they didn't, we had the option of going to court on the Chicago claims and raising the Omaha claims and results as part of our case. But none of this mattered to the FBI. They had a strong no-settlement policy on employee claims, and they were used to winning. I sent a letter directly to the director to make sure he knew what was going on, and I followed up with calls. At first, his assistants said the director would respond, but then they said there would be no response. Later, I found out that he had turned over the decision of whether to settle to the high-level FBI officials implicated in the wrongdoing spelled out in the Omaha decision.

I had to shift back into litigation gear and prepare for what looked like a difficult fight. Their only chance of winning or undercutting our claims was to completely discredit Don. I thought they would go after him in a very personal and vicious way—depict him as incompetent, disloyal, litigious, disgruntled. The case would draw some publicity, which meant their attack on Don would also. The continuing struggle would be tough on Don, with or without publicity. He was an essentially quiet, friendly person who had a deep, courageous determination when he was pushed too far. I liked him and also knew that, appearances aside, this had all taken a heavy toll on him and his marriage. I saw our choice as keeping the lawsuit relatively narrow and quiet or bringing the range of claims available and seeking active, public support. I didn't want him, or me, facing this alone or in isolation. We talked at length, and Don agreed that we would go on the offensive rather than finding ourselves defending against ridiculous accusations against him.

I planned the lawsuit on two fronts. In addition to the EEO claims against the FBI and DOJ, we would sue a couple dozen individual FBI agents for personally violating Don's civil rights. We simultaneously filed two lawsuits in Washington and one in Chicago, using a procedural strategy that made it most likely to wind up with a Washington jury. I got help from a number of talented lawyers in Washington and Chicago.[4]

I could have recruited a range of civil rights groups to support the case, but I wanted to try another avenue first. Congressman William Gray, III, was a widely respected local black leader who had recently risen to national prominence as chair of the powerful House Budget Committee. He was generally moderate and cautious and, if I could interest him, would be a great ally. I called someone who I thought might know Gray. He referred me to Gerry Mondesire in Gray's Philadelphia office, which resulted in an invitation to meet Gray after a Sunday service at Bright Hope Baptist Church in North Philadelphia, where Gray was still the pastor.

The church was large and overflowing with people singing a hymn, led by Gray. It was similar to Mary Jiles's church but more restrained, and worshipers donned more expensive suits and dresses. An usher led us to Gray's chambers, where we were told to wait for him.

Gray, a thin, tall man with short, dark hair, came in with Gerry after disrobing in an adjoining room.

"I'm pleased to meet you, Mr. Rochon and Mr. Kairys," Gray said, shaking our hands warmly. "Gerry has filled me in on this and showed me some of the materials you sent. It's terrible, what they put you through."

"Thank you, Reverend Gray," Don said.

"Hoover never did get it."

"No he didn't, and I got his legacy."

"You did, indeed. What I'm wondering, though, is why you've come to me. There's no legislative angle to this, is there?"

"No, not directly," I said. "I know this is unusual, but we've asked to see you because, given the stories they circulated about Don that make him out to be some kind of Stepandfetchit character from the early 1900s and the strategy they've pursued of attacking him, I don't want him to have to stand alone in the lawsuit. This will be a major challenge to the FBI, and Don will be vulnerable. Don is a federal employee, like you, and the FBI and all federal agencies are under the control of Congress. He's a dedicated law enforcement officer who just wanted to do his duty. The EEOC and DOJ have already found race harassment, discrimination, and retaliation. If you would stand with Don when we announce the lawsuit, it would protect him and show the public how important this is."

"You mean you want me to come to a news conference?"

"Yes, or if that is problematic, you could issue a written statement that we could distribute at a news conference."

"Well, I certainly wish you both well. I'll have to think about this, and Gerry will be in touch with you."

"Thanks."

"Thanks," Don said, "for taking the time to see me, Reverend Gray."

Legislators didn't often announce lawsuits, and Don and I didn't think Gray was going to for this one. But a couple weeks later, Gerry called to coordinate the filing date with us. As the date approached, they scheduled the news conference at Gray's office at the Capitol and then at the Budget Committee conference room, where major press conferences were held.

We filed detailed complaints on November 5, 1987, that told the story of Don Rochon's odyssey as well as set out the basis for his legal claims. The news conference followed another one announcing major Budget Committee developments; the cameras were already set up and all the major national and international media were there. Gray started by announcing that he had requested a congressional investigation of Don's allegations and a direct response from the FBI director, William Sessions. "It is," he said, "unbelievable in this day and time this kind of action can be tolerated." Don and I spoke, and we handed out a lot of copies of the lawsuits and EEOC and DOJ decisions.

The next day and for a few months the story was featured in network TV news and print media throughout the country. Don and I appeared live on *Nightline*. The FBI declined to send someone to debate us in that show's format, so Ted Koppel interviewed us for a half hour as we sat in a Philadelphia studio with earpieces that gave us Koppel's voice and a producer's. We couldn't see Koppel or see what the viewers saw. It was a strange setup, particularly after they insisted that Don sit on a phone book so he and I could appear together without a height difference. Koppel, who was supportive, quipped, "This has got to make you one of the least popular fellows in the FBI." The *New York Times* began regular coverage of the case, and I was frequently in touch with their reporters, Philip Shenon and later David Johnston.[5]

§§§

The Department of Justice assigned a team of lawyers from its top litigation unit to defend against the Chicago EEO claims. They also hired former U.S. attorneys as outside counsel for each of the individuals we sued and gave them pretty much carte blanche as far as their time and expenses. The DOJ team was headed by David Glass, a right-wing ideologue who didn't seem to accept that there could be discrimination against blacks. Dillon got as his DOJ-paid lawyer Dan Webb at Winston & Strawn, a young, Republican rising star who had been the U.S. attorney for the Chicago area. Most of the individual defense work was done by Webb's firm; a team at Kech, Mahon & Kate in Chicago headed by Scott Lassar, who would later be appointed the U.S. attorney for the Chicago area; and another team at Cohen, Gettings & Dunham in Virginia headed by Frank Dunham.

They went after Don from the beginning. He endured weeks of depositions in which each of the defense lawyers took turns grilling him and accusing him of any wrongdoing it seemed they could think of. I had referred Don to a highly reputed therapist, Sidney Pulver, who concluded that Don was suffering from posttraumatic stress disorder (PTSD), a relatively new diagnosis that was gaining acceptance at that time. Sidney thought law enforcement was like a family for Don, and the constant isolation, threats, and betrayal he experienced in the FBI over the course of years became traumatic and resulted in the classic symptoms of PTSD. This was important to our claim that Don had been rendered disabled to work in the FBI by the FBI's race harassment, discrimination, and retaliation. Sidney, who had little experience with legal proceedings, endured a week of depositions that would be good material for a psychology seminar.

The racist stories of Don's supposed incompetence, lack of common sense, and wrongdoing resurfaced, and many more were added. Like the earlier ones, they lacked any basis or truth. The ultimate phony story was put forward by Dillon and, among the defense lawyers, by Scott Lassar. They said, on the record, that Don had sent the worst racist threats to himself in an attempt to get transferred to Los Angeles.

I was not spared. The defense team refused to cooperate in the usual ways. They wouldn't select one among them for me to deal with on scheduling and other matters; I had to call them all to set deposition dates, seek postponements, and so forth. They dragged out everything, straining my limited finances while building up their billings to the federal government. One round of depositions was held in Philadelphia at a room rented at the Four Seasons Hotel, with a constant supply of fresh-squeezed orange juice, instead of at the usual law office conference room. It got petty and personal. One of them insisted on nonstop smoking at a deposition when I had my usual spring allergies. I sneezed in his direction as much as possible. A lawyer on the defense team confirmed to me many years later, with an apology, that hassling me was a planned strategy.[6] I also got phoned threats and phony mailings like Don had gotten, but I don't know who was responsible.

It went on like this for almost four years, putting a lot of stress on Don and me as we gathered more and stronger evidence.

§§§

There was a surprise at the deposition of Tom Dillon in early 1989. My strategy was, in addition to questioning on the important issues, to encourage him to talk, to tell whatever stories he wanted to. At one point, I asked him about something we had learned from a document—that he had lost one or more of his front teeth. He didn't want to talk about it. Then he said he had been beaten up in the days after Martin Luther King was assassinated, when he defended Dr. King's honor to a stranger who was insulting King on the street near Loyola University, where Dillon was a student. He said this happened in 1979 or 1980, though Dr. King was killed in 1968. I knew right away that Dillon had made this up—the deposition occurred on the day after the Martin Luther King birthday holiday—testifying under oath to whatever came to his mind. I questioned him further, without expressing any doubt or placing any importance on it. He couldn't remember who was present or whether he had then or later told anyone about it, including even his wife. He never mentioned it in response to Rochon's accusations of his racist conduct. When I persisted, he said he told his good friend James MacArthur, who was the fire chief of Elk Grove Village, Illinois. Dillon had fabricated the story and thought he could extract himself by contacting his good friend later and asking him to back the story.

I knew what I immediately had to do by the time we got back to Jeff Taren's office after the deposition, though it was unorthodox, to say the least. "This is a tape of a phone conversation," I said into a tape recorder in a conference room at Taren's office, "being made with one-party consent pursuant to a recent decision of—Jeff, which court is it?"

"The Illinois Supreme Court," Jeff said.

Federal law and the law in most states, which I was familiar with from my work on surveillance, allowed recording if one party to a call, the one doing the recording, consents, without informing the other party. I opposed such laws but wasn't going to shortchange Don's case if it was allowed in Illinois. I remembered that Illinois was one of the few states that, by statute, required that both parties consent, but Jeff told me the Illinois Supreme Court had recently undercut that statute, and he found the case when we got back to his office.[7]

"I am David Kairys," I continued into the recorder. "Also present are Jeffrey Taren and Donald Rochon. We are about to call James MacArthur, who is the fire chief of Elk Grove Village, Illinois, to check out a story that Thomas Dillon, his fraternity brother many years ago, just told under oath in a deposition. The number I am calling is—what Jeff?"

"439-3900."

"And we are in area code 312. This is just the telephone book number for the Elk Grove Village Fire Department. The time is 4:39, and it's January 17, 1989. Jeff, does this button turn on the speaker phone?"

"Yes."

The machine yielded a strong dial tone, beeps for the number I dialed, and then ringing, a click, and a woman's voice. "Elk Grove Fire Department."

"Chief MacArthur, please."

"One moment."

"Hello," a receptionist or secretary said.

"Chief MacArthur, please."

"Who is calling?"

"David Kairys."

"David Kairys, just a moment please."

"Chief MacArthur," he said, with a friendly but official tone.

"Yes, I am trying to check out a story that is rather funny of an old fraternity brother of yours, Tom Dillon." I tried to make myself sound like someone who had just heard Dillon tell a story at a bar, but I was not going to lie or misrepresent myself.

"Okay."

"About how he lost his front teeth."

"How he lost his front teeth?"

"Yes, back when, something about when he was pledging with you. You were the pledge master, right?"

"Right."

"Do you remember how it happened?"

"No I don't. I remember, I mean we go all the way back to grammar school. I remember playing hockey with him on a park rink, and he went down to block a shot, and I hit him with a hockey stick, which kinda loosened one of his teeth."

"So you started it yourself," I said laughing. "Wasn't there a fight while you all were in college?"

"A fight?"

"Yes, you were at Loyola with him, right, in the same frat?"

"Right."

"Wasn't there a fight he got into?"

"I don't recall it. Do you have more specific information?"

"It would have been 1968, and he lost his three front teeth."

"Do you know like where or when or time of year?"

"It was right near Loyola in front of a bar, and it was right after Martin Luther King got killed, like 20, 21 years ago."

"Boy, I really don't."

"You don't remember at all, chief? He's a good friend of yours, right?"

"Oh, yeah. Yeah."

"He said you would really know about this, and it was something we were all kind of interested in. But you don't recall it at all."

"No, Tom and I have gotten into a lot of things, and this one just doesn't jump right out of me. Do you remember the name of the bar or anything at all?"

"No. Do you remember at all his losing his three front teeth? You were his pledge master?"

"Yeah."

"So if he lost the three front teeth, then you would know. That would have been the talk of the frat."

"Well, yeah, there was quite a bit during our college days that was the talk of the frat, and this may have been one of them, but it's just not really coming to mind though."

"But Dillon's a talker anyway, right?"

"Oh yeah, yeah. Tom's a nice guy."

"Alright, well thanks a lot."

"Sure."

"So long."

"Bye-bye."

I hung up, and Jeff and Don burst into roaring laughter. The tape was still running, and I didn't want the laughter, any turning it off or on, or any erasure. "This is the end of the conversation," I said into the tape recorder. "That was us laughing."

I didn't like having no copy or backup for the tape, in case it got lost, stolen, or damaged. I insisted that Don and I stop by a Radio Shack store I had seen between Jeff's office and our hotel. I asked a salesman if he would copy the tape to demonstrate the new double cassette tape decks in the front window. He made us two copies, one of which I mailed to myself before we went to dinner.

Later, we deposed MacArthur, who testified, under oath, that Dillon lost his front teeth while they were in college together and Dillon got into a fight over an insult to Dr. King. He remembered a recent call from someone about it and testified that he'd told the same story in the call. That was a directly refutable lie under oath set up by Dillon. The defense lawyers went ballistic when I told them I had a tape of the call.

§§§

We had the evidence we needed for trial by early 1990, and the Washington judge, Charles Richey, set an ironclad trial date in June. We hired an expert on typewriting who used a new technology to see beneath the write-over of the typed address on the envelope that contained one of the racist death and mutilation threats. It was a match, though not conclusively, for a typewriter Miller had at his home. We had proof of numerous acts of race harassment, discrimination, and retaliation in Chicago and the pattern that started in Omaha. Agents confirmed that Dillon had set them against Don before he came, which Dillon had denied doing several times under oath. The tooth story had him suborning perjury. The theory that Don sent the explicit racist threats himself had no evidentiary support, and they seemed to back off of it. Anyway, I had a well-known linguist, William Labov at Penn, analyze the language. He concluded that they were very likely written by whites, perhaps whites trying to sound like it came from illiterate southern white racists. Historian George Frederickson at Stanford was our expert on the origins and historical development of the racial stereotypes in the ridiculous stories about Don. We were ready.

I needed a break, which I thought would come after the trial. Litigation wears on people, and this one had worn more than any other I'd been through. Every day for years the morning mail and fax machine brought missives from the DOJ and 23 individual-defendant lawyers, and there were long daily phone calls mostly consumed with bickering. The daily work was increasingly directed at issues farther and farther away from the substance of the case—discovery, procedures, evidence, scheduling. I would rally myself and sometimes get into what I was doing, but I knew I was the closest I had come to burnt out.

Fortunately, I hired Adam Thurschwell as an associate at the firm in this period. He was fed up with work at the big corporate firm he went to after graduation from law school. Without his skillful work on the Rochon case and other firm cases, and his bonding so well with me and Ilene Kalman at the office, I don't know if I or the firm could have made it to the other side. My intense, daily work on the Rochon case also meant I wasn't talking to enough new clients or bringing in my usual level of fees, and Rudy had taken off some time to help at the Public Defender office.

I ran into Bob Reinstein, dean at Temple Law School, and expressed interest in taking off a year to teach in the fall. Some time later, he got back to me with an offer of permanent employment as a full professor teaching constitutional law and civil rights and assured me that tenure would be awarded within the first year based on what I had already published. I could quit after a year or anytime I wanted. This fit the Rochon case schedule well and was an offer I couldn't refuse.

But Judge Richey reneged on his ironclad June trial date. He postponed the case to the fall, without setting any new trial date. Don and I hoped that I could get Richey to reschedule the trial for the late summer or possibly at some time when I could do part of it while still beginning my teaching duties. Don wanted me to go ahead with the Temple professorship anyway, for which I was grateful. I began to recruit other lawyers to represent Don at the trial.

Then in mid-July, with no firm trial date set, I got a call from the lawyer for an insurance company that covered some of the individual FBI defendants. He was chatting strangely, repeating a discussion we had at the beginning of the lawsuit about going to Columbia at about the same time. Then he said, "You know, the Rochon case has gone on for too long, and it's unfortunate since it seems in everybody's interest to settle."

"Yeah, I've heard that before," I said, "from myself before and after the lawsuits were filed. Remember?"

"Sure, I do, and you were right. I'm wondering if I can call everybody together and see if we can do something now."

"You mean a settlement negotiation?"

"Yes."

"Well, I'd like the idea if I had some reason to believe the government and the individual defendants were really open to settlement. I've got a lot of work to do on the case, and I don't want to waste more time."

"I can assure you right now that they are open and want to settle if we can reach reasonable terms."

I was shocked. They had no idea I was going to begin teaching at the end of August. I wondered if this was for real and, if so, whether the FBI, DOJ, or administration finally realized how embarrassing a widely publicized trial would be or whether some agents came forward and were finally willing to tell the full truth. "I'm interested, but I will need a show of good faith and interest on your part. If you really want to have meaningful negotiations, there's no reason for David Glass to be there. If we can get a high DOJ official who has authority, some or all of the counsel for the individual defendants, and no Glass, I'm willing to talk."

"I'll get back to you."

They agreed to my terms, which showed me they were very serious since you usually don't have a say about who negotiates for your opponents. Don and I prepared a list of demands that went beyond what we could get in the lawsuits. A series of meetings in Washington produced a settlement just as I began my classes at Temple.

At that time, money damages were only available on a Title VII claim if there was some salary-related loss. No damages for pain and suffering or other usual damages were allowed under the statute, and Don had no salary-related loss since he was fully paid and wasn't denied a promotion. I proposed a structure that, though unavailable had we gone to trial and won, would yield Don a considerable sum of money. He had stopped working at the FBI for his own health and was receiving a monthly disability payment based on the race harassment, discrimination, and retaliation. The government agreed that the FBI would, in addition, pay a supplemental amount that would bring the total monthly pay to the average pay received by special agents who began the same year as Don, 1981, and continued to be employed by the FBI. This was to be recalculated each year, as the 1981 class got promoted and some left the FBI. In addition, Don got about $50,000 for relocation expenses, although he would not relocate or continue with the FBI. Don's wife, Susan, who was also a plaintiff in the lawsuits, got $150,000 from the agent insurance company. I got $500,000 for counsel fees and costs. After reimbursing litigation expenses and giving a portion to some of the other lawyers who worked on the case and to my firm, I didn't wind up with much more than my regular income for the years on the case.

The settlement agreement also set out a detailed process for investigation of wrongdoing by FBI personnel, which was public since we refused to agree to confidentiality of the terms of the agreement. This resulted in the first time that the FBI disciplined high-level managers in headquarters for Title VII or employment-related wrongdoing.[8]

The hardest part of the settlement was convincing Don. He wanted it over and knew the terms were good, but, as he had said often, "They should have to create an FBI that I and other blacks can work in comfortably." That kind of resolve, commitment, and courage had carried him through all the struggles for eight years, and it was hard to let go. I had for some time noticed that my clients whose complaints were job related more often had a stronger need to vanquish the opposition than my clients who were, say, badly beaten by the police. There was something identity based, and a common sense of betrayal, when an employment relationship went bad.

My retort to Don was, "They don't deserve you. You've fought them and won for yourself and others. Now take care of yourself and your family." After many long talks, sometimes running late into the night, he decided to settle, and he has been glad he did, although there were further retaliations we have had to deal with.[9]

Not long after the settlement, Don came to a new house my wife and I were busy renovating. He helped us install a metal spiral staircase and brought a gift of a set of socket wrenches. Through the case and afterward, we've been good friends.

Epilogue

I HAVE BEEN A FULL-TIME LAW PROFESSOR at Temple Law School since 1990. The law firm has continued and done well, as Kairys, Rudovsky, Epstein, Messing & Feinberg, although I am seldom there. I've litigated some jury representativeness and death penalty cases and the city handgun lawsuits starting in 1998, but I've mostly written and taught. This is my fourth book since teaching full-time, and I've published many articles, book chapters, and commentaries. Often the focus has been civil rights, but I've also developed a novel approach to law, the rule of law, and the role of courts and lawyers in American society and culture.[1]

This memoir gave me the opportunity to relive and preserve some of the most meaningful experiences of my life, for which I am thankful. Two questions I touched on occasionally regularly come up: Why me, and what did this work accomplish?

§§§

It is hard to unravel what most influenced the course of one's life without trying to figure out the meaning of life and the mix of genes, upbringing, historical context, and circumstance that make us who we are. I'll avoid such big questions, although they're important, and resist the easy temptation to view it all as inevitable, though it is hard to imagine myself other than what I am. The puzzle is more impenetrable when there isn't a specific turning point or crucial experience in my life. I didn't have to overcome drug addiction, abuse, or deprivation; had no religious epiphany; never hit bottom—none of the usual stuff of autobiographies and memoirs. I have always been middle class, well fed, privileged, stable. My progressive, often "radical" values and my beginning and success as a civil rights lawyer developed, usually accompanied by confusion and doubt, slowly, gradually, over many years.

Among the earliest values and messages I remember from my mildly liberal parents were a Jewish identification as an endangered outcast; the evils of dictators and governments, particularly in Europe and Russia; and the great joy and privilege of life in America. My mother saw politics and the evening news largely in terms of whether events were good or bad for the Jews. So it was good that someone exposed the covert purposes of the Vietnam War by releasing the secret Pentagon Papers, but she wished it wasn't someone with "berg" at the end of his name, a Jew (Daniel Ellsberg). That could be blamed on all Jews, which, I could see on such occasions in the look on her face though it was seldom said explicitly, could lead to organized anti-Semitism and to Auschwitz.

Though we lived privileged lives and I never felt endangered, this sank in, and I took it in my own particular direction. Early on, my keenest senses focused on justice and the plight of society's outcasts, and there were some early signs of what was to come.

As a child, I often felt like an outsider and couldn't predict whether others would find my actions, insights, and observations clever or annoying. I identified with outsider family lore, mainly on my mother's side—a great-grandmother, Fruma Diamondstone, who at 15 left an abusive, arranged marriage in the Ukraine and came to America alone; a grandfather, Hyman Lovett, who invited black friends to dinner knowing it would upset the white neighbors; and two young socialist uncles, David Lovett, my namesake, and David Kairys, who became a well-known New York psychiatrist, with the same name. I sometimes openly resisted adult and peer pressures, though doing so drew anger and isolation, such as when I refused to participate in boxing matches at summer camp. I hadn't yet heard of Gandhi or nonviolence, and I was competitive, but I didn't like intentionally hurting someone or being hurt if it could be avoided. I regularly questioned authority and thought outside the box, with no clue how that might be a good thing, and sometimes said what I thought knowing it wouldn't please others. In my early years, it seemed more a curse than a gift.

I grew up in the 1950s and graduated high school without caring much about Elvis or anything to do with politics or law. My only memories of politics were the election-night parties my parents had hoping in vain that Adlai Stevenson, a vaguely liberal Democrat who was too thoughtful to be president, might win. I was moved to write a letter to the editor published by the *Baltimore Sun* criticizing my high school for putting too little emphasis on science after the Russians beat us into space with their *Sputnik*.

At a summer job in the early 1960s while I was studying engineering, I questioned a money-saving design for air-conditioning ducts that seemed to pose a fire danger. I wasn't invited back. Another summer I worked on high-tech weaponry at Westinghouse. I figured out that the sophisticated pump I was working on was not for a torpedo, as we were told, but for an underwater missile that could carry a nuclear warhead into a coastal city. I asked a seasoned engineer who supervised the work whether this bothered him and was told not to speak about it. In a design class, I fashioned an airplane with a reinforced, sealed passenger compartment that could separate from the wings, engines, and fuel tanks and float to the ground safely with parachutes and small jets, like our early space vehicles. My professor liked the design but doubted any airline would be interested in increasing ticket prices for improved safety. Had I continued in engineering, I would have been either a great success or unemployable.

The civil rights movement was at first intriguing and then became more central and, with the women's movement, changed the course of my life. But even that change, deep as it was, didn't feel like a rupture with my country's politics, economics, or culture. I held on to my parents' faith that the United States could make mistakes but was incapable of wrongdoing on the order of, for example, the greed, racism, and viciousness of Europe's colonial legacy. In hindsight, it was easy (too easy) as a privileged white person to think of segregation, as bad as it was, as a remnant of the past that we were having trouble shaking or to unfairly blame it on the South.

The Vietnam War and the antiwar movement were different and shook me to the core. My image of Americans at war was from World War

II movies, which showed us, with great courage and sacrifice, defeating warlike nations and saving the world from their wrath, their ideologies, their evil ways. It was all us and them, good and evil, with cartoon simplicity. But there was no good reason to be making war in Vietnam.

The explanations for the war kept shifting. A small North Vietnamese gunboat supposedly started it by shooting at American warships in the Gulf of Tonkin, an incident of little import that also turned out to be fabricated. Fear of communism was invoked: if South Vietnam fell to communists, all of Asia would fall. This was not convincing, and when South Vietnam did fall, Asia didn't. When we commit our military, we have to win or folks around the world will see us as soft—though our global image problem had more to do with American "imperialism" and brutality than softness. The last resort—we have to win to honor those who died—was hard to shake, except that it forecloses a reasoned or strategic cessation of a war that shouldn't have been started or no longer makes sense.

Before long, Vietnam and its people became our enemies. We assassinated anyone suspected of Vietcong sympathies and bombed provinces, villages, and homes, often with that technological marvel from Dow—napalm, which burns everything and sticks to human flesh. We targeted the civilian population. I was shocked to realize that, somewhere along the way in World War II, strategically targeting civilians became commonplace. The Germans and Japanese did it. We incinerated large cities—Hamburg, Dresden, Tokyo—and then, of course, vaporized Hiroshima and Nagasaki.

All this sank in—and felt like it consumed my 20s and my world. The hardest part for me was who was behind and supported the war. This was not a conservative or Republican war, although they rooted for it heartily and Richard Nixon escalated and continued it for many years. The Democrats, including our best allies on civil rights issues, started and sustained the war. John Kennedy, whose civil rights record is regularly exaggerated, got it going after a long French intervention in Vietnam failed. Then Lyndon Johnson, a great, courageous leader on civil rights and poverty, escalated it into a major war. Liberals, with legions of mostly Ivy League policymakers, staffers, and young corporate leaders, masterminded the defining early and middle phases of the Vietnam War, while most Americans either supported or ignored it. For a long time, there were only two opponents in the Senate, Wayne Morse of Oregon and

William Fullbright of Arkansas, and the media scoffed at war protests, if they covered them at all.

It is hard to overestimate the meaning of the Vietnam War for those of us who came of age opposing it. It seemed to fill my young adult life and felt like it would never end. One consequence for me was loss of my earlier faith that the United States is somehow immune to the inhumanity, corruption, and evil motives that plague other nations.

Living through the antiwar movement; the civil rights and women's movements; and the assassinations of President John Kennedy, Martin Luther King, Robert Kennedy, and Malcolm X left a large portion of my generation, maybe most,[2] in conflict with their families and in some form of culture or identity shock. It changed the course of lives, including mine. We questioned everything and everybody, accepted nothing—capitalism, racism, sexism, electoral politics, the plight of the poorest among us, food, music, clothes, sex. There were new theories about everything, although a lot of it was based simply on values we had been taught as children—openness to others (and do unto others), fairness, liberty, equality, democracy, avoidance of violence and war.

Thirty years of conservative dominance have cast all this negatively and taken distrust of government in a different direction. But we were the generation that finally ridded America of systemic segregation; established basic equality for women; stopped an aggressive, unjustifiable war; and effectively confronted imposed conformity in personal, spiritual, and political matters, overcoming conservative opposition every step of the way. For me, the changes were gradual and extended over a long period of time, and I was helped immeasurably by the support and encouragement of parents I didn't have to rebel against.

§§§

Thirty years of conservative dominance have also undone many of the reforms I championed and some of my most satisfying victories. For example, after many wars on drugs and crime, there are now more people held in Philadelphia prisons pretrial than when I confronted the bail system in the late 1960s, and most of them are not charged with violent crimes.[3] It is hard to imagine a contemporary governor refusing to send any fugitive convicted of murder back to a Georgia chain gang.

A scorecard based on the current status of my victories and reforms wouldn't be pretty, although there would be some remaining bright spots. But this misconceives the work I did and the nature and function of law. If you let go of the law's pretensions to separation from values and politics, it looks and acts very much like a social or political process. I described the upside of this in the establishment of our basic system of free speech, and the *Spock* case was part of a conservative retrenchment of free speech rights over the last few decades (chaps. 8 and 9). Free speech rights available to people of ordinary means—including rights at transit terminals and shopping centers and on open, public streets, sidewalks, and parks—have been limited, while free speech rights available to the wealthiest among us—those willing and able to make large campaign donations to influence elections—have been enhanced. My writings on civil rights and law have focused on how law functions based on values but appears not to and on the unusually broad power we extend to courts and the crisis of democracy I believe we face.

My civil rights litigation and writings responded to the context and epoch in which I found myself; one usually doesn't get to chose when or where one comes of age. In that era, reforms were possible, I could improve the lives of some individuals, and one of my basic functions was to facilitate movements and keep activists on the street and effective. I was also part of a larger political and cultural project that has so far survived—to change the meaning of freedom, equality, and democracy so that, for example, starting sometime after World War II, racism for the first time became wrong and the law classes I now teach are half women while the ones I attended as a student were almost all men. These successes have been so lasting and pervasive that they are hardly visible.

The struggle for freedom, equality, and democracy continues and needs partisans in every generation and every step of the way. Anyone who acts and organizes to further freedom, equality, and democracy, including civil rights lawyers, is as needed now as in any period.

The events following September 11, 2001, coming on top of the decades of steady conservative retrenchment of civil rights, demonstrated both the fragility of civil rights and the politics of law. For much of the 20th century, we led the world on the fundamental importance of human rights and insisted that other countries honor human rights even when they are in the midst of civil wars or have hostile armies poised on their borders. Then we cast off our ideals and law protecting civil rights as too dangerous after an attack by a group with no organized military or country and armed with box cutters and flight school training. They turned our technology on itself to cause enormous damage, death, and suffering. New vigilance is of course warranted, but with no real debate, we quickly renounced our own best traditions and the hard-won global consensus against preemptive war.

§§§

When I think back to my life as a civil rights lawyer or sometimes when I'm just feeling sentimental, my thoughts return to Mary Jiles, that tough, kind woman of little means or education with the gravely but resonant voice who wouldn't let the authorities send her husband back to a Georgia chain gang. It's people like Mary, Terrence O'Neill, Michael Doyle, Magarro Serrano, Ben Spock, Don Rochon, and so many others who made this work so challenging and fulfilling. I am thankful to have had work I believe in and honored to have been able to protect and further civil rights and movements for social justice, and to have known and been able to provide some help to such people.

Author's Note

UNTIL THIS MEMOIR, which I began vaguely several years ago, I was unaware of any good reason to keep so many files and documents, although my wife and coworkers pointed out some good reasons not to. But as a result, I had or was able to track down files for almost all of the cases, and for the rest I had or got at least the major opinions, complaints, or other documents. Sometimes this gave me access to minute details, such as notes, interviews, transcripts, summaries of discussions, and scribbled ideas. I also have a good memory for the cases I litigated and the people I represented. In my practice, I regularly remembered detailed quotations from the range of witnesses in a case, including words recorded in obscure depositions and documents, and time and age have been kind to that memory.

Nevertheless, on occasion I reconstructed some of the details of court proceedings, documents, or dialogue; and I sometimes modified quotations, the form and context of events and materials (e.g., presenting arguments in a brief as made orally), and the usual rules of nonfiction writing (such as rules for ellipses in quotations) to facilitate the style, voice, and flow of the book. I have done so only in instances where I am quite sure of the content and, for dialogue, of the speaking style. I have also included citations and notes in a section at the end of the book for any reader interested in documentation or further information. To avoid cluttering the text and interfering with the memoir form, I have gathered citations covering sections or portions of the book in occasional notes.

Client confidentiality limits what a lawyer can say about a case or former client, so I have not said everything I know. Fortunately, I have the consent of almost all of the clients, and in instances I was unable to find clients, confidentiality did not significantly hinder what I wanted to say. I changed the names of some clients and others, and I created some composites of two or more people, sometimes with a composite name. This memoir presents, of course, my views and perceptions, not those of my clients.

Due to space limitations, I was not able to include many significant clients and cases or to present, except in the early portions of the book, the multiplicity of cases, clients, witnesses, documents, phone calls, meetings, and so on that characterized daily work in my practice.

The lawyers, law students, and paralegals who worked with me on the various cases are acknowledged in the text or notes. Many lawyers did civil rights and public defender work worthy of an interested reader's attention. There was also a community of lawyers, activists, and scholars whose involvement and support were vital to me, particularly Rhonda Copelon, Haywood Burns, Spencer Coxe, David Rudovsky, and the National Lawyers Guild. No one does this, or probably any work of note, alone. This is a memoir—the personal story of my law practice told from my experience and perspective rather than the story of civil rights practice at my firm or in Philadelphia or beyond. And the work, of course, goes on, in public defender and legal services offices, civil and human rights offices and organizations, and law firms throughout the United States and the world.

Many colleagues and friends were an integral part of the work described in this book. Tony Amsterdam and the other fellows in Tony's program at Penn Law School, and many at the Philadelphia public defender office, particularly John Packel, were deeply involved every step of the way in events recounted in part 1. David Rudovsky founded the firm with me in 1971; we lived and breathed this work and an extraordinary string of successes together. Many contributed immeasurably to the firm and my work there: Ilene Kalman (who died suddenly in 1996), Jayma Abdoo (also a Camden 28 defendant, who died in 2006), Adam Thurschwell (without whom I don't know if I could have finished the Rochon case), Holly Maguigan, Jules Epstein, Paul Messing, Lisa Rau, Jonathan Feinberg, Julie Shapiro, Mary Elcano, Linda Backiel, June

Kapler, Tanya Smith, and, as law students, Irv Ackelsberg, Frank Deale, John Hanger, Dick Lavine, Nina Pillard, and Amy Sinden.

I got helpful suggestions and critiques of the manuscript from my good friend Kitsi Watterson and from Antje Mattheus, who also had to live with it and the boxes of documents and files. I appreciate research assistance by Temple law students Dan Linehan, Caitlin Barry, Nicole Ramos, Roli Khare, and Mark Hybner; support in many forms from Temple Law School; the work and insight of my agent, Ellen Levine; and my editor for this memoir and my first book, Phil Pochoda.

NOTES

Notes conform to the *Chicago Manual of Style,* except that references to legal materials conform to *The Bluebook: A Uniform System of Citation,* available at any law library or www.legalbluebook.com.

Introduction

1. Donald Janson, "F.B.I. Is Accused by Informer of Aiding Antiwar Crime in Camden," *New York Times,* March 16, 1972, 1.

2. For more on this, see chapter 7.

Chapter 1

1. *Necessity and sufficiency of identification of accused as the person charged, to warrant extradition,* 93 A.L.R.2d 912 (1964); Note, *Extradition Habeas Corpus,* 74 YALE L.J. 78 (1964); *Kirkland v. Preston,* 385 F.2d 670 (D.C.Cir. 1967); *Foster v. Uttech,* 31 Wis.2d 664 (1967); *Hardy v. Betz,* 195 A.2d 582 (N.H. 1963).

2. 18 Pennsylvania Statutes Annotated §4870; *Commonwealth v. Blair,* 92 Pa. Super. 169 (1927); *Commonwealth v. Viscount,* 118 Pa. Super. 595 (1935); *Commonwealth v. Dice,* 38 York 41 (1924).

3. See Nicholas Lemann, *The Promised Land: The Great Black Migration and How It Changed America* (New York: Knopf, 1991).

4. Comment, *Future Irreparable Harm: A Ground for Release in Federal Extradition Habeas Corpus Proceedings,* 25 WASHINGTON & LEE L. REV. 300 (1968); *In re Hunt,* 276 F. Supp. 112 (E.D.Mich. 1967); *State v. Wynne,* 356 Mo. 1095 (1947); *People ex rel. Barrett v. Bartley,* 383 Ill. 437 (1943).

5. Note, *Interstate Rendition: Executive Practices and the Effects of Discretion,* 66 YALE L.J. 97 (1956).

6. See "'Competitive' Drive Makes Shafer a Winner," *Evening Bulletin,* November 9, 1966; ad by Shafer campaign, *Philadelphia Evening Bulletin,* November 6, 1966.

7. See *Avery v. Georgia,* 345 U.S. 559 (1953); *Williams v. Georgia,* 349 U.S. 375 (1955); *Whitus v. Georgia,* 385 U.S. 545 (1967); *Cobb v. Georgia,* 389 U.S. 12 (1967); *Jones v. Georgia,* 389 U.S. 24 (1967); *Sims v. Georgia,* 389 U.S. 404 (1967); *Anderson v. Georgia,* 390 U.S. 206 (1968).

8. *Philadelphia Daily News,* April 7, 1969.

9. For example, "State Refuses to Extradite Escaped Killer," *Philadelphia Inquirer,* July 8, 1969.

Chapter 2

1. *Miranda v. Arizona,* 384 U.S. 436 (1966); *Gideon v. Wainwright,* 372 U.S. 335 (1963).

2. Directors of the Defender Association of Philadelphia, *34th Annual Report* (1968).

3. *Stack v. Boyle,* 342 U.S. 1 (1951); Rule 4005, Pennsylvania Rules of Criminal Procedure (1968). For a historical perspective, see Pollack and Maitland, *The History of English Law before the Time of Edward I* (1898; repr., Cambridge: Cambridge University Press, 1968), 2:582–87; James F. Stephen, *A History of the Criminal Law of England* (1883; repr., London: Routledge, 1996), 1:233–43; Caleb Foote, *The Coming Constitutional Crisis in Bail,* 113 U. PA. L. REV. 959, 965–86 (1965).

4. Rule *995, Local Rules of Criminal Procedure for the Court of Common Pleas of Philadelphia County (1965).

5. See *Griffin v. Illinois,* 351 U.S. 12, 17 (1956); *Burns v. Ohio,* 360 U.S. 252 (1959); *Douglas v. California,* 372 U.S. 353 (1963).

6. The law students were John Cole at Penn and Art Shuman and Bob Lawler at Villanova.

7. See "A Report on the Operation of the Pretrial Services Agency During the Period Between June 1974 and November 1975" (New York: Vera Institute of Justice, 1976).

8. For example, "Lawsuit May Doom the Bail System," *Philadelphia Inquirer,* April 25, 1970; "Bail System Unfair to Poor, Says Lawyer Seeking Releases," *Philadelphia Daily News,* March 12, 1969; "Penn Plan Asks Writ, Bail Cut Sought for Needy," *Philadelphia Evening Bulletin,* March 13, 1969; "Lawyer Begins Fight to Halt Jailings for Lack of Bail," *Philadelphia Evening Bulletin,* March 12, 1969.

9. David Kairys, "Constitutional 'Crisis' in Bail," thesis, University of Pennsylvania, 1971; David Kairys, "The Bail Litigation Project at the University of Pennsylvania," *Prison Journal of the Pennsylvania Prison Society* 10, no. 34 (1970); *Commonwealth ex rel. Hartage v. Hendrick,* 439 Pa. 584 (1970); *Commonwealth ex rel. Ford v. Hendrick,* 215 Pa. Super. 206 (1969).

Chapter 3

1. Act of May 18, 1976, P.L. 120, No. 53, § 1, 18 P.C.S.A. § 3104 (1976).

2. *Mapp v. Ohio,* 367 U.S. 643 (1961).

3. The questions on the card were the following: Do you understand that you have the right to remain silent? Do you understand that anything you say can and will be used against you? Do you wish to remain silent? Do you understand that you have the right to an attorney before and during questioning? Do you understand that if you cannot afford counsel one will be appointed for you? Do you want an attorney? Do you wish to go ahead and speak?

4. See Jonathon Newman and William Marimow, "How Phila. Detectives Compel Murder 'Confessions,'" *Philadelphia Inquirer,* April 4, 1977.

5. "Is Grand Jury System Headed for Extinction?" *Philadelphia Evening Bulletin,* November 2, 1970; "Grand Jury System Biased, Defenders Say," *Philadelphia Evening Bulletin,* December 28, 1970.

6. "No-Streets Judge Bids Nostalgic So-Long to Room 653," *Philadelphia Evening Bulletin,* January 5, 1982; "2 Area Judges Rise to Appellate Bench," *Philadelphia Evening Bulletin,* January 5, 1982; "McDermott Eyes High Court," October 28, 1981.

7. Stuart Taylor, "Smart, Tough, and Political," *American Lawyer* (January 1990): 50–64; decades.com, 1971–79, http://www.decades.com/ByDecade/1970–1979/10.htm (accessed July 28, 2005).

8. U.S. Dept. of Commerce, Bureau of the Census, *The Social and Economic Status of Negroes in the United States,* Current Population Reports, series P-23, no. 29 (1969), 9; *Carter v. Jury Commission,* 396 U.S. 320 (1970); *Turner v. Fouche,* 396 U.S. 346 (1970); *Witherspoon v. Illinois,* 391 U.S. 510 (1968); *Brief for Petitioners, Commonwealth of Pennsylvania v. Locke et al.,* Court of Common Pleas of Philadelphia County and the accompanying appendix of 24 exhibits; Michael Finkelstein, *The Application of Statistical Decision Theory to the Jury Discrimination Cases,* 80 HARV. L. REV. 338 (1966). The Penn statistician was James Korsh.

9. See "Grand Jury System Biased, Defenders Say, Race, Religion, Age Given Undue Weight, Judge Is Told," *Philadelphia Evening Bulletin,* December 28, 1970; "2 Phila. Judges Deny Bias in Jury Selections," *Philadelphia Evening Bulletin,* December 30, 1970.

10. See "Magistrates Now Judges; Specter Praises New Setup," *Philadelphia Evening Bulletin,* February 4, 1969; "New Municipal Court Breaks Backlog Jam," *Philadelphia Evening Bulletin,* August 24, 1969.

11. "Robert A. Latrone," *Philadelphia Evening Bulletin,* May 11, 1981; "Judge to Carry a Gun after Receiving Threats," *Philadelphia Evening Bulletin,* October 8, 1970; "Woman Who Beat Teacher Sentenced to Shake His Hand," *Philadelphia Evening Bulletin,* March 27, 1969 (trying another parent accused of assaulting a teacher who appeared without an attorney).

12. *Gideon v. Wainright,* 372 U.S. 335 (1963). The fascinating history of that case is memorably recounted in Anthony Lewis, *Gideon's Trumpet* (New York: Random House, 1964).

13. Records of the Defender Association of Philadelphia, Urban Archives, Temple University Libraries, available at http://www.library.temple.edu/collections/urbana/dfnd-181.htm (accessed August 7, 2005).

Chapter 4

1. Rule 12½, Rules of the Supreme Court of Pennsylvania (1965, amended 1969).

2. *King v. Smith,* 392 U.S. 309 (1968) (invalidating the man in the house rule); *Wyman v. James,* 400 U.S. 309 (1971) (approving warrantless searches of

homes of welfare recipients); House Report No. 615, 74th Cong., 1st Sess. 24 (1935); Senate Report No. 628, 74th Cong., 1st Sess. 36 (1935). On the man in the house rule and midnight raids, see Mimi Abramovitz, *Regulating the Lives of Women* (Boston: South End Press, 1988), 315–29; Comment, *AFDC Eligibility Requirements Unrelated to Need: The Impact of King v. Smith,* 118 U. PA. L. REV. 1219 (1970); Lucy Williams, *The Ideology of Division: Behavior Modification Welfare Reform Proposals,* 102 YALE L.J. 719 (1992). That summer of 1966 I worked at CORE through the Law Students Civil Rights Research Council and the Baltimore law firm of Fred Weisgal.

3. See *Powelton Civic Homeowners' Assoc. v. Dept. of Housing and Urban Development,* 284 F. Supp. 809 (E.D.Pa. 1968).

4. "Judge Weinrott Dies at 86," *Philadelphia Evening Bulletin,* April 2, 1981.

5. See in the *Philadelphia Evening Bulletin:* "Judge Bars Citizen Sit-ins at Drexel," December 8, 1969; "Judge Issues Warning to Powelton Group," December 12, 1969; "Judge Extends 2 Powelton Injunctions," December 12, 1969; "State High Court Upsets Injunctions Halting Drexel Protests," December 12, 1969; "Councilman Joins Fight to Block Dorm," December 16, 1969; "Court Orders New Hearings in Drexel Case," February 3, 1970; "Neighbors Bar Building of Drexel Dorm," February 6, 1970; "Drexel Sit-Ins Barred by Court Order," February 7, 1970; "Judge Frees 12 Defying Ban on Drexel Sit-In," February 10, 1970; "Judge Fines 3, Frees Nine in Drexel Protest," February 14, 1970; "Judge Forbids Protests at Drexel Gym," July 15, 1970; "Background of Powelton Dispute," July 30, 1970. See also "Woman, 90, Warned for Scaling Drexel Fence," *Philadelphia Daily News,* February 14, 1970; "Sit-Ins Un-American, Weinrott Rules," *Philadelphia Inquirer,* February 7, 1970.

6. See Rule 1531, Pennsylvania Rules of Civil Procedure (1965).

7. *Carpentertown Coal and Coke Co. v. Laird,* 360 Pa. 94 (1948); *Commonwealth v. Caplan,* 411 Pa. 563 (1963). On judicial bias and improper assignment of judges as bases, see *Chastain v. Superior Ct.,* 14 Cal. App. 2d 97 (1936); *Matushetske v. Herlihy,* 214 A.2d 883 (Del. 1965); *Park's Petition,* 329 Pa. 60 (1938); *Smith v. Gallagher,* 408 Pa. 551 (1962).

8. Brief in Support of Petition for Writ of Prohibition, *Commonwealth of Pennsylvania ex rel. East Powelton Concerned Neighbors, et al. v. Leo Weinrott,* Supreme Court of Pennsylvania, No. 428, Misc. Docket No. 17 (1970); *Lovell v. Griffin,* 303 U.S. 444 (1938); *Thornhill v. Alabama,* 310 U.S. 88 (1940); *Cantwell v. Connecticut,* 310 U.S. 296 (1940); *Edwards v. South Carolina,* 372 U.S. 229 (1963); *NAACP v. Alabama,* 377 U.S. 288 (1964); *Cox v. Louisiana,* 379 U.S. 536 (1965). On notice requirements in a free speech context, see *Carroll v. Princess Anne Co.,* 393 U.S. 175 (1968); *Grove Press v. City of Philadelphia,* 418 F.2d 82 (3d Cir. 1969) (invalidating a Weinrott injunction barring the showing of a movie).

9. The leading article on this issue had been written by Tony as a student and cited later in Supreme Court opinions. Anthony G. Amsterdam, Note, *The Void-for-Vagueness Doctrine in the Supreme Court,* 109 U. PA. L. REV. 67 (1960).

10. *Walker v. Birmingham*, 388 U.S. 307 (1967).

11. See the Web site of the Pennsylvania Historical and Museum Commission, http://www.phmc.state.pa.us/bah/dam/governors/bell.asp?secid=31 (accessed July 19, 2005).

12. Justice Cohen's order was on December 17, 1969, and Chief Justice Bell's was on February 2, 1970.

13. Redevelopment Authority of the City of Philadelphia, Court of Common Pleas of Philadelphia County, June Term, 1970, In Equity, No. 6970 (December 14, 1970); Tom Ferrick, Jr., "Drexel Is Failing to Learn Lessons," *Philadelphia Inquirer,* July 27, 2005; "Neighbors Slam Drexel U. Project," *Philadelphia Inquirer,* July 14, 2005.

14. The four different crimes were codified as 18 P.C.S.A. §§ 4827, 4829, 4834, 4835 (1963). See *Commonwealth v. Moyer,* Ct. of Common Pleas, Montgomery Co., 83 Pa. D. & C. 271 (1952): *Commonwealth v. Yocum,* 211 Pa. Supr. 17 (1967); *Commonwealth v. Bovaird,* 373 Pa. 47 (1953).

Chapter 5

1. See generally S. A. Paolantonio, *Frank Rizzo: The Last Big Man in Big City America* (Philadelphia: Camino Books, 1993); Joseph Daughen and Peter Binzen, *The Cop Who Would Be King: Mayor Frank Rizzo* (Boston: Little, Brown, 1977); Greg Walter, "Rizzo," *Philadelphia Magazine,* July 1967. The *Philadelphia Inquirer* ran a series on police corruption in November 1971. The details, including the quotes, are mostly from Paolantonio, *Frank Rizzo,* 1–79, 92–93, 99–104, 114, 175, 272, 292. "Attila the Hun" is in the column by Tom Ferrick, Jr., *Philadelphia Inquirer,* March 27, 2005.

2. "Columbia Law Students' Open Letter to President Johnson," ad in the "News of the Week in Review" section, *New York Times,* December 5, 1965; *Bond v. Floyd,* 385 U.S. 116 (1966). A few of us organized the letter informally, including my closest law school friends then and later, Tom Jones and Bob Cover.

3. The *Columbia Human Rights Law Review* was unique. We accepted only student articles and were open to student authors from any law school, and we favored articles that arose from a student's work on a real case. Tom Jones was co-founder and executive editor, and many students were instrumental in the creation and first issue, including John Lewis, Dick Howland, Bobby Lawyer, Mark Appel, and John Bruce. Our primary advocate on the faculty, who pushed a reluctant administration to recognize the journal, was Walter Gellhorn. Victor Rabinowitz wrote an important memoir, *Unrepentant Leftist: A Lawyer's Memoir* (Chicago: University of Illinois Press, 1996).

4. The ACLU also expelled Elizabeth Gurley Flynn, a leading union activist, from its board. See Jerold Auerbach, "The Depression Decade," in Alan Reitman, ed., *The Pulse of Freedom* (New York: W. W. Norton, 1975); Corliss Lamont, *The Trial of Elizabeth Gurley Flynn by the American Civil Liberties Union* (New York: Horizon, 1958).

5. The conference was a 1967 national meeting of the Law Students Civil Rights Research Council, which raised substantial funds to sponsor law student summer jobs working with civil rights groups and lawyers around the country. I was president of the Columbia branch.

6. They were Bernie Segal; Brian Appel; and our cohort in Tony's program, Lou Natali, at 1427 Walnut Street. Our first employee was Mary Elcano.

7. *Freedom Press, Inc. v. Frank Rizzo,* U.S. District Court for the Eastern District of Pennsylvania, Civil Action No. 70-3175, filed in late 1970. Peter Gale was cocounsel.

8. Paolantonio, *Frank Rizzo.*

9. The *Philadelphia Evening Bulletin* series: "Head of Rebel Paper Is Central Figure in New Left Here," July 28, 1970; "Young Activists Scorn Old-Line Communism," July 29, 1970; "City Social Worker David Gross Doubles as Free Press Staffer," July 29, 1970; "Petit New Leftist Studied for a Year in England," July 29, 1970; "Dougherty High Dropout Is a Free Press Editor," July 29, 1970; Free Press No. 2 Man Assails Bicentennial," July 29, 1970; "Visitor Reports Talk of Bombs in Powelton," July 30, 1970; "Powelton Man Denies Charges about Bombs," July 30, 1970.

10. Another Rizzo bomb-plot scare, involving a group called the "Labor Committee" represented by Rudy, looked suspiciously fabricated.

11. Stipulation and Consent Decree, *Freedom Press v. Rizzo,* U.S. District Court for the Eastern District of Pennsylvania, Civil Action No. 70-3175 (October 27, 1972). The federal government later deported Biggin to his native Canada after he lost his student status, which I couldn't stop. *Biggin v. INS,* 479 F.2d 569 (3d Cir. 1973).

12. "Ex-Fireman Prayed When Beaten by Cop," *Philadelphia Daily News,* November 18, 1976; "Cash Settles Brutality Suit," *Philadelphia Daily News,* November 22, 1976.

Chapter 6

1. U.S. Constitution, art. I, sec. 8, cl. 11; James Madison, *The Debates in the Federal Convention of 1787* (New York: Oxford, 1920), 341, 418–19, 540–41, and n. 2; Max Farrand, *The Records of the Federal Convention of 1787* (New Haven: Yale, 1911); Roy P. Basler, *The Collected Works of Abraham Lincoln* (New Brunswick: Rutgers, 1953), 1:452; Catharine Bowen, *Miracle at Philadelphia* (Boston: Little, Brown, 1986); Jules Lobel, "Foreign Affairs and the Constitution: The Transformation of the Original Understanding," in David Kairys, ed., *The Politics of Law,* 2d ed. (New York: Pantheon, 1990).

2. Three decisions in *Atlee v. Laird* were reported, dismissing Nixon, granting a three-judge court, and the final result. 336 F. Supp. 790 (E.D.Pa. 1972); 339 F. Supp. 1347 (E.D.Pa. 1972); 347 F. Supp. 689 (E.D.Pa. 1972).

3. *Pickering v. Board of Education,* 391 U.S. 563 (1968); *Perry v. Sinderman,* 408 U.S. 593 (1972); *Haverford College v. Reeher,* 329 F. Supp. 1196 (E.D.Pa. 1971).

4. Some reports of this case in the media erroneously attribute my role to Rudy, my partner. See Rod Nordland, "The Lonely, Lethal Rebels of the Law," *Philadelphia Inquirer Sunday Magazine,* November 4, 1973; "Four with Philadelphia Ties Are Among Winners of 'Genius Awards,'" *Philadelphia Inquirer,* July 15, 1986 (also erroneously attributing my role in the Camden 28 case [chap. 7] to Rudy); David Rudovsky, "Collaboration," letter to the editor, *Philadelphia Inquirer,* July 30, 1986, A10.

5. *Oetjen v. Central Leather Company,* 246 U.S. 297 (1918); *Youngstown Sheet & Tube Co. v. Sawyer,* 343 U.S. 579 (1952); *Baker v. Carr,* 369 U.S. 186 (1962); *Powell v. McCormack,* 395 U.S. 486 (1969); *Greene v. McElroy,* 360 U.S. 474 (1959); *Marbury v. Madison,* 5 U.S. 137 (1803).

6. See, for example, *New York Times,* April 2, 1972, 19, col. 1.

Chapter 7

The title of this chapter is a quotation from Supreme Court justice William Brennan.

1. On Hoover and the FBI, see generally Frank Donner, *The Age of Surveillance* (New York: Vintage Books, 1981), 80, 107, 157–59, 178–84, 374–75, 381–82; Curt Gentry, *J. Edgar Hoover: The Man and the Secrets* (New York: Norton, 1991); Athan Theoharis and John Cox, *The Boss: J. Edgar Hoover and the Great American Inquisition* (Philadelphia: Temple University Press, 1988); Kenneth O'Reilly, *Racial Matters: The FBI's Secret File on Black America, 1960–1972* (New York: Free Press, 1989). "25 Draft Office Raiders Held in Jersey and Buffalo," *New York Times,* August 23, 1971. The friends I traveled with in the Northwest were Matthew Leighton and Susan Lesser. On the Media raid, see Betty Medsger, *The Burglary of the Century: How Eight Amateur Burglars Uncovered the American Police State* (forthcoming, 2008).

2. The pretrial motion work at Georgetown was done by Addison Bowman, Michael Fayad, and Mary-Helen Mautner.

3. Bushnell's Case, 6 Howell's 1011 (1670); M. Hale, *History of the Pleas of the Crown,* ed. W. Stokes and E. Ingersoll (Philadelphia: Small, 1847), 2:312; J. Alexander, *A Brief Narration of the Case and Trial of John Peter Zenger* (Cambridge: Harvard University Press, 1963), 99.

4. Donald Janson, "The FBI Is Accused of Aiding a Crime, 'Camden 28' Informer Says He Acted as 'Provocateur,'" *New York Times,* March 16, 1972, 1, col. 1.

5. The early Supreme Court cases: *Sherman v. United States,* 356 U.S. 369 (1958); *Sorrells v. United States,* 287 U.S. 435 (1932). Cases in the recent trend either adopted Frankfurter's view of entrapment, for example, *Smith v. United States,* 331 F.2d 784 (D.C. Cir. 1964); *People v. Sinclair,* 387 Mich. 91 (1972); *Johnson v. Commonwealth,* 180 S.E.2d 661 (Va. 1971), or adopted a new defense, *Russell v. United States,* 459 F.2d 671 (9th Cir. 1972); *Williamson v. United States,* 311 F.2d 441 (5th Cir. 1962); *Greene v. United States,* 454 F.2d 783 (9th Cir. 1971).

6. *The Pentagon Papers* (New York: Bantam, 1971).

7. *United States v. Russell,* 411 U.S. 423, 431–32 (1973).

8. The defendants' and other lawyers' closing arguments were insightful, moving, and effective. I don't have space here to do them justice. Michael Doyle has published a book of letters, *It's a Terrible Day . . . Thanks Be to God* (Camden, N.J.: Heart of Camden, 2003).

9. "Camden Jurors Cite Role of U.S., Explain Their Acquittal of 17 Tried for Draft-File Raid," *New York Times,* May 22, 1973; "Acquittal Vote Protested War, Camden '28' Juror Says," *Philadelphia Inquirer,* May 22, 1973; *The Camden 28* (2006), an award-winning film by Anthony Giacchino, shown in theaters and on the Public Broadcasting System and available as a DVD from First Run Features (http://www.firstrunfeatures.com). A contrary view, that the acquittal was based on jury nullification, has been suggested by defendant Ed McGowan, *Peace Warriors* (Nyack, NY: Circumstantial Productions, 2001), and by historian Howard Zinn, based on his experience as a witness, "A Break-in for Peace," *Progressive,* July 2002; "Amazing Grace: The Movement Wins in Camden," *Liberation,* July–August 1973.

10. See Jon Van Dyke, *Jury Selection Procedures* (Cambridge, MA: Ballinger, 1977), 238–40; Alan Scheflin and Jon Van Dyke, *Jury Nullification: The Contours of a Controversy,* 43 L. & CONTEMP. PROBLEMS 51, 52–53 (1980); George Fletcher, *A Crime of Self-Defense* (New York: Free Press, 1988), 157. The comment by Justice Brennan was made in a conversation with Grady's daughter, Mary Anne Grady Flores, who told him her father was one of the defendants when they met. See also McGowan, *Peace Warriors,* 375. The leading Supreme Court decisions after Russell were *Hampton v. United States,* 425 U.S. 484 (1976) and *Jacobson v. United States,* 503 U.S. 540 (1992), which at least limited the exception, and courts of appeals have negated or narrowly interpreted it.

Chapter 8

1. *Debs v. United States,* 249 U.S. 211 (1919). Portions of this chapter are drawn from my earlier works on free speech, including "Freedom of Speech," in *The Politics of Law* (New York: Pantheon, 1982; New York: Basic Books, 3d ed., 1998).

2. David Lovett was productive and managed to touch the lives of a range of people in his short time. In 2006 I donated his papers, letters, and books to Whitman College in Walla Walla, Washington, where he taught, and Whitman established the David Lovett Collection.

3. *Whitney v. California,* 274 U.S. 357, 375–76 (1927) (concurring opinion).

4. *Davis v. Massachusetts,* 167 U.S. 43 (1897), affirming *Commonwealth v. Davis,* 162 Mass. 510 (1895) (unanimous opinion of Holmes).

5. *Hague v. CIO,* 307 U.S. 496 (1939).

6. *Flower v. United States,* 407 U.S. 197 (1972). Transcripts of Supreme Court arguments didn't identify which justice asked each question, and I have some uncertainty about it in these quotes.

7. *Greer v. Spock,* 424 U.S. 828 (1976).

Chapter 9

1. "Rizzo Asks President for Troops," *Philadelphia Inquirer,* June 2, 1976; "'Radicals' Are Coming, but Who Are They?" *Philadelphia Inquirer,* June 6, 1976; "Rizzo: U.S. to Blame If Men Denied," *Philadelphia Inquirer,* June 8, 1976.

2. *C. James Trotman et al. v. Lincoln University and Herman Branson,* 635 F.2d 216 (3d Cir. 1980). Jack Beck worked with me on the case.

3. For example, Karl Klare, *Judicial Deradicalization of the Wagner Act and the Origin of Modern Legal Consciousness, 1937–41,* 62 MINN. L. REV. 265 (1978); Alan Freeman, *Legitimizing Racial Discrimination with Anti-Discrimination Law: A Critical Review of Supreme Court Doctrine,* 62 MINN. L. REV. 1049 (1978).

4. David Kairys, "Freedom of Speech," in *The Politics of Law,* 1st ed., available at http://ssrn.com/abstract=727903. Virtually the same analysis has been presented without citation to my chapter, sometimes by writers who had read the book. See Michael Klarman, *Rethinking the Civil Rights and Civil Liberties Revolution,* 82 VA. L. REV. 1, 34–46 (1996); Michael Klarman, *Review Essay: Rethinking the History of American Freedom,* 42 WM. & MARY L. REV. 265, 271 n. 12 (2000) (after I privately informed the author of his earlier omission).

5. The information in this paragraph and the preceding paragraph is from Kairys, "Freedom of Speech."

6. Leonard Levy, *Emergence of a Free Press* (New York: Oxford University Press, 1985).

7. *Masses Publ. Co. v. Patten,* 245 F. 102 (2d Cir. 1917).

8. Leonard Levy, *Legacy of Suppression* (Cambridge: Harvard University Press, 1960); David Rabban, *The First Amendment in Its Forgotten Years,* 90 YALE L.J. 514 (1981) (received just prior to publication and added to footnotes 3 and 64).

9. Two recent books on free speech avoid the historic change in the mid-1930s. David Rabban, in *Free Speech in Its Forgotten Years* (Cambridge: Cambridge University Press, 1997), essentially ends his analysis when the "right" ideas are articulated in the 1920s by Holmes, Brandeis, and others, while, in this most recent version of his historical account, unconvincingly claiming that the change actually occurred in a 1927 case. Samuel Walker's *In Defense of American Liberties: A History of the ACLU* (Carbondale: Southern Illinois University Press, 1999) doesn't address why or how the rules of free speech changed in a history of the ACLU. See also Paul Starr, *The Creation of the Media: Political Origins of Modern Communications* (New York: Basic Books, 2004). I most recently took up the issues in *A Brief History of Race and the Supreme Court,* 79 TEMPLE L. REV. 751, 766 n. 54 (2006).

10. *Pledge of Resistance v. We the People 200,* 665 F. Supp. 414 (E.D.Pa. 1987); "Tucker Says One Group Discussed a Kidnaping," *Philadelphia Inquirer,* July 7, 1987: "City Is Sued over Police Infiltration," *Philadelphia Inquirer,* June 30, 1987; "Is the Constitution Getting Too Much Police Protection?" editorial,

Philadelphia Inquirer, June 30, 1987; "Civilian Review of Surveillance Okd," *Philadelphia Inquirer,* July 16, 1987; "A Lesson in Constitutional Values," editorial, *Chicago Tribune,* August 12, 1987; "Managing Director Must OK Police Spying," *Philadelphia Daily News,* September 16, 1987; "Story on Infiltration of Protestors Could be Sorted out in Court," *Philadelphia Inquirer,* September 9, 2000.

Chapter 10

1. Robert J. Lifton and Eric Olson, *Living and Dying* (London: Wildwood House, 1974); Robert Jay Lifton and Eric Olson, "The Human Meaning of Total Disaster: The Buffalo Creek Experience," *Psychiatry* 39, no. 1 (February 1976): 1–18.

2. "Family Plans to Sue CIA Over Suicide in Drug Test, " *New York Times,* July 10, 1975, 1.

3. Federal Tort Claims Act, 28 U.S.C. § 1346, et seq.; Federal Employees Compensation Act, 5 U.S.C. § 8101, et seq.; *Glus v. Brooklyn Eastern Terminal,* 359 U.S. 231 (1959).

4. John G. Fuller, *The Day of St. Anthony's Fire* (New York: Macmillan, 1968), 277–78.

5. The Select Committee to Study Governmental Operations with Respect to Intelligence Activities, Foreign and Military Intelligence, Sen. Rep. No. 94-755, 94th Cong., 2d Sess. (Washington, DC: GPO, 1976) (Church Committee report), http://www.mindcontrolforums.com/church-committee-drugtesting-report.htm; Victor Marchetti and John D. Marks, *The CIA and the Cult of Intelligence* (New York: Knopf, 1974). I took one other case, for the family of James Christensen, but we couldn't prove he was given LSD at a CIA interview.

6. Eric's Web site, which includes the Colby documents, is http://www .frankolsonproject.org/; H. P. Albarelli, Jr., *A Terrible Mistake: The Murder of Dr. Frank Olson and the CIA's Secret Cold War Experiments* (forthcoming, 2008).

Chapter 11

1. *Attica: Official Report of the New York State Special Commission on Attica* (New York: Praeger, 1972); Tom Wicker, *A Time to Die* (New York: Balantine, 1975).

2. Jay first published an account of these techniques, with others, in "Recipe for a Jury," *Psychology Today* (May 1973). See Stephen Adler, *The Jury, Trial, and Error in the American Courtroom* (New York: Times Books, 1994). Others have claimed and been credited with Jay's role. See Jeffrey Toobin, "The Marcia Clark Verdict," *New Yorker,* September 9, 1996 (my request for a correction was refused); Jeffrey Toobin, *The Run of His Life: People v. O.J. Simpson* (New York: Random House, 1996).

3. *People v. Attica Brothers,* 359 N.Y.S.2d 699 (1974); *Hoyt v. Florida,* 368 U.S. 57 (1961), overruled by *Taylor v. La.,* 419 U.S. 522 (1975).

4. David Kairys, Joseph Kadane, and John Lehoczky, *Jury Representativeness: A Mandate for Multiple Source Lists,* 65 CAL. L. REV. 776 (1977), incorporated with my testimony in Hearings before the Subcommittee on Improvements in Judicial Machinery, Committee on the Judiciary, U.S. Senate, 95th Cong., 1st Sess. (September 22, 1977); Joseph Kadane and John Lehoczky, "Random Juror Selection from Multiple Lists," *Operations Research* 24 (1976): 207.

5. *U.S. v. Gaona,* 445 F. Supp. 1237 (W.D.Texas 1978).

6. *U.S. v. Northside Realty,* 510 F. Supp. 668 (N.D.Ga. 1981), reversed, *U.S. v. Bearden,* 659 F.2d 590 (5th Cir. 1981); *U.S. v. Breland,* 522 F. Supp. 468 (N.D.Ga. 1981). Our statistician was Gene Ericksen from Temple.

7. *N.J. v. Ramseur,* 197 N.J. Super. 565 (Essex Co. 1984), affirmed, 197 106 N.J. 123 (1987); *N.J. v. Russo,* 213 N.J. Super. 219 (Gloucester Co. 1986); *N.J. v. Long,* 204 N.J. Super. 469 (Atlantic Co. 1985). Leading Supreme Court cases: *Duren v. Mo.,* 439 U.S. 357 (1979); *Casteneda v. Partida,* 430 U.S. 482 (1977); *Taylor v. La.,* 419 U.S. 522 (1975). The New Jersey public advocate was Joseph H. Rodriguez.

8. *Indiana v. Zolo Azania,* 778 N.E.2d 1253 (2002). I served in an unusual capacity, as an expert, and Jay Kadane was the statistician; the lead lawyer was Michael Deutsch. My work with Kadane has included Kadane and Kairys, "Fair Numbers of Peremptory Challenges in Jury Trials," *Journal of the American Statistical Association* 74 (1979): 747–53, and my chapter "The Law of Clinical Testing with Human Subjects," in Kadane, ed., *Bayesian Methods and Ethics in a Clinical Trial Design* (New York: Wiley, 1996).

Chapter 12

1. Bill Moyer, *Doing Democracy* (Philadelphia: New Society Publishers, 2001).

2. I did many cases for CEPA and its well-known leader, Max Weiner. For example, *Consumer Party v. Davis,* 606 F. Supp. 1008 (E.D.Pa. 1985), 778 F.2d 140 (3d Cir. 1986) (invalidating signature requirement for ballot access); *Consumer Educ. and Protective Assoc. v. Schwartz,* 432 A.2d 173 (Pa. Supreme Ct. 1981), 428 A.2d 711 (Pa. Commonwealth Ct. 1980) (invalidating pay raises given by city council to itself).

3. I was assisted by law students Meg Groff and Marijayne Wenck and paralegals June Kapler and Karen Detamore, and as the case progressed, Pennsylvania consumer advocate Walter Cohen came into the case on our side and attorney Philip McClelland of his office participated in the hearings.

4. Christopher Lasch, *The Culture of Narcissism* (New York: Norton, 1978), 42–43.

5. *Keystone Alliance v. Philadelphia Electric Co.,* 63 Pa.PUC 571 (1987); *Philadelphia Electric Co. v. Pa. Public Utility Comm.,* 552 A.2d 342 (Pa. Commonwealth Ct. 1989) (affirming but rejecting certain retroactive adjustments to PECO's costs); "Nuclear Sales Pitch When a Utility's Pamphlets Take Sides, Should the Customers Pay?" *Philadelphia Inquirer,* September 25, 1983; *Monitor,* NBC-TV, June 25, 1983.

6. Public Utility Regulatory Policies Act of 1978, 16 U.S.C. §§ 2611, 2623(b)(5), 2632 (1978).

Chapter 13

1. Nina Pillard, a law student working in my office, helped with legal research. NECLC, as well as the ACLU, supported the case. In *Farber v. Rizzo*, 363 F. Supp. 386 (E.D.Pa. 1973), Rudy and Jack Levine got an immediate temporary restraining order while I was in New Jersey working on the Camden 28 case, and we did the rest of the case together.

2. *Cliett v. City of Philadelphia*, U.S.D.C.E.D.Pa., Civil Action No. 85-1846, Consent Decree (April 11, 1985), Settlement Agreement (November 13, 1986); "Operation Cold Turkey: Effective, Constitutional?" editorial, *Philadelphia Inquirer*, April 10, 1985; "City Is Likely to End Drug Sweeps, Goode's Office Says," *Philadelphia Inquirer*, April 10, 1985; "Cold Turkey: The Operation That Wouldn't Fly," *Philadelphia Daily News*, November 14, 1986.

3. *Rizzo v. Goode*, 423 U.S. 362 (1976); *Lankford v. Gelston*, 364 F.2d 197 (4th Cir. 1966).

4. *Spring Garden United Neighbors v. City of Philadelphia*, Civil Action No. 85-3209 (bench opinion June 12, 1985); 614 F. Supp. 1350 (E.D.Pa. 1985); 1986 U.S. Dist. LEXIS 29688 (approval of settlement February 4, 1986); "Philadelphia Roundup Incenses Puerto Ricans," *New York Times*, June 21, 1985; "Judge: Stop Roundups in Spring Garden Area," *Philadelphia Inquirer*, June 13, 1985; "The Ban on Police Sweeps," editorial, *Philadelphia Inquirer*, June 14, 1985; "City to Pay Victims of Police Sweep," *Philadelphia Inquirer*, November 26, 1985.

5. At about the same time, some of my work seemed to receive an unusual form of recognition, a MacArthur Fellowship. But I didn't get it—Rudy did. See "'Genius Awards,'" *Philadelphia Inquirer*, July 15, 1986 ("Rudovsky's legal victories include a decision by a federal judge to declare the Vietnam War unconstitutional, the acquittal of the 'Camden 28,' a group of Catholic draft resisters, and the finding by a panel of judges that the Philadelphia prison system was cruel, inhumane and illegal."); David Rudovsky, letter to the editor, *Philadelphia Inquirer*, July 30, 1986 ("joint" award to both of us would have been appropriate). See also *PR Newswire*, July 14, 1986; *U.P.I.*, July 14, 1986; Paul Lyons, *The People of This Generation: The Rise and Fall of the New Left in Philadelphia* (Philadelphia: University of Pennsylvania Press, 2003), 230; "Putting the Innocent behind Bars," *USA Today Magazine*, May 1995; "Human Rights Hero David Cole," *Human Rights*, winter 2004.

Chapter 14

1. Portions of this chapter are drawn from my earlier works, "Why Are Handguns So Accessible on Urban Streets?" in Elijah Anderson, ed., *Against the Wall: Poor, Young, Black, and Male* (Philadelphia: University of Pennsylvania Press, 2008); "A Philadelphia Story," *Legal Affairs* (May–June 2003); "The Cities Take

the Initiative: Public Nuisance Lawsuits against Handgun Manufacturers," in Bernard Harcourt, ed., *Guns, Crime, and Punishment in America* (New York: New York University Press, 2003); *The Origin and Development of the Governmental Handgun Cases*, 32 CONN. L. REV. 1163 (2000).

2. In 2000, ATF released a comprehensive study, *Commerce in Firearms in the United States* (released February 2, 2000), showing that, nationally, about 1 percent of the dealers who sold to the public were responsible for 57 percent of the handguns traced to crimes.

3. Cohen and Makadon released internal documents to the press and waived whatever privilege there was.

4. "Lawyer Who Drafted Gun Lawsuit Quits," *Philadelphia Inquirer,* January 21, 1998; *Legal Claims of Cities against the Manufacturers of Handguns,* 71 TEMPLE L. REV. 1 (1998).

5. Paul Barrett, "Evolution of a Cause: Why the Gun Debate Has Finally Taken Off," *Wall Street Journal,* October 21, 1999; Fox Butterfield, "Suits Hold Microscope Over Gun Makers," *New York Times,* May 27, 1999.

6. *Camden Co. v. Beretta,* 273 F.3d 536 (3d Cir. 2001).

7. Protection of Lawful Commerce in Arms Act, Pub. L. No. 109-92, 119 Stat. 2095, October 25, 2005 (immunizing the gun industry from a broad array of otherwise viable legal claims).

8. "Public-Nuisance Suits Keep Companies on the Defensive, Gun Suits Start an Unnerving Trend in Corporate America," *Corporate Legal Times* (August 2004).

Chapter 15

1. On the FBI, see chapter 7.

2. Equal Employment Opportunity Act, 42 U.S.C. § 2000e-16 (a–c), et seq.; 29 C.F.R. § 1613.220(d).

3. *Rochon v. FBI,* Statement of Findings and Recommended Decision, EEOC, No. 081-086-X0054 (June 26, 1987); Dept. of Justice Final Decision (August 6, 1987). Both opinions are attached as appendices to *The Glass Ceiling in Federal Agencies: A GAO Survey on Women and Minorities in Federal Agencies,* Hearings before the Committee on Governmental Affairs, U.S. Senate, 102d Congress, 1st Sess., 276–354 (October 23, 1991), and are available at http://jurist.law.pitt .edu/pdf/kairys/RochonEEOC.pdf and http://jurist.law.pitt.edu/pdf/kairys/Ro chonDOJfinal.pdf.

4. Steve Drizin at Sachnoff & Weaver and Jeff Taren helped in Chicago, and Cindy Estlund helped in Washington. Taren was the partner of Joanne Kinoy, daughter of my friend, the great civil rights lawyer Arthur Kinoy, whose memoir is *Rights on Trial: The Odyssey of a People's Lawyer.* (Boston: Harvard University Press, 1983). Allan Stein, a law professor at Rutgers, helped with the procedural strategy.

5. For example, Joseph Slobodzian, "Black Agent Alleges Threats and Bias in

Suit against FBI," *Philadelphia Inquirer,* November 6, 1987; "Black FBI Agent's Ordeal: Meanness That Never Let Up," *New York Times,* January 25, 1988; "Racism in the FBI," *Nightline,* ABC News, January 25, 1988.

6. The most cooperative was Frank Dunham, who later represented an alleged terrorist in one of the leading post-9/11 cases before the Supreme Court.

7. *People v. Beardsley,* 115 Ill.2d 47, 503 N.E.2d 346 (1986).

8. "FBI Disciplines 8 Workers in Race Harassment Case," *New York.Times,* August 24, 1991; "FBI Disciplines 8 Agents in Probe of Harassment," *Washington Post,* August 24, 1991.

9. See "FBI Chief Backs Black Ex-Agent Criticized in Book on Agency," *New York Times,* July 12, 1994; *Rochon v. Gonzales,* 438 F.3d 1211 (D.C. Cir. 2006) (Michael Rubin at Arnold & Porter was lead counsel for Don).

Epilogue

1. Some of the leading works include "Introduction" and "Freedom of Speech," in *The Politics of Law,* 3d ed; *A Brief History of Race and the Supreme Court; Searching for the Rule of Law,* 36 SUFFOLK L. REV. 307 (2003); and "Why Are Handguns So Accessible on Urban Streets?"

2. Not all agreed on civil rights or the Vietnam War. See David Kairys, "Alito's Discrimination Problem," *Jurist,* January 28, 2006, http://jurist.law.pitt.edu/fo rumy/2006/01/alitos-discrimination-problem.php.

3. See Bruce Western, *Punishment and Inequality in America* (New York: Russell Sage Foundation, 2007); Devah Pager, *Marked: Race, Crime, and Finding Work in an Era of Mass Incarceration* (Chicago: University of Chicago Press, 2007).

INDEX

ABOUT THE AUTHOR

In the 1960s and 1970s David Kairys litigated many high visibility civil rights cases in Philadelphia and nationally, often involving significant public figures. He became renowned for his ingenious and imaginative successes, often under difficult or seemingly impossible circumstances. Kairys stopped police sweeps of minority neighborhoods in Philadelphia, won the leading race discrimination and harassment case against the FBI, challenged the CIA's drugging an unwitting scientist with LSD, won challenges to unrepresentative juries around the country, represented Dr. Benjamin Spock in a free speech case before the Supreme Court, conceived the lawsuits brought by over 40 cities against handgun manufacturers, and was the lead lawyer in the most significant acquittal of Vietnam-era antiwar activists. His cases involved such well-known figures as J. Edgar Hoover, William Colby, Arlen Specter, John Mitchell, Lester Maddox, Ed Rendell, and Frank Rizzo—as well as many others less famous but no less fascinating.

In addition to his prominence as a practicing civil rights lawyer, Kairys, now a law professor at Temple University, has become a leading author and commentator on civil rights, legal theory, and legal history. He is the editor and coauthor of *The Politics of Law: A Progressive Critique* and author of *With Liberty and Justice for Some: A Critique of the Conservative Supreme Court* and over 35 book chapters and articles, including recently "A Brief History of Race and the Supreme Court" and "Why Are Handguns So Accessible on Urban Streets?" Kairys has been the recipient of many honors and awards and has been profiled in the *Wall Street Journal*, the *Philadelphia Inquirer Sunday Magazine*, and the *Chronicle of Higher Education*.